CAMOUFLAGE CULTURES

Beyond the art of disappearance

Edited by
Ann Elias, Ross Harley and Nicholas Tsoutas

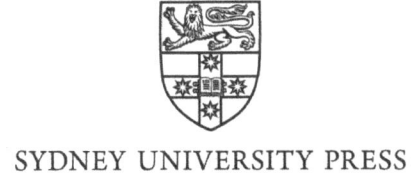

SYDNEY UNIVERSITY PRESS

First published in 2015 by Sydney University Press
© Individual contributors 2015
© Sydney University Press 2015

Reproduction and Communication for other purposes
Except as permitted under the Act, no part of this edition may be reproduced, stored in a retrieval system, or communicated in any form or by any means without prior written permission. All requests for reproduction or communication should be made to Sydney University Press at the address below:

Sydney University Press
Fisher Library F03
University of Sydney NSW 2006
AUSTRALIA
Email: sup.info@sydney.edu.au
sydney.edu.au/sup

National Library of Australia Cataloguing-in-Publication Data

Title:	Camouflage cultures: beyond the art of disappearance / edited by Ann Elias, Ross Harley and Nicholas Tsoutas
ISBN:	9781743324257 (paperback)
ISBN:	9781743324264 (ebook : epub)
ISBN:	9781743324271 (ebook : MOBI)
Notes:	Includes bibliographical references and index.
Subjects:	Art and camouflage.
	Camouflage (Biology)
	Art--Social aspects.
Other Authors/ Contributors:	Elias, Ann Dirouhi, editor.
	Harley, Ross, editor.
	Tsoutas, Nicholas, editor.
Dewey Number:	751.4

From cover image: *Jack in the Green (Lambretta-AGS 195 to Triumph-GVL2MXD),* 2013 by Shaun Gladwell. Courtesy the artist and Anna Schwartz Gallery.

Back cover image: *Hembras palito/Female sticks,* 2010 by Maria Fernanda Cardoso. Archival pigment print on 300g water colour paper. Courtesy of the artist.

Cover design by Miguel Yamin

Contents

Acknowledgments   v

Introduction   vii

1   Khaki to khaki (dust to dust): the ubiquity of camouflage in human experience   1
  Roy R Behrens

2   Camouflage and mimesis – deception, evolutionary biology and imitation   17
  Bernd Hüppauf

3   Zoos and camouflage   33
  Ann Elias

4   Australian stick and leaf insects (Insecta, Phasmida): camouflage and natural history   47
  Paul D Brock & Jack W Hasenpusch

5   Mimicking the masters: a new age for camouflage design   65
  Jonnie Morris

6   The origin of art: camouflage, anti-camouflage and de-camouflage in the appropriation art of Imants Tillers   77
  Ian McLean

7   The camouflage effect   87
  Pamela Hansford

8   Light leak   101
  Tanya Peterson

9   From Ghillie suit to glittering kowhaiwhai – contemporary New Zealand artists deploy the camouflage aesthetic   115
  Linda Tyler

10 Making visible, changing sides: the contradictory use of camouflage by artists Xing Junqin and Ian Howard — 127
    Ian Howard and Brigitta Olubas

11 Interventions in seeing: surveillance, camouflage and the Cold War camera — 147
    Donna West Brett

12 Unmasking militarism: hegemony, naturalisation, camouflage — 159
    Ben Wadham and Amy Hamilton

13 Of mimicry and hipsters — 171
    Hsuan Hsu

14 Camouflage/fashion/performance: a case study of Leigh Bowery — 183
    Jacqueline Millner

15 Hiding in the cosmos — 193
    Nikos Papastergiadis

Afterword — 201
   Shifting ground
   Ross Gibson

About the contributors — 207

Index — 213

Acknowledgments

It is due to the generous support of Sydney College of the Arts (SCA) at the University of Sydney, and the University of Sydney's International Project Development office, that we have been able to publish *Camouflage cultures: beyond the art of disappearance*. The editors would like to thank all the kind people who assisted us to stage an international conference and major exhibition of contemporary art at SCA in 2013, which led to the publication of this book: the Dean, Professor Colin Rhodes, and Professor Brad Buckley (then Associate Dean of Research) who provided seed funding; staff and volunteers who gave their time and professional skills, especially Simon Baré, Liam Garstang, Professor Ross Gibson, Priscilla Gundelach, Sophie Hague, Wendy Ju, Nerida Olson and Peggy Wallach. In addition, we thank the Vice-Chancellor of the University, Dr Michael Spence, for launching the conference, Professor Jill Trewhella, Deputy Vice-Chancellor Research, for launching the exhibition, and the International Project Development office for assisting with the book's publication. Many generous partners were involved in the project and we would like to specially acknowledge the Australia Council for the Arts, the Ian Potter Foundation, The Goethe-Institut, the University of Northern Iowa, and the University of Auckland.

Introduction

Camouflage is becoming a key topic and important critical concept in the 21st century. Emerging out of a growing interest in the connections between areas such as ecology, evolution, visual deception, and warfare, the number of publications dedicated to the subject is steadily increasing. Historically, the study of camouflage has most commonly been associated with either military or natural history research frameworks. However, over the past few years the number of critical perspectives emerging from this varied field have expanded significantly. Following the ground-breaking work of Roy R Behrens (a contributor to this volume), authors and academics in the United States and Britain have published research that embraces film studies, design perspectives, psychology, aesthetics and popular culture, as well as the more familiar areas of natural history and war studies. Most notable among these are Neil Leach's 2010 book *Camouflage* – a theoretical account of the psychoanalytic and architectural components of camouflage that connect or mediate us and our environment – and Hanna Shell's careful tracing of the mediation of camouflage by means of photography and cinema in her 2012 book, *Hide and seek: camouflage, photography and the media of reconnaissance*.

The present publication continues this trajectory, bringing together researchers from a variety of disciplines to shine new light on the way scholars and artists around the world think about and work with this expanding field. It includes contributions by thinkers who demonstrate that camouflage can usefully be considered beyond the politics of appearance, beyond the art of disappearance, or beyond simple strategies of mimicry. The contributors demonstrate a critical and insightful engagement with the concept of camouflage in ways that expand the boundaries of how we think about its history, theory or artistic deployment. As practices of deception move across the visual field and into non-representational modalities, contributors to this volume also point to an extended rubric of camouflage that goes beyond the limits of nature and visual perception.

Camouflage cultures: beyond the art of disappearance can also be viewed as a contemporary sequel to the 2011 book by Ann Elias entitled *Camouflage Australia: art, nature, science and war*. That work brought a broad historical perspective to our understanding of camouflage by concentrating on the Australian artists and designers who dedicated their service to 20th-century wartime projects of concealment and deception. By contrast, the current volume is broader in conceptual scope and more contemporary in focus. As such, our aim is to bring new insights, and to add another dimension to the broader fields of visual culture, contemporary art theory, and art history.

Contributors to this collection variously explore how camouflage theory was founded in modernity and based on cultural preconceptions about the nature of perception, as much as it was founded on historically grounded understandings of the 'nature of nature'. In an important sense, the authenticity of appearance and the possibility of its negation was once considered the principal starting point for camouflage studies. Now, in a digitally networked age of surveillance and counter-surveillance, the logic of those constructions is being fundamentally transformed by pervasive networks and global systems of code. Under these new material and cultural conditions, the centrality of figure-ground dynamics and the primacy of perception in the visual field may not play the same ontological role that they have in past understanding of how camouflage works in nature, culture and society.

At the most general level, we take camouflage to mean strategic concealment and exposure within physical, social and political contexts. Each of the contributors to the present volume reflect upon important social and cultural aspects of this concealment and exposure, which in turn sets the physical and social context for camouflage today – especially as it pertains to questions of surveillance, aesthetics, communities and animals. Subsequently, the authors assembled here investigate the many perspectives and contradictions that make camouflage a vital conceptual tool for analysing today's complex sensory world. Taken as a whole, this volume demonstrates a depth of understanding and rigorous research that helps reveal camouflage as both a contemporary working process and an arresting object of study in the 21st century. *Camouflage cultures* provides an invigorated sense of why and how camouflage is important as part of a broader cultural framework.

Approaching this subject from the disciplines of art history and theory, art practice, biology, cultural theory, literature and philosophy, this present volume greatly expands the reach of camouflage's cultural terrain. The result is a collection that makes a new and original contribution to discussions about the role that physical, artistic, and social camouflage plays in contemporary life. Indeed, the unique contribution this book makes comes from the connections it draws between diverse disciplines whose intersections open up new areas of debate and dialogue about the study of camouflage in its many guises. This new field is relevant not only to the specific disciplines that have a stake in creating the discourses concerning the role and function of camouflage; it also opens up the area to more general popular discussions that range from fashion to the military, from animals to philosophy, or from sexuality to aesthetics. Each of the book's contributors takes a different approach to understanding and interpreting the significance of specific strategies of blending, assimilation, invisibility and masking that can be found in contemporary society as much as they can be found in nature or the military.

The book is conceptually framed by two different paradigms of thinking and research regarding camouflage. The first relates to camouflage's history and principles as they emerged (in the context of modernity) out of cultural institutions dedicated to science, art and war. Modern camouflage began with naturalists and zoologists, artists and designers, military organisations and defence tacticians all trying (often for different reasons and sometimes communally) to solve problems of static and dynamic disguise. The second paradigm that frames this book raises questions about camouflage's modernist principles and proposes a new ontology of camouflage for the 21st century. Accordingly, this paradigm poses a series of new questions to help frame the contemporary context: what forms of camouflage are required in an increasingly multi-modal, networked, electronic world? How does the 21st-century 'camouflagist' mask contingent relationships in an era that seems to be less about static objects and more about dynamic systems and codes that shift through time and space?

Contributors to this book consciously juxtapose aesthetics, animals, war and surveillance, as well as social institutions and popular communities. Their visions place hipster mimicry in the United States alongside body mimicry in the life of the legendary performer Leigh Bowery; a case study of animal visibility in zoos is thrown into relief by an essay on surveillance in German war history; actant theory and contemporary critiques of evolutionary theory butt up against gestalt and evolutionary biology; industrial design is questioned by the current passion for biomimicry; one of Australia's leading contemporary artists, Imants Tillers, is spoken about for the first time alongside Abbott H. Thayer, America's leading historical artist; the politics of camouflage in the context of cosmopolitanism and globalisation is placed next to discussions concerning the politics of camouflage in bi-cultural New Zealand; militaries in China and Korea are discussed alongside militaries in Australia; and the reception of art as an act of camouflage and as a response to camouflage aesthetics is considered in light of contemporary photography, sculpture and painting.

In short, *Camouflage cultures* provides a new perspective on the developing discourse of camouflage. It asks what place the study of camouflage might have in art, science and philosophy – especially if we critically interrogate the importance of the place of the animal in this shifting framework of camouflage. Through a series of particular case studies relating to animal camouflage in zoos, in the wild, and as it is applied to human design, contributors provide detailed historical, philosophical, biological, animal-centred, and design-based analysis that sheds new light on the world of contemporary art. Taken together, the contributions contained in this volume chart the increasing importance of camouflage as a way of conceptualising the social performance of camouflage through new modes of mimicry in the 21st century.

Ann Elias, Ross Harley and Nicholas Tsoutas

1
Khaki to khaki (dust to dust): the ubiquity of camouflage in human experience

Roy R Behrens

Surveillance and the seeing eye

In writings about camouflage, it is often said that an object's visibility is primarily dependent on the extent to which it stands apart from a setting or surrounding. Known as a figure-ground relationship, it underscores the notion that we only experience a 'thing' in relation to other components. In the words of Zen philosopher Alan Watts, all experience 'is like the rainbow, for there is no phenomenon "rainbow" except where there is a certain relationship of sun, moisture in the atmosphere, and observer' (Watts 1969, 65).

Camouflage is no exception. Like a rainbow, it too can only be witnessed when an appropriate set of relations exists between a means of observation and an entity that might better survive from not being seen or, at least, from being confusing to see. 'Camouflage', said Swiss zoologist Adolf Portmann, 'implies a seeing eye from which to hide' (Portmann 1959, 9). To observe, we partake in surveillance, and, to a great extent, the history of camouflage is a dance of dynamic adjustments – a perpetual *pas de deux* between that which hides and that which seeks (cf. Shell 2012).

A recent familiar example of this is the initially puzzling adoption by deer hunters of outfits that make dual use of background matching patterns and high visibility safety orange. For purposes of camouflage, it would at first appear to be counterproductive to dress in a blatantly visible hue. As it turns out, the 'visual world' of a deer differs substantially from that of a human being. It is now assumed that deer are oblivious of (or colour-blind to) safety orange, and yet (like humans) they can be fooled by patterns that simulate green-brown foliage. As a result, two purposes can co-exist in one surface pattern: high visibility conspicuousness (safety orange, invisible to the eyes of a deer, but conspicuous to our own), and low visibility or blending camouflage (green-brown foliage patterns, which dupe both the predator and the prey).

If necessity is the mother of invention, the mother of modern wartime camouflage is technology-aided surveillance. For example, it is widely agreed that what we now call 'camouflage' was first promoted by artists serving in the French Army in the early years of World War I (Kahn 1984; Behrens 2009; Coutin 2012). While there is some confusion about which individual initiated the idea, the reasons are not in contention. Soldiers assigned to artillery teams were dismayed by the ease with which airborne enemy spotters could find and report the positions of their field artillery. In response, they proposed two countermeasures: the application of disruptive (or 'broken colour') patterns on the surface of their cannons, and the donning by those in artillery teams of sinister-looking hooded robes, called gagoules (they closely resembled the outfit worn by a French crime novel character called Fantomas (c. 1911) or darkened paint-stained versions of Ku Klux Klan ceremonial robes).

By applying broken colour to artillery, the camoufleurs' intention was to make their positions harder to spot (by subverting the continuity of the cannon's shape through high difference disruption). At the same time, by wearing dingy hooded robes, their goal was to prevent themselves from standing out (by merging visually with the ground through high similarity blending, or background matching). In relation to surveillance, all this came together because of the adoption by both sides of the conflict of concurrent innovations: the airplane (which allowed for distant observation from overhead), long-range artillery (which enabled strikes from miles away), and wireless telegraphy (by which aerial observers could report the locations of targets).

An equally crucial contributor was aerial photography, which made it possible to survey the battlefield through the non-human visual filters of the camera and photographic film. In addition, it allowed for exacting comparisons of a sequence of views of the same location over an expanse of time, which all too often gave away the subterfuge of ground-based artist-camoufleurs. Modern camouflage adapted to these and other innovations – all of which were 'game-changers', in the sense of redefining what constitutes the 'seeing eye' from which one attempts to hide.

Long-range artillery, airplanes, wireless telegraphy and aerial photography: all these things we now regard as 'technological innovations.' But throughout history, camouflage has also had to adapt to changes that were far less sophisticated – even non-technological, but no less fundamental. Of these, of particular significance is the point of observation of Portmann's 'seeing eye' (with or without technological aids).

In the 1890s, far in advance of Portmann's book, the American artist and naturalist Abbott H Thayer (who is now commonly said to have been the 'father of camouflage') fervently insisted on the importance of the viewer's observation point, which is the source of surveillance (cf. Thayer 1909; Behrens 2011b; Post 2013; Stevens & Merilaita 2011). Short of what we now regard as rigorous scientific proof, Thayer validated his theories by providing demonstrations for groups of naturalists (see Figure 1.1). These were mostly well-received, yet participants were at times dismayed by having to crouch down on their stomachs to observe his models from the presumed stalking point of view of a predatory animal. When Thayer's audience hesitated, no doubt it was partly because of the risk of soiling their clothing, but also (and, some think, far more tellingly) because it required that civilised people adopt the unmanly position of an inferior 'animal', and not – as the Great Chain of Being assumed – the dignified upright stature of a 'human being.'

A similar point has been made by art historian Ann Elias in her studies of the camouflage research of UK-born Australian zoologist William Dakin, who was clearly influenced by Thayer. For the dual purpose of observing while remaining unobserved themselves, Dakin advised World War II Australian soldiers to adopt (in Elias's words) 'the horizontal position of lower evolutionary animals using postures such as crouching and crawling which were recommended in war but not recommended in everyday civilised life because of their association with lower social types, including "servants and savages"' (Elias 2008, 254).

1 Khaki to khaki (dust to dust)

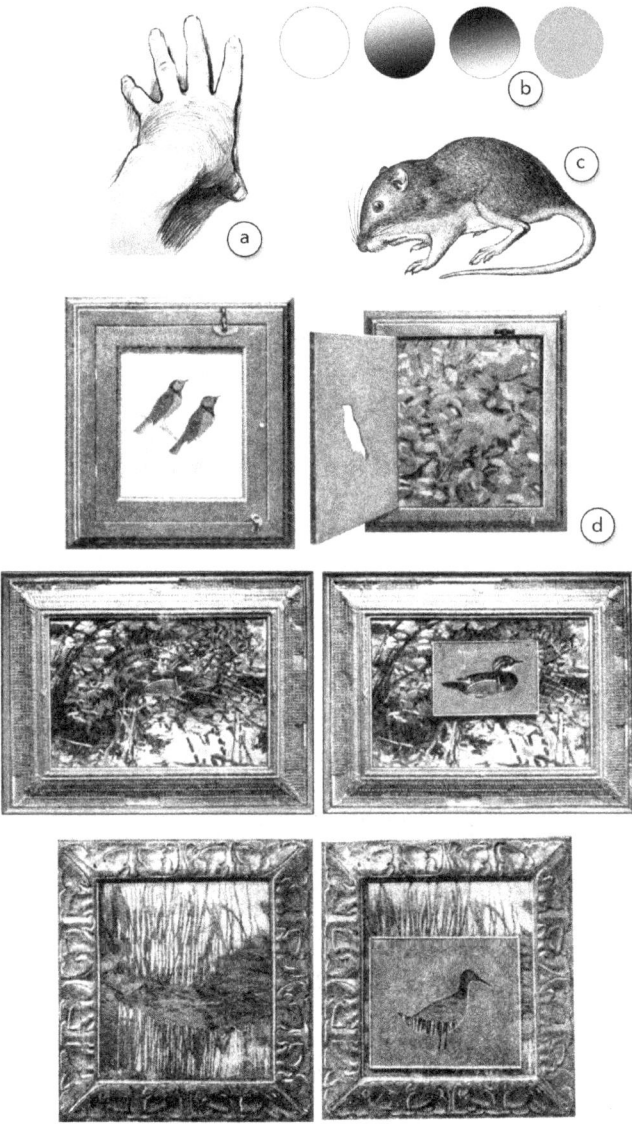

Figure 1.1 Various visual examples pertaining to the research of Abbott H Thayer, including: (a) the use of shading (a 'drop shadow') to produce the illusion of a solid, dimensional form, as illustrated in Solomon J Solomon, *The practice of oil painting and of drawing*. New York: JB Lippincott, 1910, 27 (public domain); (b) a sequence of four circles (left to right) showing flatness, shading, countershading, and the subsequent nondescript flatness (author's diagram); (c) countershading in the surface coloring of a mouse as shown in a 19th century engraving (public domain); and (d) news photographs of three interactive demonstrations (devised by Thayer

and his son) of coincident disruption in nature (figure disruption and blending combined), published in Amos T. Earling, 'Ships that pass in the daytime' in *Illustrated World*, Vol. 31 (1919), 202–15 (public domain).

In the first half of the 20th century, ground-breaking vision-related research was undertaken by Adelbert Ames II, an American artist and optical physiologist who had been a student of William James at Harvard. It is of curious interest that two of James's sons (Billy and Aleck) wanted to be artists, and had studied painting with Abbott Thayer in the years when he and his son Gerald were preparing a book on *Concealing coloration in the animal kingdom* (Thayer 1909, 1918). In later years, Aleck James was also a close friend of Ames, who spoke at Aleck's funeral.

As for Ames himself, he was not assigned to camouflage during World War I, but the army did assign him to aerial reconnaissance and to research pertaining to optics. At the war's end, he abandoned painting and devoted the rest of his life to optical physiology and perceptual psychology. He eventually became well-known for the Ames demonstrations in perception, a series of hands-on laboratory set-ups by which he showed persuasively that human vision can easily be deceived, especially when a setting is viewed through a fixed monocular point of view (Ittelson 1968; Behrens 2010). As had been anticipated by German scientist Hermann von Helmholtz in the 19th century, Ames confirmed that any number of oddly misshapen room interiors (he jokingly called them 'cockeyed rooms') could appear to be perfectly normal – providing each resulted in the same 'retinal image', a condition that could be assured by an invariant monocular peephole.

Today, when Ames's research is cited, the set-up inevitably featured is his well-known 'distorted room', in which people seem to shrink or grow as they move from one corner of the room to another (Figure 1.2a and 1.2b). In that demonstration, the right interior side wall is one half the size of the left wall, and the rear wall – although it looks rectangular – is in fact a trapezoid, turned toward us at an angle. In recent years, the Ames Room has been included in a routine by magicians Penn and Teller, in a television commercial for Quaker Oats cereal by Errol Morris, and in the opening sequence of a 2010 HBO Films docudrama (titled *Temple Grandin*) about a well-known animal scientist who had been inspired by Ames' research early in her student life.

Few people realise that Ames produced about 20 other demonstrations, including a misshapen window that looks like a normal rectangular shape when angled and viewed in perspective (Figure 1.2c). Ames called it the 'rotating trapezoid window', because its actual shape is not rectangular but trapezoidal, and in fact its shape is all but identical to that of the rear wall of his distorted room (Ittelson 1968).

Another Ames demonstration is the 'architect's room' (Figure 1.2d). To experience this, the subject is instructed to look through a peephole, to observe what initially seems to consist of a simple, square-shaped room interior, with four windows on the rear wall, and various other windows on each of the side walls. However, when the same interior is viewed from any other position, it is obvious that the actual space is long and narrow – not at all square in proportion – and, in truth, two of the windows on the facing wall are 'anamorphic' or 'skewed perspective' shapes that have been cleverly painted on the side walls. Only when viewed through the peephole do these two aberrant windows fit in (Behrens 2010).

1 Khaki to khaki (dust to dust)

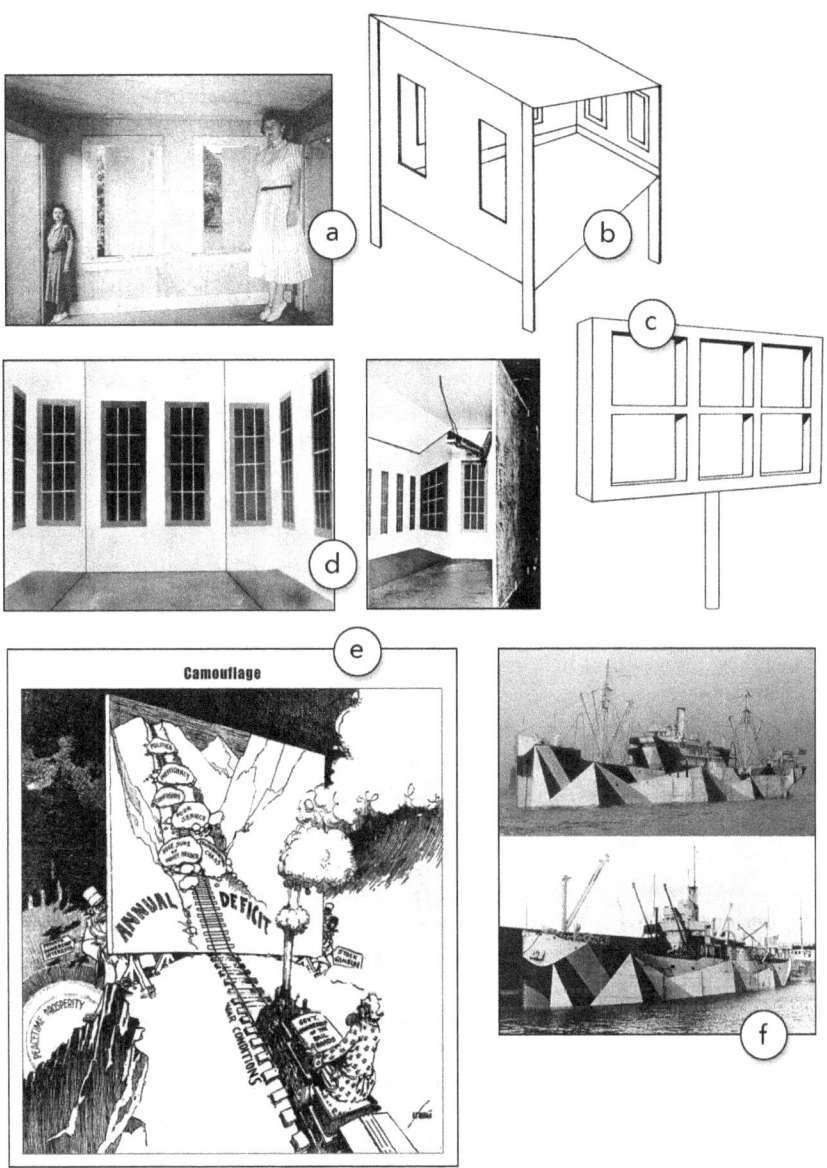

Figure 1.2 Examples of perspective-based distortion in experiments in psychology and in WWI-era camouflage, including: (a) an Ames distorted room, as viewed through the peephole (from Ittelson 1968, public domain) and (b) from the side (author's diagram); (c) the rotating trapezoid window (author's diagram); (d) two views of the architect's room (Ittelson 1968, public domain); (e) an American newspaper cartoon (c. 1918), showing a 'forced perspective' trick sometimes used (with little success) by camoufleurs (public domain); and (f) the same disruptive pattern (called 'dazzle camouflage') applied to two different US ships (c. 1919), from Naval History and Heritage Command (public domain).

While it was Ames who devised these demonstrations, the perspective distortions on which they depend have a rich ancestral past. At the very least, they can be traced to the sketchbooks of Leonardo da Vinci, who made note of his realisation one day of what he called 'accidental perspective', or, as it soon became commonly known, 'anamorphosis' (in visual art) and 'forced perspective' (in theatre stage design). In recent years, it has regained popularity in online-posted photographs of illusionistic 'street art', in which chalk-drawn sidewalk paintings look like actual dimensional objects, when viewed from a specified angle. There is a long tradition of this in Western painting, and by the time that World War I began (almost 20 years before Ames constructed his own demonstrations) those artists who were camoufleurs were well-acquainted with comparable form-distortion techniques.

Indeed, wartime drawings and photographs show that WWI camouflage artists made panoramic painted screens (most of which seem comical now) in which phony railroad tracks and crudely-made perspective screens were intended to trick the observer (Figure 1.2e). But they cannot have fooled very many, for the same reason that Leonardo rejected anamorphosis as a practicable option for artists: like the Ames demonstrations, trompe l'oeil forced perspective tricks only work optimally from the viewpoint they were designed for.

Among Ames' admirers was the Viennese-born British art historian Ernst H Gombrich, who once compared the Ames laboratory set-ups to looking at constellations at night (Gombrich 1982, 207). If observed from a location in a remote region of the universe, most likely we would never see the star groups that we know so well. It is because we are Earth-bound that, throughout history, humans have predictably tended to see connections among nearby stars, producing constellations (or gestalts) that we know as Orion, Gemini, Taurus and so on. Amazingly, the seven stars of the Big Dipper are seen as 'belonging together' despite the unfathomable distance between, for example, the farthest star Alkaid (which is 210 light-years from the Earth) and Mizar, the star adjacent to it (the distance of which is 88 light-years). To allude to Alan Watts again, constellations are akin to rainbows in the night.

During WWI, resourceful use was made of forced perspective in frantic Allied naval attempts to undermine the cat-and-mouse exchange between German submarines (called U-boats) and the slow and all too vulnerable prey of British and American merchant ships (Behrens 2011a). When within the vicinity of other vessels, for their own safety U-boats cautiously stayed submerged and maintained a considerable distance between themselves and their potential victims. The U-boat's standard 'seeing eye' was (of course) its periscope, a cyclopean surveillance device that could rise above the surface while the U-boat remained under water. But a raised periscope was itself conspicuous (in part because it left a wake as it cut across the water) so the time duration of its use was restricted to brief increments of 30 seconds or less.

Within such rigid time constraints – not to mention ocean storms, fog, haze, glare, water on the periscope lens, and the ceaseless jostling up-and-down of the U-boat and the targeted ship, all of which undermine accuracy – German U-boat gunners (restricted to their own monocular peepholes) tried to determine three critical facts: range, course and speed. In other words, how far away is the targeted ship? In what direction is it headed? And how fast is it traveling? In essence, their goal was to try to predict the position of the target ship when the torpedo eventually crossed its path.

Obviously, torpedo gunners had to aim ahead of or 'lead' the target, but not in the pedestrian way of a duck hunter. Instead they had to calculate (as quickly and carefully as possible) the probable future location of the targeted vessel. Despite ongoing improvements in periscope design, even the German Navy agreed (as confirmed by captured documents) that range, course and speed could be calculated 'with difficulty only or not at all.' However ardent their efforts, it was essentially guesswork – a process far less certain, as others have noted, than Hollywood movies would have us believe (Figure 1.2f).

Looking back, it may help to suggest a comparative link between a U-boat commander (peering one-eyed through a periscope) and a subject who is looking through the peephole of an Ames demonstration. The two situations are reasonably parallel, since both are instructive examples of how easily vision can be fooled. At the same time, it is important not to forget that while naval 'skewed perspective' schemes were adopted by the British as early as 1917, the first of the Ames demonstrations were not proposed and constructed until the mid-1930s.

As that sequence of events suggests, other artists and scientists, years in advance of Ames' research, were exploring ideas related to his for the purpose of camouflage. One of the leading contributors to this was Everett Longley Warner, an American Impressionist painter. Coming from different social classes, Warner and Ames were most likely unacquainted although both were stationed in Washington DC (in the navy and army respectively) in optics-related assignments.

What is certain is that Warner was in contact with Abbott Thayer (they even collaborated briefly on a botched attempt at ship camouflage), and that Ames (through the library of his sister and brother-in-law) was acquainted with Thayer's writings about animal camouflage. In 1917, when the US Navy chose the best, most effective camouflage schemes for protecting merchant ships, a proposal by Everett Warner was among the top six submissions and was sanctioned for official use. Soon after, he was given a second-tier leadership role in the US Navy's new Camouflage Section, in the course of which he supervised a unit of artist-camoufleurs assigned to its Design Subsection in Washington DC.

As World War I subsided, restrictions were gradually lifted and Warner was able to publish a handful of popular articles on his wartime activities as a ship camoufleur. In a 1919 essay on 'The science of marine camouflage design', he compared his unit's most fruitful approach to ship camouflage (known then as 'dazzle camouflage') to the procedure of making a physically distorted room appear to be perfectly normal, or a standard rectangular room appear to be distorted. All this can be achieved, wrote Warner, short of actually building a room, simply by applying 'op art wallpaper' (my term), using forced perspective. According to Warner, this was the most effective means of designing ship camouflage, so much so that, he noted, when 'you have thoroughly grasped this idea, marine camouflage holds no secrets for you' (Warner 1919).

In brief (keeping in mind that the truth is more complex than this), it enabled Warner's designers to make an angled ship appear to be perpendicular, or, conversely, a perpendicular ship appear to be headed at any angle. It was claimed by experts at the time that an error in course estimation of as little as ten to eleven degrees could potentially undermine the calculations of a torpedo gunner, while, according to empirical tests undertaken at MIT in 1919, the most effective dazzle ship designs could result in far more significant errors – sometimes as great as 58 degrees (cf. Blodgett 1919) (Figure 1.3).

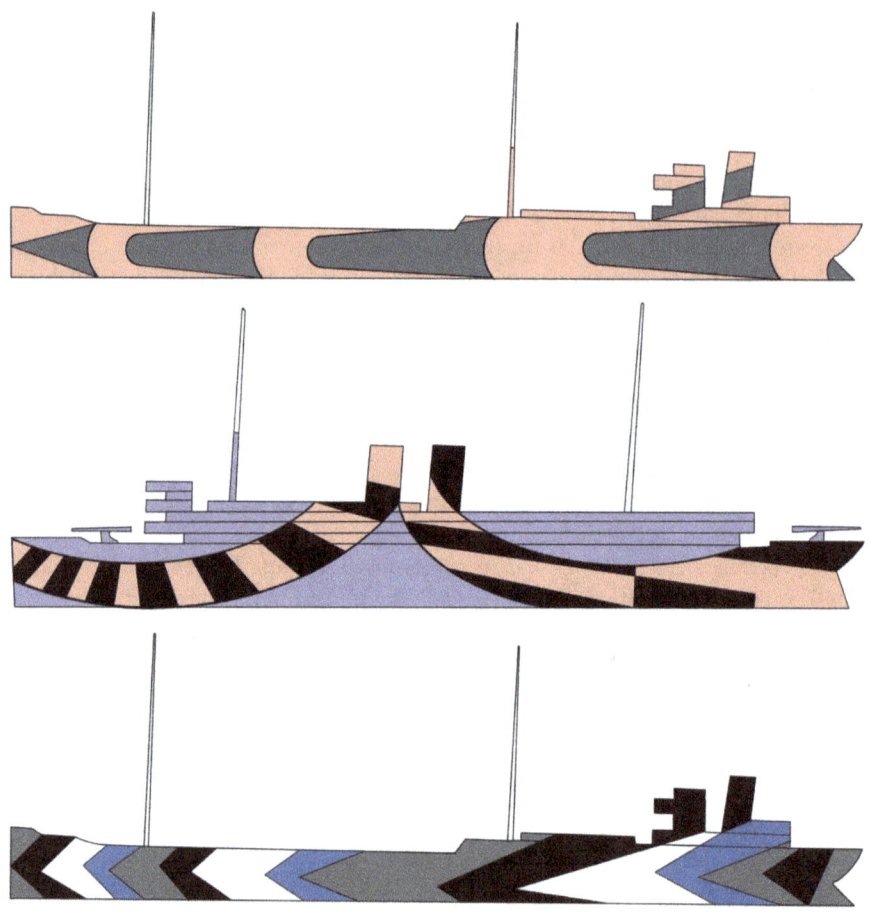

Figure 1.3 It is commonly asserted that the effectiveness of WWI dazzle camouflage cannot be verified, because it was never empirically tested. On the contrary, quantitative laboratory tests were done on painted ship models at MIT in 1919, by Leo S Blodgett (Blodgett 1919). In the most successful, perspective-based distortion schemes, he found course estimation errors as great as 58 degrees. Shown here are restored diagrams of three of the models. © Roy R Behrens, 2013.

Community and privacy

The German equivalent of 'figure and ground' is *ding und stoff*, while the phrase for the traits that contribute to that is *dingcharakter und stoffcharakter*. How is it that we experience 'things' in contrast to surrounding 'stuff'? When physicist Paul Weiss addressed that question, he replied that it 'stems partly from a biological heritage, which makes focusing on 'things', such as prey, enemies, or obstacles, a vital necessity; partly from cultural tradition; and partly from sheer curiosity, which draws our attention and interest to limited 'objects" (Weiss 1969, 5).

Like you, I even see my 'self' this way. 'I am I' and, to follow, I am not 'not-I.' Or, I am 'self' as distinguished from 'others.' We typically regard our 'selves' as permeable identities in a bouillabaisse of ubiquitous 'stuff', a surrounding that seems to a newborn, in the famous words of William James, like 'a blooming, buzzing confusion.' One wonders if this might also explain, as Ernst Schachtel suggested, why we are all afflicted by 'childhood amnesia', leaving us with little or no memory of the first years of our lives, because we lacked the 'handles' then – the linguistic categories – that enable us to 'grasp' events (Schachtel 1959). In recent years, increased attention has been paid to the various forms of 'amnesia' at the opposite end of life, including gradual memory loss, senility, dementia, and the horrifying ordeal of Alzheimer's. If the boundaries of our figural 'self' are blurred when we are newborns, perhaps we should not be surprised that the limits of our 'self' grow thin – once again – as we march to the end of existence.

As adults, we use hackneyed phrases like 'dust to dust' to imply that at birth we somehow spring from naught; that we metamorphically evolve through infancy and childhood; live out our ritualistic lives as corporeal upright adults; then slowly – or, just as often, catastrophically – 'deconstruct'; and (at last) are literally 'disembodied' in the process that we dread as death. Instead of saying 'dust to dust', it may be more in tune to say 'khaki to khaki', since it seems as if our lives consist of time-based re-enactments of a spectrum of nuanced relations between figure and ground, some or all of which pertain to varieties of camouflage.

In 1960, when Alexander Liberman reported on his interview with French painter Fernand Leger (whose WWI companions had served as camoufleurs), he recalled that the artist was wearing 'a checkered shirt, and the violent pattern of his clothes against the violent pattern of his paintings made him seem like a chameleon' (Liberman 1960, 189). According to R. Tripp Evans, whenever American Regionalist painter Grant Wood dressed in typical street clothes, instead of farmer's overalls, he could easily vanish in public. 'Such an uncanny talent for blending into the woodwork … ', continues Tripp, 'was matched by a lifelong habit of self-deprecation' (Evans 2010, 3–4). Wood even had a pet chameleon in his studio, and, during World War I, served briefly in the army as a camoufleur, in a unit whose insignia was an embroidered yellow chameleon.

Architectural theorist Neil Leach, in his influential book called *Camouflage*, proposed that we 'are governed by a chameleon-like urge to blend in with our surroundings – to "camouflage" ourselves within our environment' (Leach 2006, ix; cf. Hsu 2006). This is true enough, but there may be an opposite side of the coin. Think back to the earlier writings of another architect, Christopher Alexander, who spoke of our tandem proclivities toward 'community' and 'privacy', by which he hypothesised that not only do we need to blend with our surroundings (to belong to a community), we also need to distinguish ourselves as gated entities (our penchant for privacy), as a way to affirm our uniqueness (cf. Alexander 1964; Chermayeff and Alexander 1965).

'Sometimes I dress to fit in', writes art historian James Elkins, 'so that I can blend with the crowd and not attract attention', while at other times, 'I need to stand out; I want to be noticed' (Elkins 1997, 82). Alluding to Alexander again, we are in some ways a subset of a larger unit (a family, a city, a nation, the world) while, in another sense, we are a self-reliant 'whole.' To use a term coined by Arthur Koestler, we flourish best as a 'holon', in which we are both part and whole, both integrative and self-assertive (cf. Koestler 1967). This is true

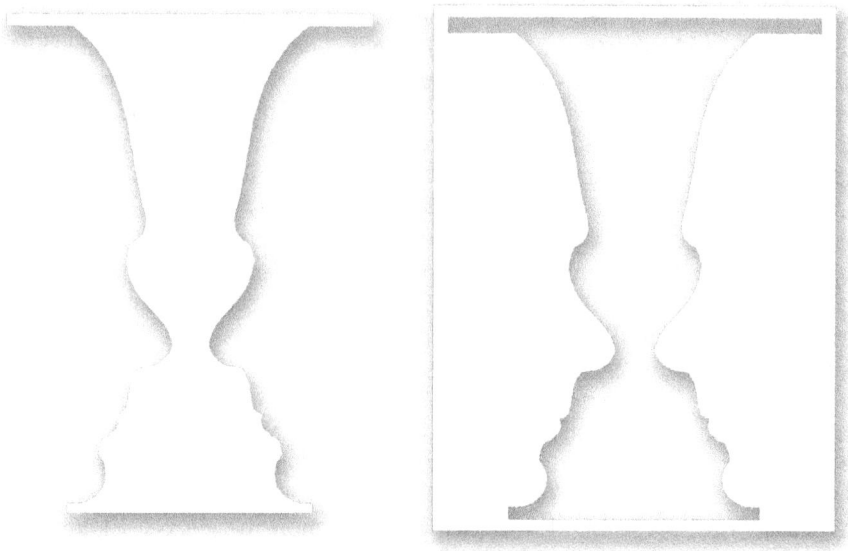

Figure 1.4 Two demonstrations of reversible figure-ground, based on comparable diagrams by psychologist Julian E. Hochberg (cf. Hochberg 1964) (author's diagram).

of all organisms, Koestler argued, a belief that was foreshadowed by Frank Lloyd Wright's insistence on 'organic form' in architecture, on the holonic interrelation between a man-made structure and its site, a building and its (literal) ground. To paraphrase Wright, a house should not be on a hill – it should instead be of a hill. To follow, a man should not live on the earth, he should instead live of the earth (Behrens 2002).

In thinking about figure-ground relationships, an image that may spring to mind is a pair of diagrams that accompanied his various writings about human vision by American psychologist Julian E Hochberg (Hochberg 1964). These were published about fifty years ago (maybe earlier), so by now they are hardly surprising. But back then they were a novel, less doctrinaire way to portray gestalt psychologist Edgar Rubin's 'vase or faces' diagram, his all-too-familiar example of 'reversible figure-ground.' In textbooks prior to Hochberg's, this had been illustrated by a flat graphic of a black vase against a white background, or of two white profiles set against a black background. It was Hochberg's innovation to reconfigure these as three-dimensional silhouette cut-outs, as if they had been made today using the layers option in Adobe Photoshop.

It is especially instructive to look at the second stage of this, in which the 'figure' is a cut-out hole through which we observe the 'ground' (in this case, a literal background). In the second half of the 20th century, this was a familiar surrealist technique among artists because of its frequent use by the Belgian painter René Magritte. But that too has its precedents. In the late 19th century, it was common for newspapers and magazines to feature 'puzzle pictures' in which a shape that initially looks like an area of little consequence became, by a switch of attention, a significant, meaningful figure. In one widely-published example, at first we see what seems to be an image of trees on the Island of Elba – and then by a switch of attention, the space between the trees becomes the profile of Napoleon in exile. In another, Abraham Lincoln, on horseback, rides through a benign grove of trees – and then, suddenly, the space between the trees becomes the ghostly figure of his assassin, John Wilkes Booth.

In the mid-1890s, as Abbott Thayer struggled to understand protective colouration in nature, and later, to adapt his findings to military camouflage, the New Hampshire painter-naturalist was all but completely oblivious to signs of the onslaught of modernism. He had no interest in cubism, vorticism or surrealism, but he was an avid follower of the daily newspapers, their cartoons, jokes and puzzles. Surely these influenced him (years in advance of the work of Magritte) as he and his son Gerald laboured to complete their book *Concealing coloration in the animal kingdom*, first published in 1909 (Thayer 1909, 1918).

Among its indelible contents is a two-page demonstration of the concealment of a copperhead snake in the context of a floor of leaves. In the book, the page on which the snake appears is preceded by a blank page that has a cut-out stencil silhouette which, when superimposed on the painting, reveals the shape and placement of the snake – in essence, the stencil extracts or 'un-embeds' the figure from the noise of the background it hides in.

Abbott and Gerald Thayer repeatedly used this approach as they devised demonstrations of animal camouflage for exhibits at European and US museums (Figure 1.1d). The elder Thayer had used it in earlier essays in which he insisted that the most effective camouflage was that in which the animal's surface pattern was (to quote one of his biographers) 'a generalization or distillation of the features of those physical settings in which the animal was commonly found' (Anderson, 1982, 116). Unfortunately, for this Thayer coined the phrase 'background picturing', which resulted in undue confusion because he surely did not mean a literal picture of the animal's habitat, but instead, as his son later clarified, something far more fleeting – a generic, abstract 'picture-pattern.'

To demonstrate this, Abbott Thayer made cut-out stencil silhouettes of birds, skunks, antelopes, zebras and even indigenous Native American warriors, whose 'war paint' he believed to be irrefutable proof of his theory.

In adapting natural camouflage for wartime purposes, Thayer took an additional, logical step. In a 1918 essay, he proposed a simple, reliable way for soldiers (or anyone) to come up with impromptu camouflage schemes. To determine the optimal camouflage for any creature – a ruffed grouse, for example – Thayer recommended that one 'has only to cut out a stencil of the soldier, ship, cannon or whatever figure he wishes to conceal, and look through the stencil from the viewpoint under consideration, to learn just what costume from that viewpoint could most tend to conceal this figure.' By the time this essay was published, World War I was ending, and camouflage was no longer a funding priority. However, when the same concerns resurfaced during World War II, Australian artist-camoufleurs, including the Sydney Camouflage Group, returned to conducting experiments with the use of cut-out stencils (Elias, 2011, 51–2).

Aesthetics and animals

In the Metropolitan Museum of Art in New York, there is a small watercolour painting by Gerald Thayer, about 20 inches square, titled *Male ruffed grouse in the forest* (Figure 1.5). At the time of its acquisition, an art critic in the *New York Tribune* described it as a 'con-

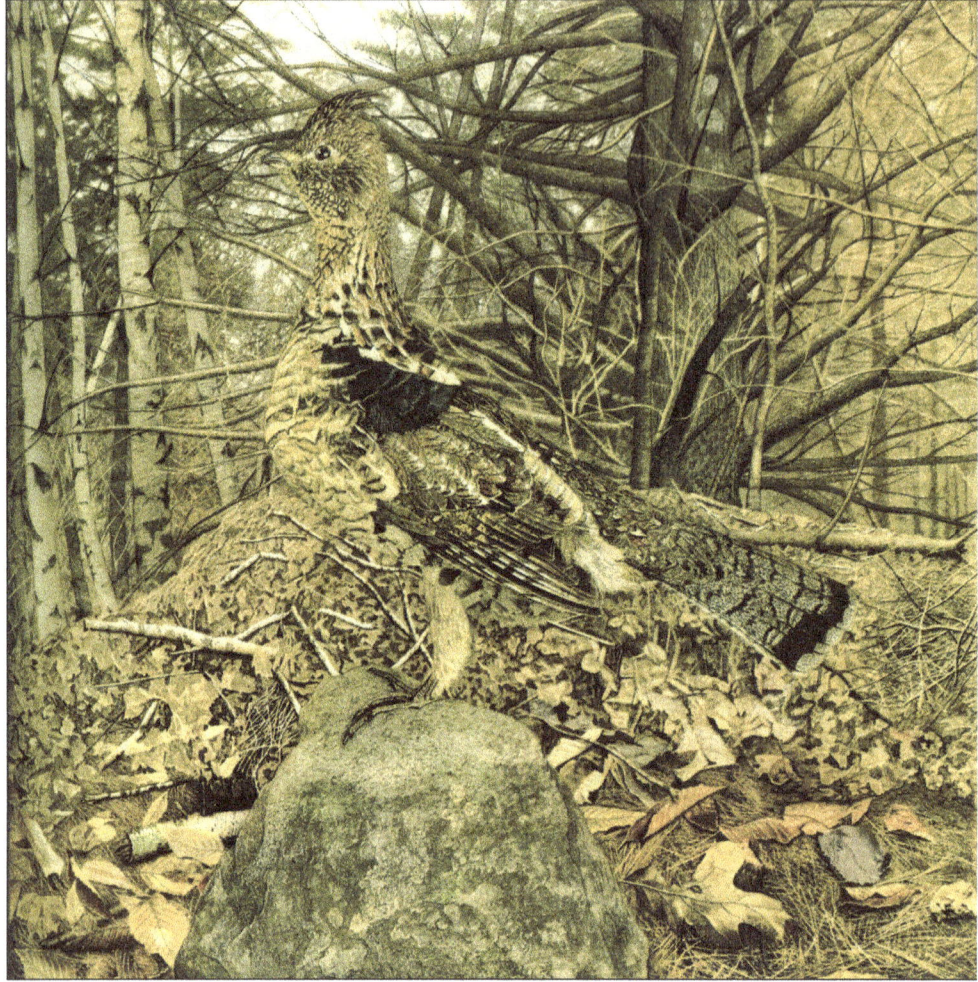

Figure 1.5 Gerald H Thayer, *Male ruffed grouse in the forest* (1907–08). Watercolour on paper. 19.75 inches high × 20 inches wide. Thayer produced this image as an illustration for his book, *Concealing coloration in the animal kingdom* (1909), Plate II, 38 (public domain). The original artwork is in the Metropolitan Museum of Art.

summate work … one of the most brilliant things of this kind since Dürer drew his famous hare' (Cortissoz, 1917, 3). No one could have known it then, but this exhaustively detailed painting was the high point in the art career of Gerald Thayer, whose woefully tragic life would end in 1939. That extraordinary painting, which took him six months to complete, is surely the finest pictorial work in his and his father's magnificent book.

As the painting's title indicates, portrayed is the elaborate feathered attire of a ruffed grouse, encountered in a woodland setting. The grouse is completely motionless (which is a common means of defence among many animals) for the same reason that the Ames distorted room works best from a rigid, 'frozen' one-eyed view. Motion is a great spoiler of camouflage, and if the grouse moves even a muscle, it will be quickly given away. Gerald

Thayer's painting looks as if it were painted from life, but in fact (accordingly to the artist) it 'was painted from woodland photographs, etc., and from a stuffed grouse in a house with lighting artificially arranged to suit the bird's countershading'.

By countershading (also known as 'Thayer's law'), Gerald is referring to his father's initial contention (in the mid-1890s) that it is a survival advantage for animals to have light-coloured undersides, with darker colouring toward the top (Figs. 1a, b and c). As all artists know, by using the technique of shading (which makes shapes lighter at the top, and gradually darker toward the base), flat shapes drawn or painted can appear solid and three-dimensional, to protrude from the surface on which they are drawn (Behrens, 2011b). Today, when we work on computers, we typically make this happen by using 'drop shadows.' We are susceptible to this trick, according to neuroscientists, because the human brain 'comes in the box' with a default setting by which we instinctively always assume that the source of light is overhead. Shading takes advantage of that; as does countershading (or inverse shading) because it counteracts or cancels out the effects of shading, and by that makes a form appear less dimensional, less 'thing-like', and less solid.

Gerald Thayer's grouse painting is extraordinary, so much so that it ought to be adopted by camouflage scholars as an occupational mascot, much like the army camoufleurs in WWI adopted the chameleon. Beyond its artistic achievement, his painting is an 'object lesson' in the most fundamental principles of camouflage (natural and military), axioms that his father described as the 'laws of disguise.'

Inadvertently, it is also a masterful lesson about other primal aspects of human vision, aspects that were first spelled out by the gestalt psychologists in the decade after Thayer's death. Those Berlin-based psychologists referred to such tendencies as 'perceptual organizing principles' and conducted extensive experiments with similarity grouping, proximity grouping, continuity, closure and so on. In 1954, one of their prominent students, Harvard psychologist and art theorist Rudolf Arnheim, published a pivotal ground-breaking book that brought all this together, titled *Art and visual perception: a psychology of the creative eye* (Arnheim 1954).

This essay began with a passage from Swiss zoologist Adolf Portmann, and it ends now with a second quote from the same author. In his book on animal camouflage, Portmann sums up the relations between camouflage and vision, which he regards as approximate parallels to disguise and display. While 'disguise and display are opposites', he writes, they are not incompatible, but simply 'two ends of the same field – here the field of vision' (Portmann 1959, 9).

In much the same way, vision is not incompatible with concealment or confusion; they are simply two opposing poles of the same continuum. Display is the figure; disguise is the ground. Vision reveals, but, in doing so, it also necessarily hides. Camouflage conceals, but it also displays what it isn't.

In fact, Thayer's laws of disguise are all but synonymous with the gestalt psychologists' perceptual organising principles (cf. Behrens 1998). They are reliable tricks of the trade that have been exploited for centuries by artists, poets, pickpockets, magicians, comedians, theatre set designers, golf course architects, fashion designers, duplicitous office-seekers – and, of course, by camoufleurs.

References

Alexander C (1964). *Notes on the synthesis of form*. Cambridge, MA: Harvard University Press.
Anderson R (1982). *Abbott Handerson Thayer*. Exhibition catalogue. Syracuse, NY: Everson Museum.
Arnheim R (1954). *Art and visual perception: a psychology of the creative eye*. Berkeley: University of California Press.
Behrens RR (1998). Art, design and gestalt theory. *Leonardo,* 31(4): 299–303.
Behrens RR (2002). *False colors: art, design and modern camouflage*. Dysart, IA: Bobolink Books.
Behrens RR (2009). *Camoupedia: a compendium of research on art, architecture and camouflage*. Dysart, IA: Bobolink Books.
Behrens RR (2010). Ames demonstrations in perception. In EB Goldstein (Ed). *Encyclopaedia of perception* (pp41–44). Thousand Oaks, CA: Sage Publications.
Behrens RR (Ed.) (2011a). *Ship shape: a dazzle camouflage sourcebook*. Dysart, IA: Bobolink Books.
Behrens RR (2011b). Nature's artistry: Abbott H. Thayer's assertions about camouflage in art, war and nature. In M Stevens & S Merilaita (Eds). *Animal camouflage: mechanisms and function* (pp87–100). Cambridge UK: Cambridge University Press.
Blodgett LS (1919). *Ship camouflage*. Thesis. Cambridge, MA: MIT.
Chermayeff S and C Alexander (1965). *Community and privacy: notes toward an architecture of humanism*. New York: Anchor Books.
Cortissoz R (1917) The personal accent in American art today. In *New York Tribune*, (April 13), 3.
Coutin C (2012). *Tromper l'ennemi: l'invention du camouflage moderne en 1914–1918*. Paris: Éditions Pierre de Taillac et Ministère de la Défense.
Elias A (2008). William Dakin on camouflage in nature and war. *Journal of Australian Studies.* 22(2): 251–63.
Elias A (2011). *Camouflage Australia: art, nature, science and war*. Sydney: Sydney University Press.
Elkins J (1997). *The object stares back: on the nature of seeing*. New York: Houghton Mifflin Harcourt.
Evans RT (2010). *Grant Wood: a life*. New York: Random House.
Gombrich EH (1982) *The image and the eye: further studies in the psychology of pictorial representation*. Ithaca, NY: Cornell University Press.
Hochberg JE (1964). *Perception*. Englewood Cliffs, NJ: Prentice-Hall.
Hsu H (2006). Who wears the mask? *Minnesota Review,* 2006(67): 169–75.
Ittelson WH (1968). *The Ames demonstrations in perception*. New York: Hafner.
Kahn EL (1984). *The neglected majority: 'les camoufleurs', art history, and World War I*. Lanham, NY: University Press of America.
Koestler A (1967). *The ghost in the machine*. New York: Macmillan.
Leach N (2006). *Camouflage*. Cambridge, MA: MIT Press.
Liberman A (1960). *The artist in his studio*. London: Thames and Hudson.
Portmann A (1959). *Animal camouflage*. Ann Arbor: University of Michigan Press.
Post A (Ed) (2013). *Abbott Handerson Thayer: a beautiful law of nature*. Exhibition catalogue. Washington, DC: Gold Leaf Studios.
Schachtel EG (1959). *Metamorphosis: on the development of affect, perception, attention and memory*. New York: Basic Books.
Shell HR (2012). *Hide and seek: camouflage, photography and the media of reconnaissance*. New York: Zone Books.
Stevens M & Merilaita S (Eds) (2011). *Animal camouflage: mechanisms and function*. Cambridge UK: Cambridge University Press.
Thayer AH (1918). Camouflage. *The Scientific Monthly*. VII: 481–94.
Thayer GH (1909, 1918). *Concealing coloration in the animal kingdom*. New York: Macmillan.
Warner EL (1919). The science of marine camouflage design. In *Transactions of the Illuminating Engineering Society*. 14(5): 215–19. Reprinted in Behrens (2011a) as The science of ship camouflage, 212–19.

Watts A (1969). *The two hands of god: the myths of polarity*. New York: Collier Books.
Weiss PA (1969). The living system: determinism stratified. In A Koestler and JR Smythies (Eds). *Beyond reductionism* (pp 3–55). Boston: Beacon Press.

2
Camouflage and mimesis – deception, evolutionary biology and imitation

Bernd Hüppauf

Mimesis and camouflage

Camouflage needs to be linked to mimesis. Mimesis and camouflage are abstract theoretical concepts, tacitly related to each other. They refer to opposing relationships to reality. Camouflage is deception yet cannot be understood without a concept of mimetic realism. They place emphasis on confidence and distrust, respectively. While designating oppositions, they also refer to identical techniques of relating to the world, resulting in repetition and creativity.

While the term camouflage was not used before the 19th century, *mimesis* can be traced back to the origin of European literature and philosophy. From Plato on, mimesis has been a concept for a disciplined relationship to reality (Auerbach 1953; Gebauer & Wulf 1992; Halliwell 2002). It has been defined in opposition to the anarchy of magic and in close proximity to realism and naturalism. The philosophical theory of mimesis created the framework for reality as realisation of the three ideals of truth, beauty, and the good. It encompasses terms such as imitation and *imitatio*, representation, replication and assimilation, and approximation. In Homer and the Bible, it has been argued, mimesis has been constitutive for creating order and, as Girard maintains, it is an order of the self in relation to others (Girard 1999).

Mimesis is an ambiguous term. It is at the same time cognition and evaluation. Its cognitive result is imitation. There is no imitation without difference. To describe an object in terms of mimesis is to acknowledge that there is no identity. It is not the thing itself. We call toy animals realistic, but not a zoo. If mimetic imitation were to be wholly at one with what it represents, it would cease to be a representation. A text that would succeed in making its words 'become' the animal they describe would be an animal breeder. Language is real, as real as a living animal, and this genuine reality is precisely the reason why it cannot *be* an animal. In this sense, all products of culture, including the most realist art, cannot be thought of without a gap of untruth.

The fact of deception is most obvious when an artist includes details that are redundant such as a precise fold in a frog's skin in order to signal an intention: 'This is a realist image.' Realistic mimesis aims at an '*effet de réel*' (Roland Barthes). Contrary to common understanding and propagated objectives, it can be called *calculated deception*. The difference creates the gap for the emergence of two distinct implications.

(1) Mimesis means more than realistic representation and more than sensuous effect. It not only shows by imitation but makes visible. It is invented for the unappeasable desire of representing an object as closely as possible but, like *nature* and *culture*, it undecidedly hovers between the real and the imaginative, evidence and value, empirical fact and cultural (constructed) fact, description and value judgment. Mimesis has the ability to create a convincing deception of perceiving an object such as an animal as it really is. To this effect it includes knowledge of the underlying *techniques of nature*. It is supposed to create an approach to life capable of grasping its dynamics which, in the age of modern science, are determined by the process of evolution.

(2) The other effect of the gap in calculated deception is the emergence of images and cultural practices of camouflage.

Camouflage is linked to and at the same time transcends the means of mimesis and can be interpreted as a fundamental characteristic of an *anti-mimetic effect* (Ott 2010, 9). It means the end of imitation and, in pretending to be something which it is not, it subverts the ideal of identification of represented distinct objects. It needs realist imitation and necessarily also includes falsification and lying.

Philosophy in the Platonic and Christian tradition was solely concerned with the concept of truth. Camouflage as a technique for deception and a form of lying goes back to the origin of representation but was not elevated to the level of serious theory building. In contrast to theories of mimesis, camouflage was a latecomer. As far as theories of the social construction of reality are concerned, camouflage has not given rise to substantial attempts at conceptualisation.

In nature, camouflage is the product of an anonymous force of deflection and departure from existing reality. Whereas mimesis is conditional upon the separation of self and other, camouflage is a term for transformation and shifting boundaries, built upon a rupture within an underdetermined self. While mimesis is built upon an operation that separates what is alike and what differs, what belongs together and what falls apart, camouflage is built upon the blurring of these differences and creates obscurity by making distinct and separate parts appear like others. Instead of imitation, camouflage refers to deviation and construction in both nature and culture. Its cultural origin is the power of the imagination and it is a product of the magical mind (Stevens 1996). Camouflage is a term that emphatically covers freedom and creativity. It is 'disorder (as are trance and ecstasy)' (Behrens 1981, 71; Bergson 1907).

Its pretence exploits a weakness of perception on the part of the viewer, both animal and human being. If we wish to comprehend camouflage as a combination of imitation and (deceiving) creation, a conception of mimesis that includes a theory of image building by perception cum deception is required.

Camouflage in nature and as cultural practice remained theoretically unaccounted for until in the late 19th century the modern scientific mind postulated that deception is a function of evolution. Observations of camouflage in nature as well as cultural practices go back to hunting, magic and rituals. Observers narrated stories and invented or recreated myths built around camouflage. Judged by the standards of modern zoological knowledge, authors prior to Darwinian theory had no understanding of their own observations as the myths collected by Ovidius demonstrate.

Evolutionary theory is, from a philosophical point of view, realism. However, it is not clear how one can represent reality which is constantly changing without striking it dead in the process of imitating it at a specific point in time. There is no reason to assume a logical link between the process of evolution and mimesis. Yet a strong connection cannot be doubted.

If Darwin's theory of natural selection is credited with creating a conceptual framework for comprehending diversity in nature, camouflage needs to be included. Once the animal was emancipated from metaphysics and granted a status of its own within a conception of life determined by evolutionary theory, theories of camouflage emerged. It is the function in the evolutionary process which allocates camouflage a position in life. As a result of theorising, camouflage was subjugated to a system of concepts and tamed. Trance and ecstasy were overruled and it was finally put to military service. World War I turned camouflage into a formidable industry. Yet until the present, camouflage retained an anarchic dimension of disorder and unpredictability that creates a problem for evolutionary theory.

This essay turns the modern zoological approach to camouflage into a problem and argues that, while evolutionary theory is the only conceptual framework for understanding camouflage, it is incapable of providing a full explanation. Camouflage is much more than purposeful mimicry and imitation. Within a Darwinian theoretical framework, a camouflaging animal can be treated as a *thing* outside of human activity. However, even in the era of the sciences animals such as the frog are not completely emancipated from magic and arbitrariness in human culture. Frogs are animals of camouflage but frog images are examples of natural selection's incapacity for full explanation. This essay argues further that camouflage has two origins: nature and social civilisation (Haraway 2007, Huppauf 2011). Their relationship is complex. They have interacted but must not be conflated. It is obvious that camouflage in nature has an impact on theories of camouflage in culture, but the one cannot be explained as the extension of the other. Man-made camouflage is often interpreted as an imitation of camouflage in nature. This is false causality. Both origin and function differ. Also, man-made camouflage has repercussions for theories of camouflage in nature. Several thousand years of imagining and imaging animals like the frog as animals of magic have not disappeared without a trace. Furthermore, it has been argued that some genetically coded behaviour has an origin in culturally determined behaviour. Yet, given these interrelationships, there is a need to distinguish between the two and to ask whether the same categories can be applied to both (Eibl 2009, Garrels 2011, Graber 1995).

Distinctions

Camouflage is not a harmless cultural technique. In his opening address of a Sydney conference in 2013 Roy Behrens refers to George Steiner's sentence that camouflage in all its forms is a means to maintain the equilibrium of the mind. I disagree. It does not belong to the theories of balance and harmony of the mind. It is irreconcilable with a Rousseauian construction of nature as a harmonious equilibrium and is set in motion by continuous competition, opposition, antagonism, and fights to gain an advantage. Camouflage needs to be extended to including conflict and the changes associated with force or violence (Boas 1911). Camouflage has never been concerned with harmony, but with power and domination and conflict on an invisible battlefield. It is part of a struggle that has not ended with the onset of the age of reason and rationality. Camouflage can be thought of as virtual visual (and sometimes acoustic) warfare. Its early philosopher is Heraclites who speaks of *polemos* as the origin of development and social innovation.

We can distinguish between four areas and conceptions of camouflage. They emerged in different epochs of civilisation, remain to a certain extent discrete, and cannot be joined together in a linear sequence. We associate, for instance, a magical concept of camouflage with phases of early human history, but aspects of it can be detected in contemporary culture; or forms of an experimental attitude can be found in the mental order of mythology.

In a *magical* conception of nature, camouflage is perceived as an implicit feature of a system of sentences revealed from a position of metaphysical authority. In this system, camouflage is the product of imagination on a high level of abstraction and requires belief in the power of magicians to be capable of suspending the laws of nature. An animal mask, for example, is neither mere pretence nor plain imitation, but has the power to transform the bearer into a different being with qualities that require and support attributes of *reality*. Customarily we call this attitude sorcery. It is more closely related to our own image of the animal and concept of camouflage (for example in fashion and the arts) than is suggested by the self-image of the era of the sciences.

In *mythology*, camouflage moves away from abstraction. It is primarily metamorphosis rather than mimicry and consists of (literary) narratives. Its means are false appearance, dissimulation, masking, semblance, disguise, concealment, and masquerade. In his *Historia animalium*, Aristotle speaks of animals changing shape and colour. There is an abundance of stories about the calculated aim of deception; for example, of Zeus camouflaging with the intent of deceiving a woman in order to have sex. Ancient Roman authors wrote about techniques of concealing and camouflaging by changing body shapes, the key opus being Publius Ovidius Naso's *Metamorphoses* (8 AD). Ovid wrote about humans, animals and plants, even minerals, changing their bodily appearance, and spoke with peasants about frogs – without, however, drawing theoretical conclusions about their changing appearance. Narration rather than explanation remained the final objective. This social practice of camouflage extends to the present during exceptional situations such as rituals or feasts.

In the *scientific epoch*, the concept of camouflage is not the result of faith or make-believe. On the contrary, scepticism *liberates* camouflage from systems of belief. Following the invention of reality based upon the concepts of fact and evidence in the early modern period, camouflage from the 19th century on was primarily observed as mimicry and imitation. It was the product of sense perception, supported by experimentation, and was made an object of scientific research. It was subjected to scientific theory-building in zoology. Results were considered a revelation of truth. Evolutionary theory conceives of camouflage as a concept that is useful to decipher mechanisms of adaptation. Scientists hypothesised that the aim of camouflage is adaptation in order to create an advantage over competitors. Its means are deceptive body shaping, marking and colouring. In addition to protection, an aggressive variant of mimicry was described (Poulton 1909).

In response to the era of empiricism and evidence, *post-industrial* culture expresses doubt concerning scientific truth and the senses. They can mislead and deceive. What is fake is not necessarily a sham or fraudulent. We simulate the world we live in. Postmodernist theory demonstrates that simulation is an element of reality. Camouflage can be interpreted as a strategy for creating reality (Schwartz 2000)[1] while authenticity is a construction and hence subject to manipulation and delusion. What we call reality may be facade and nothing else. With no value judgment passed, camouflage can then be characterised as a significant feature of reality in times of war and peace. Robert Musil spoke of modern man and a world *ohne Eigenschaften*, without qualities. In the absence of qualities, no masquerading is possible and no camouflaging necessary as there is nothing to hide. Yet, in the epoch of modern science, reality is not fixed but is made up of possibilities that call for a *Möglichkeitssinn* (Musil 1987, 16), a sense for the possible. These possible worlds appear as variants created through techniques of camouflaging with no original behind the deception.

Three basic questions

Any theory of camouflage will pursue three basic issues.

What? 'What' is the subject of camouflaging, its substratum that requires and supports attributes of nature or social culture. The 'what' has been made the object of evolutionary theory in terms of Thayer's *revelation* (Thayer & Thayer 1918). Not all animals in the animal kingdom use techniques of camouflage. Most animals do not. The technique is independent of the level of complexity of the organism. Primitive animals (of the sea), insects, caterpillars, reptiles and frogs, birds, and some mammals use camouflage. Can they be categorised in terms of an ontology? Cubism broke up the *what* into fragments with non-realistic relationships to each other. 'Under cubist attack the object first disintegrated into uncertain plains, then disappeared into an illusion of the object. The technique of camouflage assumed there was an object to camouflage, that there was a self to take on a protective colouration' (Sypher 1962, 86). This self disintegrated in the early 20th century.

The *what* can be defined in a different way. What do we perceive as the subject of camouflage? Cott distinguishes four aspects (Cott 1940, quoted in Newark 2007, 31; see also Behrens 1981, 2009; Forbes 2009). Recognition by sight, as Gestalt theory has consistently elaborated, is the perception of a contrast between a continuous field of colour and a background. The object is thrown into relief by the effect of light and shade that enables the eye to detect surface curvature. In observation, the surface of visible bodies is framed by a contour with a characteristic shape, and, finally, under most conditions, a shadow will be thrown by the object. These aspects of vision determine a phenomenology of the *what*.

The possible impact of cultural evolution on heredity is an open question. Until the late 20th century, not much was known about the impact of calculated camouflage on reproduction. Based on new knowledge, scientists at the end of the last century began asking questions about the function of genes and chromosomes for the origin of individual adaptations and adaptation as an evolutionary process (Boyd 1988; Barkow et al.. 1995; Odling-Smee et al.. 2003; Lange 2012; see also Newark 2007, 34). We have become aware of an interdependent interplay of cells, genomes, natural and cultural environments and their changes. Examples of cultural evolution have been investigated in generations of birds and monkeys. But, Dawkins summarises, 'it is our own species that really shows what cultural evolution can do' (Dawkins 1976, 190).

---

1 Authenticity and by implication camouflage is a central issue of current debate on art and fiction. There is a host of literature on authenticity and illusion from Ernst Gombrich's pioneering book *Art and illusion* (1960) and Richard Gregor & Ernst Gombrich's *Illusions in nature and art* (1973) to postmodern reflections on authenticity as fiction.

In contrast to camouflage in nature, the subject of camouflage in human societies was never fixed and needed identification. Apart from mythological animals, it has always been the privilege of gods and occasionally goddesses to change appearance and identity. Human camouflage is restricted to exceptional situations. Public celebrations, the Saturnalia and Bacchanalia, ritual dancing in Africa and Asia, Christian carnival, and the circus are based on the distinction between inside and outside. Outside of these restricted phases camouflaging is not permitted and sanctioned; inside of them special rules apply so that a different subject is constituted.

A special situation for camouflage is warfare when the *what* is determined according to the rules of organised violent conflict.

How? 'How' asks for the means and techniques of camouflaging. The magic mind has been characterised by a simultaneity of two different forms of existence. In the scientific approach to the *how* of camouflage, reductionism and causal determination dominate.

How? is a question which leads to description and includes no evaluation and no investigation of reasons and grounds. How is it possible to be hidden in *plain sight*? How do the various techniques work with which camouflage fools perception and exploits the physiology of the senses and the neural system? The probability of detection is lowered by matching background colours and textures and imitating patterns of the immediate environment. Calculated colour patterns interfere with detection. Following Thayer, Roy Behrens argues (2012) that camouflage causes confusion between an object and its background (blending) or makes a single thing divide into meaningless fragments or, and this makes mimesis a major technique, reduces differences between one kind of object and another. These are the foremost reasons for the importance of artificial camouflage in warfare.

Animal camouflage is highly successful and suggests that diverse visual systems from different phases of evolution share principles of visual organisation and basics of perception. Does the success of animal camouflage reveal universal principles that apply regardless of retinal complexity and neural systems? We customarily work on the assumption that a brilliant red on an animal's body will be interpreted as a sign of warning both by a human observer and an animal; for example, a snake looking at a frog. Is this justified? Are the means of camouflage shared by animals and humans and do techniques of perception remain identical over time?

What for? Camouflage was shrouded in mystery and fantasy. In the era of the sciences the explanation of camouflage as a means in the struggle for survival is common and convincing. It is doubtful, however, that this explanation can fully answer to the question '*What for?*'

Evolution cannot be observed because it is a theoretical construction in reference to extremely long periods of time. How do we account for the dynamics of the construction? Teleological systems offer a pseudo-explanation for change and the riddle of camouflage. Camouflage is ill-understood as long as it is considered an element of teleology. A theory of camouflage must do without macro-history and the idea of finalisation. As soon as it concerns itself with concrete issues, theory requires the observer to narrow down the scope of questions. What are the intrinsic ends of camouflage?

As far as natural selection is concerned, protection and increasing diversity are some of these ends. Is bio-diversity an end in itself? This is irrelevant in the humanities and social sciences. Can the '*What for?*' question be answered without referring to competition and struggle as the driving force? Can aesthetics, beauty, and ugliness, or negative drives such as destructive aggression provide an answer? To what extent can camouflage be an enjoyable game with no purpose and no evolutionary function? If camouflage has a dimension of play, this has seldom been considered.

Social historians customarily argue that societies create discourse in order to mask their true character; for example, an altruism discourse behind which colonial societies can hide exploitation and greed. Colonial studies engages in the project of de-camouflaging these societies and in exposing deceiving techniques during a specific period. As far as individual camouflage is concerned, the motives, dynamics and ends are less difficult to determine. Yet the problems are as difficult. Individual camouflage needs others, a group at which it is directed. Motives of this intention are often ambivalent and sometimes hidden from consciousness and consequently invite abstract theory and speculation in the approach to the 'What for?' question. What are the advantages of camouflage outside of its military applications?

Camouflage in a world of magic

Prior to a brief presentation of the modern conception of camouflage, I will introduce a concept of nature that is fundamentally different from that of modern science. In different definitions of nature, the 'what' for instance, the image of an animal, differs. The relationship between zoological and cultural images of camouflage can be made significant in terms of understanding the mental structure of a period and its relationship to nature. I will not deal with camouflage in mythology. Rather, I will focus on magic and then turn to the era of the sciences.

Magic thinking is distinct from modern scientific theory by basic differences. As far as camouflage is concerned, five major differences can be discerned. There is no compelling relationship between cause and effect and contingency replaces causality. Reality is not separated from the human will and can be influenced by thoughts, verbal formulas and rituals (using masks). Gods, spirits and heroes have the power to change natural shapes (metamorphosis) and identities and connect normally unconnected beings and events (telepathy). Things in nature (stones, plants, animals) are animated and have characteristics that can affect humans and be transferred to them. The future can be known by humans with a special relationship to transcendence; this special relationship can be established through metamorphosis.

Unlike modern scientific thought, the mental system of animism and the magic mind have no conception of evolutionary forces. Animals are not considered the product of a nature independent of human beings. They are a product of god's intentions combined with spiritual and theological discourse. In magical thought and practices, animals conform to a principle of emotionality and empathy (Frazer calls it *sympathy*) that establishes a connection of strong emotions such as love and hate, sympathy or antipathy between things and living beings that resemble each other or between beings that have been in physical or spiritual contact with each other. Stories about the instability of bodies combine human beings and animals in a common fate.

In magical and mythical approaches to nature, there can be no conception and no treatment of an animal as a *product of nature*. An animal's camouflage is not a technique for protection against predators but expression of an *élan vital*. Their image is never arbitrary but carries a meaning assigned to it by the wider and theologically defined community. It can be transferred between different contexts and from one ritual to another and has the power to motivate natural forces or can serve as a defence against malignant spirits. The animal's body is a masquerade, employed with the intention of hiding a secret. Some symbolic animals such as the eagle or lion can be understood by everyone in every culture as their strength and nobility are cultural universals. They are unambiguously recognised as royal.

Among the first ethnologists who thought about magic as a serious way of thinking were Franz Boas and Lucien Lévy-Bruhl. Boas subscribed to Darwinian theory without, however, assuming that it could be applied to culture and history without qualification. He distinguished between biological heredity and cultural constructions and focused on cultural processes. Lévy-Bruhl's study of shamanism and his concept of *participation mystique* (Lévy-Bruhl 1922) demonstrated opposition to the concept of evolutionary anthropology and evolutionary ethics. The rejection of theories of social and cultural evolution – theories which I refer to in the context of the scientific era – is often labelled cultural relativism. It was a great accomplishment and opened an avenue to comprehending camouflage.

The theory of simultaneity of two beings in one body can be supported by the observation of camouflage. The earliest humans designing camouflage, it has been speculated, were hunters in their attempt to deceive their prey. Their transformation of body appearance played on the floating line between pragmatism and belief, nature and culture. The hunter believed that changing his appearance through camouflage (a buffalo hide and buffalo horns, etc.) would have an effect on the animal (Newark 2007, 38f.). It will be fooled. At the same time, another transformation will be set in motion. By putting on attire that imitates the hunted animal, hunters not only fool the animal but also themselves. The hunter becomes the animal. The buffalo hunter believes in his self-deception. His camouflaging will bestow on him the strength, speed or prowess of the animal he pretends to be. This is the point where mimesis turns into metamorphosis and a pragmatic technique of deceiving the animal is transformed to metaphysical power. Using the terminology of modern psychology, we could say that self-deception circumvents consciousness. It is beyond the hunter's control. In this framework of thought, camouflage is much more powerful than in a world of Darwinian evolution. This is an origin of natural religion as belief in the co-existence of reality and the supernatural.

1200 years after Ovid narrated metamorphoses in myths as playful – if violent – and artistic games between gods, humans and animals, the animal–human relationship was turned into a serious theological problem (Resl 2007). The early Catholic church built its image of animals upon the perception of nature as magic. It invented a family of evil animals which included the snake, the scorpion, the frog, and other ill-willed animals all characterised by deception. For over 700 years, the frog in Europe was not the product of natural selection — Catholic theology made this animal part of a nature variegated and animated by evil spirits.

Camouflage in the age of the sciences – reductionism and evolutionary theory

In the modern period, the methodology of research on camouflage was based upon reductionism, upholding the assumption that complex systems are the sum of their elements and therefore can be reduced to smaller elements with no rest remaining. This is the precondition for causality as the principle that enables the observer to fully explain reality. Within this epistemological framework, Charles Darwin's theory of evolution was the most fruitful approach to and explanation of the riddle of diversity and increasing complexity. Evolutionary theory is the only theoretical framework that generates a language and a systematic approach to explaining camouflage in nature. With Darwin's theory, camouflage could for the first time be theoretically accounted for within an epistemological framework that excludes metaphysics and subjective agency.

In his theory of evolution, Darwin links animals changing colour and body shapes to adaptation, arguing that camouflage evolved in the process of natural selection by providing certain animals with an advantage in terms of both survival and reproduction. As soon as it is made the object of reductionist evolutionary theory, camouflage is perceived as a natural strategy for survival. Mimicry is a technique of nature for avoiding being eaten by predators. These gains make camouflage a fundamental feature of evolutionary theory of nature (Darwin 1859/1985).

The first systematic and substantial work on the subject was Poulton's *Colours of animals*, followed soon thereafter by Abbott Handerson Thayer's influential studies (Poulton 1890; Thayer & Thayer 1918). Both books accepted Darwin's categories of selection as the key mechanism behind variations of animal colouration. Thayer was convinced that he had articulated 'not theories but revelations' (Loreck 2011, 163). Expressed in less apodictic phrases, the religious overtone of this statement was (and may still be) shared by many scientists who believe that evolutionary theory reveals the truth. Thayer, an artist with a life-long fascination with camouflage, introduced basic concepts such as *countershading*. He argued that camouflage is crypsis and 'all patterns and colours whatsoever of all animals that ever preyed or are preyed on are under certain normal circumstances obliterative'. He goes on about mimicry and imitation arguing that 'not one "mimicry" mark [...] exists anywhere in the world where there is not every reason to believe it the very best conceivable device for the concealment of its wearer' (Behrens 1981). A few decades later, camouflage emerged as a practice of industrialised modernity and became a cultural technique, socially accepted and controlled. It gained military importance in the First World War.

The more an analytical approach to camouflage succeeds in laying bare its hidden forces, its origin and consequences, the more it will be in accordance with the modern ideal of cognition. In fact, there is a sense in which knowledge derived from evolutionary theory is more real than reality itself, since by bringing out intrinsic mechanisms it reveals what is essential in nature and animals. Reality, being an imperfect and messy affair, fails to live up to our expectations unless its intrinsic principles of construction are revealed or, to use Kant's imperious verb, *dictated* to nature by theory. The history of the animal–human relationship is full of dictates and misreading, some unintentional and others deliberate. It is the aim of evolutionary theory to replace this arbitrariness by a relationship of causality.

Nietzsche initiated a new reflection on deceiving and lying, suggesting a redefinition and re-evaluation (Nietzsche 1980b). Camouflage is an opposition to the ideal of truth that contradicts the value system and European discourse on ethics. From Plato on and supported by Christianity, untruth was stigmatised and all but excluded from theory. This changed towards the end of the 19th century. Nietzsche shared Darwin's basic view of a value-free theory of evolution and made delusion and deception philosophically debatable. Nietzsche and later Sigmund Freud, Heidegger, and Foucault (Eribon 1991, 328) contributed to an unwritten theory of camouflage in human history.

In Nietzsche's view, deception and untruth are part of the fabric of human civilisation. Camouflage as concealment, deception, misleading and the untruth have always been a part of the fabric of human civilisation. There is, according to this view, no human life without camouflage. Nietzsche's non-moral definition of truth and lie as *extramoralisch* are important in this context (Nietzsche 1980a).

Mankind could not exist without telling stories that cannot pass a truth test. The falseness of camouflage is a universal cultural technique and necessary for survival. Visual examples have been observed in cultures that use masks, veils, costumes and body painting as means to change the appearance of human bodies. As far as deception in camouflage is concerned, Nietzsche's view and that of Darwinists such as Poulton, Thayer and their followers are compatible.

This theory of life is based on an intrinsic contradiction. Nietzsche asks for an uncompromising tearing apart of all masks ('*abreissen*'). What becomes visible, however, is not the identical self, but a subject that is itself and at the same time something else, unmasked but not authentic, camouflaged and the product of deceit and self-deception. The subject is a multitude of subjects, and our thought and generally our consciousness are based upon their interplay and struggle, (Nietzsche 1980c, 382; 1980d, 140).

Although Nietzsche and Darwin are in agreement regarding the value problem, there are elementary differences. From a Darwinian perspective, camouflage is a dependent variable in a continuous line of evolution, whereas Nietzsche perceives camouflage as a human invention in a history of discontinuity and aesthetic play.

If camouflage adds complexity to nature in terms of deception, misleading, telling untrue stories and enforcing false images, the question needs to be asked: what is its function in the overall context of evolution? Is it functional for survival? Survival of *what*?

Fundamental is the assumption of a phylogenetic structure. From the point of view of evolutionary biology, misleading through camouflage is not an individual act committed by recognisable actors. The purpose for all living organisms is to gain an evolutionary advantage over rivals and enemies. There is no subject that can be held responsible for camouflage in the process of evolution. As a strategy of nature, camouflage is the product of selection with no intention and no aim. Its genealogy is observed within the framework of a theory of progressive differentiation.

Camouflage, seen as a means for achieving evolutionary advantage, could appear *natural*. It is not. An observer is required. It is the observer's theory that gives structure to the silent closed circuit set in motion by camouflage. This communication is a theoretical construction based on informed guesses.

Regarding the *how*, evolutionary biology describes strategies as *mimesis* (imitation or mimicry) and *crypsis*, that is, practices of a system of communication based on simulated signals. A signal is a gesture, sound or body movement that triggers a specific response in the animal receiving the signal, based on a genetically coded stimulus-response effect designed by evolution (Lunau 2002, 7–16). These signals produce the effect of indices that are causally linked to the programmed response. Mimesis can be interpreted by an observer as the appropriation of foreign signals. Mimicry is also based on appropriation, but requires three players: the animal that sends a specific signal, the imitator who sends an imitation of this signal, and the receiver of the cryptograph who is unable to distinguish between the original and the cryptic signal. Misunderstanding is the aim of the cryptograph.

An observer cannot know what happens inside the imitating animal's mind during this communication. The observer's position creates the danger of misreading signals. It is most likely that it is a value-free process of a mechanical nature pursued with no intention. Nature has no concept of truth and no agent responsible for change and therefore can have no intention to deceive. Evolution knows no lie and has no freedom to deceive as it is distinct from human history and morality. In the language of evolutionary biology, deception is an inappropriate characterisation of camouflage. Camouflage as mimicry is performed with neither good nor bad intentions. Theory consequently removes all value judgments associated with camouflage and has, at least in principle, abandoned the categories of good and evil. Terms such as sham, make-believe, fraud, falsification or trick are justified in a metaphysical context, but they have no justification in an evolutionary description of camouflage. Does an animal have the intent to feign? No. Its camouflage is not an intentional act of misleading or cheating. Does this insight govern general perceptions of camouflage?

Rehabilitation of deception as a strategy of nature: Nietzsche and Darwin

According to Nietzsche, concepts are not solid and not what they pretend to be but are based on shaky metaphors. Deception is built into the metaphorical nature of language (Nietzsche 1980a). One could call concepts metaphors camouflaged as solid foundations. The origin of civilisation's most basic concepts, Nietzsche suggests, are false perceptions. Misunderstandings and errors made in the distant past have turned out to be helpful in the struggle for survival. They were cultivated because they worked to humanity's advantage. For this reason they have been maintained. Cognition and knowledge are therefore based on deception. The basis of knowledge of the world, language, Nietzsche argues, is untrue from its origin on. This origin has conveniently been forgotten. Consequently the very term truth is untenable and nothing but a convention that says little about *true* reality.

Directing the focus away from mimesis and toward camouflage leads to shifting the intention to the creative power of the mind. This creative power is inseparably linked to deception.

Deception has two distinct meanings. The first pertains to untrue narratives and lying purposefully. An example is camouflage for military purposes, like colouring cannons or countershading battleships. We can call this its subjective dimension. Its other meaning refers to evolution. Deception is unavoidable falseness ingrained in language and practised by the symbolising species. No individual and no group are able to overcome this fundamental deception. We have no choice but to accommodate ourselves to the insight that the concept of truth is inauthentic.

Contemporary evolutionary theory has adopted Nietzsche's first and more restricted idea on lying, but linked it to evolution. The difference between, on the one hand, the long *durée* of evolution, with no responsible actor who makes decisions, and, on the other, the short-term conditions, with strategists who are able to plan and deliberately deceive, is blurred.

Robert Trivers elaborates on the idea that deceit is an integral part of the process of natural selection in virtue of its evolutionary benefits (Trivers 2011). He asks why we tend to deceive and mislead ourselves rather than tell the truth. He believes that we fool ourselves not in order to overcome inhibition and fear (singing in a dark forest), but in order to deceive others more successfully. We continuously and unknowingly fool ourselves to better fool others, because a firm belief in our own strength is more successful in making others believe in our strength and makes them behave accordingly, that is, to our advantage. The more convinced we are of our camouflage as the true indication of strength, the more successful we will be in making others believe. Selection, he argues, favours genes with a disposition for lying. In the pool of genes, those which have a disposition to self-deception are especially successful, as they create, according to Trivers, an evolutionary advantage. This is a perfect answer within the framework of evolutionary theory to the irritating observation of self-deception since it demonstrates that untruth as self-deception produces an evolutionary advantage.

Question and the answer can be turned around, though. Camouflage will then correspond with structuralist conceptions of civilisation based on power, force and anonymous authority: what is the impact of using the power of misrepresentation? What happens when we deceive by misrepresenting others? We fool ourselves by believing in our own false images or narratives about the other. This is not an evolutionary sociologist's answer, as the outcome is to our disadvantage. Strong examples are provided by wars for example, the self-deception of European nations in August 1914.

This scepticism in relation to the ideal of knowledge is rejected by the sciences. They form mighty international institutions that cannot but insist on the correspondence of scientific truth and the real.

Doubting evolutionary theory – survival of the beautiful

Can camouflage as cultural practice and habit be accounted for in terms of evolution? Attempts to maintain evolutionary theory as a model capable of producing comprehensive explanation have been criticised and, a number of philosophers argue, refuted. While evolutionary theory is not false, it fails to account for a range of characteristics of nature and animals. Evolutionary biologists insist that every single colour and mark on a living being developed because they have an evolutionary function. These biologists are blinded by the theory of natural selection. What about the beautiful and the ugly? (Menninghaus 2011). Beauty is more than a means of sexual selection in the struggle for survival. We perceive as beautiful patterns of regularities from the strictly geometrical (made famous as art in nature by Ernst Haeckel (1904) and Karl Blossfeldt (1929) commenting on his stunning photographs[2]) to the ragged in the fractal beauty of corals or trees. And what about the ugly in nature and a drive for destructive aggression that leads to camouflaging?

In a recent publication, Thomas Nagel points out that, in the Darwinian, reductionist approach to explaining the world, fundamental questions of origin and complexity remain unanswered. This approach, he writes, is 'almost certainly false' (Nagel 2012, 211). The physical sciences, Nagel argues, in spite of their extraordinary success in their own domain, necessarily leave an important aspect of nature unexplained. He focuses on mental activity and argues that, if the mind is a distinct realm of life, then physical theories about the origins of life cannot be entirely correct. Complex life cannot emerge solely, as Darwinian theory suggests, from chemical and physical processes.

The development of animal organisms cannot be fully understood through the physical sciences alone. The nature of those organisms is too complex.

---

2 See Breidbach (2006); Karl Blossfeldt wrote that 'the plant must be valued as a totally artistic and architectural structure'.

> Finally ... it follows that biological evolution must be more than just a physical process, and the theory of evolution ... must become more than just a physical theory. This means that the scientific outlook, if it aspires to a more complete understanding of nature, must expand to include theories capable of explaining the appearance in the universe of mental phenomena and the subjective points of view in which they occur – theories of a different type from any we have seen so far. (Nagel 2013)

Nagel is concerned with *mental phenomena*. They include the problem of aesthetics. Can a theory of beauty and ugliness be developed within the traditional framework of evolution? No convincing attempt has been made. The playful and fantastic aspects of camouflage, I contend, are covered by his sceptical argument. The creation of mind-driven activities (e.g. camouflage) cannot solely be accounted for by the process of natural selection. Diversity and aesthetics can be an end in itself.

The power of function in the evolutionary approach to reality fails to account for the fact that camouflage can support evolution but natural selection cannot fully explain camouflage, since it signifies aspects of nature without discernible function; for example, a bird like the peacock to be beautiful and others like the crow to be ugly, or frogs to produce disharmonic sounds or beautiful songs as is the case with some South American frogs.

Evolutionary theory will either explain camouflage by reducing it to an advantage in the struggle for life or ignore it as an optional extra, like painting a functional building in bright colours. Both approaches make it impossible to understand camouflage. The drive to pretend to be another person by imitating a beautiful body or gestures of a hero is dysfunctional in the evolutionary process, as the death of a frog in Aesop's fable of the frog that tries to inflate itself to the size of an ox drastically demonstrates.

It is apparent that the description of the functional process of mutations and selections is unable to explain diversity as a principle of nature. The rules of scientific inquiry of evolution are not sufficient to explain diversity and complexity. Why should complex organic systems with characteristics that are dysfunctional for adaptation be a product of evolution? Natural selection cannot provide an appropriate explanation for camouflage. Also, camouflage in nature and camouflage as a cultural practice do not coincide and neither can be fully grasped through a theory of evolution.

A theory which is unable to account for the playfulness, enjoyment and effects of amazement, awe and dazzle is ill-equipped to help us understand camouflage. A theory incapable of accounting for basic mind-driven activities, which go back to the beginning of human history, such as camouflage, must be reconstituted or possibly abandoned.

Natural selection as the model for cultural change?

Camouflage cannot be read in categories of reductionist science only. Even if the evolution of organisms capable of camouflaging (i.e. the *what*) could be explained in terms of physical causality, the performance of camouflage, the *How?* and *What for?*, is not reducible to physical-chemical laws.

Since neither physics nor the Darwinian concept of evolution can fully account for diversity and aesthetics, it follows that explanation by purely functional theory is inadequate and therefore they must be accounted for in different terms. Another approach is needed.

Evolutionary theory needs to be reconstituted in order to be able to include the emergence and development of camouflage.

Darwin himself has shown the way. It took him more than a decade to complete his thoughts and introduce the concept of sexual selection in *The descent of man, and selection in relation to sex* (1871). In this *second theory* of evolution, Darwin argues that some traits in nature are selected not by nature but by females. These traits are not the fittest, but the most beautiful. A colourful combination of feathers, an elaborate but *useless* song, frills, dewlaps and other characteristics of the body that females appreciate will be included in the process of selection when enough generations of males have been exposed to this preference. The peacock has its tail and the deer its antlers because females have preferred them over many generations. They are a liability in terms of strict natural selection. Yet as long as the laws of physics and chemistry make it possible, beauty, it seems, will evolve and evolves in unexpected ways (Prum & Brush 2002, 2003; Bostwick & Prum 2005; Prum 2006).

Sexual selection is a closed system. Research demonstrates that the genes for specific colours and patterns are linked to genes for a preference for that pattern in mating choice. Certainly, these patterns do have to submit to the rigor of survival by natural selection. But they also have a range of freedom. The evolutionary ornithologist Richard Prum argues that Darwin's ideas about sexual selection should be taken at face value, and not as a variation of natural selection. Dysfunctional characteristics need to be included in the basic concepts of explanation. The peacock's plumage, bowerbirds, and colourful frogs are examples of aesthetics in nature until their aesthetics are proven functional. He stresses that the female's sexually preferred trait is arbitrary, an aesthetic choice un-coupled from natural selection. The beak of the finch can crack open seeds. As the seeds change and evolve in size and hardness, the beak also evolves in order to face the challenge. The sexual display of a bird like the *manakin* functions in an entirely different way, affecting not the outside world but the mind of female birds. 'To understand how these aspects of biodiversity evolve', Prum (2012) argues, 'we must understand that the challenge is one of seducing a mind that has the capacity to evolve nearly infinite preferences. We see in sexually selected traits a much greater diversity than we see in those traits that are under strict natural selection.'

Rothenberg supports this argument. His *Survival of the beautiful* pursues the question whether colours and patterns on animals and plants can be fully defined by physics and chemistry – or are they accidental and *useless* beauty? The bowerbird's *power* is devoid of utility, he demonstrates. The bird has but one purpose: to be beautiful and to be seen by a female audience. The optical game cannot be understood without the idea of aesthetics as a dysfunctional quality.

> It's so confusing
> But so amusing
> The ruses
> One uses
> Are nature's own scheme ...
> Though we're like mirages
> We're all camouflages –
> Things are not what they seem ... (R. Gilder 1944, quoted in Behrens 1981, 64)

The mirages are an evolutionary irresponsibility and associated by Behrens with *trance* and *ecstasy* (1981, 71). Nature practised this freedom of *l'art pour l'art* long before it was introduced to art history. Camouflage can only be accounted for when its dimension of purposeless *l'art pour l'art* is acknowledged as rupture.

References

Auerbach E (1953). *Mimesis: the representation of reality in western literature.* Translated by William R. Trask. Princeton: Princeton University Press.
Barkow J, Cosmides L & Tooby, J (1995). *The adapted mind: evolutionary psychology and the generation of culture.* New York: Oxford University Press.
Behrens RR (1981). *Art & camouflage: concealment and deception in nature, art and war.* Cedar Falls, Iowa: North American Review, University of Northern Iowa.
Behrens RR (2009). *Camoupedia: a compendium of research on art, architecture and camouflage.* Iowa: Bobolink Books.
Behrens RR (Ed.) (2012). *Ship shape: a dazzle camouflage sourcebook.* Iowa: Bobolink Books.
Bergson H (1907). *L'évolution créatrice.* Paris.
Blossfeldt K (1929). *Urformen der kunst.* Berlin: Verlag Ernst Wasmuth A.G.
Boas F (1911). *The mind of primitive man.* New York, Macmillan.
Bostwick KS & Prum RO (2005). Courting bird songs with stridulating wing feathers. *Science,* 309(5735): 736.
Boyd R (1988). *Culture and the evolutionary process.* Chicago: The University of Chicago Press.
Breidbach O (2006). *Visions of nature: the art and science of Ernst Haeckel.* Munich: Prestel.
Cott H (1940). *Adaptive coloration in animals.* London: Methuen.
Darwin C (1859). *On the origin of species by means of natural selection, or the preservation of favoured races in the struggle for life.* Repr. London 1985: Penguin Classics.
Darwin C (1871). *The descent of man, and selection in relation to sex* (1st ed.). London: John Murray.
Dawkins R (1976). *The selfish gene.* Oxford: Oxford University Press.
Eibl K (2009). *Kultur als Zwischenwelt. Eine evolutionsbiologische Perspektive.* Frankfurt/M.
Eribon D (1991) [1989]. *Michel Foucault.* Cambridge, MA.
Forbes P (2009). *Dazzled and deceived: mimicry and camouflage.* New Haven: Yale University Press.
Garrels SR (ed.) (2011). *Mimesis and science: empirical research on imitation and the mimetic theory of culture and religion.* East Lansing.
Gebauer G & Wulf C (1992). *Mimesis: Kultur, Kunst, Gesellschaft.* Reinbek: Rororo; Auflage.
Girard R (1999). *Figuren des begehrens. Das selbst und der andere in der fiktionalen Realität. Beiträge zur mimetischen Theorie.* München, Wien.
Gombrich E (1960). *Art and illusion. A study in the psychology of pictorial representation.* Princeton, London: Princeton University Press.
Gregor R & Gombrich E (1973). *Illusions in nature and art.* London: Duckworth.
Graber RB (1995). *A scientific model of social and cultural evolution.* Kirksville, MO.
Haeckel E (1904). *Kunstformen der Natur.* Leipzig, Wien: Prestel.
Haeckel E (1904). *Die Lebenswunder: Gemeinverständliche Studien über Biologische Philosophie.* Stuttgart: Alfred Kröner.
Halliwell S (2002). *The aesthetics of mimesis: ancient texts and modern problems.* Princeton, N.J: Princeton University Press.
Haraway D (2007). *When species meet.* Minneapolis: University of Minnesota Press.
Hüppauf B (2011). *Vom Frosch. Zwischen Philosophie und Ökologie.* Bielefeld.
Lange A (2012). *Darwins Erbe im Umbau. Die Säulen der erweiterten Synthese in der Evolutionstheorie.* Würzburg: Königshausen & Neumann.

Lévy-Bruhl L (1922). *La mentalité primitive*. Paris: Librairie Félix Alcan. (English *Primitive Mentality*, 1923).

Loreck H (2011). Mimikry, Mimese und Camouflage. In: Anne-Rose Meyer & Sabine Sielke (eds.), *Verschleierungstaktiken. Strategien von eingeschränkter Sichtbarkeit, Tarnung und Täuschung in Natur und Kultur*. Frankfurt/M. etc., 159–84.

Lunau Kl (2002). *Warnen, Tarnen, Täuschen*. Darmstadt: Wissenschaftliche Buchgesellschaft.

Menninghaus W (2011). *Wozu Kunst? Ästhetik nach Darwin*. Frankfurt/M.

Musil R (1930/32). *Der Mann ohne Eigenschaften* (Vol.1, p 16). Reinbeck: Rowohlt.

Nagel T (2012). *Mind and cosmos. Why the materialist neo-Darwinian conception of nature is almost certainly false*. Oxford: Oxford University Press.

Nagel T (2013). The core of 'mind and cosmos'. *The New York Times*, August 18.

Newark T (2007). *Camouflage*. New York: Thames & Hudson in association with the Imperial War Museum London.

Nietzsche F (1980a). Über Wahrheit und Lüge im außermoralischen Sinn, In G Colli & C Montinari (Eds). *Sämtliche Werke*, vol. 3 (pp. 873-90), Berlin: Walter de Gruyter.

Nietzsche F (1980b). Die fröhliche Wissenschaft. In: *Sämtliche Werke*, vol. 1, ed. Georgio Colli & Claudio Montenari. Munich, 343–652.

Nietzsche F (1980c). Nachgelassene Fragmente. In G Colli & C Montinari (eds.), *Kritische Gesamtausgabe*, vol. VII/3 (p. 382), Berlin: Walter de Gruyter.

Nietzsche F (1980d). Also sprach Zarathustra. In: Georgio Colli & Claudio Montenari (eds.) *Kritische Gesamtausgabe*, vol. VI/1, Berlin: Walter de Gruyter.

Odling-Smee FJ, Feldman, MW & Laland, KN (2003). *Niche construction. The neglected process in evolution*. Princeton: Princeton University Press.

Ott K-H (2010) *Die vielen Abschiede von der Mimesis*. Stuttgart: Franz Steiner Verlag.

Poulton EB (1890). *The colour of animals: their meaning and use, especially considered in the case of insects*. London: Kegan Paul.

Prum RO (2006). Anatomy, physics, and evolution of structural colors. In Hill GE & McGraw KJ (Eds). *Bird coloration: mechanisms and measurements* (pp. 295–353). Cambridge MA: Harvard University Press.

Prum RO (2012). Aesthetic evolution by mate choice; Darwin's *really* dangerous idea. *Philosophical Transactions of the Royal Society of London*, B.367, 2253–65.

Prum RO & Brush AH (2002). The evolutionary origin and diversification of feathers. *The Quarterly Review of Biology*, 77(3): 261–95.

Prum RO & Brush AH (2003). Which came first, the feather or the bird? *Scientific American*, 288(3): 84–93.

Resl B (Ed) (2007). *The Cultural History of Animals*. Vol. 2: The Medieval Age. Oxford, New York.

Rothenberg D (2011). *Survival of the beautiful: art science and evolution*. London: Bloomsbury Publishing Plc.

Schwartz H (2000). *Déjà vu. Die Welt im Zeitalter ihrer tatsächlichen Reproduzierbarkeit*. Berlin.

Stevens P (1996). Magic. In: Levinson, David & Ember, Melvin (eds.), *Encyclopedia of Cultural Anthropology*, vol. 3. New York, 721–26.

Sypher W (1962). *The loss of self in modern literature and art*. New York: Random House.

Thayer AH & Thayer GH (1909, revised 1918). *Concealing-coloration in the animal kingdom: an exposition of the laws of disguise through color and pattern; being a summary of Abbott H. Thayer's discoveries*. London (orig. 1909): Macmillan.

Trivers R (2011). *The folly of fools: the logic of deceit and self-deception in human life*. New York: Basic Books.

3
Zoos and camouflage
Ann Elias

Animals – their behaviours, their patterns and colours – have been vital to knowledge about camouflage in the human world of science, art and war. But one thing that stands out in the standard literature on camouflage is the emphasis placed on observing animals in the wild and lack of interest in animals in zoos.[1] Why the wild animal is held up as exemplar of camouflage compared with zoo animals is of interest to the trajectory of this chapter. The answers illuminate the troubled relations of humans and animals and draw attention to hypocrisies and double standards underpinning those relations. With zoos comes the admission that these animals are not in full possession of animality since most are born in captivity, are alienated from an ecological context, and have lost the need to hunt for prey and the fear of being hunted. Once placed in concrete enclosures and cages for maximum public visibility, there is an acceptance that zoo animals have little chance (and little reason) to hide or deploy stealth. Their worth as camouflage subjects is diminished, and they become a lesser version of the wild animal who by contrast is seen as whole, complete and the source of authentic camouflage knowledge.

The rendering of animal camouflage as relatively useless in zoos and of animals in captivity as relatively useless to camouflage knowledge is one of many angles that I intend to take on the subject of zoos and camouflage. But by considering the key elements of camouflage – concealment and deception, mimicry, crypsis, and the dynamic interplay of hiding and revealing – I also discuss matters social, aesthetic, biological, and military. For instance, as pleasure-parks zoos are skilled at playful deceptions, trompe l'oeil landscapes, simulated environments and imitation nature. Therefore the very design of zoos engages with the subject of camouflage. I show how a farcical situation has arisen in the design of naturalistic zoos where the greater the success of biological camouflage the more disappointing the zoo animal is to a public craving animal visibility. And this is where the matter of cultural camouflage becomes relevant. John Berger was one of the earliest writers to claim that what is concealed in zoos is the reality that humans have made animals 'disappear' by turning them into commodities (Berger 1980). These and other camouflage matters are discussed in the following pages. My case study is Taronga Zoo in Sydney,

---

1 For example, Darwin CR (1859). *On the origin of species*. London: John Murray; Thayer GH (1909). *Concealing-coloration in the animal kingdom*. New York: Macmillan; Cott HB (1940). *Adaptive coloration in animals*. London: Methuen.

Australia, and for the period 1914 to 1950; this slice of history usefully demonstrates the complex interrelationships of zoologists, animals, war tacticians and artists in the subject of zoos and camouflage.

Taronga Zoo

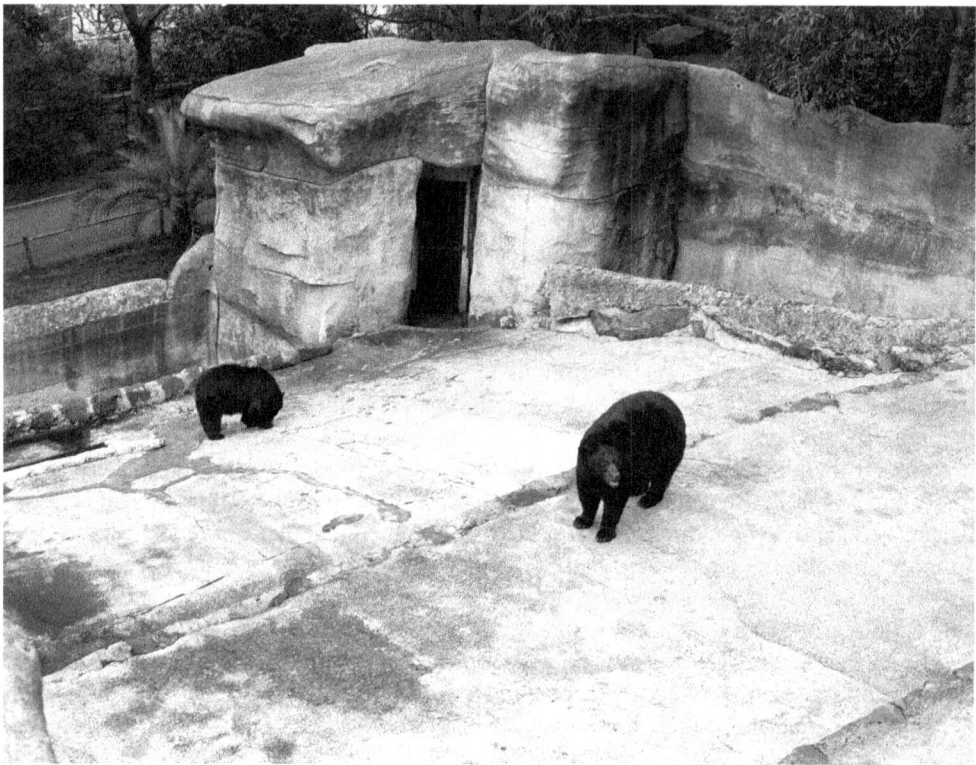

Figure 3.1 'Black bears from Canada, Taronga Park Zoo', 1946, National Archives of Australia: A1200, L6708

Taronga Zoo was originally built in 1884 at Moore Park in Sydney but moved to Mosman during the First World War and opened in its present location in 1916 (Strahan 1991). The move coincided with the zoo becoming a scientific centre. During the 1920s zoo enclosures were often simulations of caves and sandstone grottoes; bears and lions were kept in deep pits built with 'concrete walls moulded to look like rock' (Figure 3.1) (Boylan 2011, 151). In fact, despite sweeping views of Sydney harbour, Taronga Zoo in the 1960s was an austere place compared to what it has become through landscaping and planting and a contemporary approach to enclosures more attuned to animals. But earlier in its history, concrete animal enclosures offered little respite from summer heat. There were few opportunities for animals to utilise vegetation for hiding. Sir Edward Hallstrom who was honorary director of the zoo from 1959 to 1967 argued that concrete was easier to keep clean (Boylan 2011, 21).

However, the 1960s was an awakening to the question of 'the animal'. It was the first decade of sustained introspection about zoos and what they reveal about human–animal relations. Terry Boylan, veteran zookeeper of Taronga, recollected how in that decade the idea of collecting exotic animals from around the globe was seen as 'an unacceptable imperialist intrusion' (Boylan 2011, 9). Zoos were built for people to watch animals. But watching people watching animals at zoos became important in the 1960s to understanding people and societies. For example, in the United States, artist Garry Winogrand conducted an influential study at the Bronx Zoo. Writer and curator John Szarkowski said he quite liked zoos until he saw Winogrand's photographic series 'The Animals' (1969). Black and white images show bored, frustrated and dysfunctional animals but also people. It was a time of mounting dissatisfaction with zoos as places of entertainment at the expense of animal dignity. At Taronga Zoo, Ron Strahan, who was Director from 1967 to 1974, intentionally focused away from entertainment and instead on science, education, research and conservation. As a zoologist his philosophy included the view that at Taronga 'there was no place for circuses, miniature trains or roundabouts' (Strahan 2003, 477–9).

Zoologists, zoos, artists and warfare

Zoology was 'the driving intellectual discipline' within zoos and museums in the modern period (Everest 2011, 84). Zoology was also critical for the development of modern camouflage warfare, especially in the Second World War (WWII), for the simple reason that methods of military camouflage were based on zoological knowledge of animal camouflage. Therefore from 1900 to 1945 zoologists had a considerable part to play in civic affairs including military research and zoo research. Take the case of Australian zoologist William John Dakin (1883–1950). In 1931 he was a trustee of Taronga Zoo and in the same decade was President of the scientific organisation that governed Taronga Zoo, the Royal Zoological Society of New South Wales.[2] And by 1941 he was also in charge of civilian and military operations for camouflage defence in WWII, having been appointed Technical Director of Camouflage for the Australia and Southwest Pacific region.

Dakin seconded many of Australia's leading modern artists to work with him in camouflage including Frank Hinder (1906–1992) and Max Dupain (1911–1992). As Roy Behrens has made abundantly clear, modern developments in military camouflage accelerated at the same time as the rise of modernism in Western countries (Behrens, 2002, 2009). But in addition Hinder and Dupain had attained knowledge about animals and animal camouflage via cubism (for Hinder) and surrealism (for Dupain). By WWII the animal was an important subject in modern art – particularly surrealism – and among famous examples are *The Tiger* (1912) by Franz Marc, *Robing of the bride* (1940) by Max Ernst, and *Self Portrait* (1937–38) by Leonora Carrington. What the subject of the animal brought to modern art was a chance to explore and combine interests in totemism, mythology and biology. Particularly influential was Charles Darwin's theory that man is an animal. For example, while Max Dupain's most famous work, *Sunbaker* (1937), is usually discussed in terms of humanism, it can also be seen as belonging to the borderland between human and non-human. A male human figure lying on a beach is defamiliarised through foreshorten-

---

2 For biographical information on William Dakin, see: Elias; Bygott & Cable; Colefax.

ing and as a result comes to resemble as much a spider or crab as a human – the kind of animal able to move along the ground using strong front limbs (Dupain 1937).

Animals and war

Animals were the primary focus of William Dakin's career. But, although involved with Taronga Zoo, his theories on camouflage for WWII always focused on the 'wild' animal. This was true for most war literature. It was informed by an assumption that animals in ecological context are driven by the kinds of survival instincts also needed by soldiers in the field. The type of animal Dakin wanted Australian troops to emulate was one in a Darwinian state of nature, driven to:

> choose dark corners as hiding places, during the day. Above all, they have learned through thousands of years of the struggle for existence that being seen is not merely a matter of colour but far more often a matter of injudicious movement and bad choice of resting place. The correctly coloured animals of the jungle have an instinct which automatically causes them to resort to the correct background and to remain immobile whilst they wish to be hidden. The soldier has to learn both these things. (Dakin 1947, Appendix O, 7)

War justified rediscovering methods of survival practised by animals, and 'animal cunning' was held up as an important model of correct behaviour. What was admired most was the way creatures with sharp instincts utilise space, colour and light to make themselves invisible and it was Dakin's aim to equip soldiers with a similar intuition for making their bodies 'disappear'.

It was intriguing during WWII for the Australian public to learn that war tacticians were applying the study of animals, and their fitness with the environment, to warfare. They read with interest how the Australian military had, for the first time in history, begun imitating the way kangaroos, emus and insects make effective use of patterns, shadows, stillness, and silence to evade predators and ambush their prey (*The Sun* 1941, 5). A camouflage manual printed for Australian soldiers in the New Guinea jungle explained about 'The ten big sins of the hunter and the hunted': one deadly sin was 'being a conspicuous colour or shape (or both)'; another was 'being a misfit in the background pattern' (Dakin 1947, Part 3, 3).

In preparation for jungle warfare, the team of camouflage artists working for Dakin in Sydney, including Hinder and Dupain, experimented wearing different outer-skins to find ones that helped soldiers become invisible (Figure 3.2). They countershaded their bodies the way they had observed in birds and mammals: dark on top, light underneath so that gradations of light and shade create the illusion of the animal's effacement as a solid object. Like animals they utilised disruptive patterning to help their forms blend into backgrounds.

3 Zoos and camouflage

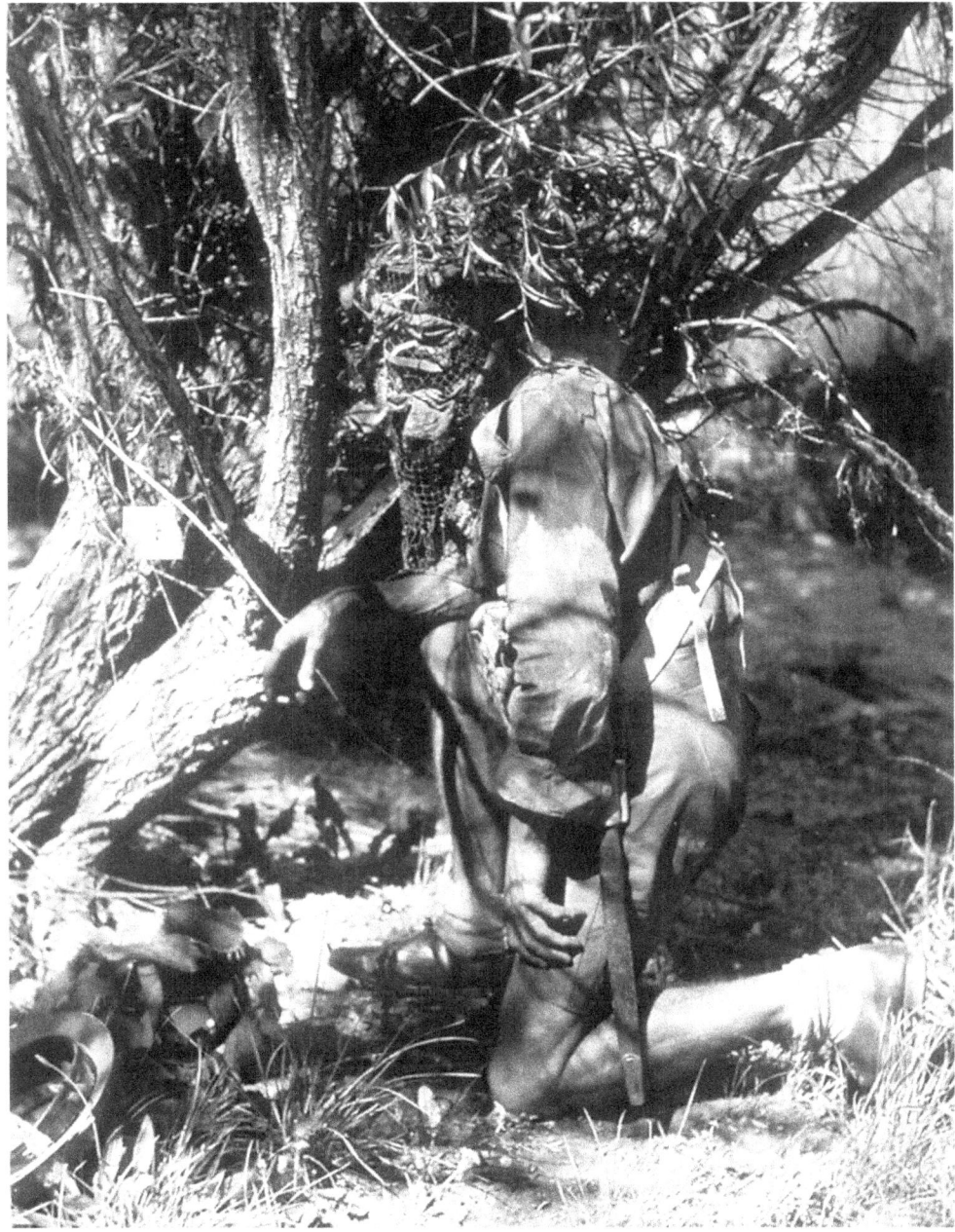

Figure 3.2 Gervaise Purcell, Frank Hinder in camouflage, c. 1943, National Archives of Australia, c.1905 T1

Because Dakin thought of war as a logical but temporary return to the animal origins of civilised man, he encouraged in soldiers the discovery of a primitive masculinity, and 'the beast within' (Mitman 1997, 262). Camouflage posters directed soldiers to behave like tigers in the wild, lying hidden in long grass before springing towards their kill. Far from serving the weak and the unmanly, camouflage as practised by predatory animals was a model of virility; which is why Frank Hinder liked to remind the troops that 'the tiger conceals to attack!' (Hinder, c. 1943). One poster demonstrated how to retreat into shadows like panthers and blacken the skin to look like 'natives' (Elias 2011, 136). Collapsing of 'the animal' and 'the native' into one was a legacy of 19th century racist assumptions about natives occupying an evolutionary level comparable to animals.[3] From this developed the theory that the native and the animal were both driven by basic survival instincts from which they perfected methods of concealment and deception. Dakin hoped that Australian soldiers in New Guinea would rediscover similar instincts. And by mimicking animals and natives he believed that Allied militaries would gain superiority in the fight for survival (Dakin 1947, Part 4, 11). He instructed soldiers in New Guinea to blend with their background, change the axis of the body to horizontal, and 'learn to crawl properly' especially to crawl like snakes 'flat on the ground!' (Dakin 1947, Part 3, 32).

Meanwhile at the zoo

It was as if war was a time of empowerment for the animal's place in the Western mind. But this was not the case. During the war the very same societies that admired the ability of animals to camouflage themselves inflicted on captive animals in zoos the debilitating states of high visibility and overexposure. At the time of WWII when animals in the wild were models for military camouflage, animals in zoos were denied the ability and choice to utilise camouflage methods. In this reversal of attitude to the animal and animality – one for war, the other for civilian life – zoos diffused and in some cases eradicated the animal's capacity for camouflage. Instead they transformed the animal body into pure visible form for exhibition.

Modern zoos, compared with contemporary zoos, were like militarised landscapes; they too were photographically mediated environments and depended on and deployed inventive processes and techniques for surveillance and exposure. Yet surveillance and exposure were the very strategies that animals (and humans at war) tried to avoid and counteract. Before naturalistic enclosures became the dominant paradigm of zoo aesthetics, the modern zoo demanded that animals be seen from the 'front, side and back' (Willis 1999, 675). This situation was once described by Ralph Acampora as degrading for making the dignity of animals disappear precisely by overexposing their bodies (Acampora 1998, 1). As a result, animals became misfits – to use the camouflage term current in WWII for bodies that don't blend with their backgrounds – but misfits socially and ecologically. In this regard it could be said that during WWII a different war was waged on animals in zoos.

---

3 For example, it was the opinion of US anatomist Jeffries Wyman that 'Negro and Orang do afford the points where man and the brute ... most nearly approach each other'. See Wyman quoted in R. Conniff (2011). *The species seekers: heroes, fools, and the mad pursuit of life on earth*. New York and London: WW Norton & Company, 237.

3 Zoos and camouflage

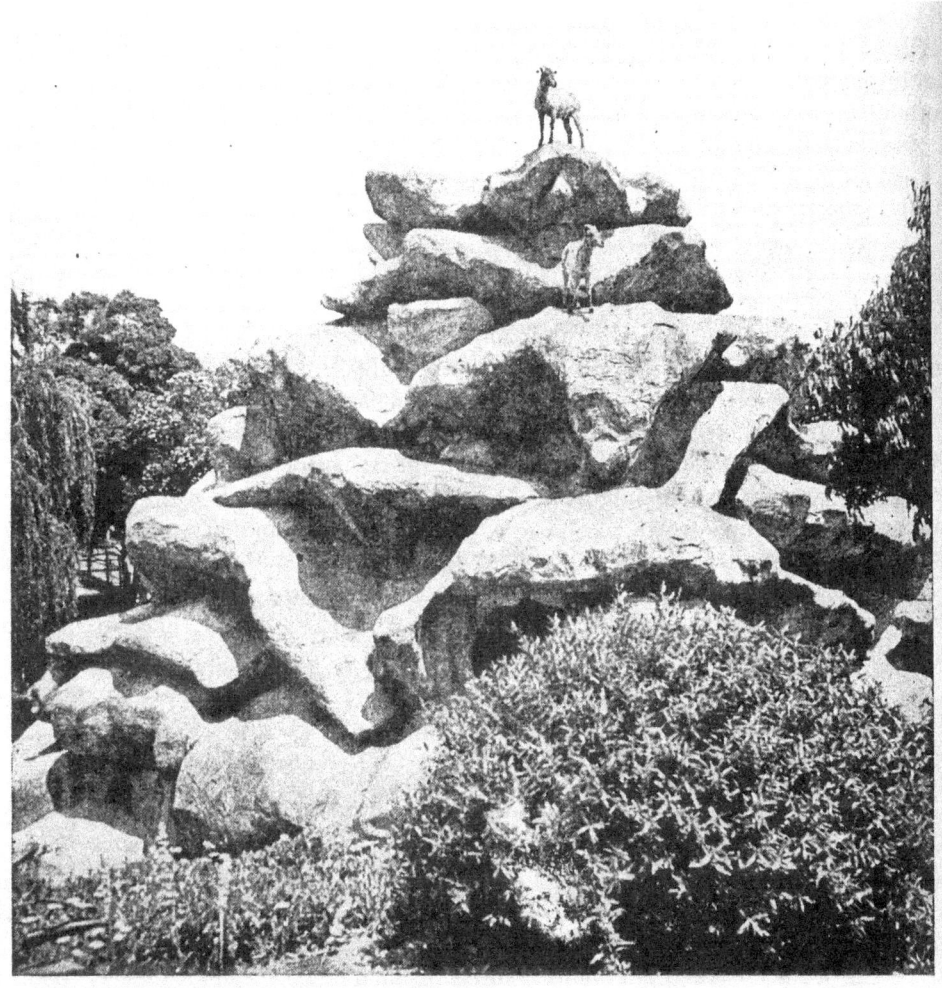

FIGURE 21.—An artificial hill made of thin layer of concrete mixture on wire netting reinforced with steel supports.

Figure 3.3 An artificial hill made of a thin layer of concrete mixture on wire netting reinforced with steel supports, from William Dakin, *The art of camouflage*, 1941, p. 50

Militarised spaces and zoo design

In Sydney it was no coincidence that the civilian space of the zoo shared affinities with military space: the same society that built Taronga Zoo also built the modern Australian Defence Force. The zoo, the army, the navy and the air force all came into existence between the time of Federation in 1901 and the establishment of the Royal Australian Air Force in 1921 (Dennis, Grey, Morris & Prior 1995). With the zoo at Mosman, and military defence forts sited nearby on the same peninsula at George's Heights, the geography was symbolically dedicated to the science and culture of observation. On this peninsula, and stretching back to the earliest years of colonisation in the 18th century, successive militaries surveyed the harbour from above, awaiting the arrival of potential enemies. In this regard the fortress of the zoo made a perfect neighbour for the fortress of the military. Both institutions are involved with protecting borders: one the national borders, the other the border between human and non-human. It could even be argued that these are similar borders since military surveillance of the harbour and surveillance of animals in zoos both involve objectifying and demarcating the other, the outsider, the intruder, and the enemy.

George's Heights near Taronga Zoo was also where Frank Hinder and Max Dupain conducted early camouflage experiments for the armed forces inside a station built by the army. During those years and together with Dakin they wrote a book titled *The art of camouflage* (1941), later used as a handbook by the Australian military. In that book they published a photograph of Taronga Zoo's Tahr Mountain which is an artificial concrete structure that even today is home to a herd of Himalayan Tahr. The mountain was built in 1932 by Thomas 'Tom' Adam, who designed many of Taronga Zoo's hollow concrete structures at a time when zoos were leaders in the design of simulated landscapes, fake installations, and trompe l'oeil objects.[4] Made to look like a genuine rocky outcrop, Tahr Mountain was included in *The art of camouflage* to show the military what was possible in terms of large-scale camouflage installations (Figure 3.3). Within a few years the same technique was deployed by the Defence Department for building constructions to hide fuel stores (including at George's Heights) and hideouts to conceal snipers. Hideouts were hollow structures designed to look like large rocks but with removable tops for entry and exit.[5]

The zoo in wartime

Fearing a Japanese air attack on Sydney, there was a sense of urgency to build camouflage installations to disguise key sites in the city and to prepare for an invasion. One worry was what would happen if Taronga Zoo was bombed and the animals, especially the big cats, escaped from their enclosures. A plan was put in place to 'destroy the lions and tigers amid fears a Japanese bomb could unleash them on an unsuspecting Sydney public' (Barlass 2011). The Sydney plan did not eventuate unlike Britain, Europe and Japan where zoo animals including snakes, lions and wolves were destroyed to prevent an escape (Itoh 2010). While the introduction of camouflage into warfare had ignited reverence for the wild animal – a master of deception – it had also struck fear into the hearts of civilians about escaped zoo animals hiding in urban space. The thought that animals could escape the fortress of the zoo, camouflage themselves and stalk human prey was unthinkable in the context of civilian life.

---

4   My thanks to Eric Riddler for informing me about Thomas Adam.
5   For an image of the sniper hideout see Elias (2011), Figure I.1. Artificial rock.

3 Zoos and camouflage

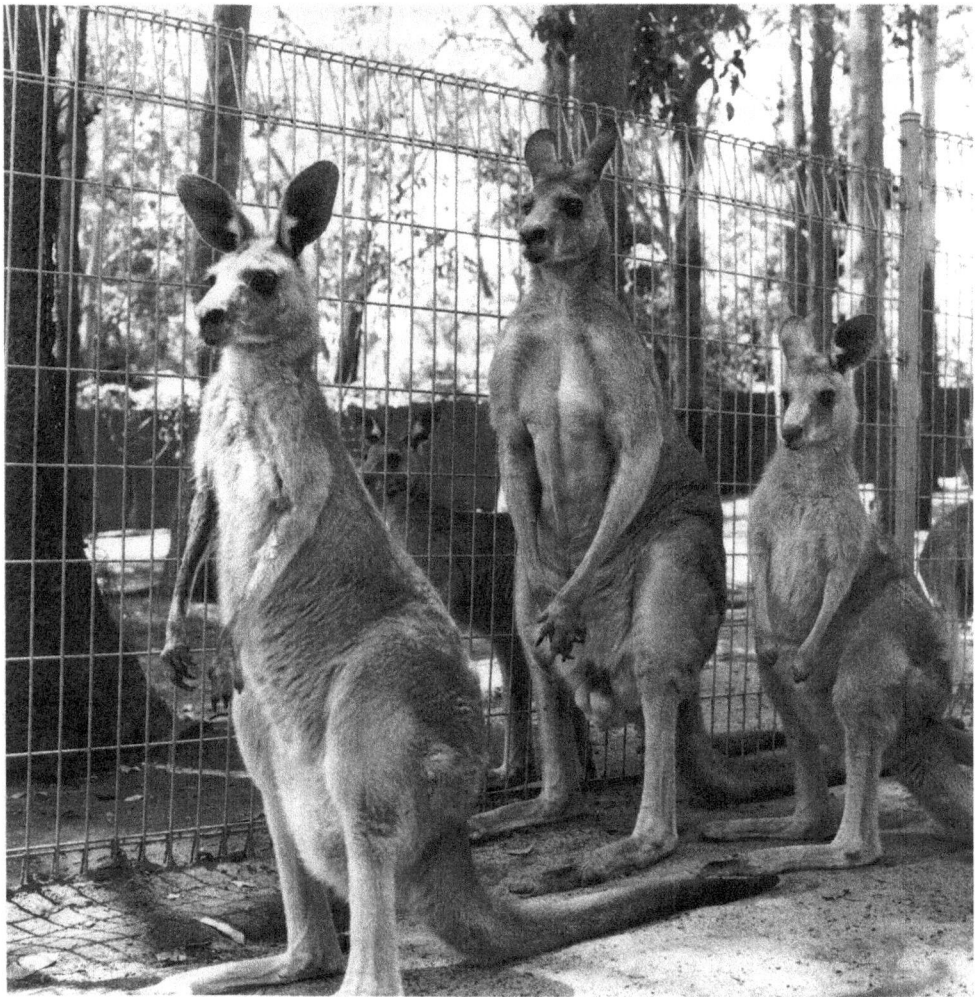

Figure 3.4 Peter Peryer, *Kangaroos*, silver gelatin print, 445 × 300 mm, 1987

High visibility

The sense of fear generated by an escaped wild animal stemmed in part from a general fear of hidden, sneaky non-human creatures. Indeed a widespread feeling of abhorrence for un-domesticated animals is partly why zoo enclosures were designed to look formidable and impenetrable. Before zoos became naturalistic, cages, pits and moats offered maximum visibility of animals and full protection for visitors. But as well they symbolised boundaries between self and other that were never to be crossed. For without zoo barriers, human beings would be denied a key experience in self-definition, namely that they are not one among animals, but superior. Some commentators, however, have thought this belief a form of self-deception which is why, when John Szarkowski first saw Garry Winogrand's photographs 'The Animals', he came to the realisation that human life is a zoo. Winogrand's photographs, he said, 'illuminate the menagerie we perform in' (Szarkowski 1969, unpaginated). By comparing the behaviours of people and animals Winogrand revealed how the would-be differences of human and animal are often hard to tell despite a clear demarcation of one from the other by zoo barriers.

Many artists and writers have consciously addressed the processes of cultural denial required to justify the objectification of animals. And many have consciously or otherwise shown how caged animals, without naturalistic enclosures, are curtailed in their ability and choice to hide using camouflage. Peter Peryer's 1987 work, *Kangaroos* (Figure 3.4), exhibits the bald fact that zoo animals in cages are not only out of place, they are also uncharacteristically exposed. Unable to make their form subordinate to space and go unseen by utilising background matching or the concealment of shadows, unable to put into practice methods of camouflage, zoo animals like these live difficult and unnatural lives. Lizards and snakes, alligators and snow leopards, animals that normally avoid being seen and are generally indistinct against their backgrounds, are often made to have high visibility in the rows of cages in zoos.

In some cases, small cages, bare enclosures, and high visibility have made zoo animals psychologically disturbed. Driven by a need to hide and blend their figure with the ground through mimicry and crypsis – but forced for the sake of a visitor's eye and camera to look solid and perfectly delineated in space – animals in zoos have become sick. Roger Caillois argued in 1935 that rather than protective, camouflage can be both the cause and effect of psychological disturbances in animals since an animal's urge to assimilate into space can lead to depersonalisation (Caillois 1984). But contemporary zoo literature points to captivity and public surveillance as the main reasons that zoo animals experience a loss of self and depression. The zoo animal's desire to withdraw and obliterate figure–ground distinctions is a form of defence. And that is why, ironically enough, some zoos today utilise military camouflage nets – objects originally modelled on the disruptive camouflage patterns of animals – to assist animals in counteracting the public gaze (Carlstead & Shepherdson 1994, 455).

The insurmountable problem, as Susan Willis sees it, is that far from finding camouflage and animals fascinating, the 'zoo wants visitors to see everything' (Willis 1999, 675). Studies confirm that zoo visitors want to see everything. In 2008 David Frede in Australia made a study about people watching animals in zoos including Taronga Zoo and the Adelaide Zoo and concluded that 'the amount of attention animals received from the viewing public is directly proportional to the animals' visibility and activity' (Frede 2008, 378). In fact, so pressing are the demands to satisfy both the eye and the camera, that even animals and their biological and behavioural characteristics can get in the way at zoos; especially if the animals don't stand out. On the rare occasion when animals are able to hide in full view, visitors find the greater the successes of animal camouflage the more disappointing the animal. Frede's study cites a tiger enclosure where the animal's markings made it difficult to see and disappointed visitors moved on quickly to the next exhibit.

The big cats are usually a major disappointment if they are not up and about: 'Where is he? Why doesn't he move? Is he dead?' wrote John Berger in 1980 about the disappointment of children in zoos and the reality that 'animals seldom live up to the adult's memories' (Berger 1980, 23). Zoo animals that lie still seem to be in the grip of depression. They don't seem to have the will to differentiate themselves from their surroundings. They fail to exhibit the same animation and distinction that people look for in their own kind. And Berger summarised: 'the felt, but not necessarily expressed question of most visitors is: 'Why are the animals less than I believed?'(Berger 1980, 23). To enliven and energise the viewing experience, Taronga Zoo includes simulated animals. These do what most bored zoo animals never do – they look at humans, not past them.[6] In this case the animate and inanimate are all but indistinguishable in the zoo setting. Zoo designers try to control our minds and emotions by setting up sudden encounters not unlike the surrealist idea of constructing uncanny situations. In zoos, artificial animals inhabit naturalistic settings and real animals inhabit artificial, theatrical worlds of simulated jungle and fake rocks, simulated bird-calls, recordings of screeching monkeys and bellowing lions to transport the zoo-goer into wild nature. In this regard zoos are all about camouflage. It is the illusion of wild nature that they seek to excite us with (Braverman 2011). It is the otherness of nature that they think visitors want.

Changes to zoo design

Zoos have changed since the 1960s. The postmodern zoo is naturalistic partly because people came to recognise that modernity was a period of 'staggering consequences' for animals (Burt 2009, 160). How much was WWII responsible for changes in zoo design? By the mid-1940s Taronga Zoo still had bear pits and lion pits where visitors looked down on animals. It was during this period, too, that Australians living in Darwin and the north of Australia, and soldiers in New Guinea and the Southwest Pacific, but also in Europe, experienced for the first time how it felt to be looked down upon during military aerial surveillance. The bombing of Darwin in 1942 created a new consciousness of the body in relation to the view of the enemy from a thousand metres above; in fact the question of how to obliterate the human body from the aerial view was the main reason that camouflage defence became an urgent priority in Australia. Could it be that subjection in WWII to the detached, objectifying aerial gaze influenced the design of zoos after 1950 by engendering greater empathy for zoo animals? Zoos began to rethink the ethics of bear pits and other forms of display that expose the animal body to the view from above and that trap it in the public gaze.

Conclusion

What happens to animal camouflage in zoos? By caging animals there is agreement that vital functions of life disappear. Cages divest animals of the need for camouflage and leave their appearances more aesthetic than protective. Their colours and markings are 'beyond camouflage and semantic functions' – beyond protection through concealment as a defence strategy, or attraction for sexual selection (Lingis 1983, 8). They are beyond pleasure for other animals. Instead the array of colours and patterns are aesthetics for human pleasure. What happens is that zoos bring to the fore the decorative nature of camouflage.[7] Yet this conflicts with the scientific and educational roles of zoos. That is why visitors are

---

6   Whereas 'other animals tend not to look at the humans looking at them' according to Susan Willis (1999). Looking at the zoo. *The South Atlantic Quarterly*, 98(4): 678.
7   Where Darwin believed in the aesthetic appreciation and sense of animals, evolutionists 'reduce the aesthetic to mere survival value' according to Wolfgang Welsch.

given textual information to learn about the markings and colours of animals as if the animals were still living within their natural ecosystem outside the zoo walls. For instance Taronga Zoo's website tells readers that the rare bongo has 'a magnificent red-brown hide, with white stripes on the shoulders and back which helps camouflage them in the jungle' (Taronga Zoo 2012, online).

This slippage between the experience of captive animals in zoos and the theory of camouflage in the wild supports Susan Willis's point that there is little difference between zoo animals and taxidermied animals in museums; both are 'body doubles, stand-ins for the real animals existing (or becoming extinct) elsewhere' (Willis 1999, 674). The example of the rare bongo also draws attention to human self-deception. By speaking of zoo animals as if they were still living in ecological context and in possession of animality, including camouflage prowess, we hide from ourselves the reality that we have diminished their distinctive qualities and attributes. But, as history shows, we have eagerly appropriated the same qualities and attributes for human ends like warfare.

References

Anonymous (1941). Nature's aid in army camouflage. *The Sun*: 1 September: 5.
Acampora R (1998). Extinction by exhibition: looking at and in the zoo. *Human Ecology*, 5(1): 1–5.
Barlass T (2011). The zoo ahead of its time. *The Sydney Morning Herald*. 9 October [Online]. Available: http://www.smh.com.au/environment/conservation/the-zoo-ahead-of-its-time-20111008-1lesf.html [accessed 21 May 2014].
Behrens RR (2002). *False colors: art, design and modern camouflage*. Dysart; Iowa: Bobolink Books.
Behrens RR (2009) *Camoupedia: a compendium of research on art, architecture and camouflage*. Dysart; Iowa: Bobolink Books.
Berger J (1980). *About looking*. New York: Pantheon Books.
Braverman I (2011). Looking at zoos. *Cultural Studies*, 25(6): 809–42.
Boylan T (2011). *The keepers and the kept: confessions of a zookeeper*. Chatswood, NSW: New Holland Publishers.
Burt J (2009). Invisible histories: primate bodies and the rise of posthumanism in the twentieth century. In T Tyler & M Rossini (Eds). *Animal encounters* (pp159–73). Leiden: Koninklijke Brill.
Bygott U & Cable KJ (1981). Dakin, William John (1883–1950). In *Australian dictionary of biography volume 8* (pp190–91). Melbourne: Melbourne University Press.
Caillois R (1984; originally published 1935). Mimicry and legendary psychasthenia. (translated by John Shepley) *October*, 31: 17–32.
Carlstead K & Shepherdson D (1994). Effects of environmental enrichment on reproduction. *Zoo Biology*, 13: 447–58.
Colefax AN (1950). Obituary: Professor William John Dakin. *The Australian Journal of Science*, 12(6): 208–9.
Conniff R (2011). *The species seekers: heroes, fools, and the mad pursuit of life on earth*. New York and London: W.W. Norton & Company.
Cott HB (1940). *Adaptive coloration in animals*. London: Methuen.
Dakin WJ (Ed) (1941). *The art of camouflage: by members of the Sydney Camouflage Group*. Sydney: Australasian Medical Publishing Company Limited.
Dakin WJ (1947). Concealment and camouflage of the individual in warfare. *Camouflage report 1939–1945 appendices k-n series 81 [77 part 3]* (pp1–40). Canberra: Australian War Memorial.
Dakin WJ (1947). Camouflage bulletin no. 7. *Camouflage report 1939–1945 appendix O)* series 81 [77 part 4] (pp7–10). Canberra: Australian War Memorial.

Dakin WJ (1947). Camouflage bulletin no 17. *Camouflage report 1939–1945, [77 Part 4]* (pp8–12). Canberra: Australian War Memorial

Darwin CR (1859). *On the origin of species.* London: John Murray.

Dennis P, Grey J, Morris E & Prior R (1995). *The Oxford companion to Australian military history.* Melbourne: Oxford University Press.

Dupain M (1937). Sunbaker [Online image]. Available: http://www.artgallery.nsw.gov.au/collection/works/115.1976/ [Accessed 21 May 2014].

Elias A (2011). *Camouflage Australia: art, nature, science and war.* Sydney: Sydney University Press.

Everest S (2011). Under the skin. In SJMM Alberti (Ed). *The afterlives of animals: a museum of menageries* (pp75–92). Charlottesville & London: University of Virginia Press.

Frede D (2008). *A tale of two zoos: a study in watching people watching animals.* Sydney: Department of Museum Studies, University of Sydney.

Hinder F (c. 1943). Teaching aids for individual concealment. *Frank Hinder Papers*, Sydney, Art Gallery of New South Wales, MS 1995.1, Box 4, Folder 10.

Itoh M (2010). *Japanese wartime zoo policy: the silent victims of World War II.* New York: Palgrave Macmillan.

Lingis A (1983). *Excesses: eros and culture.* Albany: State University of New York Press.

Mitman G (1997). The biology of peace. *Biology and Philosophy,* 12: 259–64.

Strahan R (2003). A zig-zag career. *Australian Zoologist,* 32(3): 477–79.

Strahan R (1991). *Beauty and the beasts: a fascinating history of Taronga & Western Plains Zoos and their antecedents.* Sydney: Zoological Parks Board of New South Wales in association with Beatty & Sons.

Szarkowski J (1969). Afterword. In G Winogrand. *The animals* (unpaginated). New York: The Museum of Modern Art.

Taronga Zoo (2012). Rare bongo arrival bolsters zoo conservation breeding program, 12 April [Online]. Available: http://taronga.org.au/news/2012-04-12/rare-bongo-arrival-bolsters-zoo-conservation-breeding-program [Accessed 21 May 2014].

Thayer GH (1909). *Concealing-coloration in the animal kingdom.* New York: Macmillan.

Welsch W (2004). Animal aesthetics. *Contemporary Aesthetics,* 2, [Online]. Available: http://www.contempaesthetics.org/newvolume/pages/article.php?articleID=243 [Accessed 21 May 2014].

Willis S (1999). Looking at the zoo. *The South Atlantic Quarterly,* 98(4): 669–87.

4
Australian stick and leaf insects (Insecta, Phasmida): camouflage and natural history

Paul D Brock & Jack W Hasenpusch

Remarkable camouflage strategies can be found in two Australian stick insects: *Extatosoma tiaratum* and *Anchiale austrotessulata*, both from New South Wales and Queensland. The same is true of the leaf insect *Phyllium monteithi* from northern Queensland. For example, in extreme cases such as drought where the rainforest canopy is sparse, *E. tiaratum* may vary its shape and colour mainly due to levels of light intensity, at times becoming lichen-like to better match their surroundings but retaining the ability to return to normal leaf mimics. If disturbed, *E. tiaratum* use a combination of elaborate defensive strategies, with females adopting an aggressive scorpion-like posture and using spiny hind legs in a pincer action. Newly-hatched nymphs are extremely active and mimic ants.

The camouflage strategies of stick and leaf insects – known as phasmids – make them popular in zoos and butterfly houses, for educational purposes. But due to their camouflage abilities the public can be disappointed in them, thinking the insects have 'disappeared'. When visiting a zoo or insect house, one can nearly always spot visitors trying to see something in the phasmid's cage and quickly moving onto other, more obvious subjects which actually move and fly. And although phasmids are popular as domestic pets (less so than dogs and cats though!), they are not easy subjects to display to the public. For example, photographers with the media will often misrepresent these nocturnal animals by photographing them in the daytime, in artificial conditions.

This chapter considers two things: the extraordinary range and methods of phasmid camouflage; and how phasmids are represented in visual form for human viewing. Is there a difference, for example, between the way an artist and a scientist approach visual representations of these animals? And do those representations accurately reflect each animal's natural behaviour, particularly in relation to camouflage?

We write this chapter as specialists in phasmids and their camouflage. Our studies and publications include many descriptions of new species and a field guide on Australian species. These have helped to popularise phasmids and have encouraged others to study the same animals as well as find information new to science. However, while the mainly nocturnal, plant feeding stick and leaf insects have always fascinated people, their full range of camouflage and defensive behaviour is little known and not reported in the majority of species. Previous authors have neglected camouflage for reasons that include the fact that they have not studied species in the wild, and because they have only studied dead specimens.

About stick and leaf insects and Australian giants

Stick and leaf insects belong to the order Phasmida (Phasmatodea) which includes 3065 species (Brock 2014). The ordinal name is derived from the Ancient Greek φάσμα *phasma*, meaning an apparition or phantom. Specialists cannot agree on the name of the order (Brock & Marshall 2011), with several names used over the years. Mainly found in the tropics and sub-tropics, certain stick insect species are very successful in their adaptation and some winged species have a wide distribution range, boosted, in some cases, by pet-keepers. However, many have a limited distribution and those on the edge of their range may reproduce parthenogenetically; males are not known at all in a number of species and females can reproduce without males through the development of unfertilised eggs which hatch into females. Reproduction, however, is normally sexual and the offspring are approximately equal in numbers of males and females. Males are attracted by release of pheromones; hence in some species only the males can fly. Transfer of semen is sometimes by a spermatophore, or sperm package; this applies to these stick insects and is reported for the first time in the leaf insect.

The broadened, leaf-like leaf insects are less successful with adaptation, with only 51 described species – less than two percent of the total. However, because they are little studied, there is every likelihood of finding species new to science in remote areas.

Our recent popular field guide (Brock & Hasenpusch 2009) describes 103 Australian species of phasmids including three species of leaf insect although one of these may have been an accidental importation. Most are found in tropical Queensland, including the world's longest species, the Gargantuan Stick-insect *Ctenomorpha gargantua* (Figure 4.1). With legs outstretched we estimate its length can reach up to 615 mm (Brock & Hasenpusch 2009, 106). The female is approximately 300 mm from head to tip of the abdomen, while the male is approximately 200 mm. The specimen illustrated below is the smallest female of the species seen, but is one of only a few ever recorded in Australia. Still, it is 500 mm in overall length.

The lush vegetation in Australia is, perhaps, responsible for 21 species measuring 150 mm or more in body length, a higher percentage of 'giants' than known in any other country. Many of these species feed on wattle (*Acacia* species) or gum tree (*Eucalyptus* species) leaves.

The elongated cerci, or appendages at the end of the abdomen, are designed to confuse predators; if a bird or animal grabs the 'tails' mistaking them for the front of the insect, the insect will shed them and most likely escape to safety.

When camouflage is not enough – defensive strategies

We discuss and explain in this chapter three remarkable and different survival strategies in Australian phasmids. The following are their usual defences utilised in order to avoid being eaten by predators including birds, spiders and other insects such as praying mantids (references included in Bedford 1978):

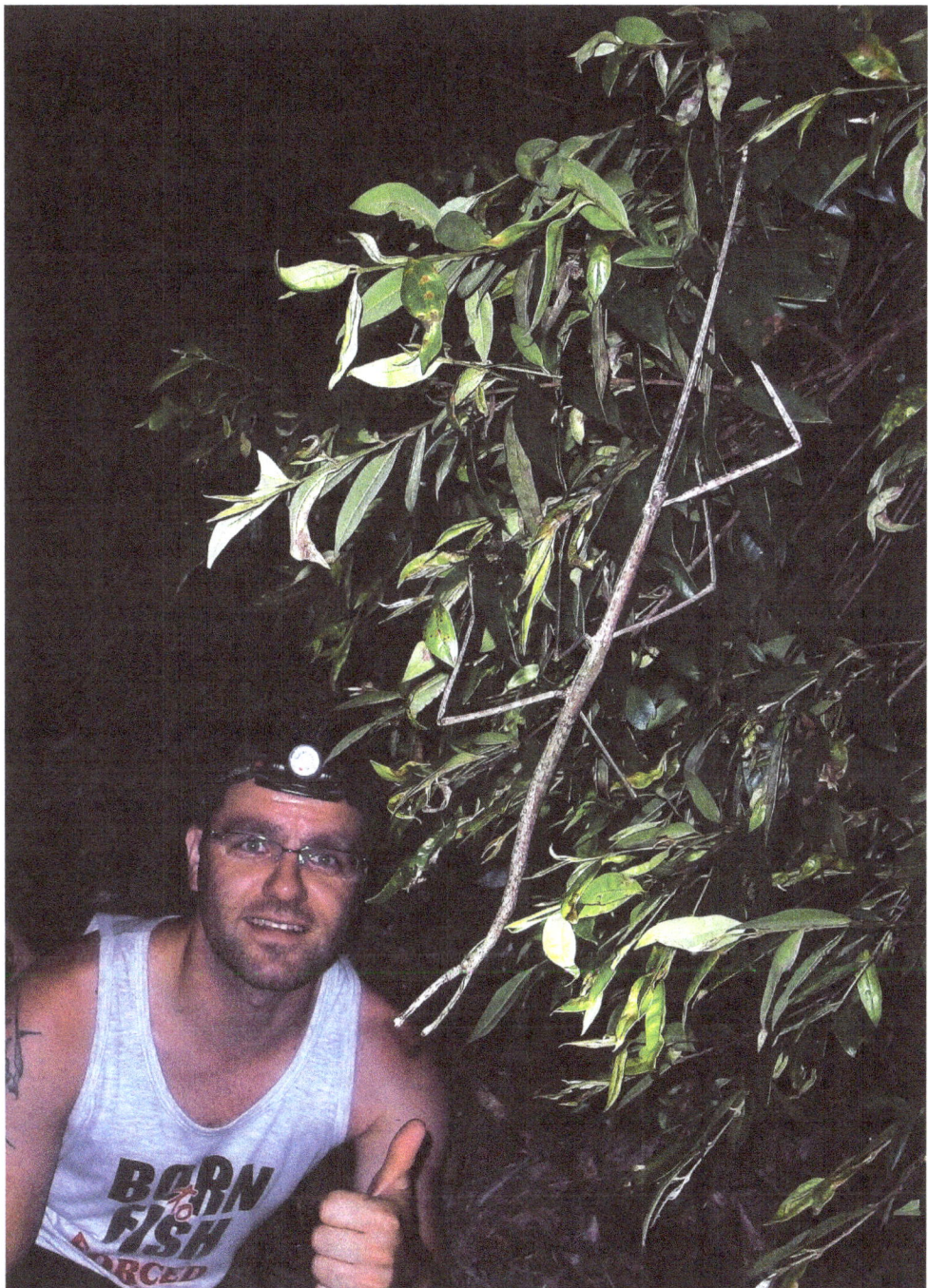

Figure 4.1 Maik Fiedel with his rare discovery during a Melbourne Museum field trip – a Gargantuan Stick-insect *Ctenomorpha gargantua* female, Copperlode Dam Road, Cairns, 20 January 2014. Photograph courtesy Maik Fiedel.

Primary defence – *procrypsis*. This involves shaping the usually green or brown body to resemble a stick or leaf, allowing the animal to blend into its background. Some species have the underside a different shade than the upperside, and some have a mottled pattern. In extreme cases a change in colour can take place in just a few hours. Even experienced insect searchers find it hard to spot phasmids in the daytime even though they often rest on or near the food-plant and may even sway from side to side in a breeze. Yet shine a torch at night and phasmids are often revealed as prolific. At night they are more likely to avoid being eaten, due to the presence of fewer predators.

When camouflage is not enough, secondary defences come into play. Handle or disturb a phasmid and it may do one of a number of things:

- *Feign death (catalepsy)* – the insect may fall to the undergrowth, tuck its legs in and remain perfectly motionless until the perceived danger has passed, however long this takes.
- *Stand its ground and display* – some winged species assume a false warning colour (pseudoaposematic) by raising the forewings and hindwings to display otherwise hidden bright colours or mottled patterns, the sudden appearance of which may startle a potential predator. Sometimes the wings are flashed open for a brief time, or may remain open for several minutes. And in more elaborate displays the flash may be accompanied by sounds produced by the rubbing of wings while other species, which have developed spines, will spread their legs. These are strategies to make the insect appear larger than it is. Threats can be real or, in some species, fake.
- *Active escape* – while many species drop to the ground and play dead (and a few jump), winged species fly and upon landing will once again 'vanish'. Other species will shed a leg in an effort to escape. *Autotomy* is commonplace, but only nymphs, namely pre-adults, can regrow a leg. The leg will remain twitching for at least several seconds.
- *Mimicry* – although a poorly studied area, it is believed that some species have the ability to resemble ants or scorpions.
- *Defensive secretion* – although not analysed in most species and not a feature in most phasmids, glands on the upper edge of the pronotum can release powerful chemicals. In extreme cases this can cause irritation or brief temporary blindness in humans. Secretions from the mouthparts are commonplace in phasmids.

Life history

The life history of phasmids is one of incomplete metamorphosis. This means there are only three stages: egg, nymph (which moults several times in order to grow), and adult. This is in contrast to other insect orders that go through complete metamorphosis by having a fourth stage: a pupa or chrysalis. Female phasmids lay up to 2050 seed-like eggs which are either dropped or flicked to the ground. But an average number of eggs for most species is 400 to 500 laid one at a time, and in some species glued to leaves and branches while others bury their eggs. The capitulum (knob) on top of the egg is attractive to ants and phasmid eggs are sometimes found in ant nests. Ants eat the capitulum, leaving the egg in relative safety beneath ground, ready to hatch in several months' time. The typical life cycle takes a year or so and, if not predated, adults live several months. In order to grow, nymphs moult five or six times before becoming adult.

The species are discussed below, each having a rather limited distribution range, with males being attracted to artificial light sources, including moth traps. Size differences can be significant, depending on food plant choice; males of phasmids are nearly always much shorter and slenderer than females and this applies to the following three species.

A 'pest' species which can strip forests bare

Tessellated Stick-insect *Anchiale austrotessulata*
Body length: 82–172 mm. Elongate, light to dark brown, sometimes green species with black and white mottled wings (shortened in female). The thorax has two rows of tubercles and several lateral, black-tipped tubercles. Habitat: Woodlands, mainly on wattle and gum trees, particularly in coastal highlands. Distribution: New South Wales, north to Gin-Gin, south-east Queensland. Season: Adults most likely December to March.

On a mini-expedition to south-east Queensland in 2011, the Tessellated Stick-insect was easily the most common phasmid, although in some areas it was localised, such as its preference for pine trees in suburban Brisbane. On 30 November 2011, however, at the Maddock Wetlands, Beerwah, southeast Queensland, we witnessed a phenomenon we had only read about: a population explosion of thousands on nearly every tree and sapling. Once we knew what to look for, they were easy to spot amongst vegetation, even in the daytime. Other previously unreported localities discovered in Queensland between 12 and 27 November 2011 by Brock and Tweed are as follows: Brisbane, Alexandra Hills, D'Aguilar Range, Walkabout Creek, Boombana, Mapleton, Montville, Lake Baroon, south of Childers, Cania Gorge, Bauple, including the National State Forest, and Tin Can Bay. All were of the normal colour and form, and were mostly adults or larger nymphs.

Camouflage in normal examples of this species, and which is typical in many phasmids, is a rather plain green or brown female (Figure 4.2) while males are nearly always brown. The folded part of the wings is reddish brown. Normally, nymphs of the Tessellated Stick-insect are green but can be brown. If disturbed, the female flashes open its shortened wings revealing a black and transparent mottled pattern aimed to startle. The wings are kept open during the perceived danger. The male has full sized wings and may attempt to fly away to live another day while the female may resort to emitting a chemical from its mouthparts and is only capable of gliding, at best. Obtaining photographs of specimens at rest is straightforward and it is useful to include in these images the insect's habitat and also to get as close as possible without disturbing the natural pose. Because the camouflage is often so notably effective it takes a trained eye to spot the insect against the vegetation. When shown images of this species during illustrated talks, even phasmid enthusiasts can fail to spot specimens at rest in bushes.

The 'high-density phase' noted by Kenneth Key in 1957 which he termed the 'kentromorphic phase' was observed during breeding experiments but also in the field. It applies to female adults and nymphs only. Females are conspicuously patterned with black, yellow and white, with the same wing pattern. Adults readily employ a startle defence; the underside showing a stunning reddish colour (Figure 4.3). Photographers find it a challenge to capture sharp images of this activity and also to represent the behaviour accurately since it happens within a split second. Many photographs of this type are taken in the studio whereas this image was taken in the wild. For naturalist photographers and discoverers nothing can surpass images taken in the wild with the animal in ecological context. A studio image rarely reflects the insect's natural pose and usually little attention is given to replicating its natural surroundings.

All adults found in the Maddock Wetlands in 2011 – approximately 10 in number – had recently moulted. The numerous nymphs ranged from newly hatched (1st instar) onwards, most with only one or two moults remaining. It was estimated that egg-laying would not start for about two weeks in early December. Of the thousands of female nymphs, about half sported the high-density phase colouration. What is the benefit of employing different colour forms? Key suggested that the high-density phase, which is not common in this phasmid, is the classical pattern of aposematic animals of all groups. It is an adaptation for large congregations and works on the basis that the 'warning' colouration has greater impact on potential predators, especially since the hordes of insects are hungrily stripping forests bare of leaves and therefore their own protection.

The DNA barcoding of populations such as this and related species from specific regions of Queensland is currently under analysis. At this the interim stage, results imply a group even more complex genetically and behaviourally than originally envisaged.

Going to the extreme: confounding the scientist – a popular pet with a full repertoire of defence behaviour

Macleay's Spectre *Extatosoma tiaratum*
Body length: 75–160 mm. The female is spectacular, a plump very spiny insect usually buff or other shades on brown, sometimes green. The abdominal segments and legs have leaf-like expansions but wings are rudimentary. The male is elongate, usually light brown and rather mottled on the wings. The legs have shorter leaf-like expansions but the wings are large, chequered in black or dark brown and whitish. Habitat: Rainforests and gardens, mainly on gum trees, but also feeding on a wide range of other trees and shrubs, including rose. Distribution: Parts of New South Wales, southeast, central and north Queensland. Season: Adults most likely December to March.

Macleay's Spectre is one of the most popular phasmids with humans, their world-wide appeal explained by their large size and unusual range of defensive behaviours. Having observed them closely for 30 years, we, as scientists and authors, have tried to understand why their colour forms are so varied. They range from shades of bright orange, brown, black, and even bright green. Most amazing is a lichen-coloured form in female nymphs and adults, which has baffled entomologists for years: what purpose does it serve and why is it different to other stages of development? There is still more to learn but years of fieldwork and observation of culture stocks have solved a longstanding mystery relating to the lichen form. More on the lichen form in a moment, but overall this species has the most extreme range of colour forms reported in any phasmid. So confused have scientists been by variations in this species that there are four synonyms, or repeated descriptions, of the one species. In the UK most culture stocks usually produce light brown females, but they vary much more in colour in their native Australia. This may relate to their food plant, or more likely their need to better match their surroundings. Food plants in the rainforest are varied, including *Callicoma serratifolia* (Cunoniaceae), *Caesalpinia sepiaria* (Fabaceae),

Eucalyptus species (Myrtaceae) and *Rosa*. (Rosaceae). However these phasmids will accept numerous plants in captivity.

Although seemingly well studied, judging by a list of approximately 70 citations in published papers (Brock 2014), this species was not even recorded in central Queensland until recently. From 13 to 30 November 2011 we (Brock & Tweed) searched for this species on a visit to south-east and central Queensland. We found nymphs in the following unreported localities: D'Aguilar Range; Walkabout Creek, Boombana; Montville; Cania Gorge; Mapleton; Maddock Wetlands, Beerwah, mostly on *Acacia*. The only adult (a male) was found at Walkabout Creek and those at Cania were much further north than previously known.

Defensive behaviour in this species is elaborate. First, the eggs differ in populations in south-east Queensland from those in north Queensland. This is normally enough to indicate a different species. And newly-hatched nymphs from south-east Queensland are more reddish in colour. Newly emerged nymphs living in north Queensland mimic large black ants belonging to the genus *Leptomyrmex*; phasmid nymphs run around in the same erratic way as do these ants. The abdomen is curled around the body, scorpion-like. There is also a *Leptomyrmex* species in south Queensland but more studies are required in this area to confirm precise associations. In any event, once *E. tiaratum* start feeding, their colour lightens in a matter of days. They also slow down in their movements and from this point on rely on camouflage. Adults from these population look the same, but despite significant differences in eggs and nymphs it is clear from DNA barcoding (Velonà et al. in preparation) that they are the same species.

Their camouflage is so impressive that the first author of this chapter only noticed a young nymph on *Acacia* in Beerwah in 2011 while checking a photograph of another phasmid. The adult female uses her spiny hindlegs in a pincer action which can cause minor bleeding when handled in captivity. Nymphs and adults lash out with their forelegs at possible intruders if still on a branch, or if they have opted to fall to the ground. In addition to the abdomen curling around in an aggressive scorpion-like posture, a clicking sound may be emitted. A chemical secretion is also released from the mouthparts; it smells rather like toffee, and a fine spray emitted from prothoracic glands smells of freshly tanned leather. If nymphs or adults fall upside down, the underside is covered in spines. This is the classic phasmid display found in horror films. The adult male uses a startle display, flashing open and beating its wings, but may opt to just fly away and 'vanish' in the undergrowth.

The distinctive female lichen form (Figure 4.4) is created by a mottled pattern and large gaps in abdominal flanges, which some past authors considered to be species specific. However, when revising the genus *Extatosoma* (Gray, 1833), co-author of this chapter Paul Brock studied the few lichen forms known and noted the eggs were identical to normal leaf mimics (Brock 2002). Accordingly, the number of species in the genus was reduced from four (two species each in Australia and Papua New Guinea) to two, listing the lichen form of each species as a subspecies or 'form'. Hence the Australian species became known as *Extatosoma tiaratum bufonium* (compared with the normal leaf mimic *Extatosoma tiaratum tiaratum*).

Very few of the lichen mimics have ever been encountered. Co-author Jack Hasenpusch saw his first female lichen mimic nymph in the 1980s in his shade house near Innisfail, north Queensland. It was planted out with *Pipturas argentus* which were covered in hundreds of nymphs of various colours and sizes. Thinking this insect was an aberration, he housed it separately in a cage for future breeding experiments. As the insect grew

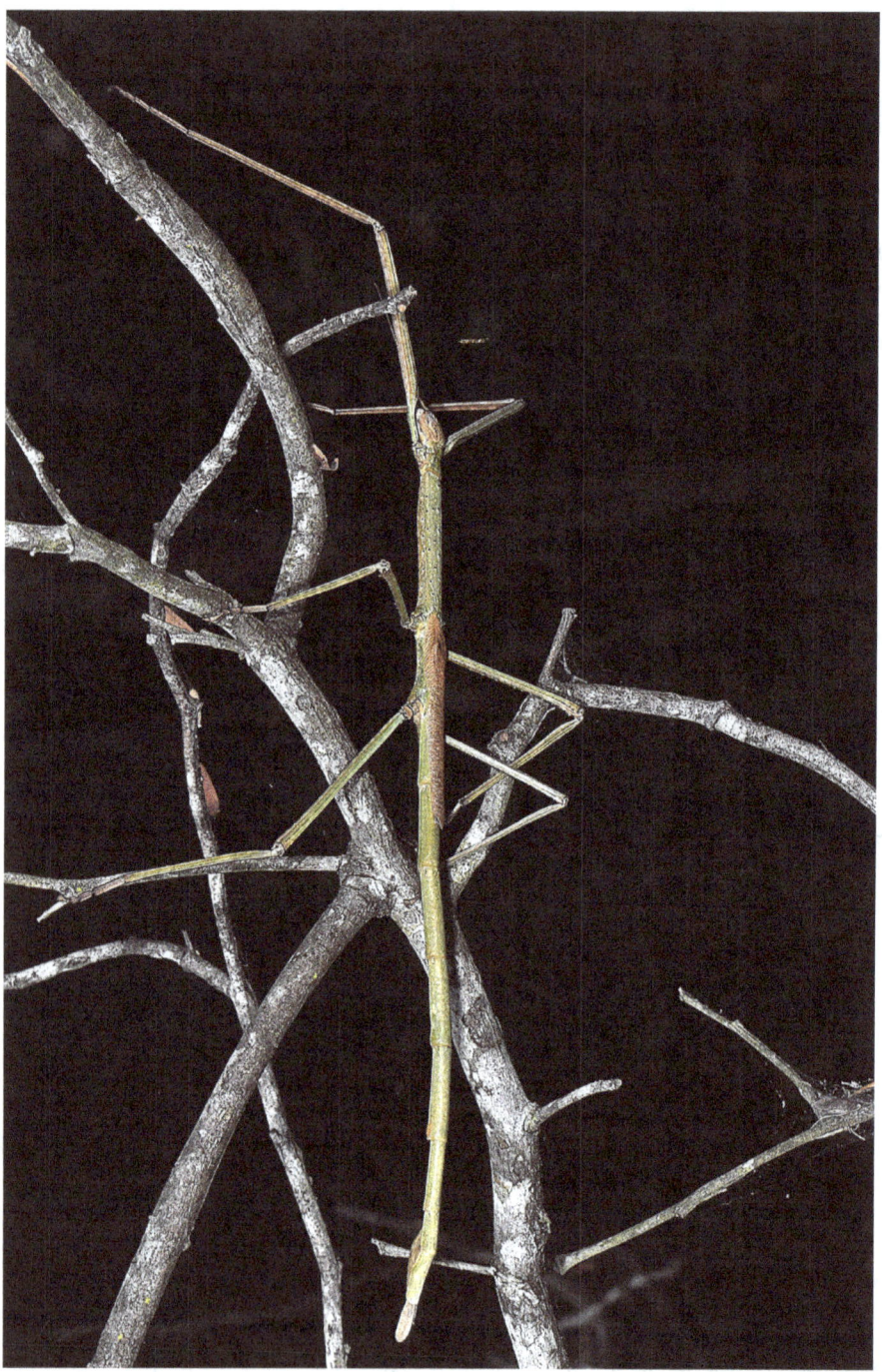

Figure 4.2 Tessellated Stick-insect *Anchiale austrotessulata* female, typical colour form. Photograph by Paul Brock.

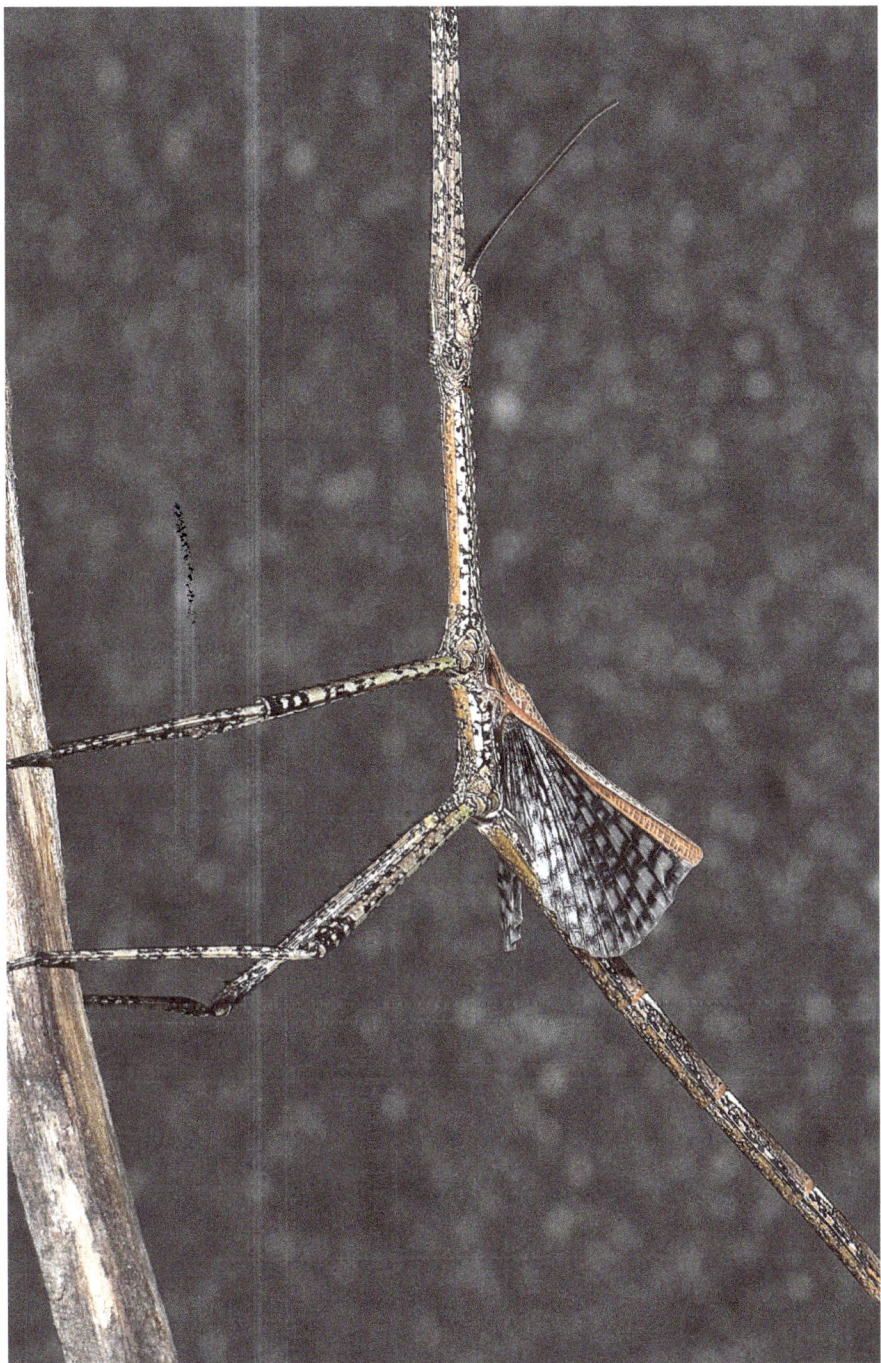

Figure 4.3 Tessellated Stick-insect *Anchiale austrotessulata* female kentromorphic phase in defence pose, showing underside. Photograph by Paul Brock.

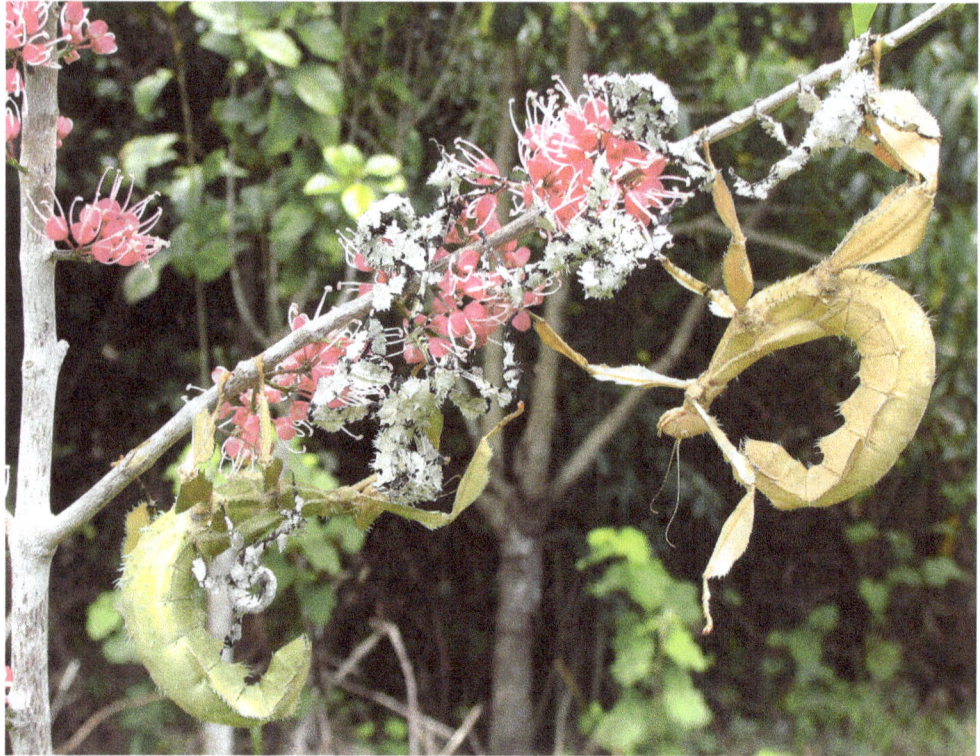

Figure 4.4 Macleay's Spectre *Extatosoma tiaratum* female lichen form nymphs (× 6) with two typically coloured adults. Photograph by Jack Hasenpusch.

she slowly started to lose the vivid contrasting lichen colouration, becoming paler with a little brown speckling. By the final moult to adult she had become totally cream coloured. Over the following years Hasenpusch continued to find the lichen forms in his shade house and watched as they developed. Again, on final moult, they reverted to a plain coloured insect. These insects are much spinier all over compared to a normal coloured nymph, with flanges on the legs larger and more elaborate/ another probable adaptation to deter predators.

In Australia, due to the risk of predation, culture stocks are sometimes sleeved onto food plants such as *Alphitonia, Calliandra surinamensis* and *Psidium guajava* using aluminium fly-wire sleeves. A number of birds eagerly eat *E. tiaratum*, as do nocturnal rodents such as the Melomy and White-tailed Rat which also stalk these insects in the canopy. It became noticeable that out of a sleeve of approximately 100 nymphs on guava or *Alphitonia,* the insects became more visible as the leaves were devoured. In this foliage one lichen form female was found, whereas on the *Calliandra* there were several. *Calliandra* is often covered in mosses and lichens ranging from various shades of green, turquoise and almost white; it has finer foliage than most plants and closes its leaves together at night making insects vulnerable to predation. The need to blend in well is vital.

Releasing dozens of *E. tiaratum* nymphs on a large potted *Calliandra* and observing them in full sun helped us obtain detailed information. It became evident that, as the female nymphs grow, their lichen colouration becomes much more intense in open sunny conditions. Even skin shed during instar change retained the darker lichen-like colouration. The males remained black, brown or ashen pale grey, even pale green. The lichen forms hanging amongst the denser foliage of the food plant hide the large gaps in the insect's abdominal flanges but retain the lichen colour.

As the insects grow so does their appetite. When the canopy becomes sparse insects need better camouflage; the lichen nymphs living on more exposed parts of the food plant adopt a different resting pose to the concealed hanging nymphs. They wrap their legs around the branch and rest on top holding their lichen-like bodies curled above them, fully exposed. After three moults nymphs reach fourth instar and have large gaps between the abdominal flanges, but by fifth instar they become paler and when they reach adult stage revert to a plain colour which is occasionally speckled. Many adults still retain the gaps in abdominal flanges. In a few cases, the lichen mimic form does not revert to normal leaf mimic, but still retains lichen mottling.

Further observations were made during Paul Brock's visit to Innisfail in November 2009. The very large *Euodia (Meliocope) elleryanna* growing behind Jack Hasenpusch's house has, since 2006, supported a considerable colony of *E. tiaratum*. Hundreds of specimens cover this tree, along with the beautifully coloured *Parapodacanthus hasenpuschorum* which is apple green and white with deep pink wings.

But in November 2009 the canopy was very sparse since Innisfail at that time was in the grip of its driest period for 90 years. As well as many green adult females with large gaps in the abdominal flanges (rather than fully flanged abdominal segments when this tree has a full canopy) there were many large lichen coloured nymphs. Searching under the *Euodia* in early December 2009 many pale coloured eggs were found and collected. But after almost a month of rain the canopy on the *Euodia* closed over and *E. tiaratum* began producing normal dark coloured eggs.

This corresponds with observations made of wild females. When placed in white boxes lined with white paper they start to produce white speckled eggs instead of the darker eggs. This takes three to four weeks. It is interesting to note that females grow noticeably larger on *Alphitonia* and *Euodia* which are pioneer trees that prefer the forest edge. *E. tiaratum* thrives in these areas, but are rare in dense forest, unlike many other phasmids in the vicinity.

The ability of *E. tiaratum* to camouflage itself within its surroundings is remarkable, especially the way it varies its shape and colour and how this extends to its eggs. These insects become lichen mimics to better match their surroundings but have the ability to revert to normal leaf mimics. This ability is attributed to the amount of foliage on the host tree and their exposure to light, making the insects much more vulnerable, hence a desperate need to blend in. It was this finding that led to the subspecies being removed and the species reverting to what is known as *Extatosoma tiaratum*. Reference to 'lichen' is subjective: extensive follow-up research confirms that the adaptation happens in trees with or without lichen growth.

But it is clear that increased light intensity influences camouflage adaptation. The insect avoids a big bulky dark silhouette since this is more likely to be noticed by birds.

The master of camouflage

Monteith's Leaf-insect Phyllium monteithi
Body length: 56–76 mm. Flat, broad bodied insects, the legs with leaf-like expansions. Wings are fully developed. Antennae very short in females, much longer in males. Habitat: Rainforests and tropical gardens where they may be specialist feeders. Distribution: Restricted to a 140 km stretch of north Queensland between Mossman and Innisfail, including locations up to 40 km inland. Season: Adults December to July.

Although rarely seen, Monteith's Leaf-insect is Australia's commonest leaf insect. There are few records. Nearly all of these males are attracted to light. Females are believed to occur mainly in the canopy, perhaps falling to lower vegetation during storms. A breakthrough in studies of this insect came in 2012 when specimens were found on *Gossia floribunda* (known as Cape Ironwood) in Kuranda. Some were cultured and are now being reared by entomological dealers and, at last, Australian educational establishments and pet keepers will for the first time be able to rear leaf insects.

Leaf insects rely on their remarkable camouflage as they lie flat on, and under, leaves. In these positions they are seldom observed. This makes life difficult for the photographer who cannot find them. Hence nearly all images of leaf insects are of captive reared stock. They vary in colour from different shades of green or yellowish green to colours that better match their surroundings (Figure 4.5). Some even have small mould spots like the leaves they feed on while others have white spots on the abdomen resembling light shining through a hole in the leaf. These colourations disrupt the outlines of insects.

Leaf insects do not have a wide range of secondary defences except that both sexes emit a fine spray of secretion from prothoracic glands. However, the much slenderer male is prepared to shed a leg to escape a possible predator and fly away, leaving the predator startled, holding a leg which still twitches for several seconds and unable to locate the leaf insect. Females cannot fly. Newly emerged nymphs have a slender very dark brown, almost black body, with red and turquoise patches on their legs; the abdomen is often curled up. They may mimic ants by walking fast, but once they feed they turn reddish-brown and, later, green. Their body becomes broader from the first moult onwards. Their eggs are brown or whitish; they are robust and resemble wood chippings or pieces of bark. They are simply dropped to the ground.

Research into the life history of leaf insects has only just begun but preliminary rearing studies indicate that each female lays about 400 eggs (approximately two a day), which hatch four months later. These are either dropped to the ground or flicked. Nymphs wander restlessly for two days before settling down and feeding. Besides *Gossia floribunda*, other host plants are *Backhousia hugessi*, *Psidium guajava* and other *Psidium* species, also *Syzigium* species (all Myrtaceae). Once nymphs begin to feed and turn green they usually rest on the edge of a leaf by three legs, resembling a piece of damaged leaf. When disturbed they will often move to the underside of a leaf, lying hard up against its surface, gripping on stubbornly. Other times they might leap from the plant, then flutter to the ground like falling leaves. Colour change is, in part, influence by host plant choice. Those on guava, for example, are more reddish brown. Instar changes (developmental stage between moults) take from 27 to 33 days depending on temperature and food plants. Five instars are recorded for males, six for females. Upon maturing, adult males can live for a further three months and females eight months. Mating takes place promptly, the male transferring a pink spermatophore to the female. Egg laying takes place 25 to 35 days after mating.

Phasmids in the media

Phasmids occasionally feature in the media but a website search is just as likely to provide links relating to stick-like women with anorexia. Recent examples of Phasmida in the media in Australia include the Lord Howe Island Stick Insect *Dryococelus australis*, rediscovered on the tiny island of Ball's Pyramid in 2001 and subject to considerable ongoing conservation efforts. However, a population cannot be released on Lord Howe Island until the ship-wrecked rats which caused their extinction have been eradicated. The media coverage (video, television, publications, animated film) has been largely accurate although posed photographs of the insects may not reflect exactly how they rest on vegetation in the wild.

Specimens kept by pet-keepers generally act in the same way as those in the wild, so it is relatively easy to obtain images of phasmid behaviour representative of the species. There are, however, numerous misleading representations in the media including blatant misidentification and errors in information. For example, a stick insect from one country may be said to be from another. The Australian Macleay's Spectre once featured in this way; it was included in a BBC film on Asian animals. Some photographers apparently care little for camouflage in nature and while it is costly to go on site and obtain footage (not to mention the difficulty in actually finding these insects), there is little excuse in obtaining culture stocks, placing them on attractive backgrounds such as flowers, bearing no resemblance to the natural habitat, or indeed food plant. Yet because stick insects can walk from the host plant and rest elsewhere, it is not always clear-cut that this is posed. Does it matter?

Are historic representations of phasmids any better? In some cases it is almost impossible to tell which species has been depicted. For example, Albertus Seba published four volumes of rather crude paintings of phasmids in 1734–65. Artistic license is taken with many including misleading body shape, length of legs or colours. The book states (Seba 2004), 'The gorgeous colours add substantially to the attractiveness of the plates, but their purpose was not just aesthetic enhancement. They had a scientific use as well.' But even in the 1700s scientists would have struggled with many of the representations. Figure 4.6, for example, shows a hand coloured engraving from 1833 which, two years later in another book, turns into Figure 4.7, an elaborate, differently coloured specimen with inappropriate habitat.

Thus, on one hand we have the approach of the scientist, expecting to see an insect in natural camouflage posing in natural vegetation and on the other the artist who shows the insect in its full glory but in an unnatural pose.

Large 'bugs' are widely used in horror films and usually with adjustments to make them look even more fearsome. And educational establishments such as zoos need to continually evaluate methods of showing these insects to the public since they usually just play dead during daylight hours. Likewise, representations in the media often include shots and images of the animals in camouflage but while these might delight the scientist there is a reasonable probability they will disappoint a public seeking insect visibility.

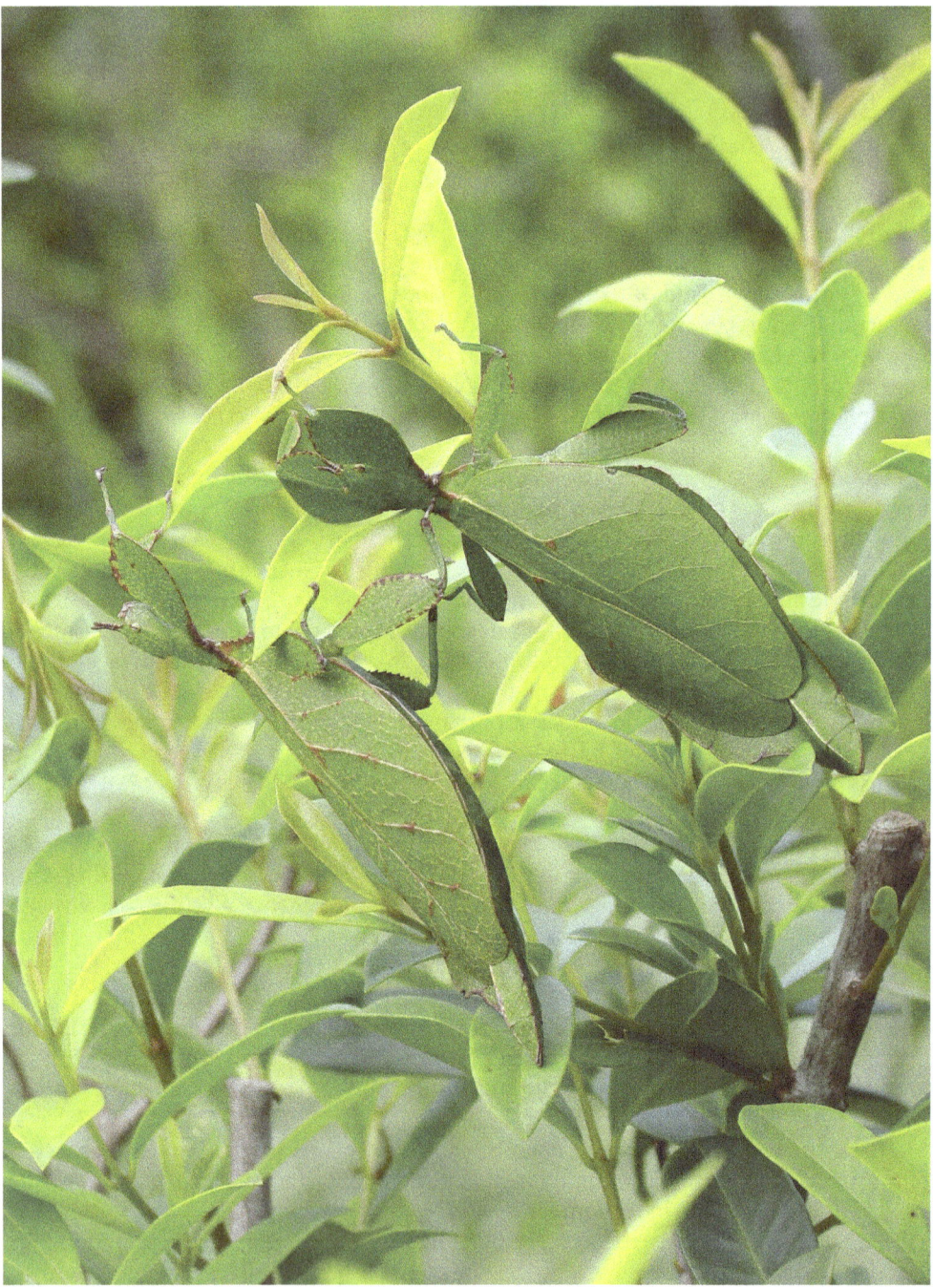

Figure 4.5 Monteith's Leaf-insect *Phyllium monteithi* two female colour forms blend in. Photograph by Jack Hasenpusch.

4 Australian stick and leaf insects

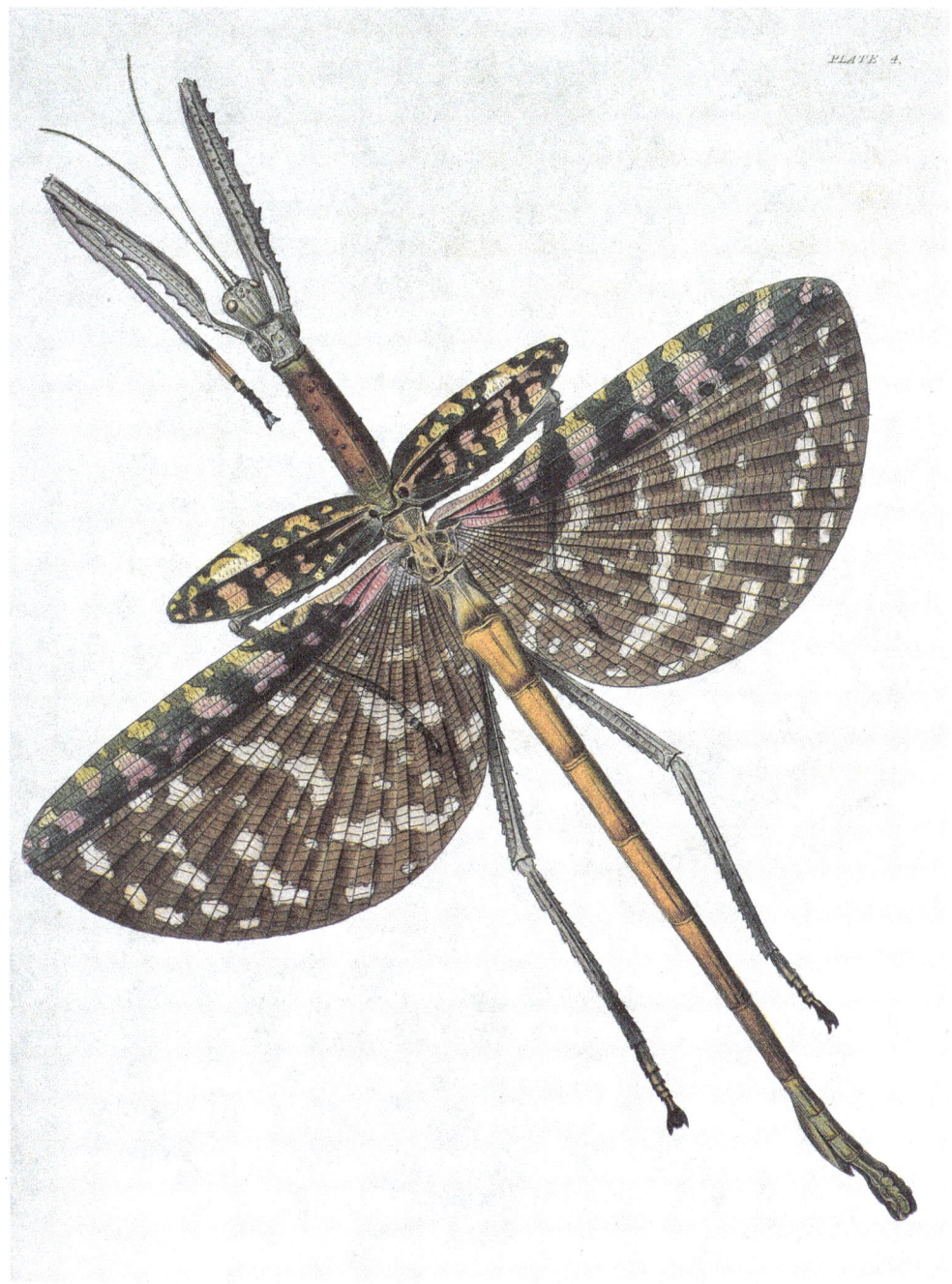

Figure 4.6 A hand coloured engraving from Gray 1833 compared with the Guérin-Méneville version Figure 4.7 from 1835 (reproduced from respective publication).

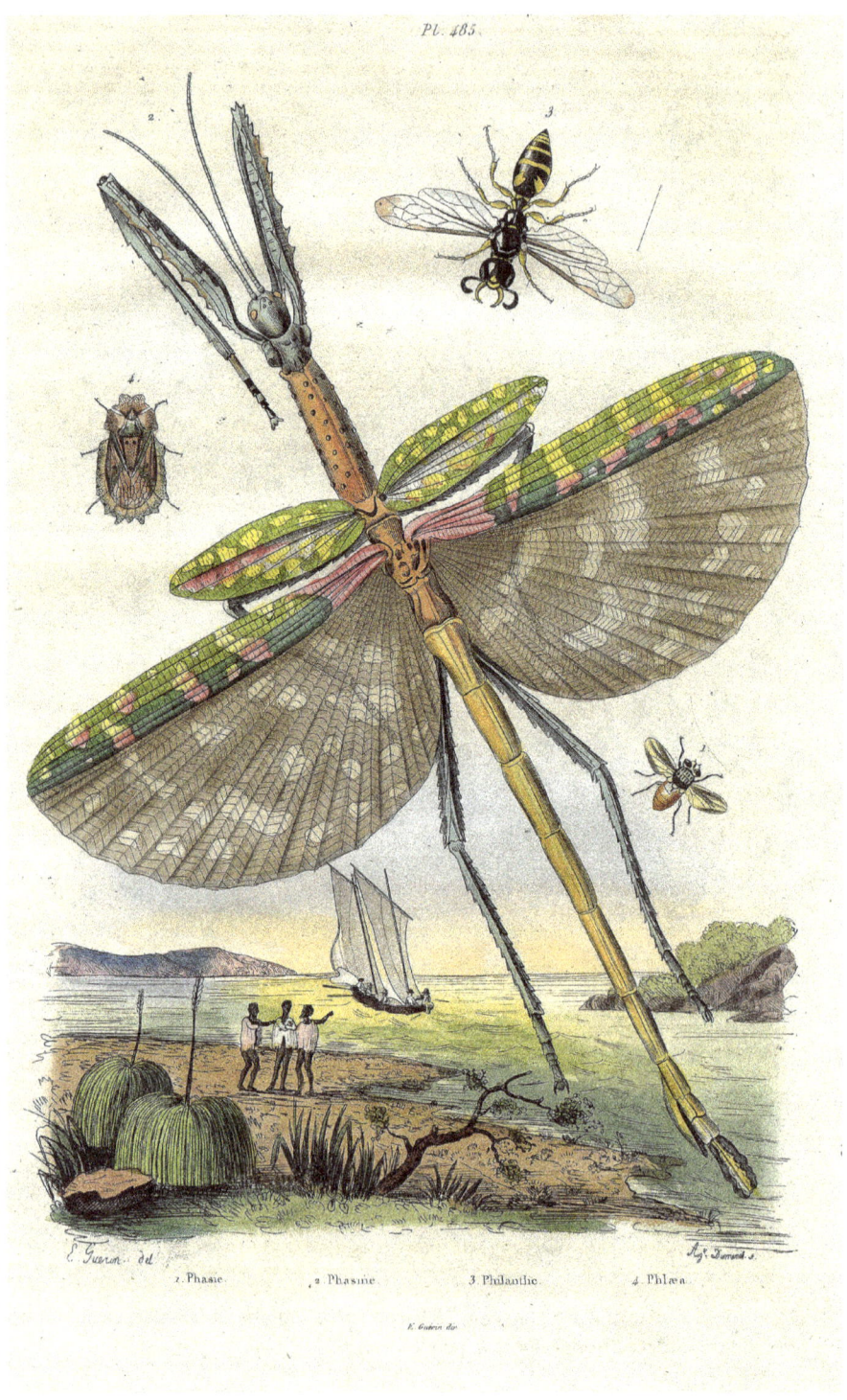

Figure 4.7 Guérin-Méneville version of the hand coloured engraving from 1835 (reproduced from respective publication).

Masters of camouflage?

Many phasmids are large and as the longest insects in the world they warrant top position as masters of camouflage in the insect world. It could be argued that phasmids are the masters of camouflage in the whole animal world but there will always be debate on this. What is certain is they have taken full advantage in adapting to resemble sticks and leaves so that even the most experienced entomologist has difficulty in spotting them in the wild. Not content with this, some species protect themselves against predators using a wider range of strategies.

As always in the natural world, there is still scope for making further studies of animals in captivity and in the wild. Many of the fascinating adaptations of phasmids are only just being understood following years of painstaking fieldwork. What happens to camouflage when *E. tiaratum* occupies different food plants? There are indications from studying the species in this chapter that some phasmids adapt to changing environments. In future this could mean climate change or habitat change will result in further camouflage adaptations. If so their camouflage will surely be effective; they have an amazing ability to change colour and body form to match differing surroundings and also to accepting a wide range of host plants. This is particularly important with insects living in the canopy, which is a phasmid habit also known to predators and where anything that does not blend in is vulnerable. But another defence is the fact that females are able to reproduce parthenogenetically if males are scarce or have died out.

In conjunction with Professor Barbara Mantovani in Bologna, Italy, the authors of this chapter will publish their DNA barcoding analysis on Australian phasmids (Velonà et al. in preparation). This will help solve further taxonomic mysteries. For example, there is currently a question mark over population differences, a dilemma especially for the genus *Anchiale*. We need to know the answers to many questions including variations in newly-hatched nymphs of *E. tiaratum* populations from southeast Queensland, compared with northern Queensland, and whether this is a mechanism to better mimic ant species present in these areas. Are female leaf insects really as secretive or rare as believed?

A conflict between the scientist requiring absolute accuracy in representation, and the poetic license and subjective views of artists and the media, is set to continue. Hollywood will continue to expand on fears of monster insects with large claws, impenetrable exoskeletons armed with spines and bulging compound eyes, of which some phasmids are ideal candidates.

Acknowledgments

Thanks to Maik Fiedel for allowing us to reproduce his photograph and Noelene Tweed for helping search for phasmids in the wild.

References

Bedford GO (1978). Biology and ecology of the Phasmatodea. *Annual Review of Entomology*, 23(1): 125–49.

Brock PD (2002). Studies on the Australasian stick-insect genus *Extatosoma* Gray (Phasmida: Phasmatidae: Tropidoderinae: Extatosomatini). *Journal of Orthoptera Research*, 10(2): 303–13.

Brock PD (2014). Phasmida species file online. Version 5.0/5.0. [retrieval date: 21 May 2014]. <http://Phasmida.SpeciesFile.org>.

Brock PD & Hasenpusch JW (2009). *The complete field guide to stick and leaf insects of Australia*. Collingwood: CSIRO Publishing.

Brock PD & Marshall JA (2011). Order Phasmida Leach. 1815. In Z-Q Zhang (Ed). *Animal biodiversity: An outline of higher-level classification and survey of taxonomic richness*. Zootaxa 3148:198.

Gray GR (1833). *The Entomology of Australia. Part 1. The monograph of the genus Phasma*. London: self-published.

Guérin-Méneville FE (1835).Dictionnaire pittoresque d'Histoire Naturelle et des phénomènes de la Nature, Paris: au bureau de souscription, imprimé de Cosson.

Key K (1957). Kentromorphic phases in three species of Phasmatodea. *Australian Journal of Zoology*, 5(3): 247–84.

Seba A (2004). *Butterflies & Insects*. Cologne: Taschen.

Velonà A, Brock PD, Hasenpusch J & Mantovani B (in preparation). Cryptic diversity in Australian stick insects (Insecta; Phasmida) uncovered by the DNA barcoding approach.

5
Mimicking the masters: a new age for camouflage design

Jonnie Morris

This chapter arises out of my practice as a documentary film-maker and the production of my latest documentary film titled *Dazzle: the hidden story of camouflage*.[1] It discusses how the natural world of camouflage influences human design, and provides examples of technologies that are based on the 'magical' skin of cephalopods, the anti-reflective eyes of moths, and the silent flight of owls. How can natural forms like these benefit society, industry, military culture, architecture, art and fashion? Bio-inspired science enables us to look at the most streamlined and efficient 'blueprints' in nature in order to re-imagine them for our own design uses. However, there is a deep chasm still separating human invention from the perfection of nature. In light of this, what does the future hold for camouflage design?

Camouflage is no longer just a tool for deception. As biologists continue to seek a deeper understanding of nature's unparalleled camouflage adaptations, technological innovations are enabling new practical applications for camouflage. With benefits surfacing in sustainable energy solutions, ebook readers, transport, and even our pre-occupation with invisibility, nature-inspired camouflage is reshaping all of our lives. However the evolution of nature's camouflage is a blind process that encompasses many different perspectives. It adopts the abstract artistic, the cellular world of biology, the architectural world of engineering, patterns of mathematics, and the survival techniques of the military. In order for us to have any hope of perfecting designs based on nature's camouflage, we too must take this holistic view or risk falling behind in our own evolution.

As early as 500 BC, with the writings of Sun Tzu's *Art of war*, the concepts of camouflage have intrigued both Western and Eastern minds (Elias 2011, 98). Imitation and mimicry have become part of the fabric of civilisation including in the disparate fields of art, science and warfare. The imaginations of artists and scientists have led to extraordinary camouflage inventions including 'dazzle' painting on First World War (WWI) ships and Yehudi lights[2] on Second World War (WWII) aircraft. But despite these imaginative

---

1 I am the writer and director of *Dazzle: the hidden story of camouflage*, currently in production for ABC television. It is the first comprehensive documentary to follow the many guises of camouflage design, from nature, through the artistry of the world wars, and to modern design technology, in the race toward invisibility.
2 Yehudi lights are lamps strategically placed on the underside of aircraft to counteract the light from the sky above, camouflaging the aircraft's black silhouette when viewed from below.

results camoufleurs[3] are limited in what they can achieve. Not only is human camouflage limited by technological capacity, but there is a tendency to assume that the 'hows' and 'whys' of camouflage are already understood (Stevens & Merilaita 2009, 423). As a senior scientist at the Marine Biological Laboratory, Woods Hole, Roger Hanlon states, 'camouflage is the least studied subject in biology that we think we already know about' (Hanlon 2011).

Of course, nature is the ultimate camoufleur. Her designs have evolved through natural selection for over 500 million years (Bhushan 2009, 1445; Parker 1999, 248; 2009, 1759; Stevens & Merilaita 2009, 423). From the moment there was light, predator and prey were locked in an evolutionary race of hide and seek, with each camouflage design tried and tested for ultimate survival (Yu, Fan, Lou & Zhang 2013, 826). While humans may never reach the same level of perfection in camouflage as animals, researchers are opening their eyes to the possibilities of a new age for camouflage design, an age defined by the fusion of art, science, military knowledge and nature, and a renewed interest in biomimicry (Salazar 2012; Stevens & Merilaita 2009, 423; Yu et al. 2013, 826).

Mimicry – a phenomenon in which one species benefits by a superficial resemblance to an unrelated species (Campbell, Reece & Mitchell 1999, 1113).

Biomimicry – the implementation of design principles derived from biology (Vincent 2009, 76).

Design is founded on recognising problems and finding solutions, and the science of biomimetics has encouraged designers to look to nature for inspiration and apply a systematic approach to camouflage interpretation (Vincent 2009, 76). The more designers understand the underlying principles and physiology of camouflage, the more likely they can efficiently recreate it. The evolution of computer science, technology and manufacturing has provided a window that looks beneath the surface of camouflage to the hidden cellular, molecular and nano world of an organism (Sing et al. 2012, 829; Vincent 2003, 1597; 2009, 78). This is a world that is measured by structures hundreds of times smaller than the tiniest bacteria cells (Shurkin 2013). It is a world with landscapes arranged in elaborate architectural hierarchies both highly functional and adaptable. This perspective allows scientists to break down the complex building blocks of camouflage into manageable parts (Vincent 2003, 81), gaining insight that allows them to quantify and mimic desired traits such as the brilliant changeable colours in octopi, the silent flight of an owl, or the light absorption properties in the eyes of moths. This is a defining new era of scientific progress where the commercial benefit of biomimicry is of great interest to industry, and where camouflage inspirations have the potential to be streamlined and perfected for use across all fields (Sing et al. 2012, 829).

The masters of camouflage

Most animals are cloaked in some degree of protective colouration, but it is the *Cephalopods* (octopus, squid and cuttlefish), Lepidoptera (moths and butterflies), and Strigiformes (owls) who create the biggest splash in the world of camouflage biomimetics. The camouflage traits of these animals not only inspire military camouflage (Stevens & Merilaita 2009, 423), but also motivate engineering advancements in our daily lives (Han-

---

3 Recognised for the first time in France during WWI, camoufleurs are the designers of camouflage.

5 Mimicking the masters

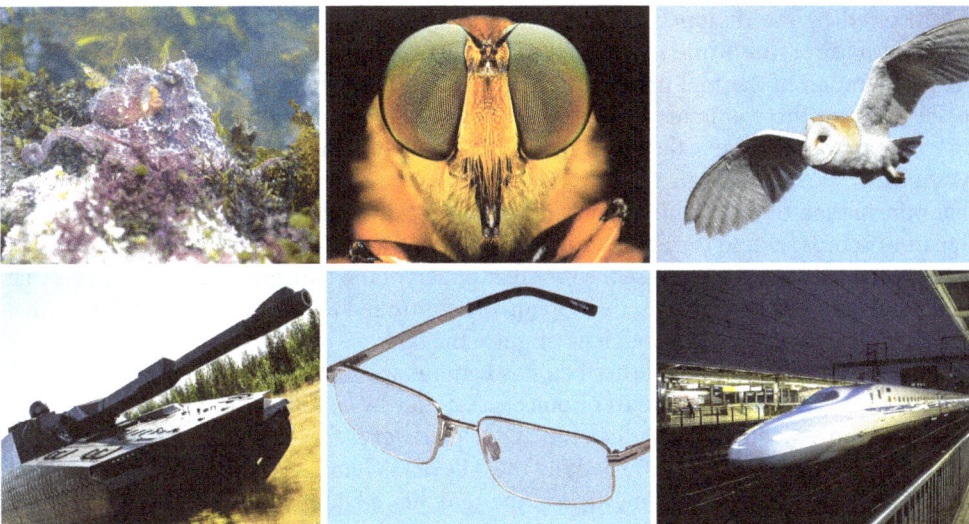

Figure 5.1 From left: An octopus displaying exceptional camouflage abilities inspires the camouflage of the BAE Systems ADAPTIV tank below; a macro photo enlargement of a moth's eyes inspires antireflective glass; an owl in stealth flight inspires the Shinkansen bullet train. Images within this sequence are reproduced with the permission of Roger Hanlon MBL, BAE Systems UK, Shikhei Goh, Evan-Amos, Anthony House and Luke Fisher.

lon 2011). From the realisation of functional invisibility cloaks, to stealthy bullet trains that produce less noise, this is camouflage biomimicry at its best.

Cephalopods

When it comes to changeable camouflage, chameleons are often the animal best known for this ability. However, the most striking examples of tuneable[4] colouration come from the underwater world of the cephalopod (Figure 5.1). Throughout 200 million years of selective pressure, they have evolved keen vision and dynamic neural control of their 'electric' skin (Hanlon 2007, 400; *Dazzle* 2013; Wardill, Gonzalez-Bellido, Crook & Hanlon 2012, 1). This essentially means that in order to escape a predator a cephalopod will analyse its surroundings, choose a 'look', and within 7/10ths of a second will effectively disappear from view (Hanlon 2011; *Dazzle* 2013; Wardill et al. 2012, 8). They are the only invertebrates with complex camera eyes similar to human eyes and with a brain capacity similar to a dog; they are believed to be the most intelligent of all invertebrates (*Wonders of life* 2013). Although they are colour blind, cephalopods employ a combination of structural colour, pigmentary colour, contrast, 3D shape, and patterning abilities, to achieve the most changeable appearance of any animal (Hanlon 2007, 403, 2011; *Dazzle* 2013). They truly are masters of camouflage.

---

4 Tuneable colourations refers to the ability to change colour either chemically or by physical manipulation.

Inspired by the disappearing act of the octopus and the chameleon, in 2011 BAE Systems[7] released the world's first 'invisible' military tank (Figure 5.1). Concerned with the proliferation of thermal imaging devices and infrared detection, the designers turned to the skins of these animals for inspiration with adaptable camouflage (*Dazzle* 2013).[8] Just as an octopus surveys the scene before changing to match its background, the tank's ADAPTIV[9] technology can read the heat signature[10] of its surroundings and transfer that information onto modular panels that form a 'skin'. Like a giant TV screen, the heat signature is broadcast to the enemy, and under the infrared spectrum the tank simply 'disappears'. This is achieved because the modular panels of the tank are made of elements that can be cooled or heated and can be individually controlled to create different patterns that when viewed through an infrared lens disguise the tank.

The designers also use another octopus camouflage method to confuse the enemy – masquerading as different animals or objects that may be less palatable. By mimicking the shape and movement of another creature, their predator is fooled and loses interest (Hanlon 2007, 403; *Dazzle* 2013).[11] By making the ADAPTIV tank display the heat signature of something as harmless as a domestic car, the tank has a better chance of being dismissed as unimportant (*Dazzle* 2013).[12]

While these design methods and concerns seem like something from a science fiction movie, in reality ADAPTIV technology still falls short compared to the original 'electric' skin of a cephalopod.BAE systems designers are yet to master the elegance and flexibility of the octopus (Kreit, Mathger, Hanlon, Dennis, Naik, Forsyth et al. 2012, 2, 11). So what is it about cephalopod skin that makes biomimicry so difficult?

Delving below the surface, cephalopod skin reveals a symphony of muscles and light interacting across three layers of pigment cells and reflectors (Figure 5.2). Each layer plays its part in the creation of visual illusion, with the entire performance consciously triggered by the animal's desire to change its appearance (Hanlon 2011; Wardill et al. 2012, 1–10). The first layer of skin reveals thousands of pigment cells known as chromatophores (Figure 5.2).

But chromatophores alone cannot achieve maximum camouflage. The next layer of skin is made up of iridophore cells which contain colourless, photonic, nanoscale structures that reflect iridescent blue, green or pink (Wardill et al. 2012, 1; Hanlon 2011; *Dazzle* 2013) (Figure 5.2). Cephalopods again show their camouflage mastery by releasing into this skin layer a protein called reflectin, that changes the hue of these living jewel-like nano structures (Fudouzi 2011, 2; *Dazzle* 2013; Wardill et al. 2012, 7). Finally, at the deepest levels the leucophore cells are found (Figure 5.2). Much like the light box of an advertising billboard, the passive structures inside the leucophore reflect ambient light, illuminating the pattern effects from the layers above (Hanlon 2011, *Dazzle* 2013).

With light, pigment and muscle control interacting at so many hierarchical levels, and with the added advantage of 3D flexibility as well as incredible goose-bump-like papillae, the possibility of humans mimicking the skin of cephalopods seems a far stretch. In

---

7   BAE Systems is among the world's largest defence contractors.
8   Interview with Mike Sweeney from BAE Systems London in 2011.
9   ADAPTIV is an active camouflage technology developed by BAE Systems.
10 A heat signature, also known as an infrared signature, is used by scientists and the military to describe the appearance of objects as they appear through infrared sensors.
11 Interview with Roger Hanlon, Marine Biological Laboratories, Woods Hole, MA, in 2011.
12 Interview with Mike Sweeney from BAE Systems London in 2011.

Cephalopod Skin Layers

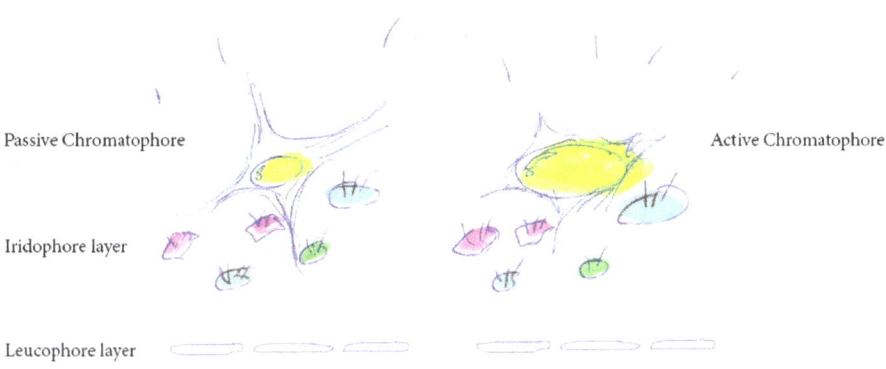

Figure 5.2 Nanoscale image of cephalopod skin layers. Top layer: Red, yellow and brown pigment patterns created by chromatophores. Middle layer: Iridescent blue, green and pink colours are reflected from the precise positioning of nanoscale structures inside iridophore cells. These structures disrupt and scatter wavelengths from the full spectrum of available light, including the UV (Fudouzi 2011, 1; Hanlon 2011; Parker & Townley 2007, 347; Wardill et al. 2012, 7). Bottom layer: Diffuse white light is reflected from leucophore cells.

addition to this, animals don't need to be plugged into a power source to generate their optical effects (Hanlon 2011; Kreit et al. 2012, 10; *Dazzle* 2013; *The point* 2012).[13] However by breaking down nature's building blocks into manageable parts, scientists are making biomimetic progress. Taking inspiration from the deep mechanics of individual cells and nanostructures, global scientists like biologist Roger Hanlon are changing the way designers think about materials. Hanlon has already contributed to the designs of engineers at Harvard and Rice universities who have made headway into producing a new class of materials that change colour and pattern using only existing light (Hanlon 2011; *Dazzle* 2013; The point 2012). Together they are drawing connections with how cephalopod camouflage can inspire human technology.

Chromatophores – mimicking the pigment layer of a cephalopod

Chromatophores are inspiring engineers to create a range of synthetic products with the potential to reach even further than camouflage design. Intrigued by the dilation of pigment discs, they have found chromatophore biomimicry useful for temperature control, active photovoltaics,[14] and colour changeability (Rossiter et al. 2012, 1). Surprisingly, e-pa-

---

13 Mindy Todd interview with Roger Hanlon and Basia Goszczynska.
14 Photovoltaics involves the conversion of solar radiation into electricity; for example, solar panels.

per technologies like the Kindle are already applying biomimicry techniques, utilising the changeable pigment abilities of cephalopod skin. The idea behind electrokinetic displays like these is to use electrofluidic and electrokinetic technologies to expand and contract pigment particles within the screen surface. This text-changing functionality could be the closest synthetic replica of a cephalopod chromatophore (Kreit et al. 2012, 9).

But chromatophore bio-inspiration doesn't end there. The same mechanism could also be used for controllable heat-sinks which manage the temperature inside computers, and are already used for improving the energy harvesting ability of solar panels by increasing sun exposure to their photosensitive elements (Rossiter et al. 2012, 1). Based on this, teams from the University of Bristol have progressed toward engineering a functional artificial chromatophore from soft compliant materials (Rossiter et al. 2012, 9). It uses carbon grease electrodes to mimic the process by which a cephalopod sends neural impulses from the brain to the muscles, and shape changing dielectric elastomers which respond quickly to stimulation and can sustain strains comparable to biological muscle (Rossiter et al. 2012, 6).

Iridophores & Leucophores – mimicking structural colours

The *pièce de résistance* for visual camouflage biomimicry belongs to structural colour effects that are not dependent on pigments, dyes or luminescence (Fudouzi 2011, 1; Yu et al. 2013, 829). Instead, they are emitted from colourless, nanoscale structures (photonic crystals and sculpted 3D architectures). Each structure is positioned in ordered and disorderly geometric patterns. This causes them to disrupt and scatter wavelengths from the full spectrum of available light, including UV which is invisible to humans (Fudouzi 2011, 860; Mathger, Senft, Gao, Karaveli, Bell, Zia et al. 2012, 1–2, 8; Parker & Townley 2007, 347; Parker 2009, 1760 & 1771).

The striking colour effects are not only found in the skin of cephalopods but also other species. The iridescent wings of the South American Blue Morpho butterfly reflect brilliant blue light from up to one kilometre away (Ball 2012a). This may appear too conspicuous for camouflage, but when ordered into broad patterns these iridescent colours are thought to be the most effective method for mimicry, communication and disruptive camouflage displays (Fudouzi 2011, 2; Hanlon 2011; Yu et al. 2013, 833 & 834). Imagine if the camoufleurs of the early 1900s had known about the potential for structural colours when painting their dazzle ships. The combination of iridescent paint and disruptive patterns would not only have been a startling effect, it may have also increased the capability of their camouflage strategy.

No longer confined to the animal kingdom, these reflective nanoparticles are finding their way into modern technology, and are even contributing to our ever-increasing desire to achieve invisibility. In fact as early as 2003 Japanese engineers were touting their invisibility cloaks as the real deal (Tachi 2003, 6). Using retro-reflective technology on what appears to be a giant raincoat, engineers set up an elaborate system of camera, computer and projector, to shine background images onto the front of their subject. When viewed from a certain angle the subject would 'disappear' (Tachi 2003, 6). But on 'reflection' the Japanese invisibility cloak is comparatively useless, considering there is only one angle from which invisibility can take effect. The genius of the design is in retro-reflective projection technology (RPT) (Tachi 2003, 4 & 5).

Based on nature's structural colouration, these retro-reflective particles, made of glass beads only 50 microns wide and without any power input, can reflect bright light directly back toward the source. This technology could benefit pilots, drivers and doctors to reveal information, rather than cloak it. For example, the material could be used to project blind spots from the exterior of a vehicle onto the interior panels, giving the driver a safer driving experience and an augmented reality of any obstacles surrounding the vehicle (*Asia brief* 2009). With RPT any driver could be a reverse-parallel-parking hero.

Structural colour effects also inspire artists like Franziska Schenk[15] to recreate nature's camouflage on the canvas. As a resident at the University of Birmingham's department of biosciences, she incorporated synthetic iridescent particles into her painted artwork to mimic the effect of Blue Morpho butterfly wings and cephalopod skin (Ball 2012b). This type of pigmentary and structural mix introduces colouration effects that can be applied to fashion, marketing materials and cosmetics (Bhushan 2009, 1477; Parker et al. 2007, 348). In fact L'Oreal has already embraced the effects of butterfly structural colours by adding them to pigment-free make-up (Kreit et al. 2012, 11). Revlon has also recognised a benefit, and have patented their intent to release cosmetic compositions with structural colour. Imagine an advertising billboard or an eye shadow that could be seen from up to one kilometre away.

At the higher end of engineering, companies like 3M have looked toward structural colours to develop films and multilayer materials that can be used in Bragg mirrors, dielectric mirrors and diochroic filters (Fudouzi 2011, 3; Kreit et al. 2012, 7). This translates to more accurate laser beam technology, fibre optics and ultra-reflective mirrors. There is even a recognised benefit to applying this type of biomimicry to the counterfeit industry (Ball 2012a; Parker et al. 2007, 348; Shurkin 2013).

Finally, e-paper technology is once again at the forefront of cephalopod biomimicry. In addition to the previously mentioned chromatophore-style ink manipulation, engineers have turned to structural colour inspiration to create screens that can project an image with little or no power. This type of reflectance means that screen technologies with a constant reliance on power sources may one day be a thing of the past. E-paper engineers are also working towards the next trend for structural colour that is as changeable as nature (Fudouzi 2011, 6; Kreit et al. 2012, 2–10). Just as the reflectin protein alters the reflectance inside iridophores, electrochemical tuning alters the spacing of nanoscale silica beads in the ink of these devices, changing the e-paper reflectance across the UV spectrum and even into infrared (Kreit et al. 2012, 7). All of this suggests e-paper is the most successfully inspired 'mimic' of cephalopod skin.

In complete contrast to the dazzling effects of adaptive colouration, another form of camouflage is making biomimetic waves. Anti-reflection is in demand across several fields from hunting to optics to architecture, and of course military camouflage, with each industry keenly embracing the benefits of eliminating glare. The roots of this burgeoning commercial interest emanates from a tiny biological phenomenon – the eye of a moth (Bhushan 2009, 1475–6; Parker 1999, 253–4).

---

15   Franziska Schenk is a contemporary artist at Birmingham City University who is exploring the relationship between fine art painting and natural sciences.

Masters of camouflage – Lepidoptera (moths and butterflies)

In nature, anti-reflection has a twofold advantage. For nocturnal animals like the moth (Figure 5.1), the light absorbing property of anti-reflection is thought to increase vision and promote camouflage by reducing surface reflections (Bhushan 2009, 1475–6; Parker 1999, 253; Parker 2009, 1759). Looking deep into the nano world of nature, we can develop insight into crucial design principles. The eye of a moth is made up of hundreds of hexagonally organised nanoscopic pillars, each with slightly rounded tips. These pillars act like a tiny sponge for light. Their precise positioning increases the refractive index, creating near anti-reflection from any viewpoint (Bhushan 2009, 1476; Parker 1999, 249; Parker et al. 2007, 347).

The greatest advantages for moth-eye biomimicry are found in combat, where the control of light, shadow and reflection is crucial to good camouflage and survival (Bhushan 2009, 1475). Glinting reflections will betray a sniper's position no matter how advanced their camouflage, and telescope optical sights on rifles are one medium where exhibiting a low visible signature is essential (Hobbs & MacLeod 2005, 349). The 'moth-eye' effect was first discovered in the 1960s and was reproduced using lithographic techniques (Bhushan 2009, 1475; Parker 2009, 1770). This essentially involved adding an anti-reflective coating (Figure 5.1) to the surface of window glass, and is currently applied to any number of products from sunglasses and binoculars to building panels and windows (Hobbs & MacLeod 2005, 350; Parker 1999, 253–4).

Today, the commercial use of anti-reflection technology has led to more accurate manufacture, with electron beam etching and fabricating microstructures directly into the surface (Hobbs & MacLeod 2005, 355). The surface texture this technology produces is close to mimicking the moth eye. Corrugations similar to moth eye pillars can even be etched onto the surface of solar panels to increase their light absorption (Bhushan 2009, 1477; Parker et al. 2007, 347). As well, glare-free computer screens can be manufactured by adding small nodules to a photosensitive lacquer with lasers.

As human beings are visual creatures, interest in camouflage is fundamentally preoccupied with visual deception. However, life on earth has evolved throughout the sensory realm, with all senses playing a role in camouflage evolution. Before there was light, organisms were most likely already dealing with chemical and acoustic camouflage techniques. Today the need to disguise smell and sound are still important for many animals, particularly those that are nocturnal. Moths not only absorb light with their eyes, their wings are also proven to absorb sound – in particular the echolocation from bats (Zeng, Xian, Jian, Jones, Zheng & Liu et al. 2011, 1). However it is another winged-form that is leading the way with auditory camouflage.

Masters of camouflage – Strigiformes (owls)

Owls are the original stealth craft (Figure 5.1). As nocturnal animals they use acoustic information to help with prey location and deception, resulting in evolved silent flight (Bachmann & Wagner 2011, 200). A large percentage of aerodynamic flight noise occurs as turbulent sound-waves are created by the wings. The owl's silent camouflage provides bio-inspiration for aviation, wind turbines and even Japanese bullet trains (Chen, Liu, Liao, Yang, Ren, Yang et al. 2012, 198; Lian, Wang, Chen, Zhou, Liang & Ren 2010, 196).

The sound suppression characteristics of an owl wing result from comb-like structures (serrations) on feathers at the outer edge of each wing (Bachmann et al. 2011, 200; Bhushan 2009, 1480; Chen et al. 2012, 194 & 195). These structures reveal an array of hooks and barbs that are woven and crossed together to form a hatched mesh. Like a tiny sieve, the effect is to break up the turbulence as it passes through, not only eliminating sound-waves but also increasing flight efficiency (Bachmann et al. 2011, 200; Bhushan 2009, 1480; Chen et al. 2012, 196). So how does this translate to human design? The most fascinating interpretation of silent flight comes from Japan. Designers of the *Shinkansen* bullet train (Figure 5.1) faced a problem when trains were prevented from travelling at their maximum speed because the resulting sounds exceeded environmental standards. However one engineer, a keen birdwatcher, sought bio-inspiration from the silent flight of owls (Ask Nature.org 2012). Simply adding small serration-like structures to the edge of the pantograph resulted in a train that meets environmental sound standards, travels 10 percent faster, and with more power efficiency (Ask Nature.org 2012; Bachmann et al. 2011, 192).

Despite the last 20 years of biomimetic camouflage advances, there is a sustained feeling that what we still know very little about camouflage (Hanlon 2011). Information regarding the particulars of biomimicry application is scarce, and articles implying military involvement are often guarded. Guy Cramer, CEO of Hyperstealth Biotechnology Incorporated, shed some light on this when I interviewed him in 2011 (*Dazzle* 2013). As a modern camoufleur, his repertoire of camouflage designs include 'SmartCamo' fabric that can change from dark green to tan at the flick of a switch; 'adaptive camouflage' materials that change shape, colour and brightness; and 'Quantum Stealth' the next generation of invisibility cloaking. However, no matter how nicely you might ask him, he will not show you any evidence. This is not to say that his claims are false, in fact quite the opposite according to military contractors ADS (Barcott 2011).

Cramer explains that camouflage studies are often commissioned by the military and are hidden from the public under strict classifications. Camouflage design falls under copyright, trademark or patents for intellectual property, and when working with the military these sensitive patents are secured or classified. For some of Cramer's camouflage designs, there is a minimum of three years before they are released to the public. For others, viewing clearances can only approved by the government (*Dazzle* 2013). Some material is so sensitive that Cramer is required to have his own security personnel present during interviews and presentations.

The implications for Cramer's claims are extraordinary and could surpass the adaptable camouflage we have so far created. His 'Quantum Stealth' invisibility cloak (Figure 5.3) supposedly bends light around a subject, is flexible, cheap and works in all parts of the visual spectrum. He equates the effect to the invisibility cloaking shown in the Harry Potter and Predator films, but 'without any shimmer' (*Dazzle* 2013). With this type of camouflage design on the horizon, can it be possible that human design might surpass the cephalopod's masterful disappearing act? In Cramer's own words, 'we can do better than nature' (*Dazzle* 2013).

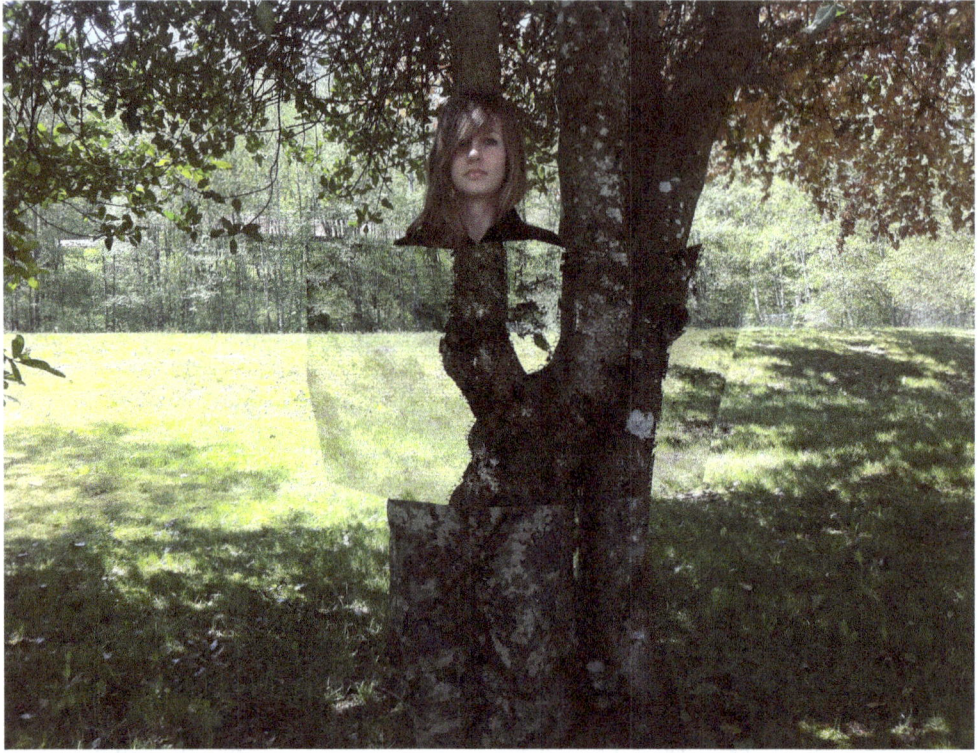

Figure 5.3 Hyperstealth Biotechnology Incorporated prototype image for the Quantum Stealth 'invisibility cloak'. Reproduced with the permission of Guy Cramer

Conclusion

Bio-inspired camouflage design is nothing new. Mimicking nature has led us toward more efficient sustainable energy solutions, quieter transport, less obtrusive architecture, e-book readers, cutting edge fashion possibilities, new artistry, and military camouflage solutions. Even while writing this paper, a company from Western Australia released a wetsuit to repel shark attacks inspired by nature's disruptive patterns.[18] These innovations are not possible without inventive problem-solving and an interdisciplinary approach to design. Information-sharing enables us to look beyond each professional silo and approach camouflage design with the same holistic regard as nature. As scientists and artists we continue to learn from recent nanoworld discoveries, and, as evolving technology facilitates new methods of manufacture, the day-to-day implications of camouflage-inspired design seem limitless. Whether our knowledge of the subject is as undeveloped as Roger Hanlon suggests, or perhaps as incomparably perfected as Guy Cramer believes, one thing remains true –whatever the future of camouflage design, it's sure to be interesting.

---

18   SAMS wetsuit design, Perth, Australia.

References

Asia brief (2009) Invisible Cloak – Retro-reflective projection technology. [Online] New Tang Dynasty Television. Available: www.youtube.com/watch?v=PD83dqSfC0Y [Accessed June 2013].

Ask Nature.org (2012). Shinkansen Train: High speed train slices silently through air [Online]. Available: http://www.asknature.org/product/6273d963ef015b98f641fc2b67992a5e [Accessed May 2014].

Bachmann T & Wagner H (2011). The three-dimensional shape of serrations at barn owl wings: towards a typical natural serration as a role model for biomimetic applications. *Journal of Anatomy*, 219:192–202.

Ball P (2012A). Understanding how animals create dazzling colors could lead to brilliant new nanotechnologies [Preview], *Scientific American* [Online]. Available: https://www.scientificamerican.com/article.cfm?id=natures-color-tricks [Accessed 21 May 2014].

Ball P (2012B). Paintings made with iridescent nanopaints change color on the spot, *Scientific American* [Online]. Available: http://www.scientificamerican.com/article/schenk-franziska-iridescent-nanopaints/ [Accessed May 2014].

Barcott B. June 2011 Invisible, Inc. *The Atlantic* online magazine source: http://www.theatlantic.com/magazine/archive/2011/07/invisible-inc/308523/2/ [Accessed 21 May 2014]

Bhushan B (2009). Biomimetics: lessons from nature – an overview. *Phil. Trans. R. Soc. A*, 367:1445–86 [doi:10.1098/rsta.2009.0011].

Campbell N, Reece J & Mitchell L (1999). *Biology*. 5th edn, California: Benjamin Cummings

Chen K, Liu Q, Liao G, Yang Y, Ren L, Yang H & Chen X (2012). The sound suppression characteristics of wing feather of owl (*Bubo bubo*). *Journal of Bionic Engineering*, 9: 192–9.

Elias A (2011). *Camouflage Australia: art, nature, science and war*. Sydney: Sydney University Press.

Fudouzi H (2011). Tuneable structural colour in organisms and photonic materials for design of bioinspired materials. *Science and technology of advanced materials*, 12:064704 (7pp). [doi:10.1088/1468-6996/12/6/064704].

Hanlon R (2007). Cephalopod dynamic camouflage. *Current Biology*, 17(11):R400–R404

Hanlon R (2011). Dynamic octopus camouflage: art, science and technology, November [Online]. Available: http://tedxtalks.ted.com/video/Roger-Hanlon-TEDxWoodsHole-Dyna [Accessed May 2014]

Hobbs DS & MacLeod BD (2005). Design, fabrication, and measured performance of anti-reflecting surface textures in infrared transmitting materials *SPIE 5786–40 Window and Dome Technologies and Materials IX*, 349 (June 22, 2005); [doi:10.1117/12.604532].

Kreit E, Mathger LM, Hanlon RT, Dennis PB, Naik RR, Forsyth E & Heikenfeld J (2012). Biological versus electronic adaptive coloration: how can one inform the other? *J R Soc Interface*, 10: 20120601.

Lian G, Wang J, Chen Y, Zhou C, Liang J & Ren L (2010). The study of owl's silent flight and noise reduction of fan vane with bionic structure. *Advances in Natural Science*, 3(2): 192–8.

Mathger LM, Senft SL, Gao M, Karaveli S, Bell GRR, Zia R, Kuzirian AM, Dennis PB, Crookes-Goodson WJ, Naik RR, Kattawar GW & Hanlon RT (2012). Bright white scattering from protein spheres in color changing, flexible cuttlefish skin. *Adv. Funct. Mater*, 1–10: [doi: 10.1002/adfm.201203705].

Parker A (1999). Light-reflection strategies. *American Scientist*, 87: 248–55 [doi140.159.34.46)].

Parker A (2009). Natural photonics for industrial inspiration. *Phil. Trans. R. Soc. A*, 364: 1759–82 [doi:10.1098/rsta.2009.0016].

Parker A & Townley H (2007). Biomimetics of photonic nanostructures. *Nature Nanotechnology*, 2: 347–53.

Dazzle: The Hidden Story of Camouflage (2011). [Documentary Interview]. Jonnie Morris Productions [In production 2013].

Rossiter J, Yap B & Conn A (2012). Biomimetic chromatophores for camouflage and soft active surfaces. *Bioinspiration and Biomimetics*, 7: 036009. [doi:10.1088/1748-3182/7/2/036009].

Salazar J (2012). Janine Benyus: Biomimicry is innovation inspired by nature. [Online]. Available: earthsky.org/human-world/janine-benyus-biomimicry-is-innovation-inspired-by-nature [Accessed 3 June 2014].

Shurkin J (2013). Butterflies inspire anti-counterfeit tech [Online]. Available: http://www.foxnews.com/tech/2013/06/10/butterflies-inspire-anti-counterfeit-tech/#ixzz2XnW82txE. [Accessed 21 May 2014].

Sing AV, Rahman A, Kumar NVG S, Aditi AS, Galluzzi, M, Bovio S, Barozzi S, Montani E, Parazzoli D (2012). Bio-inspired approaches to design smart fabrics. *Materials and Design*, 36: 829–39.

Stevens M & Merilaita S (2009). Animal camouflage: current issues and new perspectives. *Phil. Trans. R. Soc. B*, 364: 423–7.

Tachi S (2003). Telexistence in Retro-reflective projection technology (RPT). *Proc. 5th Virtual Reality International Conference (VRIC2003)*, 69:1–9.

The point (2012). Mindy Todd [Radio Interview]: Roger Hanlon and Basia Goszczynska. Cape Islands and NPR Stations. A service of WGBH.

Yu K, Fan T, Lou S & Zhang D (2013). Biomimetic optical materials: Integration of nature's design for manipulation of light. *Progress in Materials Science*, 58: 825–73.

Vincent J (2003). Biomimetic modelling. *Phil. Trans. R. Soc. Lond. B*. 1597–603 [DOI 10.1098/rstb.2003.1349].

Vincent J (2009). Biomimetic patterns in architectural design. *Architectural design*. 79(6): 74–81.

Wardill T J, Gonzalez-Bellido P T, Crook R J & Hanlon R T (2012). Neural control of tuneable skin iridescence in squid *Proc. R. Soc. B*, 0: 1–10.

Wonders of life (2013) Episode 3: endless forms most beautiful. [Television broadcast] UK: BBC 2.

Zeng J, Xian N, Jian L, Jones G, Zheng Y, Liu B & Zhang S (2011). Moth wing scales slightly increase the absorbance of bat echolocation calls. *PloS ONE* 6(11): e27190. [doi:10.1371/journal.pone.0027190].

6

The origin of art: camouflage, anti-camouflage and de-camouflage in the appropriation art of Imants Tillers

Ian McLean

'The origin of something is the source of its essence.' (Heidegger 1993b: 143)

Animal camouflage is a classic proof of the theory of natural selection. Thus a book that puts into conversation ideas about camouflage in nature and art is an invitation to entangle two discourses that have a troubled relationship. The trouble stems from different attitudes to the relationship between nature and culture. Where science tends to see continuities, art theory generally makes a sharp, even ontological, distinction. This chapter doesn't argue one way or the other, leaving the question on hold. However, in the spirit of the book, the chapter employs Richard Dawkins's notion of memes and other evolutionary concepts. This doesn't amount to an evolutionary theory of art. Rather, evolutionary tropes are used for their explanatory power in the interpretation of the copy in contemporary art and in particular appropriation art. While short lived as an art movement, appropriation art's poetics of the copy established the ontological ground of art that followed, in much the same sense that cubism prepared the way for modernism. Today artists think through acts of repetition, doubling and camouflage. What is the origin of this poetic sensibility and what does it mean?

Appropriation art

Douglas Crimp is credited with discovering appropriation art in 1977 (Crimp 1977), though it wasn't until 1980 that the term began to take hold when the influential New York art journal, *October*, championed it as the quintessential style of postmodernism (Crimp 1980; Owens 1980). Postmodernism, said Rosalind Krauss, is 'the discourse of the copy' rather than originality (Krauss 1981, 66).

Modernism now appears as a brief aberration in the history of human poetics, with postmodernism returning the artist to the traditional role of imitator. Down the ages art has invariably been conceived as mimesis, as a doubling. Indigenous artists, for example, copy designs that originated from the hands of ancestral beings. Medieval artists did much the same when they took God's creation as a model of their designs, as if this was a way to 'mediate the special ontological status of … traces of the divine on earth' (Guérin 2013, 54). However, the discourse of the copy that postmodernist critics had in mind derived from the ubiquity of photographic reproduction, which seemingly challenged the ontological condition of modernism's aesthetic regime (Owens 1978). Crimp, Owens and Krauss interpreted appropriation art as the legacy of minimalism's critique of the egoism of the modernist avant-garde – what Krauss called its fiction of 'the self as origin' (Krauss 1981, 53).

If postmodernism is a poetics of the copy – of disguise and camouflage – avant-garde modernism is one of anti-camouflage or attention seeking. In this respect avant-garde art is akin to the colourful displays of various male birds that Darwin said evolved to attract the attention of a mate (sexual selection). This apparent quirk of nature seemingly defies the tendency of natural selection to evolve (through the heritable information of genes) biotechnologies that insinuate (camouflage) the subject into the background environment. Whatever metaphysical lessons that philosophers and art theorists have taken from the poetics of the copy, evolutionary theory is more prosaic: camouflage provides a disguise from predators.

Avant-garde modernism and peacocks seemingly resist the evolutionary tendencies of their inheritance. 'Avant-garde originality', said Krauss, 'is conceived as a literal origin, a beginning from ground zero ... to be born – without ancestors – a futurist' (Krauss 1981, 53). While the peacock evolved its anti-camouflage by the same genetic copying process as its well-camouflaged cousins, it is the result of the repression of those alleles (variant genes) that through natural selection produce camouflage. What once was dominant became recessive. Similarly, argues Krauss, avant-garde originality represses 'the ever-present reality of the copy as the underlying condition of the original' (Krauss 1981, 58). 'What would it look like' today, Krauss asked (in 1981), 'not to repress the concept of the copy ... to produce a work that acted out the discourse of reproductions without originals?' Her answer was the work of Sherrie Levine, as it 'seems most radically to question the concept of origin and with it the notion of originality' (Krauss 1981, 64).

Krauss was referring to Levine's recent photographic facsimiles of American modernist photographs by Edward Weston, Walker Evans and Eliot Porter. Mainly known as reproductions in books, they are the single most important icons of the postmodern turn, the bread and butter of every introductory art course on postmodernism. When the Metropolitan Museum of Art hung all six of Levine's photographic series *After Ed Weston* (1980) and eight of the 18 photographs from the series *After Walker Evans* (1981) in its 2009 exhibition, 'The pictures generation, 1974–1984', they seemed too small and innocuous for the heavy theoretical attention they have received. About a quarter the size of the original prints, and photographed from reproductions, their diminutive token-like presence only quickened the desire to experience the real thing (unlike Warhol's replications of Campbell's soup cans).

However, in reproduction we can't tell the copy from the original. Neither can the law. The estates of Weston and Evans hold the copyright on Levine's images. Because postmodernist theory also hinges on the undecidability between original and copy, the more their difference is narrowed the better it works. Then, as Douglas Crimp commented: 'the original cannot be located, is always deferred' (Crimp 1980, 98).

After Ed Weston and *After Walker Evans* have achieved such iconic status in the annals of postmodernism because of the completeness of their disguise, which effectively renders the relationship between the original and copy reversible. Each becomes a replicant of the other. In this way Levine transformed an artwork into an image, indeed a sign. They are not 'pictures', as Crimp called the 1977 exhibition that is credited with first announcing this move, but signs; their aim being 'to determine how a picture becomes a signifying structure of its own accord' (Crimp 1977, 3).

In transforming pictures into signs, Levine's images are examples of memes. In defining a meme as a 'unit of cultural transmission' (Dawkins 1989, 192), Dawkins effectively gave it the status of a semiotic sign (Deacon 1999). As units of transmission their job is to replicate information as accurately as possible. A meme, then, is heritable information. This is why the seriality of *After Ed Weston* and *After Walker Evans* is important. Levine is interested in their shared heritage, not the individually differentiated phenotype of each picture. Thus she numbers rather than individually identifies the name of each work she copies, shifting our attention from the aura of the actual work (phenotype) to its underlying memetic origin. The seriality reduces each individual work to a sign, to 'an Ed Weston' or 'a Walker Evans'; that is, to the heritable meme that the names of these authors signify in art world and especially modernist discourse.

Dawkins coined the term 'memes' after mimesis (copy), and also because it rhymed with genes, his point being that memes acts like genes. Each is heritable information because each is a function of language. Generated from a code, the gene and the meme can theoretically be copied perfectly ad infinitum. Semiotically, Levine's perfect copy (sign) of the Weston meme makes it a signifier in her own work. Levine thus created what Roland Barthes called a 'second-order semiological system' (Barthes 1982, 129) – a seminal concept in postmodern theory. In this way she draws our attention to Weston's 'second-degree' poetics, which descends in this case from the formal play of the classical nude. In similar fashion *After Walker Evans* signals the pedigree of social realism in Western art. According to Barthes, a second-order semiological system is the structure of myth (Barthes 1982, 129). Levine, in effect, discloses the myth of modernism: 'the ever-present reality of the copy as the underlying condition of the original'.

By narrowing the gap between the copy and the original, Levine enhances the 'infinite play of substitution', as Craig Owens described (in 1978) the new game in town. However, if the gap is completely closed, the play cannot begin. The original must still be seen to haunt the copy like a ghost in the machine, as the copy is as dependent on the original as the original is on it. This ambivalence of mimicry, which at the same time authorises and subverts the original, is the trademark of postmodernist deconstruction (Bhabha 1994). Owens aptly called it the Derridean '*mise en abyme*', which reads 'a book within a book, an origin within the origin, a center within the center … a photograph within a photograph' (Owens 1978, 77). Levine's photograph is precisely a photograph within a photograph. However, her disguise is so complete – the photograph in the photograph is at the same time the photograph – that the original cannot be located, not because it has been deferred but because it has been repressed. If, as Krauss accused, modernism repressed the copy, Levine represses the original. Levine's memetic replication is equivalent to the evolutionary dead-end of cloning genes.

Imants Tillers had covered much the same territory two years earlier in *Untitled* (1978), in which two photographic reproductions of a typical picturesque landscape, but greatly enlarged, were hung side by side. Tillers of Sydney and Levine of the American mid-west share a fascination with reproductions, which to them had a greater auratic presence than the original artworks available in their local art museums. However, the point of Tillers' appropriation was subtly different from Levine's. The serial doubling of *Untitled* was not perfect. Made by order in a factory that produced mural-size images with a computer-controlled paint-jet system, Tillers had enlarged two different reproductions of *Summer*

(1909), an iconic Australian landscape painting by one of Australia's most popular artists, Hans Heysen. The meaning of *Untitled* derives from the memetic virulence of the image in Australia and Australian collective identity, but it also hinges on two formal aspects of the work (as opposed to the image). Firstly, about nine times larger than the original Heysen watercolour, its scale announces the image as a public transmissible sign, as a sort of pop billboard – so different from Levine's small works, which in their intimacy seem like an obscure private language. Secondly, the subtle differences of colour registration – one yellowish and the other purplish – between the two reproductions of *Summer* introduce the notion of variant memes, which like variant genes or alleles produce slightly different skin colourations in the phenotype. Tillers' focus is not the perfect heritability of memes but their variance.

Variability is the most important factor in evolution. Without it there would be nothing to select and evolution would not occur. The random lottery of mutation (imperfect copies) may have been the initial basis for genetic variation, but because genetic variability is such an asset, processes that enhance it have been selected for (i.e. evolved). These weighted dice are sexual reproduction, which increases the possibilities of gene combinations, and inherited variant genes stored in the genotype's chromosoms. Every genotype has two or more versions or alleles of the same gene that compete for dominance – a balance of power between dominant and recessive genes, which is the reason that animal camouflage can evolve. In a similar fashion to genetic variation, memetic variability is a factor of imperfect copies (akin to mutation); cross-cultural exchange (akin to sexual reproduction), which increases the possibilities of variant meme combinations; and inherited variations within memes (akin to variant genes or alleles).

Like postmodernism, the theory of memes (and genes) challenges the notion of a creator. New memes arise from the inherent variability of memes as well as imperfections in the copying process – what Tillers called 'the triangle of doubt' (Tillers 1982a). Artists might exploit the poetry of these variabilities and imperfections, but the forest of signs they inhabit forever delimits their moves, sublimating ego in a discursive effect. This relationship between variability and discursivity (coding) is a hallmark of Tillers' investigations.

Like Levine and other appropriation artists, Tillers enacts the disguise of mimicry. He begins by copying an artwork. However, the main focus of his enterprise is unpacking the inherent variability of the copying process. Tillers' interest in variability and the systematic nature of its processes is evident in one of his earliest works, *Permutant* (1971). It consists of 180 wooden tiles arranged in a grid on the floor like a Carl Andre installation. On each tile was fixed a photographic image of a complex patterned drawing (made by Tillers) that resembled microscopic organisms. The photographs were taken at varying distances from the drawing. The result was a camouflage-like surface made from memetic variations or repeated permutations of the same image.

These early investigations culminated in *Conversations of the bride* (1974–75). It is difficult to think of an artwork that better models how variant memes replicate. Consisting of 112 panels of painted images (each 8.5 × 11.8 cm) supported on aluminium stands so that the panels are at eye height and arranged in an ordered installation, viewers circulate through the images looking for a key, a way in, until they realise they are already in, part of the code. A clue is the reflective mirror backing of each panel, so that one's own visage hovers in this field of fragmented images. The two main sources of these images are Heysen's *Summer* and Duchamp's *The bride stripped bare by her bachelors, even* (1915–23). Broken down into a quasi-systematic format, the images are repeated in varying combinations like re-arranged signs or letters of the alphabet. Each panel is numbered as if a catalogue of the variant replications, and distributed in non-linear sequences across a grid that maps the rhizomic pattern of memetic replication. The variation not only occurs within each image or meme, but between two cultural formations that then was known as the 'provincialism problem' (Smith 1974) – the Duchamp meme of the centre and the Heysen meme of the periphery. Tillers, who has an eye for these things, was no doubt aware of the poetic crossovers of each artist's life spans: Duchamp (July 1887 – October 1968); Heysen (October 1877 – July 1968).

Graham Coulter-Smith identified *Conversations of the bride* as a 'prototype' of Tillers' *Book of power*, his ongoing project (since 1981) of drawn and painted appropriations on canvasboards. At the time of writing, Tillers has completed about 93,000 canvasboards, each a unit that appropriates a segment of another artwork. Each canvasboard is numbered, making the *Book of power* an encyclopaedic codex. In this it resembles the genotype. We might call it a memotype: 93,000 memes and still growing. Currently about four times the size of the human genome, theoretically the *Book of Power* has no end. Tillers refers to these 93000 canvasboards as one painting but 'cloven' or split into 'innumerable and intra-and intertextual couplings' (Coulter-Smith 2001, 5). Its very excess of appropriations creates a relational network of variant copies (memes) that fragments the will to power of any one ego or subject. Where better to hide ego than in a forest of egos? Tillers (the postmodernist) has chosen the fate of Echo (the double of Narcissus, who is the mythic archetype of the modernist): he will only speak by repeating the words of others. So rigorous is his commitment that it seems like a spiritual discipline by which he hopes to liberate himself from ego. This huge network of variant copies appears as a type of cubist fragmentation that, like camouflage, insinuates his ego into the pattern of surrounding voices.

Compared to Levine and indeed any other appropriation artist, Tillers probes much more deeply into the ontological questions raised by the discourse of the copy. His project is not to de-mythologise or deconstruct modernism – though this might be one of its effects – but to rethink the ontology of art. So excessive is his appropriation of artworks that it recalls Heidegger's Dawkins-like tautology that the origin of the work of art is not the artist but art (Heidegger 1993b, 143).

The *Book of power* began after Tillers completed *One painting cleaving*, a set of works painted between 1980 and 1982. The very title evokes cellular division, and indeed the work has several versions. The unseen womb-like cavernous interior of its central image, the Cathedral of Assisi, houses the origin (memes) of Western art. Appropriated from a postcard in which the colour printing is misaligned, Tillers uses this effect to create what seems a time-lapse photograph of the church shaking just prior to its collapse in the earthquake that occurred 15 years after the work was completed. Tillers described the project as an exercise of triangulation designed to locate a point of certainty – here the point of the origin of Western art. Tillers' point was that such triangulation always fails. He was at the time interested in Göedel's concept of undecidability – what Tillers called in reference to this painting the 'triangle of doubt' (Coulter-Smith 2001, 139–49).

The fragmentation of *One painting cleaving* makes it appear cubist, a camouflage design. Actually hidden under the outer layer of the painting is an image of a boy appropriated from a Latvian children's book. Tillers, who is of Latvian decent, was also triangulating his own origins. At the time, Tillers' invoked the fanciful triangulation of Duchamp, Arakawa and de Chirico, which he said was 'three lines of influence (moving in the direction of melancholy)' and converging on 'Böcklin's painting "The Island of the

Dead" – this island being the triangle of doubt' (Tillers 1982a). In an essay written several months later (published in mid-1982), Tillers repeated the metaphor in another triangle of doubt (postmodernism, Australian art, Aboriginal art) and its melancholy history, suggesting that Böcklin's painting might be an effect (as per Bell's Theorem) of the 'extermination of the Tasmanian aborigines by the white settlers' (Tillers 1982b, 57). Tillers wrote this just before he began work on one of his earliest canvasboards, *Island of the dead*, which replicates a photograph of an Aboriginal rock painting – which can be taken as another origin image from a cavernous interior.

These breakthrough works were made when Tillers was involved with his *n*-space projects – a series of improvised exhibitions between 1980 and 1983 that placed invited artists in varying situations to which the meaning of their work was effectively subordinated. In Tillers' Duchampian mind, '*n*' referred to the mathematical *n*-dimension – i.e. a space of variable dimensions, potentially a quantum space, hyperspace or 4th dimensional space. *N*-space venues ranged from a telephone which the viewer rang to hear John Nixon's anti-music, a pole (at Documenta 7), the cottage on the west coast of Ireland that Wittgenstein stayed in for several months in 1948, an artist's studio, a lighthouse in Sydney, a small Victorian garden pavilion in Melbourne, and a contemporary art gallery in Sydney. These were temporary clearings in which sounded an unfolding of voices that offered an alternative perspective to the avant-gardist 'self as origin'. They were also a type of camouflage in which Tillers could conceal his role as the conceptual producer of the events.

The main theoretical document that Tillers published at this time, 'Locality fails', is an apt summation of the thinking behind *n*-space. Its references to Bell's Theorem (1964), which proved that quantum particles can be in two places simultaneously, reflected Tillers' long-held interest in mathematics and physics and his own experience as an artist in Sydney. The meme of appropriation art had simultaneously emerged in Sydney and New York because it replicated in images that were reproduced across the world. Tillers envisaged *n*-space as a similar quantum event in which ideas or memes could be in more than one place at the same time and so have unexpected effects from a distance – as evident in the final *n*-space project, *Waiting for technology*, which juxtaposed four of Tim Johnson's paintings of Papunya Tula artists with their canvasses and the actual paintings. It was an example of the unlikely shuffling of dissimilar cultural memes, creating the variable memes of cross-cultural formations.

The composite fragmented space of the juxtaposed canvasboards that Tillers began working on at this time provided a ready-made relational schema for the provisional and multiple conversations that Tillers sought to generate with *n*-space. The canvasboard system demonstrated Bell's Theorem: that a local event – the canvasboard – is a site of simultaneous global effects. Further, the canvasboards provided Tillers with a framework that echoes the technology of appropriation. Not only were they ready-mades, manufactured multiples, the repetition of the boards invokes the duplication processes of appropriation (as well as the replication of memes), and the ensuing grid references an age-old copying device that Tillers actually employs.

6 The origin of art

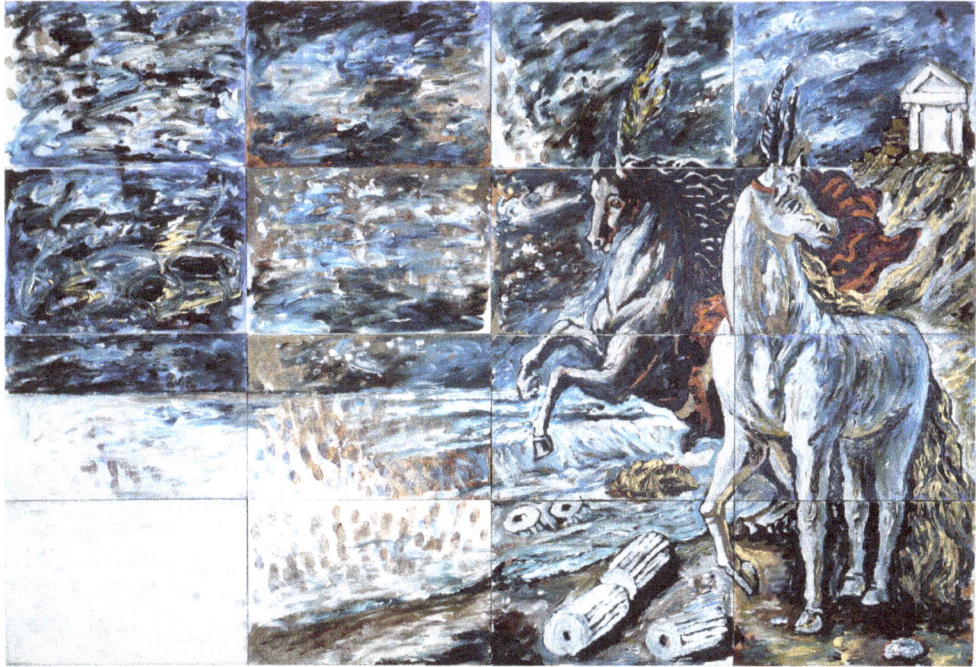

Figure 6.1 Imants Tillers, *The dichotomy*, 1984. Synthetic polymer paint on 16 canvasboards (10 × 15'), 101.6 × 52.2 cm. Panel numbers: 4028–4043. Collection of the artist

The canvasboard system, as in *The dichotomy* reproduced above, comprises two discrete systems that interrupt rather than reinforce each other: one a painterly two-dimensional image – the copy (disguise) – and the other a three-dimensional object – the surrounding environment. The first consists of copies of images of existing artworks rendered in a painterly manner on canvasboards. The second comprises the same canvasboards butted together in the form of an object. This creates a grid across the copied image, thus interrupting or fragmenting the cohesion of its disguise. It also gives the overall work an objecthood. Thus the canvasboards are not so much paintings as installations, a point that Tillers at first emphasised by the manner in which they are sometimes exhibited. However, the essential element of the canvasboards is neither system in itself, but they ways in which each interrupts the other – like the trade-off between natural and sexual selection.

As with the *n*-space project, the starting point of Tillers' canvasboards is existing discourses already put into play by others. There is also a striking resemblance between Tillers' canvasboard system and Krauss's seminal (previously-mentioned) essay, 'The originality of the avant-garde: a postmodernist repetition' – as if his system is itself an appropriation of her argument. Tillers developed his canvasboard system shortly after the publication of Krauss's essay in 1981.

Krauss identified two main signifiers of avant-garde originality: the 'illusion of spontaneity' (Krauss 1981: 63) exemplified in the expressive hand of Rodin and Monet – the artist as origin – and the ubiquitous grid of post-cubist modernist art – the picture plane as origin. Despite their apparent differences, both, she argued, repressed the copy in the name of originality. This was especially the case with the grid, which promises the autonomy of an originary self-referential ground in which artists, she said, thought they 'could hear ... the beginning, the origins of Art' (Krauss 1981, 54). However, she argued, in duplicating the coordinates of the squared surface of the canvas, 'the grid ... does not reveal the surface, laying it bare at last; rather it veils it through a repetition' (Krauss 1981, 57).

If Tillers appropriates Krauss's argument, he also seems to deliberately misread it, as his canvasboards combine the spontaneity of expressive brushwork with the modernist grid, thus doubling the modernist repression of the copy. Tillers' introduction of his hand – the sign of ego – is a deliberate deconstruction of minimalism's repression of the artist's hand. Levine's photographic appropriations are, as mentioned earlier, a direct legacy of minimalism. In a reversal of modernism's quintessential meme, Levine represses her own hand. This, paradoxically, has become her claim to originality. The minimalist Carl Andre had already done something similar in the 1960s, but through the technology of the grid. For example, in 1966 he purchased – could we say appropriated – 120 bricks from a local brickyard. In 1972 he sold them to the Tate as his own work, and at enormous profit. The Tate could have more easily and cheaply purchased the bricks directly from a local brickyard, without the middlemen (artists and dealer). However Andre's dealer didn't just sell a stack of bricks, he also sold Andre's signature. By now Andre's grids of industrial manufactured units, such as steel sheets and bricks, had become synonymous with his 'hand' – his signature style. What he apparently kicked out the door – ego – had sneaked back in through the window, like the proverbial return of the repressed. This was also the fate of Levine's appropriations. In the age of ego, ego is not so easily dismissed, and certainly not through its repression.

Tillers' use of canvasboards is his signature style. However, unlike the above artists to whom his work is closely related, Tillers' painterly appropriations introduce a counter element in their dealings with ego. Paradoxically, Tillers gives us his hand in the archetypal modernist form of painterly brushmarks. This is an act of anti-camouflage. However, with Tillers it is a feint, a decoy, to forestall the return of the repressed ego that he has expelled in his copies of reproductions of existing artworks. Tillers here engages in a subtle dialectic with the archetypal expressionist mode of modernism identified by Krauss.

If in withdrawing their hand, Andre and Levine inadvertently revealed it, Tillers interrupts this withdrawal through a series of counter movements between the image and the grid, between two- and three-dimensional formats, and between painterly marks and reproductive processes of the copy and the grid. No matter how expressive his marks, they uncannily disclose their inherent systemisation. Tillers thus conceals and reveals ego in a double movement. This simultaneous camouflage and anti-camouflage is, to use Heidegger's term, an act of 'un-concealment', which refers to an inherent delay, even short circuit, caused by a double movement, a crossing back.

How or what do we name this un-concealed when, caught within a perpetual delay, it never properly shows itself. What does it hide? This is the ontological question that Tillers has been circling throughout his career. The origin of the work of art might be art, but as Heidegger added, this origin, art, only 'unfolds in the artwork'. It 'prevails in an actual way' (Heidegger 1993b, 144). This circular movement, Heidegger argues, cannot be avoided: the conundrum must be entered into: thus Tillers' incessant trade-off between camouflage and anti-camouflage: a poetics of de-camouflage that in neither fully concealing or fully revealing bears witness to the enigma of an ancestral event.

In ancient times such a place was marked with a ring of columns in the middle of which was placed a statue of a God – such as an ancient Greek temple. If God, the Creator, is a name no longer in our lexicon, we are left with the statue, with the work of art and its ineffable origin. A more apt example for us today of this place than the ancient Greek temple is the field of dotting in Western Desert paintings, which don't so much conceal an ancestral being but announces in a suitably minimalist fashion the place in which it is unconcealed. The optical shimmer of dots is a de-camouflage that warns us to look away or be dazzled, blinded. Heidegger – and Tillers is the most Heideggerean of artists – called such a place the 'fourfold', the folding of human, God, earth and sky. This folding, he said, is the way that humans 'dwell' on earth (Heidegger 1993a). He sometimes denoted the 'fourfold' as 'being' (crossed) or 'Dasein', which literally means 'being there', or existence. Being (crossed) denotes not the negation or crossing out of being but the delay of its 'un-concealment' or 'gathering' in a particular event – like a work of art – denoted by the fourfold (Eldin 2001, 82-4). In dismissing ego, Tillers had found Dasein.

Dasein denotes that gap between camouflage and anti-camouflage where being emerges. Like the trade-off between heritability and variability in genetic reproduction, this is a creative moment – a movement of creation. This gap (and its processes) is the ground that Tillers' art attempts to occupy. For him appropriation or replication is not a deconstruction of the codes of representation but the means by which being becomes.

References

Barthes R (1982). *Mythologies*, trans. Annette Lavers (New York: Hill and Wang).
Bhabha HK (1994). Of mimicry and man: the ambivalence of colonial discourse. In *The Location of Culture* (pp 85–92). London: Routledge.
Coulter-Smith G (2001). *The postmodern art of Imants Tillers: appropriation en abyme 1971–2001*. Southampton: Fine Art Research Centre, Southampton Institute & Paul Holberton publishing.
Crimp D (1977). 'Pictures', *Pictures* (pp 3–29). New York: Committee for the Visual Arts. Inc.
Crimp D (1980). 'The photographic activity of postmodernism.' *October*, 15(Winter): 91–101.
Dawkins R (1989). *The selfish gene*. Oxford: Oxford University Press.
Deacon TW (1999). Editorial: memes as signs. *The Semiotic Review of Books,* 10(3): 1–3.
Eldin S (2001). *Mapping the present: Heidegger, Foucault and the project of a spatial history*. London: Continuum.
Guérin S (2013). Meaningful spectacles: gothic ivories staging the divine. *The Art Bulletin*, XCV(1, March): 53–77.
Heidegger M (1993a). Building dwelling thinking. In DF Krell (Ed). *Basic writings: revised and expanded edition* (pp. 347–63) London: Routledge.
Heidegger M (1993b). The origin of the work of art. In DF Krell (Ed). *Basic writings: Revised and expanded edition* (pp. 143–212) London: Routledge.
Krauss R (1981). The originality of the avant-garde: a postmodernist repetition. *October*, 18(Autumn): 47–66.
Owens C (1978). Photography 'en abyme'. *October*, 5(Summer): 73–88.
Owen C (1980). The allegorical impulse: toward a theory of postmodernism. *October*, 12(Spring): 67–86.
Smith T (1974). The provincialism problem. *Art Forum*, 13(1): 54–59.
Tillers I (1982a). One painting cleaving: triangle of doubt. In S Grayson & S Nairne (Ed), *Eureka! Artists from Australia* (p. 36). London: Institute of Contemporary art and the Arts Council of Great Britain.
Tillers I (1982b). Locality fails. *Art & Text*, 6(Winter): 51–60.

7
The camouflage effect
Pamela Hansford

Contemporary meanings of camouflage are situated in contexts where rapid adaption to complexity, change and unseen risk has become a norm. Fluid and swift adjustments are hallmarks of this camouflage culture, and disguise, mimicry and disruption are the adaptive strategies humans and animals use in response. This chapter examines the means, ends and meanings of camouflage in environments that generate unstable forms of being.

Preliminaries

The phenomenon of camouflage is evident in art, war and society and it crosses the boundaries of human and animal, animate and inanimate. It is present, though not always apparent, in acts as diverse as the pyrotechnical disguise of cuttlefish, in the magician's sleight of hand, in the joke's masking of unconscious intent, in a dazzled warship's defensive cover, in the delicate oscillation between cultural absorption and independence, and in the immune system's responses. In all these instances camouflage is a response to risk,[1] and its function is preservation of the self.[2]

The essence and origin of the camouflage phenomenon is obscure, a fact which is evident from the slipperiness of its key concepts, multiple genealogies and contested significance. Unsurprisingly perhaps and with some notable exceptions,[3] most of the literature directly concerned with camouflage focuses on its technical dimensions, including the optical and perceptual (such as reversals of figure and ground in gestalt switches, and surveillance media), animal concealment and mimicry, and of course the famous military camouflage patterning to which an entire encyclopaedia is devoted.[4] Relevant philosophi-

---

1 Risk, or its inverse, risk aversion, may be 'hard-wired' into perception: 'Without … hard-wired tendencies toward unit-making and unit-breaking we could not so easily be deceived by camoufleurs, or magicians or pickpockets or artists. In all these instances camouflage implies an [immanent] seeing eye from which to hide.' (Behrens 2013).
2 In the case of the magic trick the preserved 'self' is figurative, maintaining the integrity of the illusion.
3 Including Leach (2006), and Hsu (2006) in review of Leach's book *Camouflage*.
4 Unsurprising not least of all because the term itself only came into widespread usage after World War I: 'The term "camouflage" gradually spread from French into all languages after the First World War

cal literature essentially ignores these technical aspects, and eschews the term itself while nevertheless energetically pursuing the significations of its key elements: mimesis, mimicry, recognition and misrecognition, distinction, assimilation and blending, erasure, invisibility, masking, veiling and the like.[5]

I use the concept 'camouflage effect', the title of this chapter, as a marker for an inclusive idiom to capture responses to rapid adaption to complexity, experiment and risk. I argue that camouflage self-fashioning is not primarily a negative self-defence *strategy* but simply a necessary part of being a self per se. This is true at the microbiological immune system level, and also at the level of emotional response, awareness, identity and perception. We engage camouflage mechanisms such as mimicry and adaptation in a constantly shifting inter-relationship with human and nonhuman environments.

One of the fundamental ideas pursued in the chapter is that the 'camouflage effect' is a marker for the limits of the human. It is both a feature of subjective responses to experiment and risk, and a leitmotif – a salient reminder of the current instability of animal and human life. The chapter proposes the humble cuttlefish as an icon – a necessary reminder of the precariousness of the human as a stable state of being. In the possible loss of the cuttlefish with its marvellous and pyrotechnical displays of camouflage, I read the animal origin and the animal end of humanity. This increasingly fragile existence is expressed through the 'camouflage effect' with its rich repertoire of self-fashioning, which is an unacknowledged dimension of and perhaps a precondition for the present of self-preservation.

The first part of the chapter briefly notes camouflage elements at work in re-fashioning post-human subjectivities via the extension, contraction and re-identification of bodily existence. Here camouflage mechanisms function to loosen and re-figure the boundaries between the animate and inanimate, such as in crossovers between biology and electronics and informatics evident in genetic engineering. In the second part of the chapter I apply the concept of a 'camouflage effect' to readings of several artworks to foreground processes of self-production in the moment of art reception. I argue that in general art can function to stimulate adaptation (camouflage) and that some artworks make this process itself more apparent.

Camouflage and dynamic self-fashioning

Whether we know it or not we encounter and engage with camouflage phenomena on a daily basis in many different ways. Haraway (1991) and Esposito (2011) argue there is one iconic encounter that particularly engages the subject in processes of adaptation, mimicry etc – this is the immune system, which is the literal and figurative emblem they

---

(WWI) when France was the first nation in military history to establish a formal section de camouflage. By 1925, "camouflage" was increasingly used to identify animal concealment and deception, science's terminology having become enmeshed with military lingo. Before the war, however, common biological terms were "mimicry" and "concealing" ... Rather than "camouflage", Breton and his associates throughout the 1920s and 1930, including writer and sociologist Roger Caillois, favoured the older terminology "mimicry" used by 19th century naturalists, Charles Darwin and Alfred Wallace.' Elias (2012)
5   Mimesis is a central plank within the semiotic chain of the camouflage phenomenon, and derives from the Greek mimesis, meaning to imitate. Darwin's *The origin of species* (1859) is an especially notable reference in showing that all life is mimetic (Norris 1980; Grosz 2011).

use to explore the negotiation of human subjectivity. In seeking to extend the relevance of immunity from the somatic and ontological into the epistemological, politico-legal and environmental realms, Esposito emphasises that in maintaining organic integrity the immune system actively modifies the *identity* of the subject. He argues that immune functions are a form of self-fashioning and adaptively open the self to the challenges of specific environments, and are progressively and ultimately conditioned by them. Immune system processes could be said to be, or to instigate, a kind of recognition so sophisticated that if it is successful it protects the body by preventing a negative response. Immune 'tolerance' is one example of this,[6] but there are multiple, complex and as yet unknown ways in which camouflage phenomena are associated with immune system relationships. For example, certain viruses disguise themselves in the host cell when they infect and replicate in 'dressed' cells derived from the host cell machinery to appear like 'self' to the immune system. But another connection to camouflage is the ways viruses constantly evolve/mutate to make them unrecognisable to the immune system; for example, influenza viruses evolve from one season to the next, which prevents our immune system recognising it in the next infections. Viruses also constantly shape-shift within an individual host – the virus rapidly mutates, preventing the immune system from expelling it, for example, RNA viruses, of which HIV is one. In both cases there are co-evolutionary and co-adaptations between the virus and immune system, whereby each progressively change in relation to the other.[7]

In addition to these material manifestations, the immune system can also be understood on a figurative and collective level as signifying 'an elaborate figurative icon for principal systems of symbolic and material "difference" in late capitalism ... a "map" drawn to guide recognition and misrecognition of self and other ... to construct and maintain boundaries' (Haraway 1991). Haraway also sees the strategies of camouflage (though she never names them as such) – blending, assimilation, masking, mimicry, and disruption of recognition, in the fashioning of new bodily existences using implants (both organic and inorganic), plastic and cosmetic surgery, chemical therapies, terminalisation of the body in the internet and genetic engineering. For example, xenotransplantation is a technique of deliberate camouflaging that scientists engage in while coaxing the immune system not to reject pig cells/organs. This is done either by coating them with something uninteresting to the immune system[8] or by genetically engineering pigs to make their cells more 'human' looking to the immune system – both instance of camouflage as blending in.[9]

Such new surgical and engineered constructions preserve and extend human life (and impact the life of pigs farmed and tested for this purpose), and radically transforms the experience and signification of human subjectivity. In particular they come at the cost of overturning the individual conceived in the classical sense as a stable term, as something that cannot be further divided. This is a paradox noted by Esposito: 'in order to preserve

---

6 Immune tolerance is (medically) understood as a specific suppression of the immune response induced by previous exposure to an antigen. 'Self' antigens are usually well tolerated by the immune system, which has been educated to non-reactivity against the structures normally present. 'Non-self' antigens can be identified as invaders from the outside world or modified/harmful substances present under distressed conditions, and only these are supposed to be attacked by the immune system.
7 See Waldby (1993). I am grateful to Rachel Carr for providing me with this example.
8 Scientists use an alginate coating on cells for this purpose.
9 A concern for virologists, however, is that this may also provide any viruses with an effective camouflage. I am grateful to Rachel Carr for providing me with this example, and for her own and Professor Catherine Waldby's valuable contributions to this paper.

itself human life must transcend itself – no longer in a sphere that is external to it, as theology would have it, but inside itself. It must objectify itself – and therefore exteriorise itself – in forms beyond its simple coming into being' (Esposito 2011, 13). In these instances camouflage processes (alarmingly) grease the boundaries between biology, electronics and informatics, making them more permeable and fluid. In this material and figural dismantling and multiplication of the body, what we are facing is 'a radical restructuring of what until now we have called "body" … there is no doubt the body is experiencing a state of profound alteration, down to its essential fabric … on these lines, the subject is no longer an originary given but a functional construct' (Esposito 2011, 148).

It is something of an understatement to say that notions of 'bodily integrity', 'organism' and 'individual' are being rendered dynamic and problematic, and it is also not a new insight. To paraphrase De Beauvoir's famous dictum in *The second sex* (1949) originally applied to describe 'woman': one is not born an organism, one *becomes* one. What has changed in the intervening decades is the intensification and pace of technological development, the degree to which it routinely penetrates, transforms, doubles and mimics life, and how dramatically and publicly the preservation of life is threatened: 'What we are talking about is not just the overturning of the relations of mastery between subject and instrument dreaded by a long anti-technological tradition … rather this is an interaction between species, or even between the organic world and the artificial world, implying a veritable interruption of biological evolution by natural selection and its inscription into a different system of meaning' (Esposito 2011 201, 150). The theme of a morbid fascination with assimilation, 'mimephobia' (Norris 1980), is familiar from Caillois' *Mimicry and legendary psychasthenia* (1935); for example, when he cites Flaubert's *The temptation of Saint Anthony* where St Anthony surrenders to the mimicry present in nature: 'Plants are no longer distinguished from animals … Insects identical with rose petals adorn a bush … And then plants are confused with stones' (Caillois 1935, 27). Baudrillard (1988) also pursues a mimetic pathology associated with a lack of boundaries when he observes that the sensible texture of human experience more and more comes to resemble simulated events rather than real things. In his assessment of this, Baudrillard fluctuates between a celebration of the artificiality and malleability of this 'postmodern condition', and despair at the crudity of its representations. At the other end of excessive assimilation of otherness is auto-immunity, whereby the immune system defines self in a too limiting way that causes disease for the organism as a whole.[10]

In the construction of unstable bodily and cultural configurations, camouflage is both a condition and a strategy. It is a conditioned response to change and risk, perhaps an instinctive legacy that humans share with other animals, and an energetic and strategic means of adaptation to a rapidly changing environment, experiments and new technologies. This is evident not only in the increasing fragility of life that humans globally share with other animals, but also in practices such as xenotransplantation and the future threat of industrialisation of genetic engineering, and in the present global industrial practices of human fertility commerce (Cooper & Waldby 2014).

---

10   Thanks to Rachel Carr for this point.

The camouflage effect in the production and reception of art

Processes of self-fashioning – mimesis, erasure, blending, invisibility, merging and adaptation – are recognised as fundamental traits of camouflage. Although we are essentially unaware of them they are indispensable parts of everyday life: combined perception and recognition (or misrecognition) actively produces self, other, and identity in immune system responses; the unstable post-human body is divided, doubled and recreated from techniques such as xenotransplantation; and human and animals adapt in response to risk to preserve and extend themselves. But camouflage phenomena are also important (yet under-acknowledged) features in the reception of an artwork. This is one aspect of the aesthetic and symbolic dimensions of the camouflage effect and involves the construction and eradication of various stages of awareness, observation and identification required to connect with works of art. For example, Leach articulates camouflage as a means for inscribing the individual within a cultural setting, not as disguise but as a medium to relate to the other. He also points out that camouflage is not restricted to a visual domain, but is visceral:[11] 'it can be enacted within the domains of the other senses, especially smell and hearing. Perfume is precisely part of the masquerade of self-representation that defines the operations of camouflage. So too is music … the example of walking into a space and hearing music which makes us feel "connected"' (Leach 2006, 241).

The important theme of connection as surrender to the other, and the threat of a consequent dissolution of identity, is famously worked through in *Mimicry and legendary psychasthenia* (Caillois 1935). The text is often cited for its original use of a philosophical anthropology that draws on sympathetic magic in the work of Frazer, Hubert and Mauss (Leach 2006, 69), surrealism, and naturalism. Caillois' argument is complex; at one level he sees the endowment of concealment in animals, mimicry, as a primitive vestige retained in human beings through the use of objects and machines. Mimicry is maintained to assist us in the assimilation or distinction from our surroundings. At another level, mimicry can lead to pathological 'psychasthenia', which is a loss of distinction between the self and its environment. On an individual level this amounts to the inability to balance distinction and assimilation and in extreme cases may lead to psychosis; on a collective level it is a temptation of the masses: fascism.[12] Either way Caillois concludes: 'The ultimate problem … is that of distinction: distinctions between the real and the imaginary, between waking and sleeping, between ignorance and knowledge … among distinctions, there is assuredly none more clear-cut than that between the organism and its surroundings' (Caillois 1935,

---

11 Here Leach differs from Shell (2012) who limits her concept of camouflage as both a time-bounded concept – an adaptive logic of escape from photographic representation – and as an accumulation of perceptual devices for self-fashioning.

12 The intellectual closeness of Caillois to the surrealists is important in appreciating anti-rationalist and anti-war themes in this text. Elias (2012, 4) comments: 'Surrealism emerged in the 1920s in reaction to a western military culture that fetishized camouflage like none before … and never before had abstraction and trompe l'oeil played such a big part in war aesthetics … Concealment and deception, in intellectual and organic forms, became central to Surrealism through two intellectual channels. First, through Darwin's theory that through natural selection animals evolved physiological attributes to conceal themselves and deceive predators; second, through Freud's theory that the unconscious is a defence mechanism for concealing and disguising traumatic memories.'

59).[13] Avoiding the 'temptation of space', which involves merging totally with the other (mimicry in overdrive), is what (negatively) drives the camouflage phenomenon.

If self-adaptation is visceral and emotional in the negative ways described by Caillois, it can also equally be a dynamic that involves the subject positively and creatively in its relations with both animate and inanimate being. Leach makes a similar point when he follows Walter Benjamin in observing that responding to art involves a form of surrender (2006, 13). In the reception of art the mechanisms of camouflage operate to facilitate identification and de-identification, a merging with and demarcating boundaries between the self and the work. Following Shklovsky (1917), it might be said that the reception of art takes place both as spectator and spectacle, a complex form of self-fashioning mediated by the artist through the inter-textual boundaries established by the work. Art creates dynamic and experimental environments, which are present to us as a kind of double, and in this space there is the opportunity to acknowledge conditional effects that influence the changing sense of who we think we are, were or aspire to be. The 'camouflage effect' highlights the roles camouflage elements play in encounters that engage the subject in boundaries set out by an artwork.

Certain artworks stimulate a self-fashioning 'camouflage effect' more so than others and this is evident in *Coin* (Armanious 2013) where what we see first of all is the absence of a coin via techniques of cut-out and stamping. As touch is usually forbidden in art museum display systems, and impossible in the domain of reproduction,[14] another technique is relatively invisible (at least to the eye if not the touch), because although the main object in Figure 7.1 appears to be cardboard it is actually made of cast bronze. Fooling the eye links with at least two kinds of deception or theft: firstly, the magic of material transformation in *Coin* is a reference to the connection between alchemy and art, although in *Coin* base metal remains base metal; additionally, the coins have disappeared so we must be content with our imagined idea of them, presuming they have remained bronze masquerading as cardboard rather than the gold promised by alchemists. Secondly, the combined logic of the camera and the security systems of the gallery has stolen away our sense of touch. In using our eyes alone we are obliged to falsely conclude that *Coin* is made of something it is not.

At a second closer glance, perhaps we see a small beige dot above the main object, but perhaps we also miss it because it is very small. This turns out to be a so-called coin, a coin masquerading as a cracker. Like the other object this is not what it seems. The expectation of something edible is confounded by its materiality – inedible resin.

---

13 Lacan (1991) follows Freud and Caillois in understanding identity as a dialectical movement between distinction and assimilation.
14 In being obliged to respond to *Coin* as a reproduction, we rely on norms established by the camera even if we are not aware of them. Likewise, if we could touch the cuttlefish we would instantly know it was not seaweed, sand or coral, but its visual evanescence, speed and the protective environment of the sea combine as powerful barriers between us and it. Thus we depend on absent norms established by cuttlefish enthusiasts and marine scientists to photograph and film the cuttlefish for us, and on YouTube, Google and wildlife documentaries to present the cuttlefish to us.

7 The camouflage effect

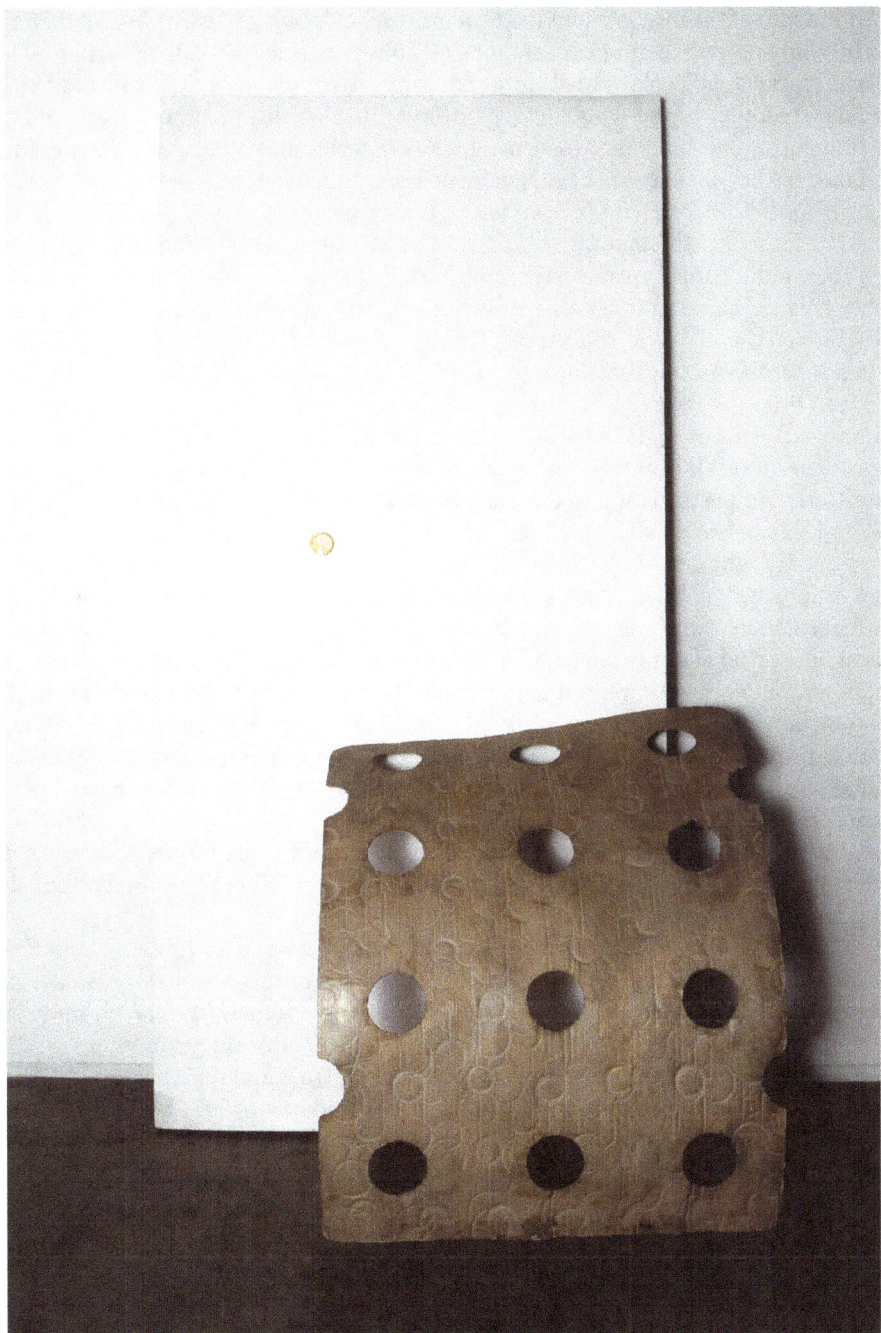

Figure 7.1 Hany Armanious, Coin, 2013 (cast pigmented polyester resin, cast pigmented polyurethane resin, cast bronze, 240 × 134 × 80 cm). Courtesy of the artist and Roslyn Oxley9 Gallery, Sydney

The conundrum of the missing coin made of bronze but looking like cardboard, then being found but only partly meeting expectations of 'coin-ness' (being made of resin and looking like a cracker), is displayed within a museum system where touch is forbidden. This inserts the reception of the work clearly within anti-sensualist traditions of thought, but while rationalism has tended to treat the gaze as superior and a means to downgrade the importance of the other senses, it is equally possible to understand 'looking' as one of the emotions, so that intentional objects are the things we think about, see, imagine and so forth. In order to 'get the picture' in relation to *Coin* we must become involved with the possibilities and meaning of materials, finish, size and placement. Such engaged looking not only creates the thing it sees by means of selective attention, but our identity is also affected, adapted and subtly re-formed. Through the emotion of surprise we realise that *Coin* is not cardboard but brass and resin. We might even say, with Sartre (1943), Lacan (1991), and others working in the shadows of the phenomenological and psychoanalytical traditions, that lived being is in effect being seen by an 'other', so that we are both spectator and spectacle. In this instance the other is an inanimate object, the boundaries set down by the work, and our participation in *Coin* is mediated through the nature of a second nature, the second skin of the artistic layer itself.

In fact under the camouflage-effect of *Coin* we become aware of a series of conditioned and conditional selves. There is the self who was temporarily fooled by brass masquerading as cardboard, there is the one who missed the coin/cracker, or a self-irritated at the games the artist has played at our expense, and the self-subjected to the disciplinary norms of the museum and photographic reproduction. And if we don't reject these as strange impressions, they become present to us as a kind of double. They are our concealed selves, the camouflage effect of our self, selves we live but do not always know and can never master (Freud 1905). This is not to say there is a 'true' self that might provide an original point of reference to ground camouflaged selves, but that not unlike the pyrotechnics of the cuttlefish, and the dynamics of the immune system, we constantly adapt ourselves in response to an environment. One might imagine the self as a swarm of perceptions, emotional and visceral responses constantly shifting in relation to a milieu.[15]

The logic of camouflage is also evident in works by Mikala Dwyer, *Uniform* (Figure 7. 2), Justene Williams, *Your boat my scenic personality of space* and *I am what you see* (Figures 7.3 and 7.4), but these effects are figured differently than in *Coin*. To understand this difference, imagine the aesthetics of concealment as points on a continuum of difference where the dynamics of disguise are utilised to construct and maintain boundaries. At one end lie examples of camouflage modelled on bio-mimesis. This is a space occupied by animal powers of active invisibility, the conditioned control over real-time strategic concealment possessed by the cuttlefish and our own immune system. With Caillois (1935) we can understand activities where an organism merges seamlessly with its milieu as dangerous, a pathological evacuation of identity. But equally, identity formed in this way can be vital rather than pathological. Like the immune response, we might describe it in figurative terms as an endlessly dynamic and transforming community with a system open to challenges of the outside world, and indeed ultimately formed by them. This is a system mediated by complex principles, such as immune tolerance, continuously forging what can only ever be provisionally understood as self and other, a dynamic genesis of conditioned and conditional groupings. In this domain there are parallels with Deleuze's principle of

---

15   My thanks to Rachel Carr for this observation.

difference (Deleuze 1968), and his example of wasp and orchid as they create a becoming or symbiotic emergent unit (Deleuze & Guattari 1980).

At the other end of this imaginary continuum are figurative fantasies of semblance: the literary and sci-fi world of replicants, cyborgs, aliens and transformers who translate the logic of camouflage into the realms of shape shifting, supernatural and horror. Think HP Lovecraft's *Necronomicon* (1924), or Ridley Scott's *Alien* (1979). Lacking naturally proscribed boundaries, these inventions have the capacity to drill into the column of reality and to figuratively re-compose being. I would place *Coin* at the softer end of this part of my scale.

Between these two extremes there is a large middle ground with numerous examples of concealment based in humorous subterfuge. This face of camouflage has a fertile comic history, rich in the traditions of trompe l'oeil, irony, mimicry, identity swaps and aural jokes. For example, think of technologies of surveillance and their spoofing in popular media: *Dad's army* comes to mind, with quaint dress-up attempts at hiding using grease paint, leaves, netting, twigs – old-fashioned, ready-to-hand cloaking; or *Inspector Gadget*, Inspector Clouseau, *Get smart,* the *Benny Hill show,* and *Some like it hot,* where disguise incorporates a grab bag of cross-dressing opportunities, 'passing', tacky prosthetics and amateur faking. This point on the continuum typically favours low-tech materials, and so-called low-life types, and artefacts. The sophistication of dynamic masking and dynamic modelling found at the extreme ends of the scale translates here into fumbling, bumbling, farting and imperfect impersonations. All manner of matter and materials – from the humble to the grandiose – feature here and it is the artist's role to discover how they can be revealed in all their richness. This is the comic territory of the camouflage-effect, one where Dwyer and Williams feel right at home.

Figure 7.2

The work in Figure 7.2 is *Uniform* by Mikala Dwyer. Of her use of costumes such as those we see here the artist has written: 'My mother always made fabulous costumes for school plays, fancy dress parades and parties. My favourite was a Bunyip costume made of a dyed sheet covered in hundreds of separated rubber glove fingers. Costumes for me are a sort of cubby house, they create an "elsewhere" to inhabit while simultaneously being in the "here"; a sort of cloaking device of extreme visibility and at the same time hiding and disappearing. Even though they are not necessarily wearable they are easily inhabited by the imagination.'[16]

Using this work, and the artist's description of her relationship to costumes as channels to the past, I can powerfully recall my own childhood, and especially those moments when I believed I was invisible, yet with the benefit of hindsight realise I clearly wasn't. The materials in *Uniform*, the colours and fabric, are not opulent. In fact the costumes are somewhat plain with large sagging orbs, the 'eyes', attached like targets to the front. But the relatively featureless aspect of the work acts as a tabula rasa in allowing my projected imaginary thoughts to infiltrate from the past. I remember childhood camouflage pranks, swapping identities in a seamless fashion, hiding and disappearing. My concealed selves emerge as a double, a camouflage effect, a form of complex self-fashioning that comprises

---

16   Mikala Dwyer, GoldeneBend'er, ACCA, Melbourne, 2013, p. 68.

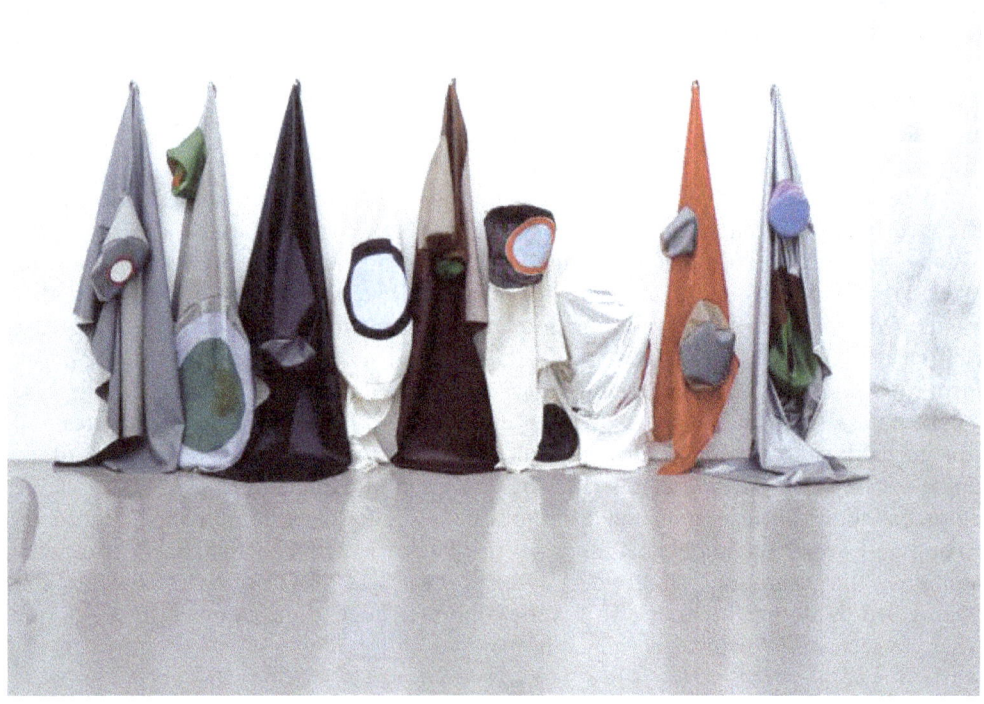

Figure 7.2 *Uniform* by Mikala Dwyer

the community of selves I live every day but which I can never comprehensively know. With *Uniform* as my guide this community mixes with selves from the past, some of which may now be ghosts, merging figure and ground; my 'camouflage condition' one might say.

Figure 7.3

Figure 7.3 is a still from Williams' *Your boat my scenic personality of space* and here we are on more familiar ground, in the sense that this image has clearly literal as well as conceptual connections to camouflage. Taken comprehensively, camouflage is an elaborate icon whose modalities map the disruption of bonds between being and appearance, recognition and misrecognition. While it mobilises repertoires of dynamic masking and dynamic modelling, camouflage also has the dubious privilege of having been fixed, formatted as camouflage patterning. Blechman's *Disruptive pattern material: An encyclopaedia of camouflage* (2004) chronicles the virus-like spread of camouflage patterning beyond the boundaries of military badging, to anti-war protest, couture and street fashion, contemporary art and consumer paraphernalia, from cakes to pencil sharpeners. Camouflage pattern is shorthand for combat but also an issue of mass-produced figure–ground erasure,

7 The camouflage effect

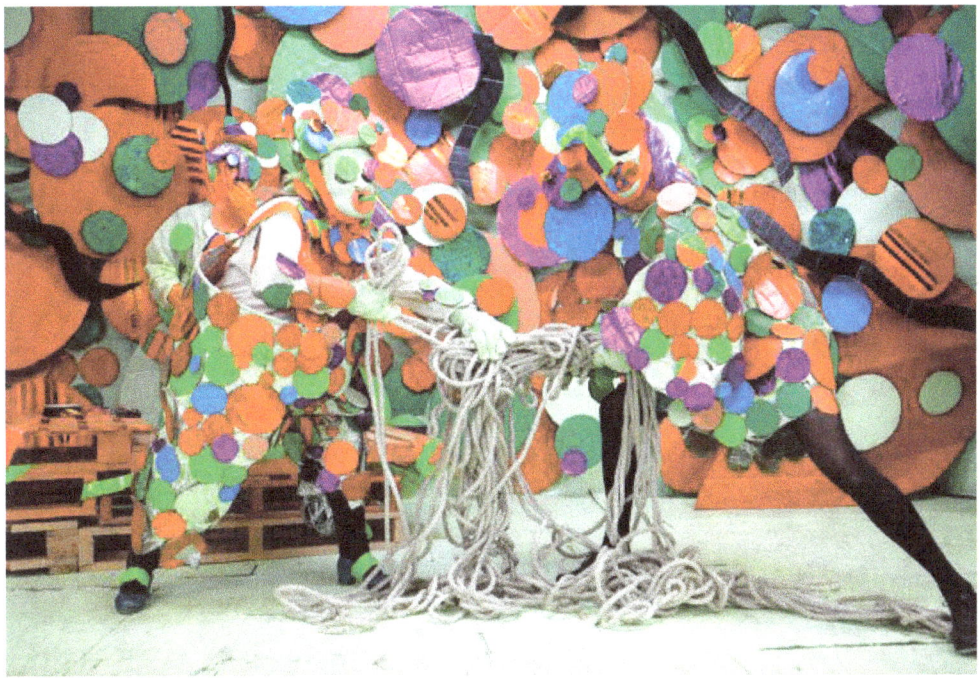

Figure 7.3 a still from Williams' *Your boat my scenic personality of space*

something immune-system philosophers, bio-political pundits, psychoanalysts and cultural theorists would all consider symptomatically invasive.

Certainly this work by Williams references that kind of erasure; it overtakes us, engulfing the senses, space and actors in an avalanche of low-tech materials and garish colours. The visual effect is strangely droll but at the same time odd and menacing, and I am reminded of Roger Caillois' mimephobic observation that as a mode of being figure–ground erasure shares a common dimension with psychosis. The terms of engagement are singular and uncompromising. This camouflage-effect is repetitious, brutal, and sadistically comic all in the same breath. We are undone by space.

Figure 7.4

Figure 7.4, Williams, *I am what you see*, is a glamorised tinny.[17] The reflective surface of the wrapped tinny lets us see ourselves as we are and, paradoxically, makes us see differently because we see what the boat sees. The boat's eyes are low-rent optics, Mylar adhesive film, but they nevertheless dynamically reflect changes in the boat's surrounding milieu, including us. To put ourselves in the picture however, we are obliged to adopt the boat's aspect, which is very low-slung to the ground and then we wholly appear within its line of vision.

In boat-land we are seen as squat and distorted beings, rather fat and awkward, which is curious only if we consider ourselves to be thin, beautiful and powerful. No doubt

---

17 'Tinny' is used here as Australian slang with a double meaning: a metal boat and a beer can.

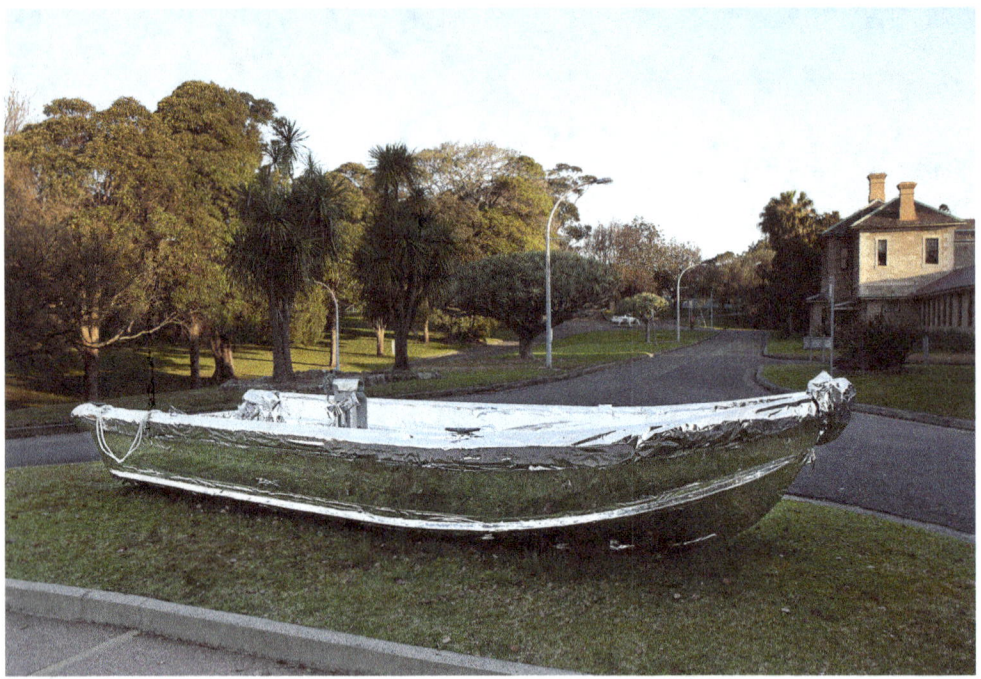

Figure 7.4 *I am what you see*, Williams

like immune system reactions, or rather non-reactions to 'self' antigens, we tolerate these unflattering yet harmless aspects of ourselves, and move on. Like all the other camouflage-affected selves we encounter on a daily basis, they seamlessly mix and mingle with our dynamic sense of who we think we are, were or aspire to be.

In the orbit of this art-event my concealed selves emerge as a double, a camouflage effect, a complex form of self-fashioning that comprises the community of selves I live every day but which I can never comprehensively hope to know, let alone to master. With *the work* as my guide this community mixes with selves from the past, some of which may now be ghosts, merging figure and ground: my camouflage condition, a self that is provisional and dynamic, a becoming of conditioned and conditional groupings. In participating in this unceasing process of erasure, merging and adaption, perhaps we are a lot closer to the cuttlefish than we think, and after in fact I would go so far as to say that we are cuttlefish or we are nothing: 'The animal is a necessary reminder of the limits of the human, its historical and ontological contingency; of the precariousness of the human as a state of being, a condition of sovereignty, or an ideal of self-regulation. The animal is that from which the human tentatively and precariously emerges; the animal is the inhuman destination to which the human always tends. The animal surrounds the human at both ends: it is the origin and the end of humanity' (Grosz 2011, 12).

References

Baudrillard J (1988). *America* translated by Chris Turner. London: Verso.
Behrens R (2013). *Khaki to khaki (dust to dust): The ubiquity of camouflage in human experience.* This volume: Sydney.
Blechman H (2004). *Disruptive pattern material: An encyclopaedia of camouflage.* Richmond Hill, Ontario: Firefly Books.
Caillois R (1935). Mimicry and legendary psychasthenia, translated by John Shepley. *October*, 31(Winter, 1984): 16–32.
Cooper M & Waldby C (2014). *Clinical labour: tissue donors and research subjects in the global bio economy.* Durham: Duke University Press.
De Beauvoir S. (1949). *The second sex*. (trans. Green P) 1977. London: Penguin.
Darwin C. (1958 [1859]). *The origin of the species*. New York: New American Library.
Deleuze, G (1968). *Repetition and difference*. (trans. Patton P). New York: Columbia University Press, 1994.
Deleuze G & Guattari F (1980). *A thousand plateaux* (trans. Massumi B). Minneapolis: University of Minnesota Press, 1987.
Elias A (2012). Camouflage and surrealism, *War, Literature and the Arts*, 1(24): 1–25.
Esposito R (2011). *Immunitas: the protection and negation of life*. Cambridge: Polity.
Freud S (1905). *Jokes and their relation to the unconscious*. London: Routledge & Kegan Paul, 1976.
Grosz E (2011). *Becoming undone*. Durham: Duke University Press.
Haraway D (1991). The bio-politics of postmodern bodies: determinations of self in immune system discourse. In DJ Haraway, *Simians, cyborgs, and women*. London: Free Association Books.
Hsu, H. L. (2006). Who wears the mask? *Minnesota Review*, (67), 169– 175,183.
Lacan J (1991). *The four fundamental concepts of psychoanalysis*, Jacques-Allain Miller (ed), Alan Sheridan (trans). New York: Norton.
Leach N (2006). *Camouflage*. Cambridge: MIT Press.
Norris, M (1980). Darwin, Nietzsche, Kafka, and the problem of mimesis. *MLN*, 95(5): 1232–52.
Sartre JP. *Being and nothingness* (1943). New York: Doubleday (1970).
Shell H R (2012) *Hide and seek: camouflage, photography and the media of reconnaissance.* New York: Zone Books.
Shklovsky V (1917) *Art as technique*. Accessed 30/11/2013. Accessed from http://web.fmk.edu.rs/files/blogs/2010-11/MI/Misliti_film/Viktor_Sklovski_Art_as_Technique.pdf
Waldby C (1993) *AIDS and the body politic: biomedicine and sexual difference*. In *The Politics of Aids*, Vol 3, Monument Press.

8
Light leak

Tanya Peterson

There are dead stars that still shine because their light is trapped in time. Where do I stand in this light, which does not strictly exist? (De Lillo 2003, 155)

A man stands motionless on a subway platform. The number '14' is marked on the column behind him. A train has pulled into the station, but unlike the commuters around him, the man's focus is drawn to the camera's lens. This is his connect. The moment unfolds across a sequence of six black and white photographs. And as the frames advance, a haze of light begins to intensify and envelop the man. He is becoming invisible. He is becoming light. By the sixth frame, his body is a spiralling galaxy of stardust – a return to origins. These six intervals of time depict the cycle of a life and universe, bound to an order of light – both celestial and photographic. Like the fixed analogue of time behind the man's head, where the clock hands remain at eight past nine across the sequence, the indexing of light is depicted as a force of time moving towards a future anterior. In this series by Duane Michals, *The human condition* (1969) is told through a narrative of light as camouflage – a simultaneous obliteration and creation of life, governed by the light.[1]

Michals' series was undertaken in the late 1960s, against the televisual backdrop of the first moon landing and the collective imagination of space travel. Just over half a century later, our vision of space has travelled much further towards the origins of light and time through photography. NASA's Hubble Space Telescope has now captured data to create the eXtreme Deep Field (XDF) image – the deepest reaches of space ever photographed. The combination of 'more than 2,000 images of the same field' taken over the last ten years is like 'watching individual frames of a motion picture … [and] the emergence of structure in the infant universe and the subsequent dynamic stages of galaxy evolution' (Garner 2012). From the stop-motion frames of Michals' world becoming stardust in six instants to NASA's collapsing of a decade's light into a single composite, light of time keeps changing through the camera's lens. How do different temporalities of light operate to conceal and

---

1 While there are innumerable writings on photography as a history of light, of note amongst these is Melissa Miles' book, *The burning mirror: photography in an ambivalent light*. It provides comprehensive and insightful analysis into the variable ways our understanding of light, in and through (primarily analogue) photography, is reflected in the medium's histories and theories (Miles 2008).

reveal the shifting dynamics of selfhood alongside our changing notions of photography and the eight - world we make through it?

In this chapter I will explore how different strategies of camouflage can help us rethink our experiences of navigating, negotiating and participating in contemporary photography as an affective process. I will consider the questions: how do bodies and images intersect under photography's light in the late 20th and early 21st century? And how might the concept of camouflage provide a way of understanding this experience?

Anterior light

Possibly the most famous reflection on photography's light and the body is Roland Barthes' description of a photograph as something 'that has been' (Barthes 1982, 80).[2] In the chapter titled 'Luminous rays, colour', from his book *Camera lucida*, Barthes elaborates further on photography's causality at the point where the medium's indexicality becomes alchemical. He says:

> The photograph is literally an emanation of the reference. From the real body, which was there, proceed radiations which ultimately touch me, who am here; the duration of the transmission is insignificant; the photograph of the missing being, as Sontag says, will touch me like the delayed rays of star. A sort of umbilical cord links the body of the photographed thing to my gaze: light though impalpable, is here a carnal medium, a skin I share with anyone who has been photographed. (Barthes 1982, 80–81)

Works like Christopher Bucklow's *Wakening guest 4:03 p.m. 29 November 1996 [JG]* (1996) – part of his ongoing *Guest* series (Figure 8.1) – appear to exemplify Barthes' idea of photographic light as denoting an index of an absent body. To make these works, Bucklow draws around the silhouette of a figure and then transfers the outline to a foil sheet. The foil sheet is then repeatedly perforated with a pin to form a pattern that delineates the body's form. It is subsequently placed over an elementary type of box camera pre-loaded with photographic paper, and taken outside where it is exposed to light. As the sun's rays pass through each tiny aperture a dazzling figure registers itself on the photographic ground. There are roughly 25,000 points of light on each print, the equivalent number of days in an average human life (around 70 years) – a measure of mortality in light (Hambourg 2004).

His use of the silver dye bleach printing process registers the body as a shimmering field of light, a positive image cast upon a dark ground. And yet, the resultant interplay of light also suggests an emanation coming forth, as if from within the image. This creates a perceptual confusion. By inverting the body's silhouette from its conventional figure/

---

2   There has been much analysis and debate around this idea of Barthes', especially on the status of photograph as an indexical sign, which most often draws on Charles Sanders Peirce's' definition of an index as 'a sign which would, at once, lose the character which makes it a sign if its object were removed, but would not lose that character if there were no interpretant' (Peirce 1984, 9). For key discussions around the definition of the index see Rosalind Krauss' seminal essays: 'Notes on the index: part 1' and 'Notes on the index: part 2', both in her book: *The originality of the avant-garde and other modernist myths* (Krauss 1985, 196–219). Geoffrey Batchen offers an incisive review of the index in photographic theory, via a Derridean re-reading of Peircean semiotics in his book, *Burning with desire: the conception of photography* (Batchen 1997, see especially 194–8).

8 Light leak

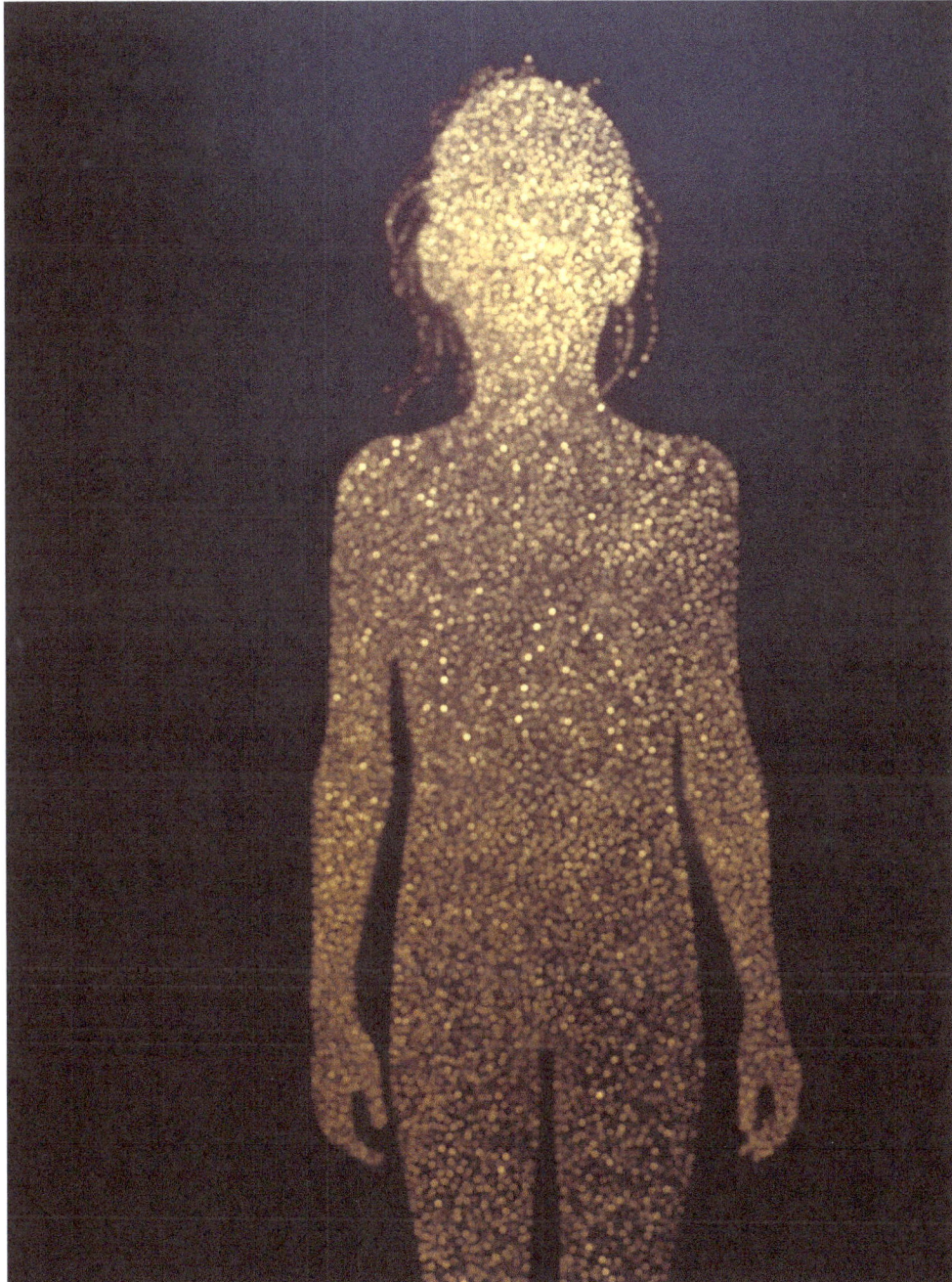

Figure 8.1 Bucklow, Christopher (b. 1957) © Copyright *Wakening Guest 4:03 p.m. 29 November 1996* [JG]. 1996. Silver dye bleach print, 101.6 x 76.2 cm (40 x 30 in.). Gift of Christopher and Susan Bucklow, in memory of Fred Zinnemann, 1997 (1997.218). Image copyright © The Metropolitan Museum of Art. Image source: Art Resource, NY.

ground relationship, from cast shadow to luminous mirage, Bucklow disrupts a conventional reading of the image's causal signification. Through this play of reversals the work pivots on an axis of ambiguous light. Poised at the threshold of (im)materiality, is the radiant figure an emergent being coming to light or a diminishing constellation of the past? Or to put it another way: at what point does light leak beyond the image into our field of vision? How can we begin to lose ourselves in the light of photography as a shared skin?

It's a question that extends to Barthes' perception of photographic light as inextricably bound to the medium's indexical status as an analogue of the world. Underpinning Barthes' argument is a *temporal* collapse of bodies falling into and against one another at the threshold of photography's light. The 'touch' of a past light, its 'residual sensitivity', is contained as an affective charge within the past transcription and present transmission of the photograph – a form of contiguity between the body depicted and the viewer.[3] As Margaret Iversen has noted, Barthes' fascination with photography's contiguity suggests an experience of vision and selfhood that is both lost and found in light. It's a perceptual state that she proposes could be translated as: 'I may see objects, but I am also enveloped by a light or gaze that unsettles the position I want to occupy as source of the coordinates of sight' (Iversen 2009, 69). It is a momentary spatio-temporal dislocation brought on by the 'magic' of photography's 'emanation of *past reality*' (Barthes 1982, 88).[4]

Barthes' conception of photography as an affective medium, where time and the body are conjoined through light, is grounded in an understanding of the medium as a residual or indexical trace and its affective potential. In Barthes' writing and Bucklow's imagery, photography is a spectral light, where things are there and not there at the same instant, like the 'delayed rays of a star'. It is an affect that has close links with Neil Leach's definition of camouflage as 'a double moment from a temporal perspective', where 'life folds into death and vice versa' (Leach 2006, 246).

Barthes alludes to camouflage in another way, further on in the 'Luminous rays' chapter. He makes the distinction between this type of photography and the 19th century technique of hand-colouring black and white images. For him, hand colouring creates a disagreeable condition he calls 'superadded light' (Barthes 1982, 81). He deems hand-colouring an excessive light because it is applied after the image is taken, an overlaid artifice that condemns the photograph to a second, eternal death, like a painted 'corpse'. Barthes argues it is an addition of time, which works only to garishly overcompensate for the past's pallor – a type of bad camouflage.

But what of Barthes' idea of an embodied experience of photography in a digital age? What if both the image and body were always, already perceived as constant companions in the *same time*, and not contingent upon a causal link from past to present to generate an affective potential? What if superadded light wasn't perceived as an add-on, but had now become an underlying condition of how we experienced light more generally as already photographic?

---

3 Barthes discusses these ideas of photography and affect further in *Camera lucida* through his concept of the 'punctum' (Barthes 1982, 43–59). Recent critical analysis of this concept has been undertaken by Rosalind Krauss; Eduardo Cadava and Paolo Cortés-Rocca; and Geoffrey Batchen (Batchen 2009, 187–92; 105–39; 259–69 respectively).
4 Italics in the original.

Readymade stars

From a contemporary perspective, one way to reconsider Barthes' idea of photography as a metonymic body is in relation to the ongoing synchronicity between forms of natural light and artificial light, particularly those of real-time, digital technologies – light that's on '24 / 7', as Jonathan Crary describes it in his recent book of the same name. For Crary, this is the light of late-capitalism and a tool of ideological control, where stock markets and the military never sleep, enabled by technologies that provide around-the-clock, illuminated visions of the world (Crary 2013). In this world, photographs tend to function less as historical markers to be revisited later, and more as continuous, networked, (re)transmitted, image streams. They visualise time's interminable pulse as opposed to its arrest, where any access to the delayed rays of the past is only an Instagram™ filter away.

Thomas Ruff's work appears to reflect this contemporary condition of photographic vision and light. Many of his images suggest that the way we see is *a priori* photographic. In his practice, Ruff frequently appropriates and re-presents the mechanics of viewing and knowing the world through photography. Many of Ruff's images are like ready-mades – copies of copies, where life appears caught in a second-hand halo of light.

In his series *Sterne (stars)* (1989–2), he uses select details from telescopic images of stars, purchased from the European Southern Observatory's archive of the Chilean Andes, to create the large-scale portraits of the cosmos (Figure 8.2) (Pohlen 1991, 116). The resultant images present a microcosmic snapshot of a larger galaxy – portals of scattered light that beckon and overwhelm our vision with their exhaustive detail.

Ruff's work, however, isn't merely another iteration of what already exists. His *Sterne* images convey a sort of glitched reciprocity, where the photograph reveals itself as a self-reflexive image of our vision in a photogenic world. Ruff describes his reworking and reframing of the image as a process of 'transformation' from a scientific to artistic context which 'brings about interferences' (Ruff 2013, 87). And in his *Sterne* images it could be said these interferences show us the way in which photographic light acts as a form of camouflage. More specifically, the idea of interference is not just a change in context, but also one that momentarily places us out of time, out of step, with the image. If, however, as Ruff's images indicate, our vision of the world is already photographic – is then all photography a form of 'superadded light'? Is it an excessive spectre that camouflages the world, only animating it as a residual glow of technology? Where do we stand in this light?

Often the answers to these types of arguments put forward a dichotomy of photography and temporality based on a postmodern inversion of semantic causality, where the representation dictates the ontological status of the referent or the 'real'.[5] However, I'd like to consider a slightly different way of thinking about contemporary photography's temporal impact and its links to concepts of camouflage. It's an idea that's less concerned with ontological debates about the world and its signs or photography as inverted mirror, and one that's more focused on asking: how can certain approaches to photographic light create temporal effects of camouflage, which in turn have the potential to reconfigure photographic images as a network of affects?

---

5 For example, Jean Baudrillard's seminal book on the simulacra, *Simulations* (Baudrillard 1983).

Figure 8.2 Thomas Ruff, *Stern 11h 12m/−45°*, 1989, Chromogenic print, 102 3/8 × 74 inches (260 × 188 cm), courtesy David Zwirner, New York/London, © Thomas Ruff/Bild-Kunst. Licensed by Viscopy, 2014.

Speculative light

Konstellation / Constellation (2000) is a work by Thomas Demand that begins to hint at another partial answer to this question (Figure 8.3). It's a photographic image that forecasts *what will be*. Demand describes it as a 'projection of the sky over Switzerland on 12 January 2300', a conceptual prediction of stars aligning 300 years in advance of the date and the location it is exhibited (Demand 2000, 47). He goes on to say:

> Photography is always supposed to describe the past, never the future. I wanted to do the opposite. As for the date, why 300 years? Because 2300 is sufficiently remote so that no one can imagine living then, but not so remote that we have no idea of how people will live. Moreover, it is very likely that photography won't be there then either. I had wanted to take a photo of the future for years, and it took me two hours to do it. (Demand 2000, 47)

Like Bucklow's *Guest*, Demand's work also uses apertures created by pins through paper to give us light, but there's a difference. Demand's image is not operating as the registration of a specific light and time that frames the body as absent and a moment 'that has been'. In *Constellation* we have the idea of a photograph that depicts its own fate, as a writing of light before the moment has unfolded, and maybe even more crucially, one that also acknowledges that fate (the stars and photography) as *speculation*. And it is the work's speculative proposition that provides a clue to thinking about ideas of the physicality and abstractions at play in the world's temporal camouflage through photography.

Demand begins many of his works by sourcing existing images circulated by the mass media. He then recreates a life-size paper sculpture of his chosen scene. The paper architecture is crafted with a forensic precision, but one that abstracts the smaller details of the scene. Constructed as a façade specifically for the camera's point of view, once complete, the sculptural facsimile is then photographed – translated into another iterative paper representation and exhibited, while the sculpture itself is typically discarded.

Generally the photographs Demand makes are face-mounted and installed without frames, which makes the surfaces of the images appear slick and frozen, in contrast to the paper worlds which sit beneath them like half-forgotten memories. In each image, the retranslated scene is there – the architecture of a narrative – but the details remain persistently and deliberately vague. In Demand's photographs, the materiality of the work, the reduplication of a fragile (paper) world, petrified again under the sleek face-mounted veneer, initially evokes an endless cycling of photograph-to-world-to-photograph – a looped circuit of causality. And the empty façades solicit the viewer to fill in the missing details – to remember the scene in their own way – to almost mentally duplicate Demand's process of narrative reconstruction, complete with details that refuse to be recalled.

This aspect of interiority and self-referentiality in Demand's work has, in recent years, been most notably championed by Michael Fried, who describes Demand's work as an 'ontologically exceptional project' (Fried 2008, 276). Fried uses the terms 'intentionality' and 'intendedness' to characterise the production process underpinning the conceptual framework of Demand's photographs (Fried 2008, 271–2). Specifically, he positions the work as an index of Demand's labour. For Fried, this 'intendedness' is the artist's 'inscrutability', a turning away from the world and looking inwards (Fried 2008, 271–2). It's an approach that allows him to read the work as a form of self-referential allegory.

Figure 8.3 Thomas Demand *Konstellation / Constellation,* 2000 C-Print/ Diasec, 130 x 180 cm © Thomas Demand/VG Bild-Kunst, Bonn. Licensed by Viscopy, 2014.

And it locates Demand's practice as a process that is contingent upon an internalised logic for its meaning, which for Fried eclipses all other inferences and thereby frames the work as 'anti-theatrical', in other words autonomous or 'complete' (Fried 2008, 271). Fried sees Demand's work as cool and distanced, operating without reference to the external world or a 'beholder' looking in – in a sense, it positions the intent of Demand's imagery as always out of time with the work's immediate, physical presence. The photographs, Fried argues are:

> so saturated with his [Demand's] intentions ... they leave no room for anything else, [which is] why indeed the viewer instinctively recognises that he or she is called upon by the image to do nothing more than register the 'madness' of all the objects on view and of the place in which they exist. (Fried 2008, 271)

Fried's choice of the word 'register' is telling. It sets up another mode of self-referentiality, this time between the viewer and image, whereby Fried argues the viewer can only have a photographic experience of the work, i.e. 'register' its 'madness', if they recognise the work as a 'straight (that is indexical)' photograph (Fried 2008, 272). It's an argument that also allows Fried to call on the opinion of another writer, Régis Durand, and his claim that:

> the quality [Demand's] photographs convey [is] of wanting nothing from the viewer, of giving him or her no opportunity for empathic projection of any kind, indeed of contra-

vening the very possibility of imagining any relation to the depicted scenes other than one of mere alienated looking. (Fried 2008, 272)

These are two interesting propositions, a photographic effect created inside and outside the work (the 'register' of 'madness'), which in turn sets up a condition of 'alienated' looking. And while interesting, they are also somewhat limited. What if, instead, the photographic effect in Demand's work wasn't just alienating? What if there *was* also an empathic counterpoint to be found behind it?

Demand's own discussion of his work implies that the empathic relationship between the viewer and the work occurs, not at the level of figuration, but precisely at the level of photography's materiality. Of his specific use of paper, Demand says it's:

> mainly because everybody knows it, everybody has an experience about it and everybody has done something with it … So many things are made out of paper, cardboard. You rip up things in cardboard, and somehow I like the fact that we share the experience about the material already, which is very different from [the] computer for instance, because the computer always has this rhetoric of technology which is inaccessible for most viewers and I didn't want to have that. I wanted to make it very easy to enter. (Demand 2013)

Demand's reasons for privileging touch over technology through the use of paper in his work, and its links to the world from which the images were derived, recall similar arguments the artist and theorist Hito Steyerl makes in her essay 'A thing like you and me' (Steyerl 2012). Steyerl's arguments are useful to draw on at this juncture as a way of further exploring photography's contingency of light and the stars in relation to Demand's practice and his work *Constellation*. And they may also provide clues as to how we may rethink and expand Barthes' definition of 'superadded light' and the basis of Fried's ontological argument, within the context of contemporary photography.

In her essay, Steyerl looks to reorientate subject–object dichotomies towards participatory 'intensities' (Steyerl 2012, 51). Instead of seeing the body's objectification through imagery as a negative form of subjectivity, she rethinks this conventional dichotomy, by considering contemporary representations of subjectivity as both part and product of networked flows of information in constant exchange, rather than static, disembodied signs. As opposed to searching for notions of authenticity in representation, she instead looks at how the commodification of the self functions as part of a networked economics, and how this approach can potentially open up ways of thinking about the relationship between the self and its representation, between subjects and objects. She argues this perspective is possible with the democratisation of the self as a 'thing', and hence as 'some' 'thing' that is interchangeable with the status of images. From another perspective, one might say that the implied reciprocity of this arrangement and argument is the notion of images and objects becoming animated as other types of bodies – like a re-imagining of Barthes idea of the photograph and the body. Specifically Steyerl considers this representational exchange not as a form of identification but as *participation*. In particular, she looks at the prevalence of photographic imagery across both online and offline platforms, the commodification of desire and the self-recognition it is designed to solicit, and asks:

> What happens to identification at this point? Who can we identify with? Of course, identification is always with an image. But ask anybody whether they'd actually like to be a

> JPEG file. And this is precisely my point: if identification is to go anywhere, it has to be with this material aspect of the image, with the image as thing, not as representation. And then it perhaps ceases to be identification, and instead becomes participation. (Steyerl 2012, 49–50)

What seems to be at stake in Steyerl's position is a countering of the image as an objectified (and hence) dead reality, and a rethinking of figure–ground distinctions. Understood in this way, Steyerl's argument also presents us with an affective model of camouflage, where images are made and unmade as a matrix of bodies – embodied ideas as opposed to just bodies becoming signs and signs becoming bodies. Viewed from this perspective, Steyerl's arguments can be likened to Leach's understanding of camouflage 'as a productive exchange' and the 'corporeality of aesthetic engagement that points toward the bond that might be established between the individual and the world' (Leach 2006, 242–3).

Resonant light

In her consideration of an image's materiality, Steyerl argues for a corporeal understanding of it in which it is perceived as vulnerable and open to things like decay, destruction and agency. In this way, she explores ways to reframe our perception of the online image as one which is not separate from or running parallel to the material (paper) world. In effect, she's trying to cut through the kind of 'rhetoric' of technology described by Demand. She therefore puts forward an argument based on equivalences – one where bodies and images are part of the same flows and transactions, the same materiality, the same temporalities, the same mutabilities. She says:

> To participate in an image – rather than merely identify with it – could perhaps abolish this [identificatory] relation. This would mean participating in the material of the image as well as in the desires and forces it accumulates. How about acknowledging that this image is not some ideological misconception, but a thing simultaneously couched in affect and availability, a fetish made of crystals and electricity, animated by our wishes and fears – a perfect embodiment of its own conditions of existence? As such, the image is – to use yet another phrase of Walter Benjamin's – without expression. It doesn't represent reality. It is a fragment of the real world. It is a thing just like any other – a thing like you and me. (Steyerl 2012, 51–2

Steyerl's reference to Benjamin here, and throughout her argument, is important to understand because it defines participation as a refractive mode, whereby '[t]he image is the thing in which senses merge with matter. Things are not being represented by it but participate in it' (Steyerl 2012, 58). While Steyerl is drawing specifically on Benjamin's essay 'The concept of criticism', we can extend her uptake of his ideas to photography. In *Words of light*, Eduardo Cadava has noted that for Benjamin the representation and bringing to light of an idea was to witness its death (Cadava 1997, 30). And it was the metaphor of stars which Benjamin chose to translate this process of thinking – ideas developing (like photographs) and coming to light from darkness (Cadava 1997, 26). Specifically, Benjamin says:

ideas are the stars, in contrast to the sun of revelation. They do not shine their light into the day of history, but only work within it invisibly. They shine their light only into the night of nature. Works of art are thus defined as models of a nature that do not await the day. (Benjamin 1997, 30)

The split between day and night, latent ideas (stars/night) brought to light (by the sun/day), is the difference between life and death – that is, to bring something to light, like a star (or a photograph) is to witness its death like a ruin of meaning (Cadava 1997, 30). We might, therefore, understand Steyerl's idea of an image as 'a thing like you and me' as the reanimation of images and the affective re-imaging of selfhood through definitions of interface which remain open and changeable, specifically through the act of camouflage. As Leach has argued, camouflage is 'an interactive process of becoming – of becoming one with the world, and of becoming distinct from that world – where both states are locked into a mechanism of reciprocal presupposition' (Leach 2006, 245).

In a similar way, might we see Demand's use and deployment of paper as undertaking double duty? Not only does it render the world figuratively, but it affectively expresses the making of the world's materiality (our feeling and understanding of it) as a form of shared experience, and one that, of necessity, also begins from a point of erasure. His works are a process of unmaking the details of the representational work, of emptying out the traces of specificity, of subjectivity. Like Benjamin's description of Atget's photographs of 19th century Paris, Demand's work is 'empty, as it should be … like a lodging that has not yet found a new tenant' (Benjamin 1997, 251).[6] It is this quality of emptiness which Benjamin asserts 'sets the scene for a salutary estrangement between man [sic] and his surroundings' (Benjamin 1997, 251). Emptiness and estrangement: what do these entwined concepts of Benjamin's have to do with the affective dynamic of camouflage and Steyerl's concept of 'participation'?

Brian Massumi's discussions of embodied experience and sensation offer a model of affect with affinities to Steyerl's argument (after Benjamin) of identification as a participatory act. Massumi argues that affective experiences define the self through 'resonation', which embodies the experience of sensation as 'a qualitative transformation of distance into an immediacy of self-relation' (Massumi 2002, 14). He uses the spatial dynamic of an echo to describe how the internalised experience of sensation occurs as a proliferation of affect, which acts in and beyond the body as 'a relay between its corporeal and incorporeal dimensions' (Massumi 2002, 14). And he makes the point that:

An echo, for example, cannot occur without a distance between surfaces for the sounds to bounce from. But the resonation is not on the walls. It is in the emptiness between them. It fills the emptiness with its complex patterning. That patterning is not at a distance from itself … It is a complex dynamic unity. The interference pattern arises where the sound wave intersects with itself. (Massumi 2002, 14)

If we think back to Demand's work in light of this description, it is his particular process of making which engenders an affective resonance within the viewer, precisely because it also leaves the image empty 'like a lodging'. Tamara Trodd has argued that the fact Demand's

---

6 Tamara Trodd has also discussed the connection between Demand and Ateget's work in relation to memory, interiority and embodiment (Trodd 2009, 954–76).

images are drawn primarily from media imagery is part of why we get 'a sense which cannot be pinpointed precisely as a specific memory – that these pictures seem to have come somehow from "inside us"' (Trodd 2009, 962). Building on this assumption, I would argue that the sometimes inexplicable recognition of Demand's work, both through his choice of subject matter and process of making, is what can trigger an embodied experience of his work – where the image seems to be generated inexplicably from 'inside' us – enacting a form of 'reciprocal presupposition' within the viewer.

In this context, Demand's *Constellation* can be read as a model not only of the stars, but also of camouflaged light – one that has the potential to keep changing both itself and us. If we, therefore, consider the implications of the affective exchange Steyerl is arguing for, it is possible to extend her argument further through the concept of camouflage. We can speculate that to creatively engage with an image, then, is to not only render its representation momentarily invisible, it is to also camouflage oneself through affect – that is, to not see the exchange between body and image as a new form of representation, but rather to consider the potential of images as part of a network of intensities which are all in states of becoming 'a thing like you and me' and vice versa. And taking this idea one step further, we might even say that the potential of contemporary photography lies in our becoming through light.

References

Barthes R (1982). *Camera lucida* (trans. R Howard). New York: Hill and Wang.
Batchen G (1997). *Burning with desire*. Cambridge, Mass./London: MIT Press.
Baudrillard J (1983). *Simulations* (trans. P Foss et. al.). New York: Semiotext[e].
Benjamin W (1997). *One-way street* (trans. E Jephcott & K Shorter). London/New York: Verso.
Cadava E (1997). *Words of light*. Princeton, New Jersey: Princeton, University Press.
Crary J (2013). *24/7: late capitalism and the ends of sleep*. London/New York: Verso.
Delillo D (2003). *Cosmopolis*. London: Picador.
Demand T & Quintin F (2000). There is no innocent room. In F Bonami, R Durand & F Quintin. *Thomas Demand* (pp. 36–68). ex. cat. Paris/London: Fondation Cartier pour l'art contemporain/ Thames & Hudson.
Demand T (n.d.). *I work with paper – Thomas Demand clip 5* [Online]. Available: http://cybermuse.beaux-arts.ca/cybermuse/docs/DemandClip5_e.pdf. [Transcript of the video recording: http://www.gallery.ca/cybermuse/collections/artist/media_f.jsp?imediaid=7711] (Accessed 21 May 2014).
Fried M (2008). *Why photography matters as art as never before*. New Haven/London: Yale University Press.
Garner R (2012). Hubble goes to the extreme to assemble farthest-ever view of the universe. Available: http://www.nasa.gov/mission_pages/hubble/science/xdf.html. (Accessed 21 May 2014).
Hambourg, MM & Mellor DA (2004). *Guest: Christopher Bucklow*. ex. cat. (unpaginated). New York: PowerHouse books.
Iversen M (2009). What is a photograph? In G Batchen (Ed). *Photography degree zero: reflections on Roland Barthes's 'Camera lucida'* (pp. 57–74). Cambridge, Mass. London: MIT Press.
Krauss R (1985). *The originality of the avant-garde and other modernist myths*. Cambridge, Mass./London: MIT Press.
Leach N (2006). *Camouflage*. Cambridge, Mass./London: MIT Press.
Massumi B (2002). *Parables for the virtual*. Durham/London: Duke University Press.
Miles M (2008). *The burning mirror: photography in an ambivalent light*. Melbourne: Australian Scholarly Publishing.

Peirce C S (1984). 'Logic as semiotic'. In R E Innis (Ed). *Semiotics: an introduction anthology* (pp. 3–11). Bloomington: Indiana University Press.
Pohlen A (1991). Deep surface. *Artforum*, 29(8): 114–6.
Ruff T & Famighetti M (2013). Thomas Ruff: photograms for the new age. *Aperture*, 211: 82–87.
Steyerl H (2012). *E-flux journal: the wretched of the screen*. Berlin: Sternberg Press.
Trodd T (2009). Thomas Demand, Jeff Wall and Sherrie Levine: deforming 'pictures'. *Art History*, 32(5): 954–76.

9

From Ghillie suit to glittering kowhaiwhai – contemporary New Zealand artists deploy the camouflage aesthetic

Linda Tyler

Painted rafter patterns form an integral part of customary Māori decoration of the wharenui or meeting house, an architectural form introduced to allow large gatherings, Early meetings were arranged to resist the appropriation of land during colonisation in the 19th century. Rafter patterning is known as kowhaiwhai, and represents the fern frond or koru shape (which symbolises the family) dying and being replaced by another, newer shoot. A simple and strong alternating of black, white and red tints derived from ochre and soot was painted on the curved surface of a whitened half-tree trunk which supported the roof structure. Painted kowhaiwhai was Op Art *avant la lettre*, providing a syncopation of positive and negative forms which moved and reformed when viewed from below in flickering lamp light, camouflaging structure through pattern. Called the geometry of Aotearoa, the designs were inherently mathematical, and could be used to trace lines of descent. Now part of the artistic language of a bicultural country, kowhaiwhai, with its inherent camouflage quality, has become a metaphor for New Zealandness, shorthand for a shared postcolonial heritage which cannot be simply stated as black and white. A newer New Zealand has emerged in the 21st century, succeeding a vexed period of reconciliation and reparation based on claims made by Māori under the terms of the 1840 Treaty of Waitangi. A working partnership has emerged where tangata whenua (Māori, or people of the land) have asserted their sovereignty, and agreed to accommodate in Aotearoa tangata tiriti (the people of the treaty), those immigrants whose right to dwell in Aotearoa was established by the treaty. To complicate matters, Māori now dominate the military, routinely wearing camouflage, and changing military culture with the introduction of haka, the ceremonial war dance of their ancestors. All these aspects – genealogy, history, the uneasy partnership of Māori and European under the treaty – combine whenever a camouflage pattern appears in contemporary New Zealand art. Never mere decoration, its use is freighted with the politics of biculturalism.

When painter John Reynolds appeared above decks on the HMNZS *Otago* clad in a Ghillie suit as part of his response to the artist's brief for the 2012 Kermadec exhibition, the naval rankings around him were discombobulated. A Ghillie suit is a form of clothing where the textile is designed to appear like foliage, and can have actual branches woven into it. Was he ridiculing military strategy? Or trying to fit in? Surveying the uses of camouflage tactics in art produced in Aotearoa New Zealand in the last two decades, three discrete strands emerge. First, there is the foregrounding of the relationship between mapping and camouflage, using the metaphoric associations of the map as a device for rendering three dimensions in two through symbolic representation of contour. Second, camouflage is used by artists to symbolise culture's attempt to emulate nature, and even dominate it. Third, the visual effects of dazzle and disrupt are used not only because of 'the allure of its power as a conceptual tool for cultural critique' (Elias 2011, 199) but also to create installations where painting undergoes a 21st-century reassessment. How the encounter with camouflage is mediated by New Zealand artists, and why, builds an argument for a negotiation with a local history of difference which is complex and distinctive.

Mapping difference

Colour photographs of the artist's own tongue were collaged together to emulate a cordiform projection or heart-shaped map titled *Lingua Geographica (Geographic tongue)* (1996) as Ruth Watson's contribution to the Asia Society's exhibition 'Paradise now? Contemporary art from the Pacific' in 2004. While the exhibition as a whole questioned the continued validity of constructions of the Pacific as a south seas paradise, Watson's work continued her interrogation of the way that maps shape human understanding of geography. Pink and glistening, the tongue's surface cracks appear magnified, hiding their living, human origin as the unexceptional texture of a love heart. A sensory organ, the tongue, provides an analogy to the way that mapping affects the intellectual apprehension of the world and also how it is experienced. Those that make the maps make the world, the power relations obscured by the camouflaging cloak of dissemination of European science.

Whereas Watson shows how a mapping a place can impinge on the person, Korean New Zealander Jae Hoon Lee fabricates a map of human skin digitally which both conceals and reveals ethnicity, hiding the individual behind the screen of the crowd. Making digital recordings which he structurally alters using image manipulation technologies, he compounds visual and sound effects to build up a composite artwork that questions the shared nature of lived experience and perception. *Camouflage* 2003 is a mosaic of skin that has almost no register of scale within it, but is a mural-sized one-channel video projection that gently segues through a palette of differently coloured flesh and skin patterning. The tones morph together to create a mottled mosaic that begins to form a recognisable camouflage pattern as it progresses. As skin tags float past, the distinctive whorl of that marker of difference and identity, the fingerprint, comes into focus before a galaxy of wrinkles on a full body skin replaces it. The soundtrack is the grinding, repetitive ping/hum sound of a flatbed scanner.

Although the skin is not all the artist's own, the skin series started as a process of documenting his daily life, almost diaristically, using a scanner to capture fragments – sometimes his face, a bit of stubble, a nick from shaving – but not all of them recognisable. The project grew as he recorded the skin of other New Zealanders he met, and eventually included complete strangers whom he invited to donate a sample image of their skin. The computer's memory operates as a storage container, with the artist mining his archive of skin samples to create a synthetic compound structure which is the camouflage. By combining ethnicities, ages and genders, he shows how the memory of difference cascades down generations while his contemporary sampling creates a history of New Zealand which is a product of its time.

In a corollary project, Lee made a series of skin photographs based on images of Asian women from internet pornography sites. Each anonymous woman looks out of the image directly at the viewer, but their skins have become a carpet of mottled multiculturalism, marked by consumption. He describes these works as democratic, considering that the technology used to sample them makes the viewer omnipresent and omnipotent through virtually interconnected locations of time and space. He manages to extend the decisive moment of conception of photography to become a time lapse of lived experience. Breaking the human body down into its constituent parts, he creates a new entity where identity is successfully concealed.

Natural disguise

Just as Watson and Lee use camouflage tactics to expose cultural ideologies of racism and European hegemony, New Zealand artists have also used camouflage patterning ironically. Bill Hammond's large painting *Camouflage* (1997) relates the unhappy narrative of the near-extinction of an indigenous flightless bird, the Kakapo. It was the attractiveness of the protective yellow-green colouration of the Kakapo's plumage which led to it becoming a hunting trophy in the 19th century. Only 126 individual birds have been identified as surviving today, and fears are held for the continuation of the species because introduced predators endanger both eggs and chicks. Hammond's work depicts the Yellow Kakapo being captured near Fiordland in 1873, and immediately killed and mounted as a taxidermied specimen for study. It was purchased by ornithologist Walter Lawry Buller for his son, who considered it to be 'the most beautiful thing in the bird line that I have ever seen' (Norman 2012, p24). The devastating effects of human populations on biodiversity are also the concern of collagist Peter Madden, who has minutely painted the bodies of dead houseflies with tiny skulls so that they masquerade as the death moth, patterning other flies with traditional camouflage patterning in a work that he titles, *Beelzebub, the Lord of the Flies*.

Commissioned to make art in response to the Pew Environment Group's Global Ocean Legacy project to create a marine park to safeguard the environment of the Kermadec Trench, John Reynolds went ashore on Raoul Island's Oneraki Beach wearing a bowler hat and a Ghillie suit, a symbol of science and the human impulse to understand circumstances. Described by curator Gregory O'Brien as 'A piece of human flotsam or a life-form dredged from a B-grade science fiction movie' (O'Brien 2011), Reynolds wanted to embody the twinned roles of the artist and the scientist in exploration and discovery, and in particular to draw attention to what is expected from artists: 'The Kermadec project has such a strong political component to it. It galvanizes you as an individual and as an artist ... the perils are sloganism and some kind of trite reference to issues that are complex – but a greater peril is not taking that risk' (Reynolds 2011). By camouflaging himself, he appears in documentation as no longer John Reynolds, the artist, but as a human actor in the natural realm. As he points out, the scientists that travel there have their own conventions, ideas, formalities, languages and materials. Artists and scientists do similarly intense research which 'couldn't be more diametrically opposed [yet] the purpose is the same. We are both intensely looking at aspects of the world ... ' (Reynolds 2011). Dressed in the appurtenances of the London stockbroker and the duck shooter or military sniper in the field, Reynolds began numbering rocks on the beach with chalk, starting at one and ending at 10,000 in what has been described as 'aberrant seaside mathematics ... a Sisyphean sham science project' (O'Brien 2011). Around the artist's neck hung a quotation from Marcus Aurelius: 'Soon, very soon, thou wilt be ashes, or a skeleton, and either a name or not even a name; but name is sound and echo ... the things which are much valued in life are empty and rotten and like little dogs biting one another, and little children quarrelling and laughing and then straight away weeping. But fidelity and modesty and justice and truth are fled.' Disguised as someone else, Reynolds invites us to consider what an artist's role, or a scientist's role, might be in relation to an endangered environment. He resolves, 'our role is to point at something, and we do this by making art work' (Reynolds 2011).

Dissemblance

Georgie Hill appropriates camouflage patterning from its military and male context and deploys it as a strategy of feminine resistance, and concealment. Her most recent series of watercolours, collectively entitled *Feint*, adapt visual disorientation strategies used in a military context and perceptual psychology and bring these ideas into the domestic arena, deploying furniture and architecture as ciphers for female agency. In fencing or military terminology, a feint is a manoeuvre designed to mislead an opponent by suggesting then deferring a certain course of action. Hill's paintings adopt similarly deceptive strategies. Her watercolour and graphite works on paper conflate optical experience and the understanding of pictorial space – what can be seen, experienced or felt within or through a painting – and equally importantly, what can be concealed.

Methodically planned and executed, Hill creates her paintings within designated parameters of scale, colour, and spatial devices based on imaginary architectural interiors, often domestic spaces. To conceal and fracture both the surface of the painting and its imagery, she introduces a camouflage pattern which breaks up the legibility of the forms. She takes her lead from protective colouration used to distract predators in nature – the contrasting patches of colour on the wings of a moth – paralleling the gendering of social spaces and the cultural concealment of women. In Figure 9.1, a vanity seat by German designer Émile-Jacques Ruhlmann tangles with Eileen Gray's Transat stool, gesturing to the way in which Eileen Gray's contribution to modernism was eclipsed by male modernists until her work was recuperated from obscurity, being made visible by monographs and exhibitions which illuminate Gray's career. Hill's use of Eileen Gray to symbolise the gendering of the historical record allows Hill to pattern over her work with surface decoration as Gray did, at a time in which Adolf Loos had condemned ornament as crime.

Koru as chameleon

As well as being used to point to gender relations in cultural production, camouflage has recently been used to interrogate the supposed biculturalism of New Zealand and in particular to examine issues of appropriation of Māori motifs in European art practice. In 1999, Andrew McLeod created a uniquely Aotearoan version of camouflage pattern, mixing the woodland and arid colours of traditional camouflage with kowhaiwhai patterns derived from customary Māori art, coining the neologism 'camouwhaiwhai' (Figure 9.2) to describe the effect as his commentary on the appropriation debate.

9 From Ghillie suit to glittering kowhaiwhai

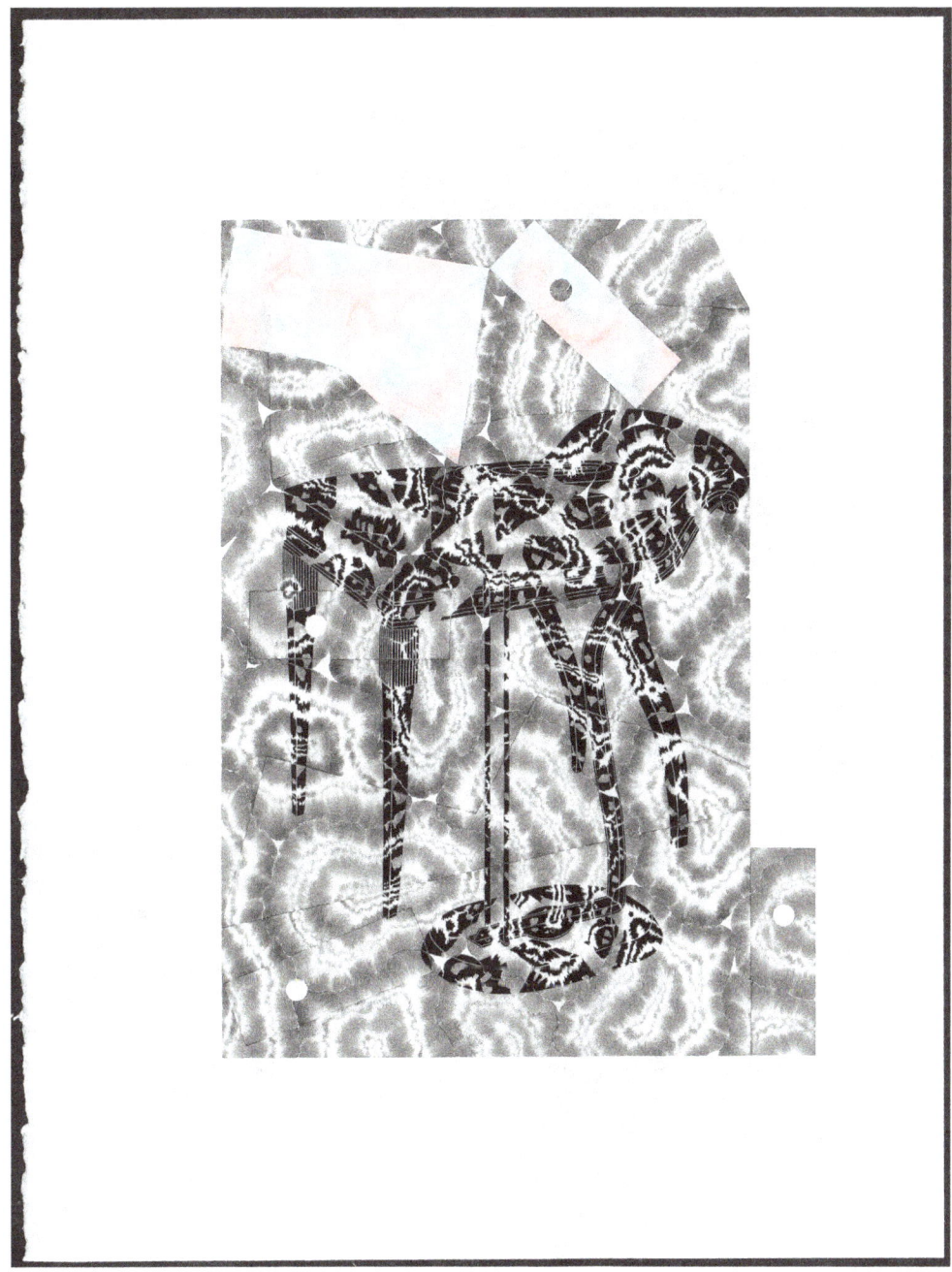

Figure 9.1 Georgie Hill, *Boudoir/studio (Eileen Gray stool with Ruhlmann vanity seat)*, 2013, watercolour and graphite on paper, 318 × 386mm. Photograph Sam Hartnett. Collection of the artist and reproduced with permission.

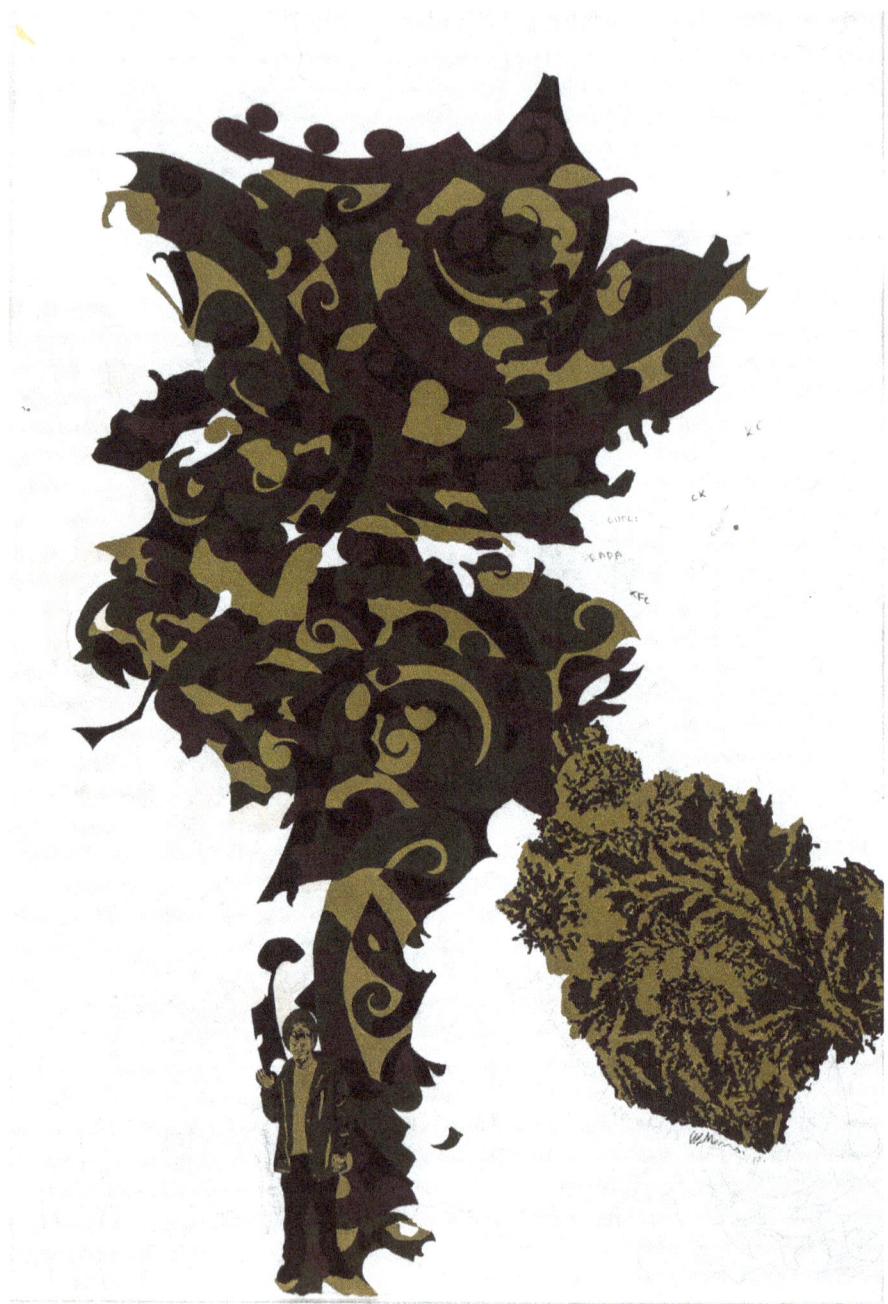

Figure 9.2 Andrew McLeod, *Camouwhaiwhai*, 1999, acrylic, pencil and letraset on paper, 1040 × 740 mm. Collection Anna Miles and Richard Fahey, Auckland. Photograph Sam Hartnett. Reproduced with permission of the artist.

Ngai Tahu artist Chris Heaphy is interested in the way in which introduction into the sphere of the fine arts causes an inevitable change or slippage of meaning of the symbol of camouflage, and the pattern becomes a chameleon itself. Fellow Māori artists Shane Cotton and Wayne Youle are also interested in the ubiquity of Māori in the armed forces in New Zealand, and use the pattern to denote the hybridised nature of ethnic identities.

Ultimately, camouflage pattern seems well suited to artworks with political intent created by Māori artists. Using tactics that include marrying mottle and disruptive patterns with the koru motif, Reuben Paterson (Ngai Tuhoe, Ngati Rangitihi) not only uses camouflage as a vehicle for identity politics as a young, urban, gay Māori artist but as a metaphor for post-fiscal envelope[1] politics in New Zealand. With considerable irony, he refers to governmental attempts to reconcile tangata whenua and tangata tiriti by using an aesthetic practice based on optical illusion. Drawing attention to the innate impulse to visually sort and assimilate objects as part of a larger group, while at the same time distinguishing units within that perceptual field, Paterson's abstract forms reflect and refract into fragmented configurations. They challenge the eye to resolve issues of depth through deceptive perspective effects and contradictory use of foreground and background patterning. This shifting black-and-white opticality challenges binary views on issues such as Māori land ownership and history, with the fragmented perspectives opening up a multiplicity of readings.

Commissioned to work on Bethells Beach on Auckland's West Coast, Reuben Paterson dug into the glistening black sand an undulating grid within a circle. As the tide advanced and the full moon rose, an enveloping froth briefly made the grid gleam under the moon, whose lunar pull causes the ebb and flow between land and ocean.

Evoking Robert Smithson's interest in entropy and processes of time, and his early use of glass to form refractive crystalline structures, *There goes the moon* briefly formed a Narcissus figure of the moon gazing at its own reflection. Its circular form, inscribed in sand in a modulated grid of alternating sections, recalls the black and white optical illusions that emerged in Paterson's practice with *Whakatata mai: do you see what I see?*, a 2004 SCAPE commission for the ground outside Riccarton House in Christchurch (Figure 9.3), and the subsequent 2005 *Narcissus* exhibition at Gow Langsford Gallery. The pared-back colour scheme and resultant optical effects draw from early 20th century German Gestalt psychologists' studies of perception and illusion, which identified our innate contradictory desires to visually sort and assimilate objects as part of a larger group, and to distinguish units within that perceptual field. Paterson's abstract forms reflect and refract into fragmented configurations that challenge the eye to resolve issues of depth through deceptive perspective effects and contradictory use of foreground/background colouring.

The optical energy of the *Narcissus* works refers to the underlying power that ripples beneath the land we occupy, with its ever-changing layers of history. The swirling, kaleidoscopic forms suggest the magnetic pull that held the hypnotised Narcissus as he tried to catch his own reflection in a pool of water. Situated in the Riccarton Reserve, traditionally known at Putaringamotu (Irish 2005), the Christchurch installation acknowledged the energies, life force and history embedded in the land by local whenua, visualised as undulating rhythms or a vortex into the past.[2] In particular, as a visitor to the area, Paterson's work honoured the intrepid journeys taken in the Lake Wakatipu area by local iwi Ngāi

---

1 After the sesquicentennial commemoration of the Treaty of Waitangi, the 'fiscal envelope' was the term used to put a price on solving Maori grievance over land loss with financial compensation. Like the item of stationery, it was finite and enclosing, and intended to tidy things up.

2 Putaringamotu means 'severed ear' or 'the place of an echo' referring to a clearing where a suitably skilled person could hear approaching footsteps by putting their ear to the ground.

Tahu to collect precious pounamu. Similarly, the subtle addition of diamond dust in the *Narcissus* paintings recalls stories about Rua Kenana's discovery of Te Kooti's hidden diamond, the guardian-stone of the land. It is in these buried details that Paterson's work signals energy beneath the surface, picked out from the darkness.

This shifting black-and-white opticality also challenges binary views on issues such as Māori land ownership and history, with the fragmented perspectives opening up a multiplicity of readings. Historian and anthropologist Dame Anne Salmond has spoken of her need to discover this Māori world in a visceral way, through the skin – with the soles of her feet walking the land (Wichtel 2012). With this in mind, Paterson has noted the rich history of Matata, the ancestral home of Paterson's Ngati Rangitihi rohe (sub-tribe), as the location of New Zealand's last land war conflicts and a burial site for many who fell in those battles, now subject to substantial urban beachfront development (Mason 2005). *There goes the moon* was intended as a tribute to Matata. As the rising tide slowly filled hollowed out sections of the work, it gently eroded and caressed away the shapes; a soft destruction that commemorated Matata's 2005 flooding and land-slides, which left a prominent scar in the landscape and exposed sacred burial sites.

Paterson's earlier works reference both his gay identity and Maori heritage with glitter-on-canvas depictions of traditional kowhaiwhai motifs and, later, designs based on fabrics worn by his family. Kowhaiwhai are designs usually found on the rafters of a wharenui (meeting house), considered the ribs of an ancestral body and depicting local events and journeys. Each curled koru is a reminder of an ancestor that has been there before, connecting one generation to the next through the flowing patterns.

One notable painting from this series is *The pubic hair of Hinenuitepo* (2003). Named after the goddess of death, it shows a silhouetted Pacific island scene at twilight, a tropical fantasy caught in the flux between night and day. This design was given new life as part of a series of glitter suits Paterson designed for fashion house World's 2003 Auckland Fashion Week show, literally becoming a memory to be worn. *Hinenuitepo* was translated into the large installation, *When the sun rises and the shadows flee*. The image comprised large mylar 'shimmer disks', like giant sequins, loosely fixed to the wall on rows of nails so they can flutter, animated by a breeze caused by an industrial fan to create a spiritually charged dance of reflected light and dark.

Since his 2010 *Dear beauty, dear beast* exhibition at Gow Langsford Gallery, Paterson has increasingly looked to figurative imagery, particularly that of animals. *Dear beauty, dear beast* featured predatory panthers, lions and tigers, paired with softer motifs including floral bedspreads or a table cloth. Like the Pacific scenes in his fabric works, the animals are also derived from (or make reference to) textile designs such as the budget glamour of animal-print bedspreads (in Korean Mink) or synthetic blankets, common in lower socio-economic homes – images of exotic wonder that provide a surface covering of glitz in a depressed setting. The pairing of masculine and feminine combined with domestic references suggests an intimate and volatile mix of emotions. This was the first time Paterson directly addressed issues to do with gay culture, and these works challenge an underlying culture of homophobia and racism, making reference to murder cases that have successfully used the provocation or 'gay panic' defence as a means to reduce a murder charge to manslaughter.[3] A panther titled *Nigger* makes an unmistakeable reference to the radical Black Panther movement that became a key player in North American racial politics in the 1960s and 70s, as well as the Polynesian Panthers in Auckland, inspired by the American struggle.

9 From Ghillie suit to glittering kowhaiwhai

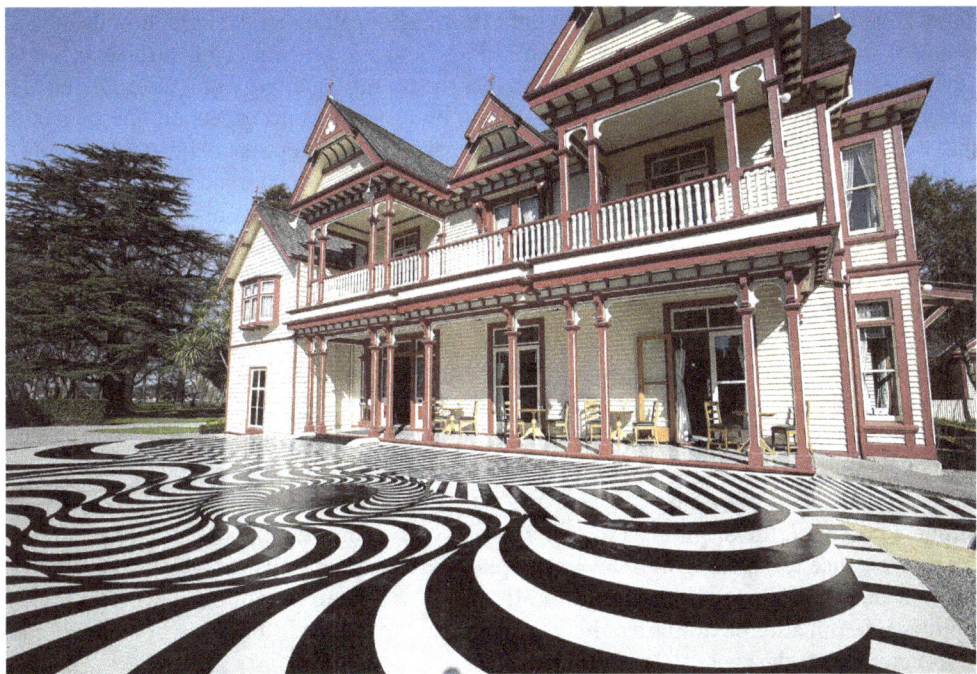

Figure 9.3 Reuben Paterson, *Whakatata mai: do you see what I see?*, 2004, hand cut domestic vinyl, 1520 mm squared, installed at Riccarton House, Christchurch. Commissioned for the Art and Industry Biennial 2004 SCAPE (now dismantled.). Photograph by Lightworkx Photography. Reproduced with permission of the artist.

The water between us, his following show at Milford Galleries that same year, also brought an overt approach to politics, this time to do with land use. Whereas previous works used glitter to depict flat, textile-derived motifs and abstract patterns, these made use of photographic effects to portray perspective, depth and volume, so it's interesting that Paterson has chosen the liquid environment of the Karangahake Gorge for his most figurative works to date, which depicted sparkling water surfaces, a gushing waterfall, and riverbed environments. Continuing his exploitation of the fluid properties of light through metallic glitter to address social and political issues to do with histories of the land, the works consider the legacy of gold mining at the Gorge (one of the most industrialised sites in New Zealand) on waterways that were previously a major food source for iwi, as well as an important traditional route and territorial divider. As well as referencing the precious metals in the riverbed, the gold toning of these works suggest the nostalgia and loss found in historic old sepia photographs. Former prominent gold mining towns are also now gone, washed away in the ongoing flux of time.

Water has been a recurring reference in Paterson's work, as the cleansing spring of *Rehua*, the bubbling waters of soft drinks and alcohol, or the implied storage within tradi-

---

3 David Broker makes connections between gay activism and Maori land rights in the introduction to his story 'Kaleidoscope culture: Reuben Paterson' in *Contemporary Visual Art and Culture Broadsheet*, Vol. 38, no. 4, 2009, pp. 274–6.

tional gourd containers that now project light from mylar sequins. Like light, liquids have a transient form and deceptive depths, often hidden beneath a shimmering surface. It is another state of flux that defies easy definition, like the pounding energy of a waterfall, or the threatened ecosystems contained by a sparkling blue stream, and especially the constant shift of histories that traverse the ever-changing waters. These depths are brought into play with the flatness of Paterson's images, which gain spirit from the charged medium of light.

In 2007 Paterson began to diagonally divide his canvases to combine different fabric and kowhaiwhai motifs, allowing different emblems of his heritage to mix in new combinations to build something new from the past. Then came kaleidoscopic distortions to further fragment the distinctions between one world and another, causing patterns to combine and multiply in acknowledgement of his mixed Māori-Scottish heritage and the instability of how we situate ourselves in the world. This strategy culminates with *Whakapapa: Get down upon your knees*, an 8×8-metre, 16 panel work he produced for the sixth Asia-Pacific Triennial, taking three different split panels and further interweaving them in a kaleidoscopic array that reflects and rotates in all directions. The intense darkness of the void, an idea also explored by Māori artists Ralph Hotere and Lisa Reihana, is a space of limitless potential, the originary moment out of which comes the big bang of possibilities; a creative pause released by light and multiplied into endless transformations like the effect of a kaleidoscope spiralling outwards. This becomes Te Ao Marama, the world of light, a physical realm and the domain of being, as opposed to the traditional realm of Te Po, the Māori concept of darkness (Clarke 2012).

The movement of time and energy important to the creative process itself, and Paterson's latest works, the swirling fabric motifs of his 2011 *Flow* exhibition, mark the ebb and flow of inspiration as distortions bend and flex into each other with a new form of fluctuation that suggests undercurrents pulling through the canvases. With titles such as *Anxiety for the sake of boredom* or *Arousal for the sake of apathy*, they draw from the flow theory of Hungarian psychologist Mihály Csíkszentmihályi, which associates the state of happiness with spontaneity, surrounded by boredom, relaxation, anxiety or arousal. Marrying mottle and disruptive patterns from camouflage's rich history with the trajectory of the koru in modernity, Reuben Paterson uses camouflage as a vehicle for identity politics as a young, urban, gay Māori artist.

While artists who are tangata tiriti, the people of the treaty, use camouflage to extend their artistic projects of mapping cultural understandings, gender politics and environmental concerns, Māori artists such as Andrew McLeod, Chris Heaphy, Shane Cotton and Reuben Paterson seem to be developing a practice based on camouflage for its metaphoric value. Ultimately it is the inevitable change or slippage of meaning of the pattern of camouflage itself that is so useful – a chameleon itself. As an adaptive mechanism to avoid detection and recognition in the work of these contemporary New Zealand artists, camouflage operates as a Trojan horse, smuggling a message about the unstable nature of New Zealand's biculturalism into public consciousness.

References

Clarke C (2012). A Māori perspective on the wearing of black. In D de Pont (Ed). *Black: The history of black in fashion, society and culture in New Zealand*. Auckland: Penguin Books.
Elias, A (2011). *Camouflage Australia: art, nature, science and war*, Sydney: Sydney University Press.
Irish G (2005). Collaborating with spirit, SCAPE: from a different angle. *Art New Zealand*, 115: 60–97.

Mason N (2005). Open for interpretation: the art of Reuben Paterson. *Art New Zealand*, 116: 64–105.

Norman, G (2012). *Buller's Birds of New Zealand: The Complete Work of JG Keulemans*, Wellington: Museum of New Zealand Te Papa Press.

O'Brien G (2011). *Kermadec: Nine artists explore the South Pacific*. Tauranga: Pew Environmental Group in association with Tauranga Art Gallery.

Reynolds J (2011). A voice and an echo. In Bronwen Golder and Gregory O'Brien, *Kermadec: nine artists explore the South Pacific*. Tauranga: Pew Environmental Group in association with Tauranga Art Gallery: 116.

Wichtel D (2012). A way of being. *NZ Listener*, 3740: 24–9.

10
Making visible, changing sides: the contradictory use of camouflage by artists Xing Junqin and Ian Howard

Ian Howard and Brigitta Olubas

It has long been understood that camouflage is used across the plant, animal and human kingdoms to modify appearances in order to deceive; disallowing or distracting easy and clear recognition of the object in view. This distracting role of camouflage – to deceive by minimising *presence profile* – is of course only half the story; the very same mechanisms of contrived outwardly appearances also work to attract attention – for instance in plants that use colour to entice insects for cross-pollination, or animal mating processes such as the peacock's feather dance or indeed the ever-changing costume of modern-day humans. More dramatically, modern humans make use of camouflage in the theatre of war to distract, compel or elude attention in a strategic dance of here and there, back and forth, choreographed from afar. Camoufleurs of the First World War often covered vital equipment with canvas painted in a way to belie what was beneath. Conversely, in the Second World War, in the Africa campaign, a number of heavy tanks spotted from aircraft were in fact light trucks covered with timber frames and stretched cloth. Representing an object, partaking in mimicry through working directly on or from its surface, is an age-old practice. The endless double play of attraction and distraction, compulsion and rejection is clearly at the heart of camouflage, extending across the domains of nature and culture, surface and depth, as artists and art critics have insisted time and again over the last century.

This chapter seeks to build on the insights of theorists and art historians who have worked to generate a rich commentary around the aesthetics of camouflage (see Behrens 1981, 1988; Taussig 2008; Elias 2011) in order to provide an account of a large body of work that has been completed on and around the idea of visual camouflage by two contemporary artists: Ian Howard, a Sydney-based academic artist and Colonel Xing Junqin of the Chinese People's Liberation Army. Howard and Xing have worked separately and collaboratively on a number of projects around the visibility and materiality of national military and security deployments, scrutinising the scope and the limits of the state, the points where the bodies of citizens encounter its force and impact. Both artists use the capacity of camouflage to deceive as a mechanism to make the invisible visible rather than the other way around. Further, both work to extend the practice of camouflage beyond the visual and into conceptual and performance domains in order to attract rather than distract, to foreground display, and the shifting meanings of display within the changing contexts of inter/national military engagement and artistic collaboration.

In her recent monograph on Australian military camouflage, Ann Elias observes that 'camouflage is cryptic and paradoxical. Invisibility is simply visibility in disguise. It is the outcome of a process of visual transformations in which the deadly appear innocent and the innocent deadly,' (xiv) highlighting the chiastic complications of camouflage's deceptive specularity. Michael Taussig aligns camouflage's regime of visuality with a persistent colonial desire, tracing what he calls 'the complex of attraction and repulsion in the violence displayed' in his reading of Marlowe's meditation on 'the fascination of the abomination' in Joseph Conrad's *Heart of Darkness*, and thence to the horrors of the spectacle and the secrecy of Abu Ghraib at the other end of the century. More broadly, Taussig directs attention to the ways the acts of looking and looking away come together in the face of camouflage, for instance in photographs of 'dazzle-painted' British warships from 1918:

> They are surely among the most brilliant artefacts of mankind, these ships, all stripes, no stars, set at conflicting angles to one another hundreds and hundreds of feet long. You can stare at them for a long time. Meant to destabilize vision in real life, they mesmerize when looked at in pages of a book. Why mesmerizing? I do not know. Perhaps it is because we see here humans out of desperation enjoy interfering with nature, painting it 'out' in grandiloquent swathes. Perhaps it is because we, who come after, have such fun in seeing through the deception and marvel at the disingenuousness of man's ingenuity? We see it twice over. We see the camouflaged thing, and then we see the thing 'behind' the camouflage and admire both our cleverness and that of the designer, not to mention God who contrives nature in such a way, our eyes included, that it includes its camouflaged deceptions of selves that are not-selves as well. (109–10)

Taussig here works the compulsion to look and indeed to look hard at a mysterious and 'mesmerizing' image against camouflage's initial intention to occlude and distract. He sees the viewer's attention turning away from the object and toward the processes of construction whereby things become images and artworks. This is to confound the more familiar story sequence that sees cubist and surrealist art practice pre-empting and informing military practice, as encapsulated in Picasso's famous claim on observing camouflage zig-zags painted on guns that, 'We invented that.' Picasso was surprised, as Roland Penrose explains, 'to see that his discoveries in the breaking up of forms should have been pressed so rapidly into military service' (quoted in Behrens 1980, 18). Both stories depend of course on the unexpected reversibility of cause and effect, or of original and copy, event and consequence; at the same time, it's important to note that the intimate connection between art and war is itself not in doubt in either scenario. Indeed Taussig proposes a further point that 'Clausewitz got it only half right. War is art carried on by other means' (104). Srinivas Aravamudan takes this point further in his discussion of what he calls the 'perpetuity' of war, proposing that war's alignment with technology pushes the question of display relentlessly into the foreground:

> Because the history of war is inseparable from the progress of technology, the meaning of war changes dramatically as killing machines and human lifeworlds increasingly imbricate each other. War names an unconcealment that Martin Heidegger called technē. (1506)

Here Aravamudan refers to Heidegger's complex account of the work of 'unconcealment', the 'presencing' or 'bringing-forth' of that which has been concealed in a movement of 're-vealing': 'The Greeks have the word *alētheia* for revealing. The Romans translate this with *veritas*. We say "truth" and usually understand it as the correctness of an idea' (Heidegger 1977, 11–12). Both stories of cause and effect in the relation between art and war in the development of camouflage thus speak also to the ways that camouflage might attest to the world, the ways it might speak truth and deception at the same time while continuing to compel viewers in and out of context in that chiastic sequence already noted. And this question of truth relates not only to the camouflage artworks to be discussed in this chapter, but also very particularly to Ian Howard's extensive series of large-scale 'rubbings' of military technologies: vehicles, fixtures and fragments from across the Cold War and post-Cold War globe, where the exhibited work is the literal imprint – the index – of the object itself. In this way, camouflage impels a collision of truth and deception.

This collision is at the heart of Howard's collaborative practice with Xing Junqin, as he makes clear in the following observation:

> As an image-maker I have always been struck by the capacity of two-dimensional imagery to convincingly represent concrete things: objects, people, landscapes. Additionally, I recognise that this representation can carry multiple layers of meaning, open to interpretation. And finally, I am bemused by relatively simple images that can represent complex matter and experience. As painters interested in capturing the nature of landscapes of our time and place, Colonel Xing Junqin and I deal with these issues and potentialities every day, gathering from within our fields of vision and experience and processing them in a more focused way in our studios in Beijing and Sydney. Landscapes of our time and place include military personnel, equipment and installations.

More particularly, Howard has differentiated four overlapping categories in the use of camouflage across his and Xing's shared body of work: first, camouflage as a motif to signal time, place and position; second, camouflage as a device to interface various disparate cultures; third, camouflage as a conceptual tool for exploring landscape globally; and finally, camouflage as a performative act in advancing relationships towards productive and mutually beneficial outcomes, both in terms of artist collaboration and of intercultural understandings. Each of these will now be addressed in turn.

Camouflage as a motif to signal time, place and position

Highly effective camouflage, within its designated surroundings, melts into the background, becoming almost invisible. Necessarily, the colouring and patterning are maximised towards mimicking their host environment. Outside this intended setting, however, the visual effect is severely compromised, even reversed, with the camouflaged object now contrasting with and standing out from its new background. Xing Junqin uses this interplay of visibility or readability of camouflaged figures to great effect. On the one hand his soldiers are totally camouflaged, from head to toe; on the other they appear as arresting, even startling figures on a large canvas exhibited in an elite cultural institution, an art gallery, as seen in the works *Life* and *Second Squad* (1997) (Figure 10.1).

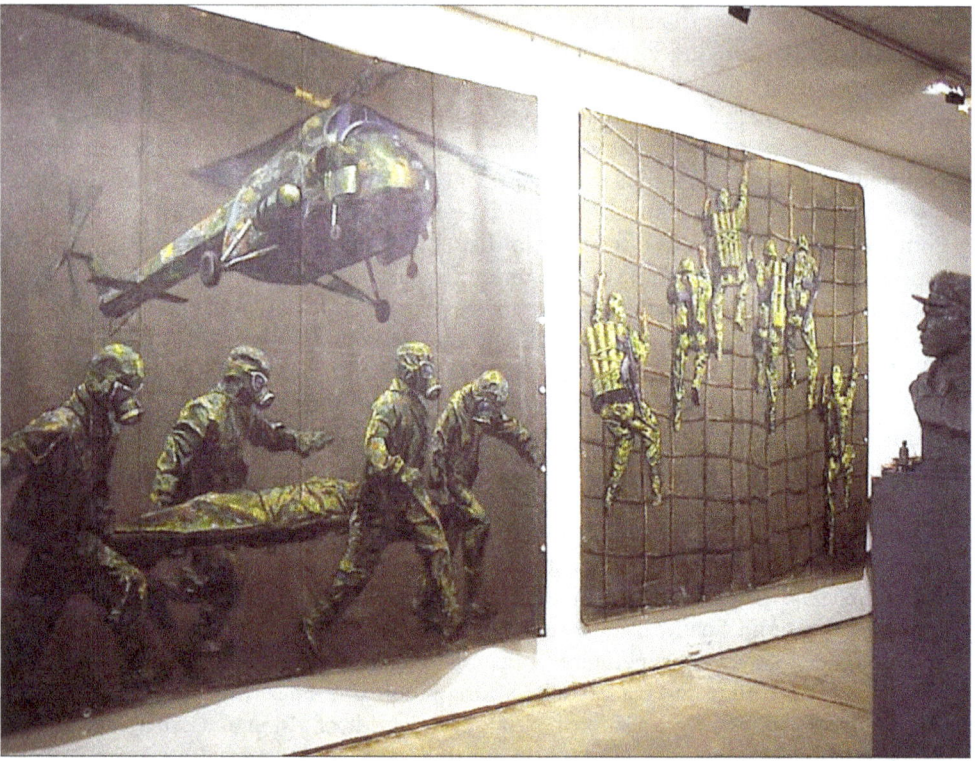

Figure 10.1 *Life* and *Second Squad* (1997)

The pictorial directness of Xing's camouflaged figures provides for instant, confirmed recognition; recognition, that is, of the artist's place in the world, of his era, his position, status and likely value set, establishing his place as official military artist. Howard has used camouflage and the device of camouflage in a similarly direct way to speak to his own location as artist. Given the opportunity in the UK in the mid-1970s to make a rubbing of either of two first World War tanks, he chose the one carrying the hard edge vegetation green, soil brown and sky blue colour-field patterning in *Mark.1 male (heavy)* (1973) partly because of the deliberateness and clarity of the design, but largely in response to the irony of how close this patterning seemed to be to late-modernist hard edge and colour-field painting which had dominated his art school training (Figure 10.2).

Some years later he created a series of collage/paintings that brought together 'kitsch' paintings of landscapes, always excessively painterly and emotive, and images of advanced military hardware sourced from highly technical aviation industry publications. The rationale for the choice of pairs was that they were pictorially similar, such that with each pair one *camouflaged* the other into an integrated whole, creating, in effect, another landscape. The convincing assimilation of images spoke to Howard's sense of his situation as a citizen of a world where military and civilian cultures seamlessly coexisted, a central theme taken up by much of his art across this period.

10 Making visible, changing sides

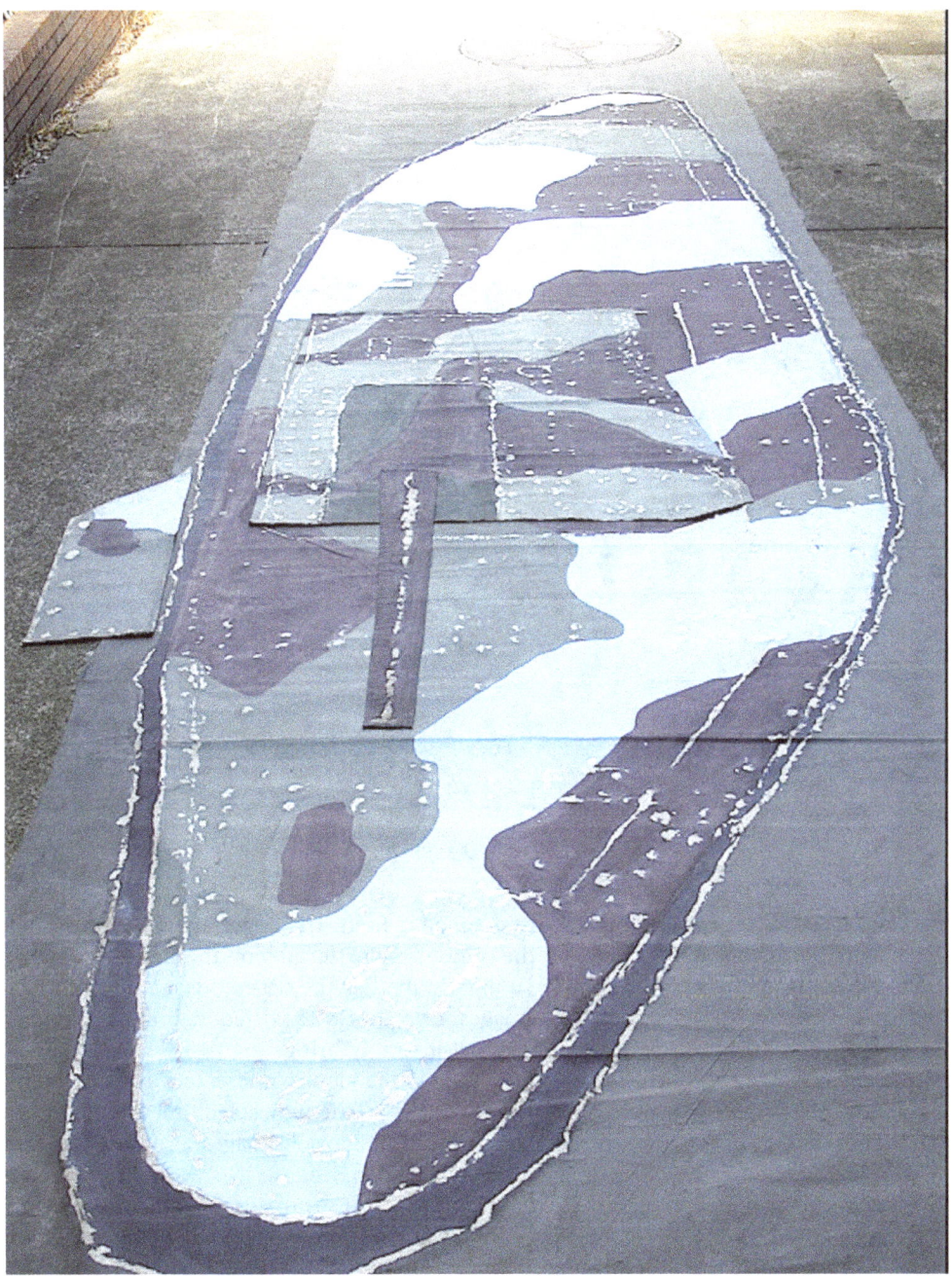

Figure 10.2 *Mark.1 male (heavy)* (1973)

In *Rockwell engineers check out turn of century painting prior to flight-testing B.1 bomber* (1994) (Figure 10.3), the mix of cultures is extreme, with an experimental Rockwell B1 bomber – in 1994 a pinnacle of aerospace technology design and achievement – being readied for flight by technicians on the ground and test pilots in the cockpit alongside a

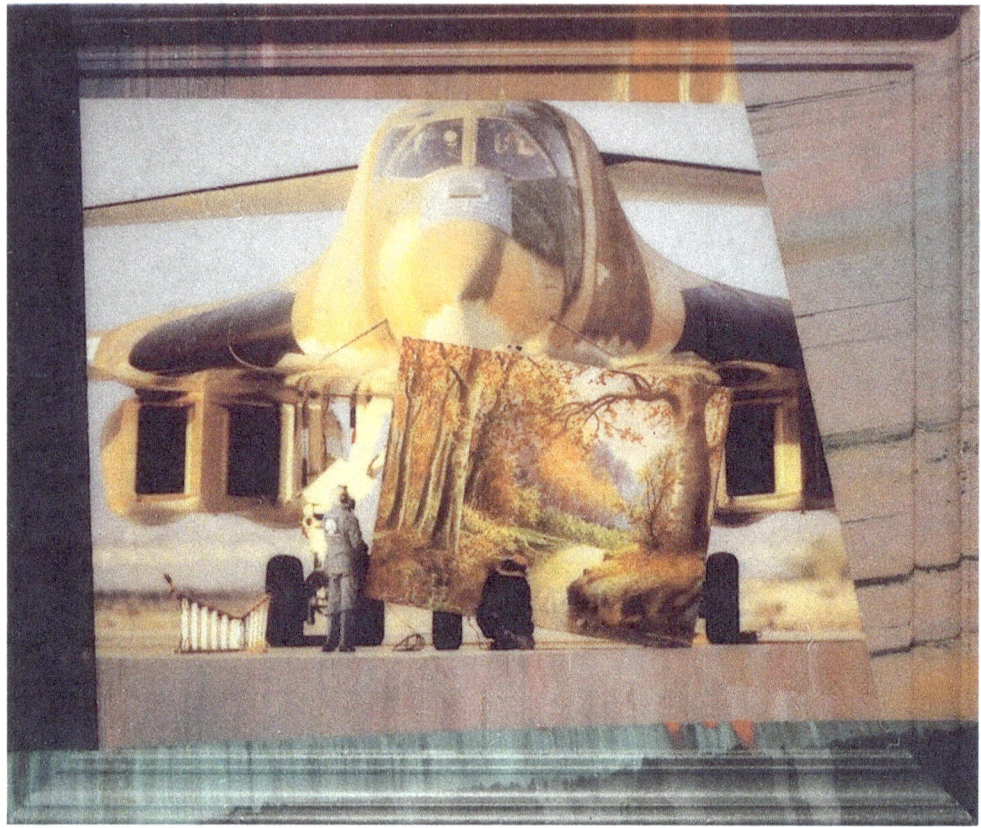

Figure 10.3 *Rockwell engineers check out turn of century painting prior to flight-testing B.1 bomber* (1994)

mass-produced image of a romantic forest dappled in light. The larger image is dominated by sunlight, seen in the ways it picks up the camouflage patterning on the aircraft fuselage, while the landscape work sees similar sunlight stippling the vegetation and landforms. Under the one sun, it seems, these two images have always coexisted, nature and culture jaggedly aligned; Howard's painting insists that it simply brings the two worlds together into the same image space. The literal submerging of the picture frame, in a unifying paint surface and colour palette which variously encroaches on the subjects, ultimately pressures them into a vortex of oneness. The edgily resolved paradox of images also relies on the work of humour, for instance in the low-tech stepladder lying on its side and the second Rockwell technician crouching down to get a closer look at the treatment of the river in the landscape painting. Here, the visible works alongside as well as against the readable, with the divisions between the two unsettled.

Camouflage as a device to interface disparate cultures

Xing Junqin's paintings see camouflage patterning spread easily across uniformed People's Liberation Army figures, engulfing the entire picture plane, the whole compliant land-

10 Making visible, changing sides

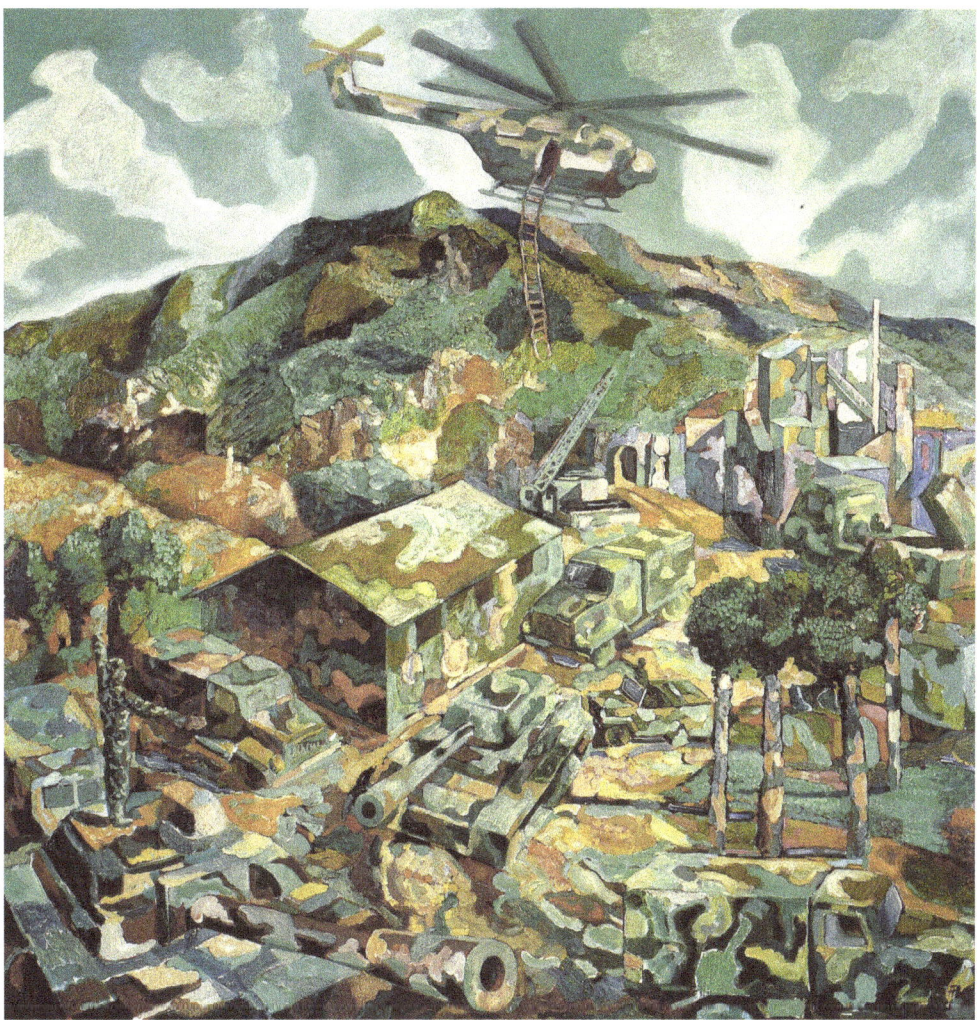

Figure 10.4 *Series of Camouflage – Highland* (1997)

scape. These works (for example, *Series of camouflage – Highland* (1997) (Figure 10.4)), are but a few brush stokes away from the landscapes of Cezanne and the cubists, bringing another temporal layer to the sequence of the breaking up of visual form and the military deployment of camouflage noted earlier. The paintings mark the start of Xing's ongoing dialogue with Western art – or as Howard terms it, his 'respectful and sometimes not so respectful "attack" upon icons of Western art' within which the collaborative practice between Howard and Xing has developed. Through the use of the camouflage device, Xing rapidly developed a schema in his painting that would see his responsibility as PLA artist align with other, disparate elements of interest. Thus he could paint landscape, military hardware, atmospherics, spirituality and ideology into one integrated and unified, albeit subtly shifting, camouflage pattern.

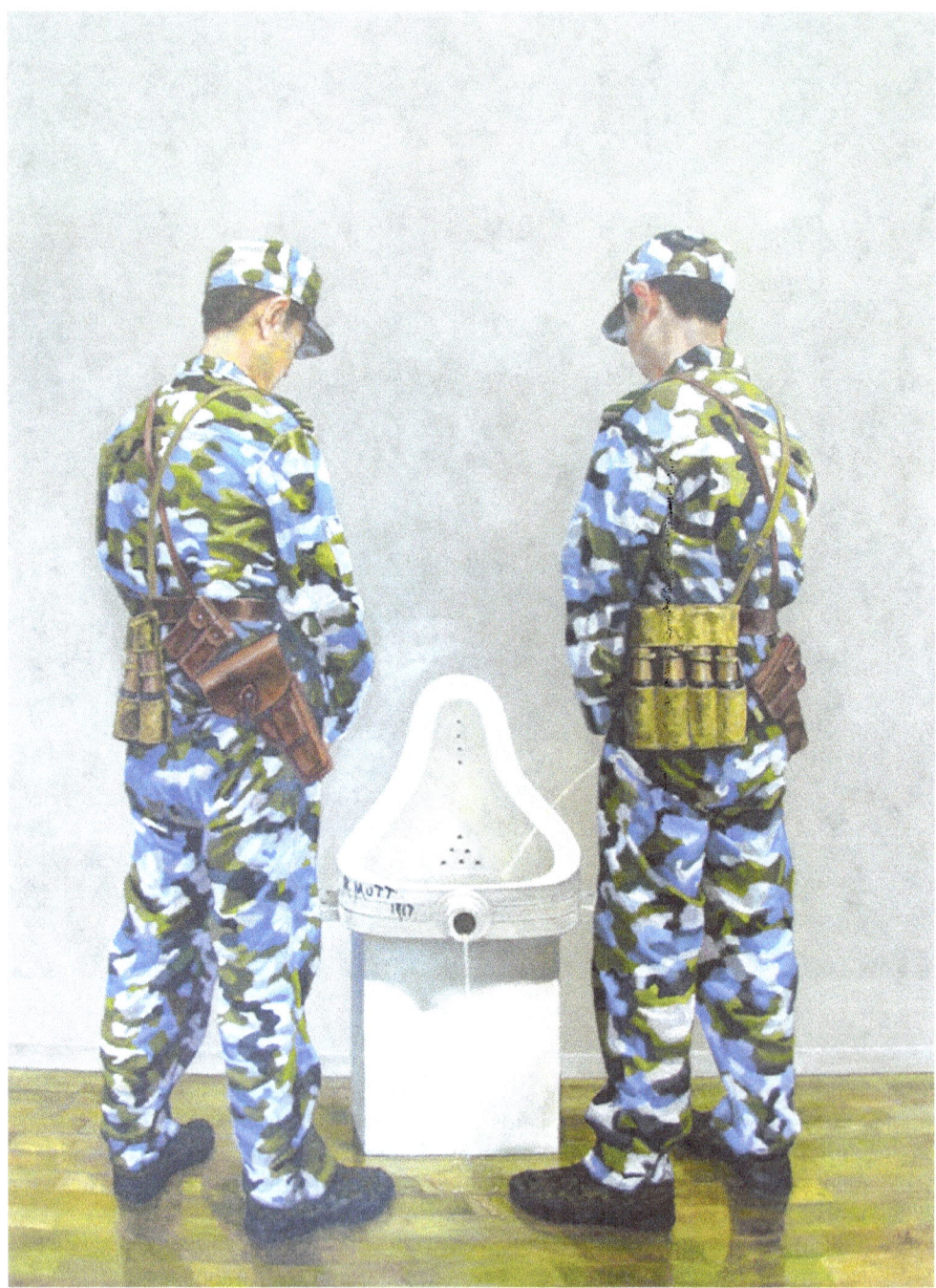

Figure 10.5 *Duchamp Syllogism (Spring)* (2005)

Rapidly catching up with, or perhaps just aggressively shadowing European culture, his later works have 'taken on' the icons of Western modernist art. In one work, *Duchamp Syllogism (Spring)* (2005), two PLA soldiers are depicted 'using' the R Mutt urinal (Figure

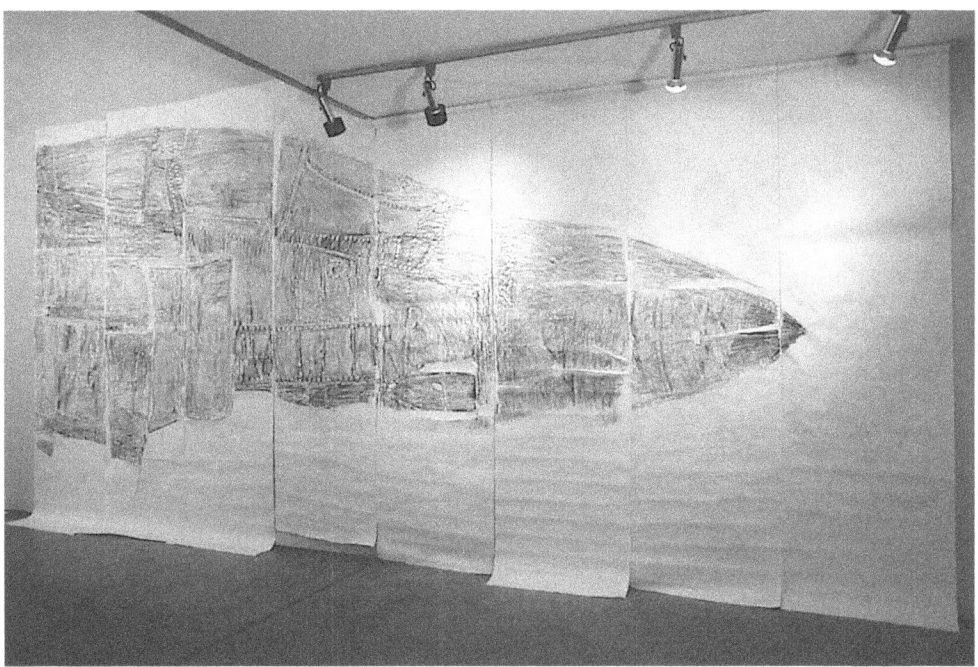

Figure 10.6 *F4 Phantom U.S. Navy* (1975)

10.5). Both soldiers wear dramatic camouflage, appearing not as clandestine or concealed figures so much as vibrantly costumed court jesters, poking fun at – making visible – tensions in the relationship between a new and emerging China and an older, weakening Europe, a culture in decline. Viewers are also perhaps reminded of the story recounted by Roy Behrens, where Picasso told Cocteau that the camouflage effects of military uniforms would be heightened and improved if the men were dressed in harlequin costumes (Behrens 1980, 17). The camouflage pattern on the soldiers' uniforms codes the painting's realism while at the same time directing attention to the not so sly irony at play here. Thus for Xing, camouflage speaks to the need to see otherwise. As well as compelling viewers to look hard, camouflage thwarts and distracts vision, creating something new in the gap. If these are ponderings made visible through this painting, there also lies realistically within the imagery of the leaking urinal the playful irony that such faulty plumbing still exists in China.

Howard's series of military rubbings speaks eloquently to his belief that:

> It is important to have strong links between Civilian, and Defence cultures, and military equipment constitutes a significant part of our landscape. I have for many years used the rubbing process to 'capture' such objects in image form. Although the object is momentarily hidden, camouflaged by the covering material, the process of transfer is direct, and little is lost in this quick translation. The military object, often kept remote from public scrutiny, is in this approved and appropriate way made visible.

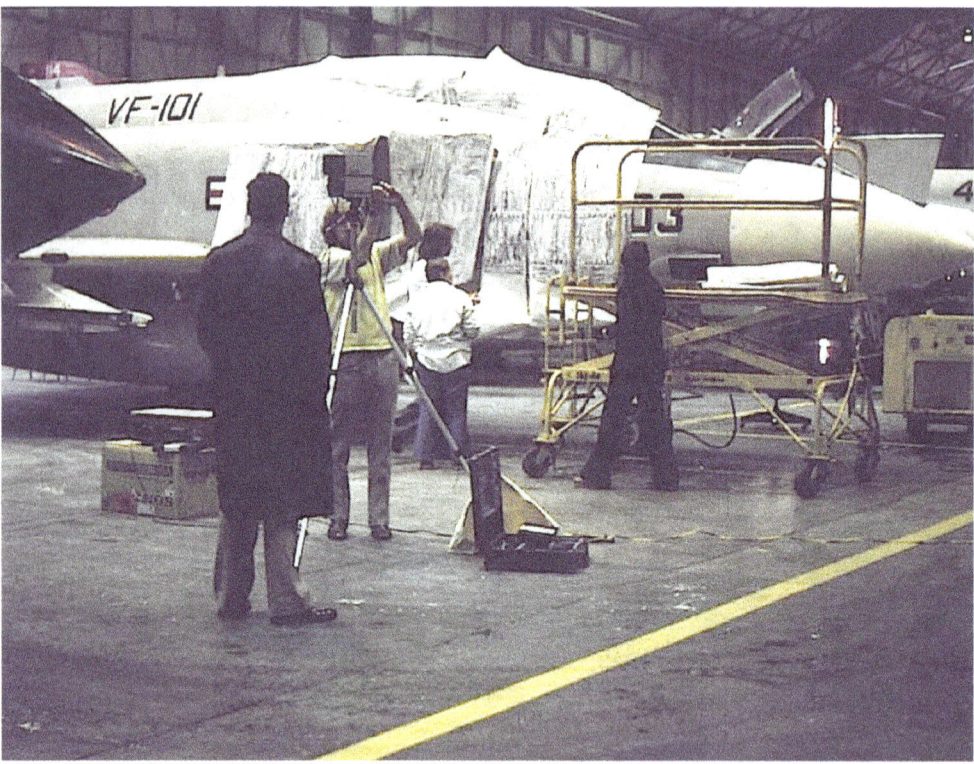

Figure 10.7 The rubbing to create artwork, undertaken during the Vietnam War

The collaboration between Xing and Howard works to stage within this military/civilian domain an intercultural dialogue, providing unexpected – unforeseen – points of connection and conversation between artists working within separate cultures. At the same time, it speaks to the divide but also the overlap between civilian and military establishments. More broadly across the work of both artists, this overlapping of otherwise separate or hostile contexts, the encroachment on one by the other operates, according to Howard's thinking outlined above, if not as a mode of literal camouflage, then as a way of making visible the military object, bringing it into view of the civilian public, and transporting it away from its place of authorised concealment. Such a process is seen in Howard's rubbing *F4 Phantom U.S. Navy* (1975) (Figure 10.6). The rubbing was approved and then, astonishingly, carried out during the Vietnam War. Howard recalls how the context of doing the rubbing impacted in tangible – indeed visible – ways on the finished work (Figure 10.7):

> The field work, undertaken at Naval Air Station Oceana, Virginia Beach, was a little frantic because there was a typhoon threatening and all aircraft had to be brought into hangars…in a hurry. I had approved local media and art students on base, so it was quite a coming together. The work, now with the NGA [National Gallery of Australia], was as rough as my rubbings get…as a consequence of the limited time and very high humidity, which sent the rubbing process and the fragile paper into a bit of a spin.

The work of technē brings together once again the domains of 'killing machines and human lifeworlds' (Aravamudan, 2009) in a process of unconcealing.

Camouflage as a conceptual tool for exploring landscape, globally: 'just in case'

One of the most significant collaborations between Howard and Xing is centred on the extensive possibilities of camouflage as a marker of national distinctiveness. Gertrude Stein remarked on this quality of camouflage in 1933:

> Another thing that interested us enormously was how different the camouflage of the French looked from the camouflage of the Germans, and then once we came across some very very neat camouflage and it was American. The idea was the same but as after all it was different nationalities who did it the difference was inevitable. The color schemes were different, the designs were different, the way of placing them was different, it made plain the whole theory of art and its inevitability. (187)

In the aftermath of the Second Gulf War Howard reasoned, with a sense of irony to match Xing's R Mutt camouflage painting, as follows:

> With the perceived increase in the likelihood of a terrorist attack occurring anytime, anywhere in the world, and with hostilities breaking out in various countries and regions, it would seem prudent to have a camouflage pattern ready and available for each country of the world. In 2005 I set out to make a camouflage pattern for every country, based on the topography of the landscape, natural and/or man made depicted in a single photograph representing each country. These representative national images were then worked on by Xing who added suitably camouflaged military personnel, vehicles or installations.

The geographical distance between the two artists' workspaces is thus factored, literally, into the construction process. The enormity of the task – 202 camouflage patterns and the same number of militarised country images – made apparent to both artists, and in turn to viewers, the nature and scale of territorialisation that has seen the earth divided up into such a large number of often minute nation states. And once again, this work pushes viewers into the domain beyond what can literally be seen. As Howard observes:

> Realities of such complexity and magnitude are difficult to realize and contemplate without a synthesizing mechanism. The mechanism in this case was a concept-driven symbolic imaging gesture employing camouflage to make visible, to render comprehensible, the otherwise unimaginable.

The process here began with Howard sourcing an accessible and legally usable image for 'every country', a task requiring considerable time and effort. Howard then developed a camouflage pattern responding to each. The country images were sent to Xing in Beijing, who over-painted them with his predictive military presence which invariably included camouflaged figures and/or vehicles (Figure 10.8).

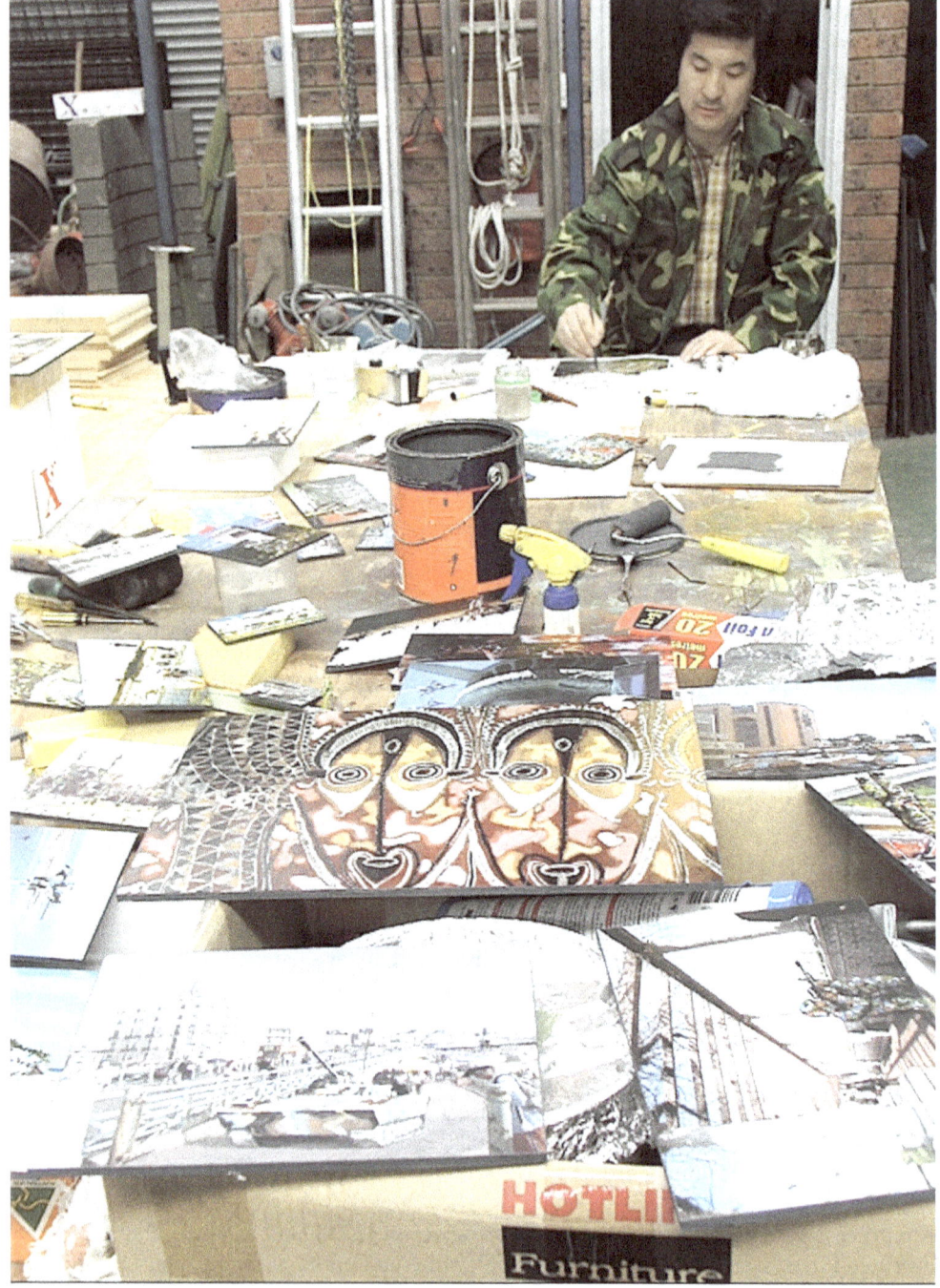

Figure 10.8 Xing Junqin over-painting rural landscapes with predictive military presence

As Howard sourced the images it became apparent that, even though they had been randomly gathered, there was nonetheless a clear consistency in the messages conveyed. In

10 Making visible, changing sides

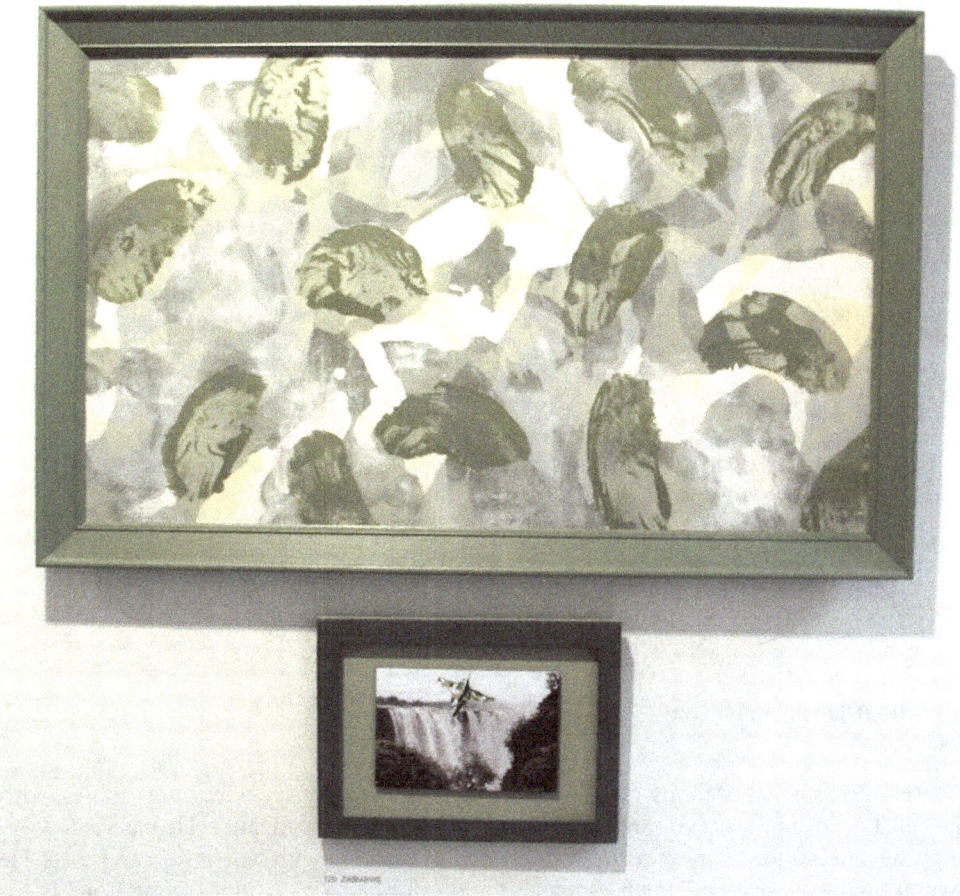

Figure 10.9 *Zimbabwe* (2004)

Caribbean and African countries, for instance, there was a clear legacy of colonial buildings and public spaces, now decaying; while in developed countries it was property of all sorts in the form of private real estate or other substantial and contemporary object possessions such as vehicles with their messages of status and commodification that predominated. In other instances it is landscape once again which provides the template for camouflage, for instance in *Zimbabwe* (2004) (Figure 10.9). The iconic image of Victoria Falls signals both sublimity and disaster in the points at which it overlaps with the camouflaged aircraft. There were additional complications for Xing and Howard in that the exhibition was difficult to hang, with 404 pictures, a point highlighting the very issues around scale and complexity that had prompted the 'Just in case' project (Figure 10.10). A selection of countries and their camouflage patterns were shown at the 2005 Beijing Biennale, further compounding the ways this project tracked the shared terrain between national and global formations, with the camouflage process operating as the visible interface between separated or hostile domains.

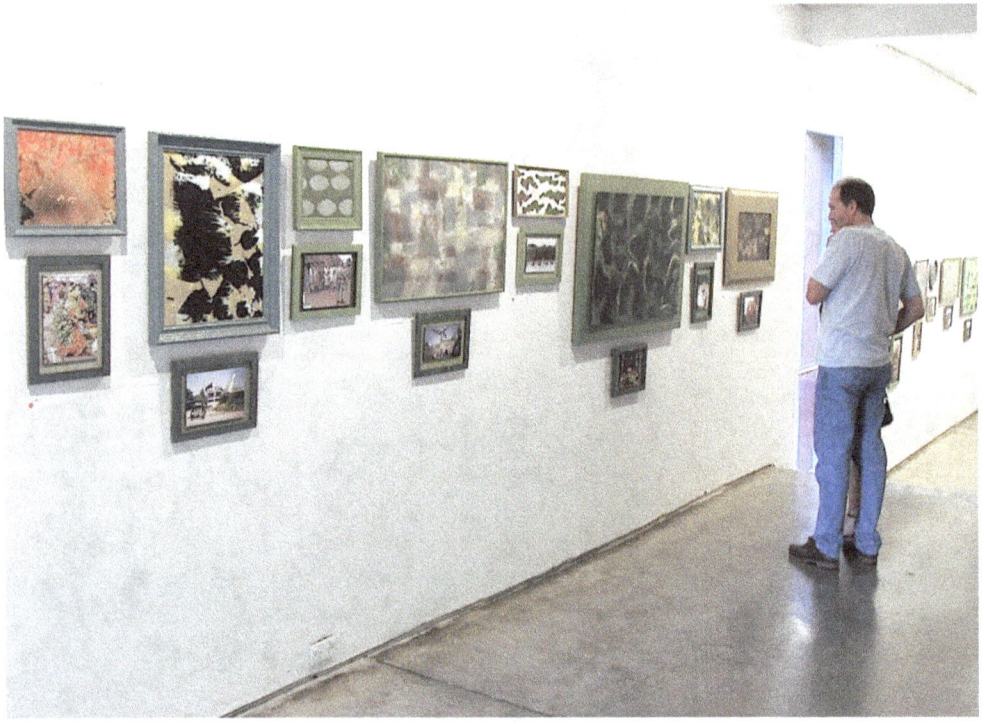

Figure 10.10 'Just in case' project

Howard's collaborations have at times focused on very specific topographies, with the collaborative process not always able to be determined in advance. He has visited Pyongyang and has for many years been interested in working with North Korean artists. He owns a small collection of North Korean art and exhibited a piece by Ri Dong Kouk in his 2009 exhibition at Watters Gallery, Sydney, 'North Korea, War with Flowers'. Frustrated by the difficulty of working directly with these colleague artists, Howard developed a plan to undertake a joint landscape painting, a four-metre impression, that would be made from a two-metre rubbing of either side of the China and North Korean border at Changbai Mountain. His aim was to rub the landscape on the Chinese side of the border while a North Korean colleague would execute the work on the North Korean side.

Changbai Mountain was chosen as the site because it powerfully symbolises cultural and military relations between the People's Republic of China and the Democratic People's Republic of Korea – as a border marker it has been shared since a declaration by Mao Tse Tung in recognition of the North Korean hostility towards the US. It is a spectacular landscape and, importantly, the area is so remote there is no physical border fence, wall or barrier to restrict the free movement of an art project. Although the plan was put forward through official channels in Pyongyang, there was no North Korean participation on the day of the rubbing and Howard was strongly advised to move back from the borderline. He compromised by undertaking the landscape rubbing only just, but wholly, within China (Figure 10.11). The finished work, although complex in structure and detail, belies any reference to a border. The pattern and colouring indicate the richness of the volcanic landscape but camouflaging any reference to geopolitical tensions. Instead of direct representation of national entities and borders, what we get in the rubbing of this site is something that dramatically shifts both scale and orientation – we might be in a spaceship gazing down at a lost earth, or indeed contemplating minute flora or other life-forms on a microscope slide. These literal impressions preserve an elemental binary of earth and sea, recalling the 'here and there' of camouflage, visible and veiled, confounding the viewer's sense of location on the earth itself (Figure 10.12).

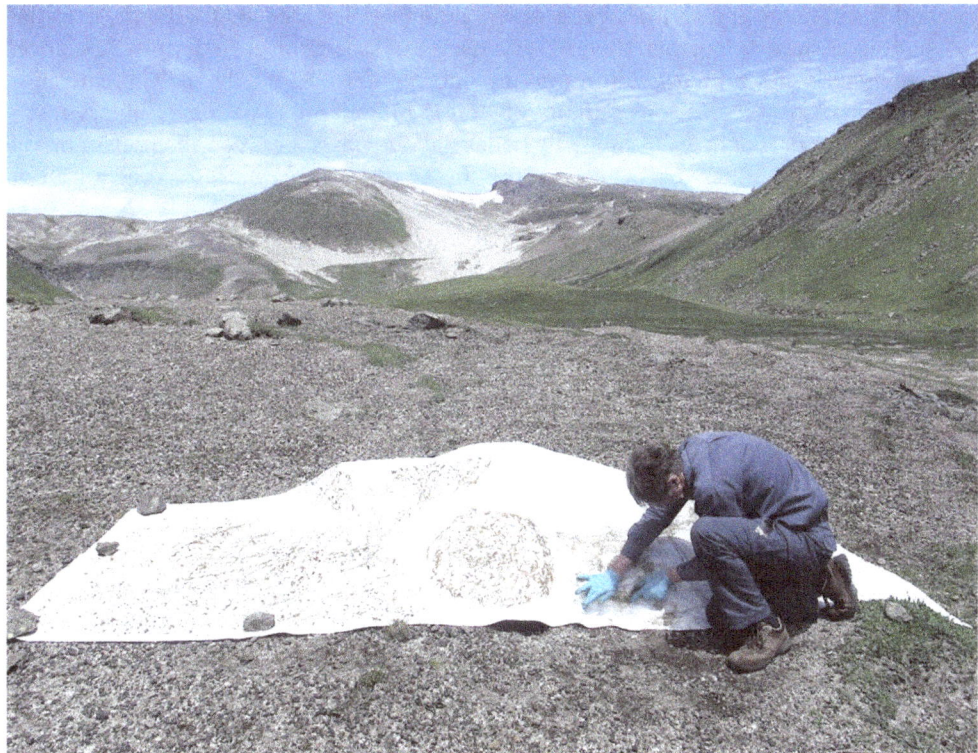

Figure 10.11 Landscape rubbing within China

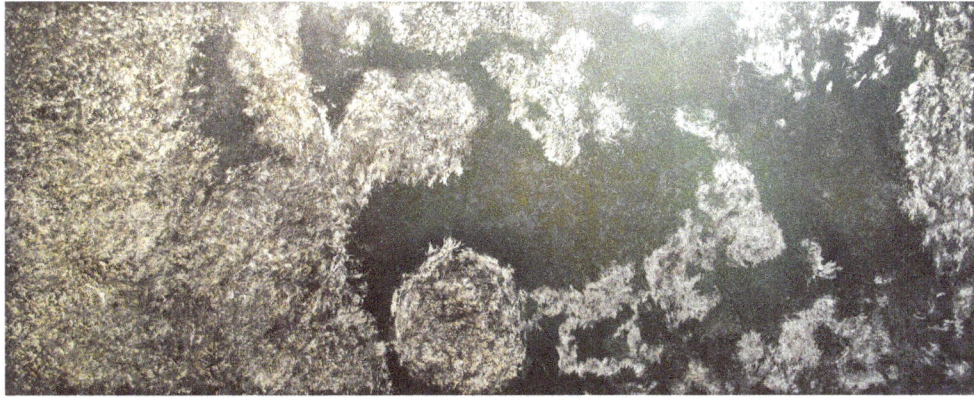

Figure 10.12 Bird's eye view of the earth, showing the 'here and there' nature of camouflage

Camouflage as a performative act in advancing relationships towards productive and mutually beneficial outcomes

Howard argues that while regrettably it is not the norm for artists to work actively and productively in contested landscapes, the very fact that they are contested would suggest that these are the arenas that require examination, evaluation and interpretation resulting in considered expression and communication and further assessment. Equally, cultural policies and institutions regularly neglect areas of 'human experience' that fall outside of the conventions of the arts. Further, there exists a degree of suspicion, even desirable distance, between civilian and military cultures in any one country and finally, more predictably, there is deep suspicion and constraint in relation to bi- and multi-national military institutions forming productive and mutually beneficial outcomes, between themselves or via third parties that is, unless particular defence forces are part of a bloc, forming a pact of strategic cooperation.

Within this sensitive environment, what Howard calls *overt camouflage* is used to negotiate the constraints and restrictions that individual predilections and institutional settings can otherwise dictate. Overt camouflage therefore speaks to the formalisation, the dressing up, of purpose, procedures and intent in producing artworks out of a civilian-military relationship. While conventional camouflage works to conceal, often for *malevolent* reasons, usually through misrepresentation or other artifice, making the significant insignificant, overt camouflage on the other hand reveals through over-representation, making what is insignificant – and therefore more easily dismissible – significant. And as the purpose of this negotiated relationship is for the mutual benefit of each party, the concealment, or rather the indeterminate element – the camouflage, indeed – remains steadfastly *benevolent*. This relationship can be seen in the photograph of the artists, clad in almost identical western civilian suits, at the Military Museum of the Chinese People's Revolution in Beijing in October 2008 (Figure 10.13). Colonel Xing is to the left of picture, his commanding officer, a general, to Howard's right and Jin Hua, translator and now the head of the International Office at the Central Academy of Fine Arts in Beijing, is to his left. The discussion focused on plans for a rubbing of a PLA Air Force Chengdu J-10, which eventually took place three years later.

The logic of exchange here suggests that as Howard has been able to work as an Australian citizen artist within a Chinese military milieu, then Colonel Xing Junqin ought likewise be able to work as a People's Liberation Army military artist within an Australian civilian and military context, and indeed this has taken place with Xing undertaking artist-in-residence programs at the Australian Defence Force Academy in Canberra. During his most recent residency in September 2010, he undertook a major painting that explored the peacekeeping role of the PLA. Central in the completed painting was an image of the recently acquired first aircraft carrier for the PLA Navy. Xing repainted this ship onto a small canvas as a gift for Kevin Rudd, who as Shadow Minister for Foreign Affairs in 2002 had officially opened a Howard/Xing joint exhibition in Sydney. As part of that address, Rudd observed, in English and then Mandarin, according to John McDonald's review of the exhibition: 'that to gain any indication of where post-ideological China is heading, we must look to its emerging art and literature, and its film industry.'

The painting depicts the aircraft carrier, the *Liaoning*, from the waterline to the deck. It is heading directly towards the viewer, the line of the deck exactly matching that of the horizon, the foundational meeting between the sea and sky. This meeting point is inesca-

10 Making visible, changing sides

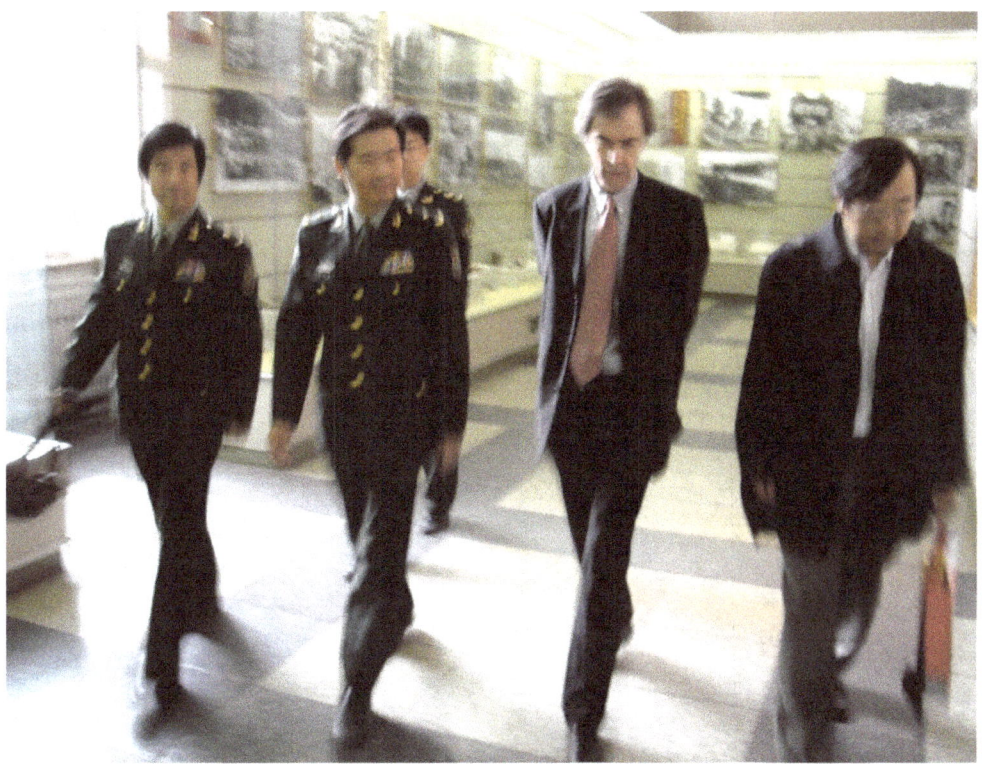

Figure 10.13 Artists at the Military Museum of the Chinese People's Revolution in Beijing in October 2008

pably part of the militarised terrain of national topographies, borders and contact zones as Suvendrini Perera has argued, 'The horizon is simultaneously a threshold and a border. It marks a divide and an illusory, ever-receding point of meeting, and holds possibilities of both promise and threat' (114). There is no superstructure on the ship in Xing's painting, no aircraft on the flight-deck; rather, it carries imagery, painted in a traditional manner, of the picturesque Guilin Mountains, resplendent with waterfall. Decidedly this image is a work of camouflage. The understood, commonplace role of an aircraft carrier is subverted, transformed into an ocean-going, forward-projected emissary of Chinese culture and good will. The offering of the work as a gift takes us back once again to the sense of camouflage as a point of interface or overlap between opposed or differentiated domains, emblematised in the practices of collaboration by artists at the scenes and sites of war. Kevin Rudd accepted the painting during a formal ceremony held at the College of Fine Arts, UNSW, in May 2012 (Figure 10.14). One is unsure as to what degree the ceremony itself was also a work of camouflage. Regardless, Howard and Xing were present (Xing via video), bringing together layers of cultural, technological, institutional and formal governmental connections across nations.

At the ceremony, Xing spoke as follows:

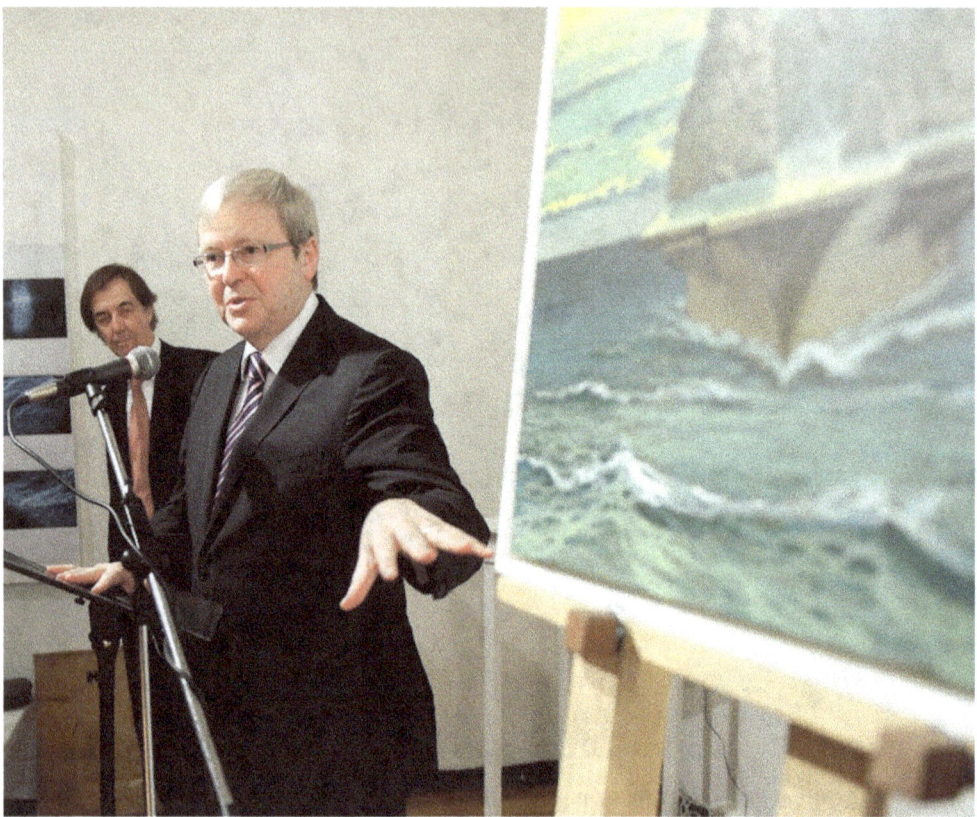

Figure 10.14 Kevin Rudd accepted the painting during a formal ceremony held at the College of Fine Arts, UNSW, in May 2012

I have communicated with Australia for ten years. During this period of time Ian and I worked together on lots of projects. Many joint exhibitions. But what impressed me most was the first exhibition we had. The opening of that exhibition was hosted by Kevin Rudd and he also cut the ribbon for us. His correct Mandarin pronunciation and knowledge about Chinese culture touched me very much. So I came to Australia now again. While I was artist and visiting scholar in residence at the Australian Defence Force Academy, I made a piece of artwork, and would like to send it to you, Kevin Rudd, as a gift. Hoping that Kevin could remain his love about Chinese culture and art, to remember Chinese culture and art.

The artworks of Xing Junqin and Howard constantly make use of and reference camouflage in a range of ways, distracting, highlighting, and *unconcealing* objects and figures. Camouflage is employed to make known their disparate identities, while serving also as a device to bridge cultural divides, and as a tool to explore the nature of global relationships across a worldwide landscape. And finally, within the literal, material space of collaborative art practice, camouflaged behaviour works not simply to deceive and constrain but also to facilitate understanding. This engagement, never utopian, is endlessly hedged about by constraining factors generated by political, geographical, institutional and aesthetic entities. Nonetheless, as camoufleurs, Xing Junqin and Ian Howard have exposed their intentions through art, their desire to talk to the other side.

References

Aravamudan S (2009). Introduction: Perpetual War. *PMLA*. 124 (5): 1505–14.
Behrens R (1980). Camouflage, art and gestalt. *The North American Review*, December: 9–18.
Behrens R (1988). The theories of Abbott H. Thayer: father of camouflage. *Leonardo*, 21(3): 291–96.
Elias A (2011). *Camouflage Australia: art, nature, science and war*. Sydney: Sydney University Press.
Heidegger M (1977). The question concerning technology. In M Heidegger. *The question concerning technology and other essays* (pp. 3–35). Transl. William Lovitt. New York: Garland Publishing.
McDonald J (2002). Painting politics: on the march between two worlds. *The Australian Financial Review*. May 30: 55.
Perera S (2009). *Australia and the insular imagination: beaches, borders, boats, and bodies*. New York: Palgrave Macmillan.
Stein G (1933/1961). *The autobiography of Alice B. Toklas*. New York: Vintage.
Taussig M (2008). Zoology, magic, and surrealism in the war on terror. *Critical Inquiry*, 34(2): S98–S116.

11
Interventions in seeing: surveillance, camouflage and the Cold War camera

Donna West Brett

The Wall, we might conclude, stands not on the outside of the GDR society, but right in its center, and is invisible. It is present, it is felt, but nobody dares describe what they see. They see walls everywhere, but the Wall is not seen. (Koepke 1996, 85)

Ways not to be seen

In his *Denkbild* titled 'Ways not to be seen' the German philosopher Ernst Bloch ruminates on a phenomena that he refers to as 'unseeing'. As an example of how unseeing can take an object below the horizon of perception he recounts a story of the Prussians in Paris in 1871 in search of the *Mona Lisa* painting, which was hidden behind a wall in the Hotel des Invalides by a canny protector. As the spiked helmets burst into the junk room concealing the painting, the soldiers instead found a rare map that satisfied their objective, whereas a few steps away, the *Mona Lisa* remained hidden with her face to the wall, unseen. Bloch considers this strategy of making something unseeable as diverting the covetous gaze from the main objective by satisfying it with something less; the gaze is satiated before it finds its target (Bloch 2006, 82–3).

This concept of unseeing resonates with various strategies of camouflage such as visual deception, concealment, blending or the psychological effect of hiding things in full view. The concept also informs my reading of surveillance photography of the Cold War and the role of the Berlin Wall in defining the scopic realm of the German Democratic Republic (GDR). The following analysis accounts for the photographic restrictions in East Germany, which contributed to an underground of socialist photographers and a heightened state observation culture, resulting in an explosion of surveillance tactics that employed extreme camouflage techniques to ensure their success[1] (Wedler 1962, 100–2). I explore this tendency toward camouflage and surveillance through the work of German contemporary photographer Arwed Messmer who employs the unseen archives of the GDR and the Ministerium für Staatssicherheit, (MfS) (Stasi) to comment on the secrecy of this regime. Messmer's photographic engagement with images from these archives explores issues of

---

[1] Photography of public places was severely limited from 1961 to 1989. A list of restrictions was published in *Die Fotografie* in 1962.

propaganda and concealment in relation to the erection of the Berlin Wall, attempted border breaks and their associated crime-scenes, and brings into view heinous actions of surveillance activities against German citizens. Combined with the relatively unchartered limits on seeing in Germany, both in the national socialist period and the Cold War, the photographic archival projects discussed here take on new meaning and can be read as engaging with a specific photographic seeing, which is to look at looking itself. The analysis of these 'unseen' photographs of the GDR and the Stasi archives engages with Bloch's concept of 'unseeing' as a repression of the visible and investigates the physical and psychological effects of surveillance and camouflage activities in the former GDR.

The Berlin Wall

Photography in Cold War Germany was used as a strategic and political device to analyse activity along both sides of the Berlin Wall, to record attempted escapes and citizens' daily actions in a way that would define and limit what could or could not be seen in East Germany from 1961 to 1989. The Berlin Wall is discussed here specifically in terms of its enabling effect of the extensive surveillance control methods of the GDR government and its secret service agency, and its role as a unique camouflage device. The erection of the Berlin Wall and the ways in which the government controlled the public eye had significant effects on the field of vision and led to a range of Wall-induced pathologies with several sociologists considering the erection of the Wall, and its resultant limits on seeing, as violating expectations of normality. Known as *Die Berliner Mauerkrankheit* (Berlin Wall disease) individuals suffered from depression and other psychological ailments reacting directly to the shock of the Wall's erection.[2] German writer Matthias Flügge describes his experience as a teenager living in East Berlin in the 1960s as being defined by the Wall. 'For me the wall back then was a form of normality. In its omnipresence it was somehow possible to blot it out of our everyday lives for periods, just like the whole of West Berlin' (Gröschner & Messmer 2011, 34). As architectural theorist Neil Leach so aptly describes, 'camouflage refers to both revealing and concealing' (Leach 2006, 244) and the Wall as a visual camouflage device, although physical, psychologically blended into its background.

In the early 1990s, German photographer Arwed Messmer and former East German writer Annett Gröschner were undertaking research in the Militärisches Zwischenarchiv in Potsdam, which housed the archival records from the GDR period, when they came across rolls of exposed and developed 35mm film in a rather ordinary cardboard box. The negatives show the Berlin Wall in the early days of its construction in 1966 when the border troops of the GDR photographed its length from Treptow to Pankow in order to assess areas of weakness. There were also negatives of watchtowers, border guards, surveillance activities and escape attempts taken for the Berlin City Command office. The films had been developed, archived and forgotten.

Several years later Messmer and Gröschner rediscovered the material and they ventured into a project to investigate who took the photographs and why.[3] This research has

---

2 Dr Dietfried Müller-Hegemann noted the impact of the Wall on the psychiatric stability of his patients. See *Die Berliner Mauer-Krankheit zur Soziogenese psychischer Störungen,* Nicolaische Verlagsbuchhandlung, Herford, 1973. See also the work of Polly Feversham, Leo Schmidt and Christine Leuenberger.

11 Interventions in seeing

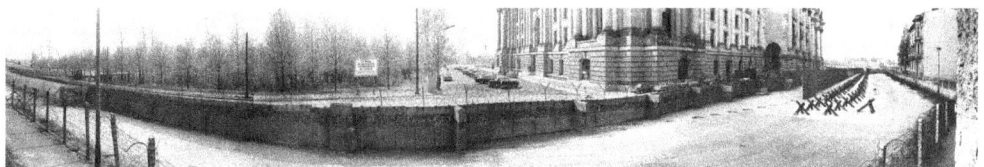

Figure 11.1 [Clara Zetkin-Straße, 9.00 a.m.] Clara-Zetkin-Straße/Ebertstraße. A West Berlin policeman: 'Is it as cold over there as it is over here?' Source: BArch, DVH 60 Bild-GR35-10-020 bis 026; BArch, DVH 60 Bild-GR35-09-069 bis 073/NN/. Interpreted and reconstructed by Arwed Messmer; author Annett Gröschner.

revealed elements of a regime that was consumed with surveillance and camouflage activities and includes incredible stories of escapes from East Germany and of deception, cruelty and death. The cultural impetus to explore such archival material and its concomitant ethical concerns only adds to the complexity of showing and seeing these photographs. Messmer considers that the photographs 'tell us much more about the Berlin Wall than the propaganda photos of both sides that were produced for public consumption at the time' (Gröschner & Messmer 2011, 61). Their determination to reveal these archival photographs provides a nuanced view of the city and its aberrations, but more importantly the images question the cultural, psychological and physical obfuscation of vision and reveal the role of camouflage in the communist regime's surveillance of the GDR.

These images of the Berlin Wall are unique given the rigorous photographic restrictions of the border and public spaces in the GDR. Other than photographs taken in secret by Detlef Matthes (who was imprisoned for several weeks for his actions), very few photographs of the Berlin Wall from the eastern side exist. The photographs are not of the Berlin Wall that we have all come to know from the media, but rather are of a structure in the making, which in 1966 consisted of a border made of ruins, building façades, tangled barbed wire, horizontal concrete strips and heavy timber fences (Figure 11.1). In using existing infrastructure, much of the Wall was camouflaged against a background of extant ruins and industrial wastelands. Erected to stop both the perceived ongoing threat of fascism and to stem the flood of East Germans fleeing to the west, the barrier that was the Wall enclosed the east, erased the west and defined the field of vision for over 40 years.[4] The profound emotive presence of the Wall is in stark contrast to the almost banal archival photographs of grey wastelands emptied of people, and, in their amateur aesthetic, they reveal something of a political mindset in which the gaze was designed to be non-reciprocal.

The panoramic view that Messmer creates from these archival records accounts for the scopic field of 'seeing' with two eyes, reflecting the way in which the body physically and visually encounters the city and references the height parameters of the Wall itself. In reinterpreting this photographic material Messmer reinvigorates a lost pictorial memory of Berlin, shifting its ambivalent nature into the realm of historical significance. Curator

---

3   The project resulted in an exhibition and catalogue titled *The other view: the early Berlin Wall*, 2011. Messmer digitally manipulated the negatives to form 324 panoramic photographs spanning 250 metres accompanied by narrative captions written by Gröschner based on border guard reports.

4   Over four million people left for the west to escape the political and ideological pressures of the Socialist Unity Party of Germany (Sozialistische Einheitspartei Deutschlands, SED) with over 1.35 million East German refugees processed from 1953 to 1990 through the Marienfelde Refugee Centre, Berlin.

Florian Ebner comments in a conversation with Messmer and Gröschner that, although the photographs were taken as evidentiary documentation for the maintenance of the barrier, they have now become 'documents that provide evidence of a regime of surveillance and control, which leads to questions about how to assess them today' (Gröschner & Messmer 2011, 60). They respond with a consideration that frames the photographs in terms of their documentary and evidentiary nature, as dumb witnesses to a provisional state of the Wall in construction by a regime whose gaze was relentless. The project represents an attempt to reconcile a fractured visual field, with artist and author coming from the west and the east, considering that this other view of the Berlin border makes their specific visual image of the Wall complete.[5]

As a concrete manifestation of political and social control the Wall is often represented in the abstract in literature and art; more precisely it is represented by its absence. The Wall, as a representation of state control over what is seen or not seen, found a kinship with literature and in Cold War espionage novels as an acute expression of the global rift between Cold War ideologies and as the epitome of a divided nation. As German literary and cultural theorist Jürgen Kamm considers, given the physical presence of the Wall, it is difficult to account for its startling absence in German literature after 1961. While GDR writers used camouflage tactics in their writing to escape censorship, as did photographers, with the exception of Uwe Johnson, Günter Grass and Gruppe 47, writing about the wall meant embracing the ideological rhetoric of the political adversary (Kamm 1996, 17). Likewise, in many photographs of East Berlin during this period the Wall is made strangely present by its absence. On all levels, in politics and art, the Wall was made invisible and yet it is the Wall that made possible the political mindset of extreme camouflage and surveillance activities on the west and on GDR citizens.

Looking at looking

The physical presence of the Wall contributed to the isolated and contradictory position of impeding vision and being constantly watched. The presence of the border guards and military looking out, the West Germans and Allies looking in, and the invisible Stasi observing everything, compounded both the level of surveillance and the number of photographs taken. As the science and espionage historian Kristie Macrakis writes, in 1978 alone the United States Military Liaison Mission took over 195,000 photographs and over 500,000 infrared photographs in their spying activities against the east (Macrakis 2008, 241).

Along the length of the Wall border guards recorded all activity and carried radios, binoculars, a reconnaissance journal and a 35mm Praktica camera. The military historian Gordon Rottmann notes that the guards photographed everything and everyone on the west side of the border and recorded sightings in their journals. Thousands of photographs were sent every week to the MdI (Ministry of the Interior), and then filed by date and border sector. 'Guards recorded the time and location of sightings, activity, descriptions of persons (uniforms, equipment, organisation), types of military/police vehicles and their bumper numbers, NATO patrol formations, new construction and so on' (Rottmann 2008, 52). Much of this, as Rottmann describes, was intended to be low-level intimidation, with

---

5 The project was funded by the German Federal Cultural Foundation and the Federal Foundation for the Reappraisal of the SED-Dictatorship.

11 Interventions in seeing

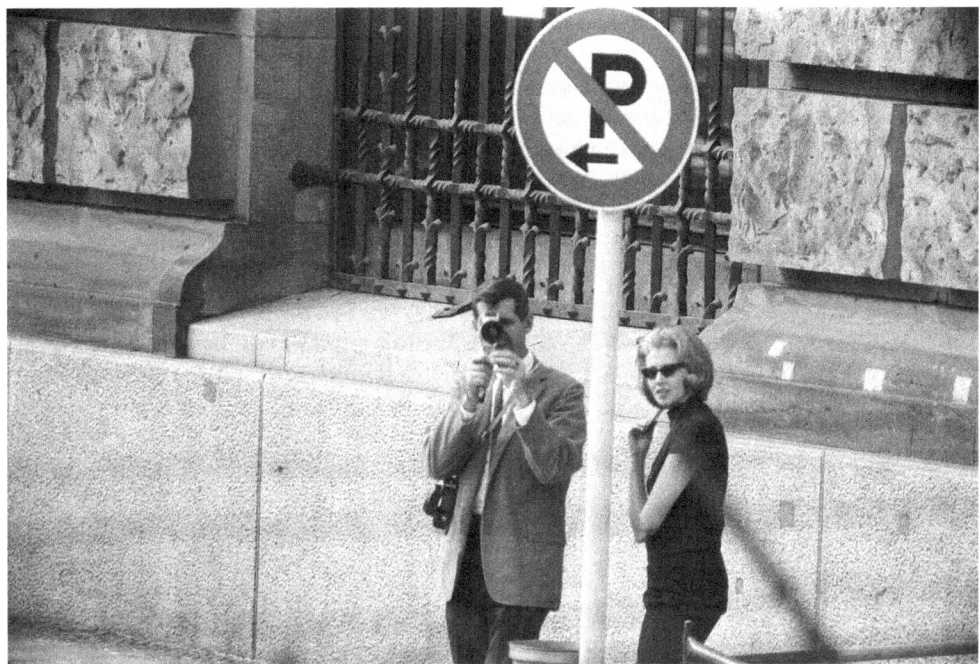

Figure 11.2 BArch, DVH 60 Bild-GR35-10-016 /ohne Angabe. Courtesy Arwed Messmer and the German Federal Archives.

the border guards often pointing the camera toward the west without shooting, and obstructing the view whenever NATO personnel made attempts to photograph them. Despite the distance of the guards from their subjects, the gaze is often returned with alarming effect. The Wall in this case becomes the focus and the site at which the gaze of the west and that of the east meet with the photographs conveying a sense of urgency and a perception of invisibility.

Several such surveillance photographs were taken on the same day by a border guard intent on observing the activities on the western side of the Wall in the vicinity of the Reichstag and the Tiergarten. The Reichstag was located right next to the Wall and after its Baumgarten renovation of the 1960s it reopened in 1971 for special exhibitions, ceremonial events and parliamentary congresses[6] (Foster et al. 2003, 124). Any commotion around the Reichstag created tensions between West and East Berlin and caused a flurry of activity amongst the Allies who are the main subjects of these photographs. Among this odd array of images are two pictures of a couple standing between a building and a street sign intent on photographing the Wall and the border guard in what appears to be a photographic standoff (Figure 11.2). Shot in black and white, the couple posing as tourists are framed to the right of the image with the focal point located somewhere behind them, indicating a hasty photographic opportunity. In the first frame, the woman is looking away but by the time the second image is taken a few seconds later her attention has shifted to-

---

6   In 1961 Paul Baumgarten was commissioned to refurbish the interior of the Reichstag after it had lain in ruin since 1945. It reopened on 21 March 1971.

wards the Wall, while her companion keeps photographing the border guard. The tension between the two photographers on either side of the barrier is palpable, mirroring the tensions between the British and Russian sectors.

The surveillance tactics at the border not only targeted activity to the west but also traversed the no-man's land toward the border on the east, the prime target being attempted escapes by GDR citizens. As one border guard wrote, 'following orders, we concentrated on staring at the hinterland through our binoculars all night, with instructions to open fire if anyone approached the wall without authorisation. That was a relatively rare occurrence, however, for any "border violators" were usually caught back in the hinterland. The surveillance system was so finely graduated that not even a mouse could have crept through' (Gröschner & Messmer 2011, 699). Despite this observation, many barrier breaks were successful as the archives show in photographs of evidence found at the sites: tunnels, tampered-with barbed wire, ladders or belongings left behind in the haste to get over, through or under the Wall. After each attempt of escape a team would arrive to examine the site; *fluchtskizzen* (escape sketches) were made and photographs taken in order to analyse the weakness in the barrier and for evidence of the attempted 'barrier breaks' (Rottmann 2008, 52). The escape sketches provide an overview of the site and details of the route taken, the proximity of watchtowers, guards and other surveillance, and the date and time of the incident. The photographs, however, are quite abstract in their information; often taken at night, they are blurred and grainy and also focus on small details rather than the overview provided by the sketches. Hence, the 'evidence' is photographed in isolation from the crime scene and includes objects such as a blouse, a watch, footprints or a briefcase that lies discarded on a brick-paved path (Figure 11.3). Inside the briefcase are the possessions of its owner who has escaped over the Wall to the west. On the associated sketch an arrow was drawn showing the direction of the escape from the top of the ministry building at the corner of Niederkirchnerstraße across the Wall to land near the corner of Wilhelmstraße on the block of land now hosting the Dokumentationszentrum topographie des terrors, previously the site of the Nazi SS.[7] Here is the story of Günter H. and his parents retold here by Melanie Huber.

Abseiling from the roof of power
Günter H, nine years old, is squatting next to his mother on the roof of the middle building at the House of the Ministries at Leipziger Straße. Günter is tired. It is shortly after midnight, 29 July 1965. The family came up to Berlin from Leipzig early that day. Günter had to spend the whole day with his parents in the House of the Ministries, that enormous building at the border in which his father sometimes has work to do, and where he and his mother were allowed to come along today. Günter has spent the day leafing through books, watching his mother have her hair done, and eating in the canteen. And then he waited through the afternoon and into the night in a small toilet in one of the upper stories.

His father, 34-year-old Heinz H, is standing near the edge of the roof at the rear side of the building complex. He can see the Berlin Wall, and on the other side he can vaguely make out brief bright signals. Heinz knows that they are waiting for them. He puts his hand into his light-brown traveling briefcase, which, as a qualified economist, he always

---

7 The Ministry building was formerly the Third Reich Aviation Ministry and is now the Ministry of Finance.

carries with him when he is on business for his company. Today it contains the entire life of his family on paper: reports and references, tax documents, inoculation certificates, their declaration of quitting church membership, the family tree, party documents. There is also a Pentacon F camera, a blouse, and a skirt. Heinz puts leather gloves on and takes a torch out of the case, with which he flashes signals at the other side of the wall. Then he fixes a nylon rope to the building's flagpole and throws it down across the wall, where it can be attached by helpers on the other side. Then Heinz H can silently slide down an eight-millimeter steel wire using rope clamps. The wind is howling around his ears – it is really too stormy for their attempt tonight. His wife, Jutta H, 32 years old, is preparing the loops of hemp rope that they intend to use to abseil down. Günter is very quiet. Then his father waves him over. He picks Günter up and holds him in his arm. The roof is twenty-five meters above the ground, the steel wire runs at an angle of thirty to forty degrees down into the darkness. Heinz takes one of his leather gloves off so he can hold his son tightly. With his other hand he wraps a loop of rope around the wire and then jumps into the darkness. Now it is his wife's turn. She lifts up her arms to attach her loop to the wire. Her dark gray coat is taut around her chest. She takes it off, picks up the briefcase with one hand, and grabs the rope with the other. As she is sliding down, she drops the briefcase, which falls onto the pavement in front of the wall at Niederkirchnerstraße.

This is what might have happened.

Later two West Berlin policemen will shout over to the border soldiers at Otto-Grotewohl-Straße: 'Throw the bag over!' It is 4 a.m., and the astonished border soldiers are left with only the steel wire, some pieces of hemp, a few tools, one leather glove, a dark gray coat, and the documents in the light-brown traveling briefcase[8] (Gröschner & Messmer 2011, 655).

The story of Günter H. and his parents reads like a 'how to' for camouflage tactics. Günter and his mother Jutta disguise themselves as visitors while they wait for Heinz who blends into his surroundings by conducting usual business activities. They later conceal themselves in the toilets waiting for darkness to come to camouflage their escape. As Leach observes, camouflage 'acts as a device for us to define the self against a given cultural setting through the medium of representation – either by becoming part of that setting, or by distinguishing ourselves from it' (Leach 2006, 244). In turn, surveillance depends on the processes of camouflage, the hidden camera, the disguised observer and the target all playing their roles in a game of tactics.

In developing his enquiry into the GDR archives, Messmer turned to issues related to the psychological space of surveillance photography taken by the Stasi; in particular, photographs of attempted escape re-enactments.[9] As Messmer explained in an interview with the author, when GDR citizens were caught attempting to escape they were often forced to re-enact their attempt for the Stasi record. Part of this re-enactment included cruel psychological torture of exacting detail that was recorded in photographs. In one image a family is shown curled up in the back of a Kapitan car, the parents hugging their small children close to them (Figure 11.4). Having discovered the small group attempting to escape the east by hiding in the boot of the car, the culprits were made to demonstrate their attempt for the photographer, knowing that in doing so they were able to hold their children for the

---

8 Source: BArch, DVH 60-3/19917668.
9 This new series of photographs are drawn from records in the Stasi archive.

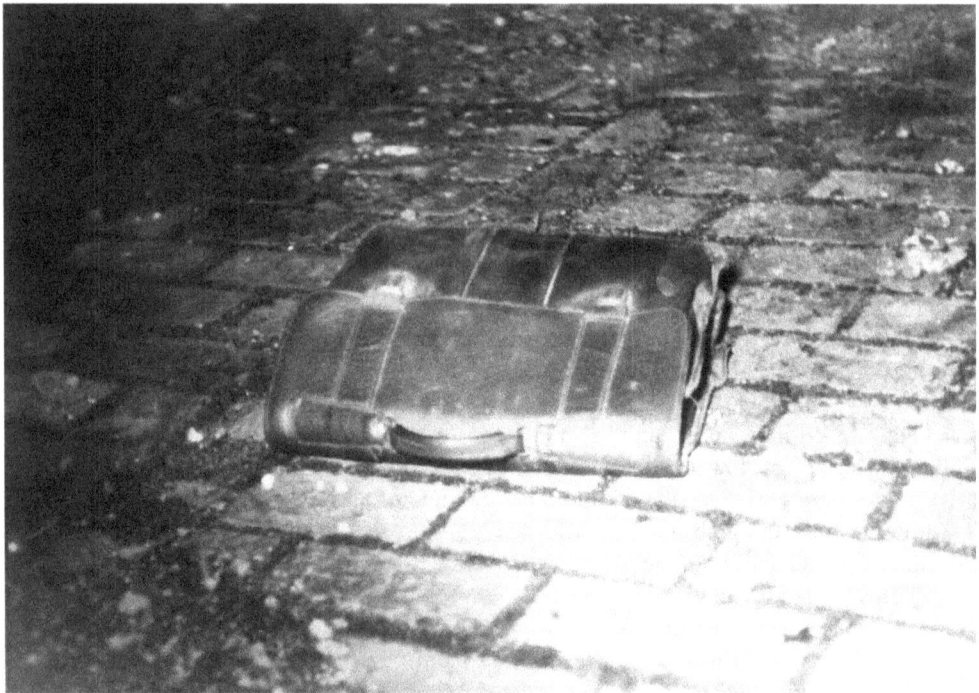

Figure 11.3 BArch, DVH60-3/19917, BI.144.1/ohne Angabe. Courtesy Arwed Messmer and the German Federal Archives.

last time before being taken to prison. As GDR historian Karin Hartewig and others have pointed out, the Stasi were accused of being human traffickers, for such prisoners were often sold to the west for hard currency (Hartewig 2004, 74–5).

In the 1980s there were only eight or so legal exits via road or railway to cross the German border and time after time individuals attempted to escape via land, sea and air; attempts that were often foiled by informers, border troops or friends (Hartewig 2004, 74). Each failed attempt was documented in reports, sketches and in photographs with the events re-enacted in a tableau as if the forced confessions were not enough. Hartewig refers to such 'documentary' photographs of absurd single frames and enigmatic picture stories as both strange and grotesque spectacles (Hartewig 2004, 74).

The Stasi surveillance machine

In addition to escape attempts, the Stasi took photographs of cultural figures, musicians, writers and others suspected of adverse behaviour, and of people's belongings during secret house searches. (Betts 2010, 194) The BStU archives' written and photographic documentation were inseparable with the photographs utilised in interrogations because of their perceived veracity[10] (Macrakis 2008, 228). In the late 1950s the Stasi established the Technical Operations Sector or OTS where they trained their agents in camouflage, microphotography infrared, and surveillance photography (Macrakis 2008, 227). As with

11 Interventions in seeing

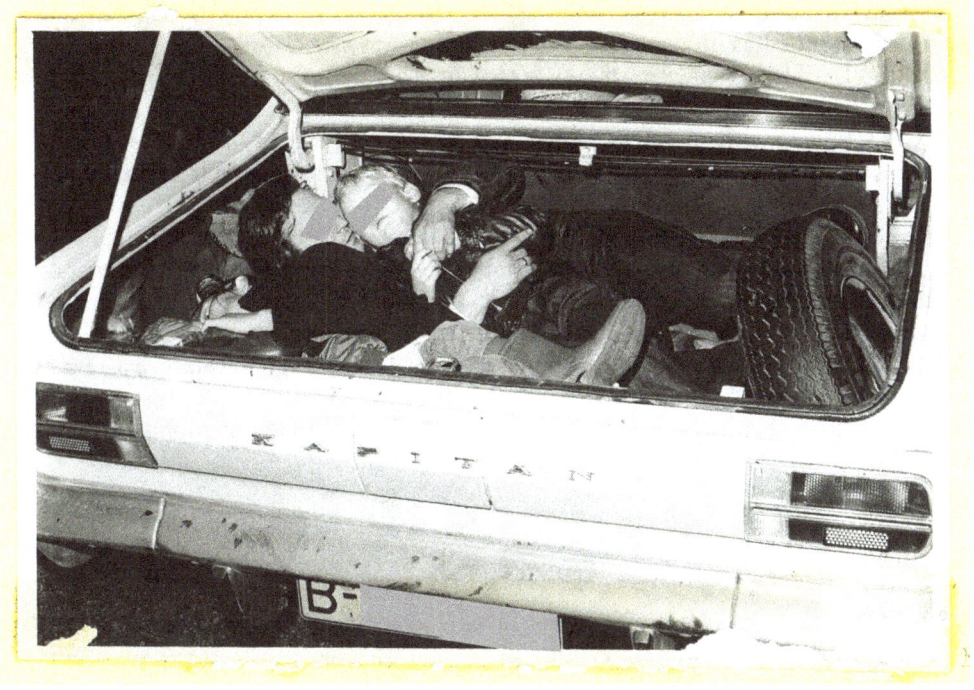

Figure 11.4 MfS-HA-IX-Fo-2180-Blatt-0003. Courtesy Arwed Messmer and BStU.

the border guards, observers were trained at the special observation and photography school where they mastered the theoretical principles and practice of taking effective photographs. In addition, the observation teams learned how to camouflage cameras and themselves by posing as tourists, businessmen or secretaries. Cameras were placed inside refrigerated trucks, in handbags, coats, and money holders, in gloves or inside bras with the shutter release situated in a dress pocket (Macrakis 2008, 226–7). Furthermore, miniature cameras were hidden in flowerpots, watering cans, tree trunks and other containers in order to watch what was known as dead letter drops or to observe individuals' daily activities.[11] Photography was instrumental in recording search operations and officers took four types of images: orientation, overview, focused and detailed. Often using Polaroid cameras, a photograph would be taken of an entire room, followed by cupboards and the placement of objects before the search began. The Polaroids were then used as comparative markers to replace objects in their original positions, while photographs of highly incriminating evidence, such as radios, codes and documents, were taken using larger film cameras (Macrakis 2008, 247).

From 1957 to 1989 Erich Mielke held the then prestigious post of minister for state security in the GDR, heading the infamous organisation of the secret police that at its height had approximately 100,000 employees, equating to one full-time operative for every 165

---

10 Federal Commissioner for the Records of the State Security Service of the Former German Democratic Republic. BStU, VIII, 6677, fol. 107 as quoted in Macrakis.
11 As seen in the Stasi Museum displays, Berlin, October 2013. See also Simon Menner's photographic series *Images from the secret STASI archives*, 2011.

inhabitants. In addition, historian and East German expert David Childs suggests that an estimated ratio of Stasi informers to the population was seven times that of the Gestapo during the Third Reich, equating to an average in 1986 of one informer for every 120 GDR citizens (Childs 1999, 93–4). In his ground-breaking study on East German photography Karl Gernot Kuehn also observes that whether from fear or opportunism, close to one out of every 30 East Germans became informers, many of whom were photographers (Kuehn 1997, 21).

The extent of the surveillance activities of the Stasi is difficult to comprehend however, after the fall of the Wall and with the opening of the archives, the extent of the operations began to become clear. The archives contain over 180 kilometres of documents, including 35.6 million card indexes containing personal details, and hundreds of thousands of photographs, tape recordings and videos (Childs 1999, 104). Although the Stasi's existence was acknowledged in the east, Childs remarks that they were written out of history prior to 1990 and remained largely invisible, their success due largely to highly sophisticated physical and psychological camouflage tactics.

Conclusion

In his short prose, 'Ways not to be seen', Bloch considers that 'unseeing' can be effected very deliberately (Bloch 2006, 82). Although written between 1910 and 1929, his musings on the notion of unseeing could well have been applied to the varying concepts of camouflage such as disguise, hiding in full view, masking and blending. All of these tactics were employed to profound effect by the GDR regime, principally through the erection and maintenance of the Berlin Wall and through the activities of the Stasi. Ironically, it was the building of the Wall that precipitated Bloch's departure from the east to Tübingen in the west, where he and his wife were staying in August 1961 and where he remained until his death in 1977.

As Leach observes, the logic of camouflage is often performative, immaterial or temporal, operating on many levels of masquerade and concealment (Leach 2006, 244–6). Camouflage is also a psychological space that inhabits being and place, infiltrating every level of existence so that the act of camouflage is itself invisible. The various strategies employed by the GDR regime are made evident through the photographs discussed here that present a tension between seeing and not seeing. From the Wall as a camouflage enabler, the disguise tactics of border control, Stasi operatives and informers, to the actions of concealment employed by escaping GDR citizens, it is clear that the processes of camouflage were operating at every level of society in the former East Germany.

In a country in which the memory stakes are high, turning to the archive for alternative narratives is fraught with issues, particularly given the sensitive nature of these images. For Messmer and Gröschner these archival projects offer a means in which to expose the insidious actions of the GDR and the archive itself as yet another form of camouflage and concealment. The banality of the photographs and the affective nature of the subject however, present conflicted readings of the images; the space between the viewer and the subject, creates a distance that like the Wall itself complicates both the act of witnessing and the act of seeing.

The author acknowledges the generosity of Arwed Messmer in assisting with this research.

References

Betts P (2010). *Within walls: private life in the German Democratic Republic*. Oxford: Oxford University Press.
Bloch E (2006). *Traces*. Anthony A Nassar (Trans) Stanford: Stanford University Press.
Childs D (1999). The shadow of the Stasi. In PJ Smith (Ed). *After the Wall: eastern Germany since 1989*. Boulder and Oxford: Westview Press.
Foster N et al. (2003). *The Reichstag Graffiti*. Berlin: jovis Verlag GmbH.
Gröschner A & Messmer A (2011). *The other view: the early Berlin Wall*. Ostfildern: Hatje Cantz Verlag.
Hartewig K (2004). *Das auge der partei: fotografie und staatssicherheit*. Berlin: Ch. Links Verlag.
Kamm J (1996). The Berlin Wall and Cold-War espionage: visions of a divided Germany in the novels of Len Deighton. In E Schürer, M Keune & P Jenkins (Eds). *The Berlin Wall: representations and perspectives*. New York: Peter Lang.
Koepke W (1996). The invisible wall. In E Schürer, M Keune & P Jenkins (Eds). *The Berlin Wall: representations and perspectives*. New York: Peter Lang.
Kuehn KG (1997). *Caught: the art of photography in the German Democratic Republic*. Berkeley: University of California Press.
Leach, N (2006). *Camouflage*. Cambridge MA: MIT Press.
Macrakis K (2008). *Seduced by secrets: inside the Stasi's spy-tech world*. New York: Cambridge University Press.
Rottmann GL (2008). *The Berlin Wall and the inner-German border 1961–89*. Oxford: Osprey Publishing.
Wedler R (1962). Photography prohibitions (or: unlawful photography). *Die Fotografie*, 3:1962. In JP Jacob (Ed) (1998). *Recollecting a culture: photography and the evolution of a socialist aesthetic in East Germany*. Boston: Photographic Resource Center at Boston University, Staatliche Galerie Moritzburg and Halle Landeskunstmuseum Sachsen-Anhalt.

12
Unmasking militarism: hegemony, naturalisation, camouflage

Ben Wadham and Amy Hamilton

The 'coalition of willing' nations have just engaged in the most sustained series of military actions since the Vietnam War. Explicit militarism has become an ever present and daily imposition on Western consciousness: a palpable force, an inescapable presence. Weapons of mass destruction (WMD), the war on terror and operations from Iraq to Afghanistan sit aside global military engagements, conflicts and peacekeeping activities. As this 'coalition' moves out of Afghanistan the war memorial becomes more poignant, particularly as Australia moves to its centenary celebrations of World War I in 2014 extending into 2015. The manner in which war and militarism are represented expresses the logic of global democratic capitalism – the dominating cultural order. This is a militarism designed by particular subjects with particular ends in mind.

Some scholars have described the politics of contemporary war as 'camouflaged politics' (Messerschmidt 2010; Hunt & Rygiel 2006). The War on Terror, or border control measures such as the contemporary *war* on people smugglers entitled Operation Sovereign Borders, are represented in terms of security, the protection of a way of life, the authority of the nation or preservation of national character.

The discourse of militarism that is employed in justifying and rationalising military adventures is established upon a profoundly naturalised set of meanings, concepts and assumptions about the military and its relationship with the state, and its implications for the nation. War is a practice of militarism, and camouflaged politics extends to the militarisation of national identity and the naturalisation of militaries in fraternity with the state.

Despite Western militaries being marred by sex scandals, violence and murder or sexual violation on peacekeeping missions, or at home, they appear remarkably resilient to sustained critique (see Wadham 2013; Razack 2004). Our aim is to begin to decamouflage militarism and its implications in national governance and nationalism. This chapter will take the following form. We begin by developing the notion of camouflage in the context of camouflaged politics – the camouflaged character of war stories and their search for legitimacy. We then use this to describe the ANZAC mythology and then the institutional accounts of military misconduct that have plagued the ADF over its history.

Camouflage, naturalisation, hegemony: distortion

There have been two recent texts on the military, war and war talk published that have actively used the term camouflage. Krista Hunt and Kim Rygiel's *(En)gendering the war on terror: war stories and camouflage politics* bases its intentions upon Miriam Cooke's *Women and the war story*. The intended aim of Hunt and Rygiel is to: 'challenge the officially sanctioned war stories and the politics they camouflage by providing feminist counter-narratives about the war on terror' (2006, 4).

The structure of the war story evolves through familiar dichotomies that work to naturalise and legitimise war and the way in which it is waged. It is this naturalisation that we argue lends this analysis to the concept of camouflage. These authors attempt to decamouflage the social realities of war by unmasking the relations of race, class, sexuality, gender, nationality and religion (Messerschmidt 2010; Sharma 2006; Eisenstein 2006).

In the book *Women and the war story*, Miriam Cooke (1996) explains that wars are conducted and legitimised through the articulation of the war story. Hunt and Rygiel explain:

> The war story gives order to wars … by evoking certain familiar dichotomies ('beginning and ending; foe and friend; aggression and defense; war and peace; front and home; combatant and civilian') as the natural order of things. This 'natural' order of things, however, is a deeply gendered one … (2006, 4)

It is this notion of natural order, or naturalisation, that communicates most forcefully with the notion of camouflage. The military as taken-for-granted reifies militarised national identities camouflaging the social realities of war. This militarism produces an Australian national identity that is seemingly naïve of war, and its violence and hegemony, yet clearly established upon it.

Similarly, criminologist and critical masculinities scholar James Messerschmidt in *Hegemonic masculinities and camouflaged politics: unmasking the bush dynasty and its war against Iraq* sought to uncover the ways in which dominating and hegemonic masculinities are employed by the Bush dynasty in the United States. Messerschmidt implied in the terms 'camouflage' and 'unmasking' that he sought to penetrate the appearances of society and the world that the Bush men gave us through their political rhetoric.

Messerschmidt analysed the Bush war speeches over the 18 years of war on Iraq. He outlined how their dominating masculinities are established through the rhetoric of the 'heroic rescuer' of a feminised Kuwait or the 'heroic succurer' there to protect the feminised American citizenry, against the villainous toxic masculinity of Saddam Hussein' (Schippers 2011, 343). In this sense these concepts and discourses are masks that hide ideological origins and cultural implications.

Both texts provide fascinating insights into the ways that war talk or narratives of war construct naturalised versions of the world, its subjects, its conflicts and its resolution. However, neither develop the notion of camouflage in any incisive manner. Camouflage means simply to hide. How then can a deeper exploration of the history and field of camouflage helps us to more precise about the technologies of war narratives, and the stories of militarism and nationalism?

The aim of this chapter then is to take this idea of the war story as a form of camouflage of the ruling elites in order to legitimise their production and execution of war, and its foundation of militarism.

Camouflage as cultural critique: on the science of doubles

Depending on the source consulted, the French word camoufler means to 'conceal, cover up, disguise', to 'put on makeup', or to 'blow smoke' (to disguise oneself for illicit purposes). It can be traced back to a 16th century French slang word *camouflet* meaning 'a practical joke'. In this initial description we can see that this notion is characterised by a kind of double-play in the construction of meaning. Camouflage is a useful notion in that it shares the dualistic character of the military in many societies, expressing relations of presence and absence. Whatever is camouflaged is present, but its presence is clouded, distorted or blended.

On the one hand militarism is celebrated, through ANZAC Day, the returning troops or the Victoria Cross (VC) winner for example; on the other it is an entirely expected element of national security and home defence – 'How could we not have a military?' In other ways the military is clouded, hidden and peripheral – army bases are closed locations, civilians disappear into the military, military bases have their own police, hospitals, churches and shopping complexes. Military secrets are state secrets, silenced by legislation or protocol as operationally significant or the techniques of warfare. These relations of visibility and invisibility, of presence and absence, are well described by the notion of camouflage (see Wadham & Hamilton 2009).

Militarism is an expression of the relations of dominance. Camouflage is an ensemble of technologies used to maintain that dominance by contributing to the normalisation or the naturalisation of the matter at hand. The social realities of war and militarism are hidden, masked, distorted, represented in particular ways. The narratives of war are represented through rhetorical techniques like the combatant lying in ambush blending into his background, or the geometric dazzle paintwork on the navy warship, distorting its position on the horizon (see Behrens 2002). In this way camouflage is a military technology used in the art of war, but also, and more to our point in this chapter, the art of representation, or the expression of the narrative.

Camouflage subsequently also lends itself to the project of cultural critique that seeks to uncover the ways in which highly reified regimes of meaning and practice generate totalising fictions of the world. These are narratives and representations expressed in global gender, sex, race and class relations (Hunt & Rygiel 2006, 4–5). Camouflage is in the business of doubles. That is, camouflage is inherently structured by processes of foregrounding and backgrounding, making some things visible and others invisible, or in the domain of discourse generating some truths at the expense of others. How representation and perception are distorted, manipulated, engineered to produce particular ways of seeing, hearing or being in the world is particularly important in terms of the construction of nation, and the relations of gender, race and sexuality. Militarism is its medium.

One of the principal doubles in the field of camouflage is the impulse to totality and the production and/or disruption of wholeness. Camouflage is in this sense an instrument of masking – that is, by constructing a series of elements so as to appear as a whole, perception is distorted, distracted or some elements are rendered invisible – it is a process of aggregation (or gestalt) and mimicry. Lacan's explanation relates this to the social theory of identity:

> The effect of mimicry is camouflage ... It is not a question of harmonising with the background, but being against a mottled background, of becoming mottled – exactly like the technique of camouflage practiced in human warfare. (Lacan cited in Bhabha 1994, 121)

As a theoretical notion, however, it opens up the potential of unmasking or de-camouflaging.

Theodor Adorno alerts us to the Western epistemological preoccupation with totality when he declares: 'the whole is false' (1996, 398). In a discursive sense articulated through the politics of identity, the writing and speaking of war as inescapable, or an inevitable consequence of contemporary circumstances, is achieved through a technology of camouflage.

This instrumentalisation of war is achieved by drawing the nation's attention to the whole, and through a sleight of rhetoric distracting our attention from its parts. These are the facts that counter the seamless narratives of military action; for example, there are no weapons of mass destruction, there were no children thrown overboard.

To decamouflage is to, at least in part, acknowledge that the subject does not correspond to the object. The whole is disaggregated and the mask is lifted. It is a strategy to expose mimicry.

The field of camouflage has emerged from the domains of art, science, nature and militarism (Elias 2012; Behrens 2002). Camouflage is not simply 'hiding', it is an ensemble of technologies and strategies employed to hide, distract, distort, subsume or blend. Our intention is begin to articulate their discursive expressions through the articulations of language and identity.

This can also be further developed through semiotics, through notions of mimesis, metonymy or synecdoche – technologies of representation and meaning-making that establish particular cultural rules to the constructions of truth regimes or versions of reality. The field of biology, for example, has alerted us to the technologies of the natural world that has informed the development of military camouflage. For example, camouflage is the disruption or reification of that whole through the distortion of the elements of a totality, what has become known as dazzle, or through the subsumption of difference into the totality, what is known as blending, or the development of selective attention – countershading.

In the field of criminology the question of accounts of violence or criminality has generated a field of endeavour looking at how 'delinquents' or 'deviants' legitimise their behaviour. Sociologists Sykes and Matza (1957), developing the idea that crime was learned in social contexts as opposed to being 'devils of the mind or stigmas of the body', studied the 'deviant's' *techniques of neutralisation*. These are the ways in which the transgressor uses discursive tricks to generate a subject position that absolves their responsibility, distracts our attention from their responsibility or hides their culpability.

The following discussion will look at narratives of the ANZAC cult and military misconduct as a means of explicating the discursive technologies of camouflage.

Nation: the ANZAC myth

Militaries are highly naturalised institutions but they are not universally accepted. Elements of populations support the military and other elements resist and reject the institution and its premise. Nonetheless, the doxa (Bourdieu & Eagleton 1994:268) of militaries is one of an honourable, professional, upstanding and dutiful institution that propagates and cultivates the national character and its core values. In this sense camouflage does not only extend to war stories and the legitimisation of state violence but also the place of militarism within the domestic realm. What has become referred to as the ANZAC mythology is a clear expression of the link between the domain of war and the cultivation of the national character in the domestic realm. In this context the notion of mythology adopts the technologies of camouflage (see Barthes, 1972). How does this mythology sustain the dominance of militarism in our national identity?

One example of the way camouflage perpetuates our misrecognition of the social reality of the military is evident through the ANZAC folklore. The ANZAC has over time represented the Australian soldier and his place in combat through the tropes of courage, sacrifice and mateship. The ANZAC figure was forged on the beaches of Gallipoli and has come to represent a national identity and way of life. This is well described by leading war historian Peter Stanley who explains that the Gallipoli campaign:

> occupies a central place in Australia's national mythology, identity and memory, the landing on the peninsula has been portrayed by commentators across the political spectrum as representing the place and time when Australia became a nation. (Stanley cited in Gare & Ritter 2008, 311)

ANZAC has truly become such a powerful mythology that it is rarely questioned and, when it is, it is considered treasonous.

Former Prime Minister Paul Keating was willing to question this mythology, describing the campaign as a farce, and its correspondence to the birth of nation as preposterous:

> Dragged into service by the imperial government in an ill-conceived and poorly executed campaign, we were cut to ribbons and dispatched – and none of it in the defence of Australia. [That] the nation was born again or even was redeemed is an utter and complete nonsense. (Salusinszky 2008)

The ideal of a nation-defining moment portrayed in glorifying terms masks a campaign that was a debacle, where the British command sent our men out to slaughter.

Roland Barthes elucidates the ways that myths naturalise but also the means by which they use technologies of deception, or camouflage, to represent particular stories as real and enduring. In terms of the ANZAC mythology:

> a conjuring trick has taken place; it has turned reality outside, it has emptied it of history and has filled it with nature, it has removed from things their human meaning so as to make them signify human insignificance. The function of myth is to empty reality: it is, literally, a ceaseless flowing out, a haemorrhage, or perhaps an evaporation, in short a perceptible absence. (Barthes 1972, 142)

The mythology of the ANZAC uses dazzle camouflage, the story is not entirely emptied of history but the history is recast in different dimensions that distort the view of this event on a timeless horizon. The significance of the senseless slaughter of Australian men at the behest of a feckless British command is founded upon an imperial illusion of the nation as a man, built upon manhood, and war as warding away the effeminacy of a nation devoid of trials by fire and blood.

Camouflage, developed in this way, is a tool of critical theory and/or deconstruction. Camouflage is principally about generating misrecognition. Misrecognition or more specifically meconnaissance is a notion that Bourdieu (1977, 6) uses to describe the ways social realities are concealed or masked. Mahar, Harker and Wilkes explain:

> participants do not conceal a practice by dressing it up as something else (in the sense of disguising it), but rather render it invisible through a displacement of understanding and a reconstrual as part of other aspects of the habitus 'that go without saying'. (1990,19)

This is a reference to a process of naturalisation or what Eng (2000) as an envoy of the anti-essentialist cultural turn describes in terms of essentialism: the rendering of something as taken-for-granted, natural, or without alternative.

Consequently, there is no alternative for the acolyte of the cult of ANZAC:

> There is no place in the Anzac legend for any deviation from the image of the resolute, heroic digger. Bean does not mention the deserters, the men with VD and those sent home in disgrace. Nor does he refer to the numbers of men who returned home and shot themselves with their service revolvers. The myth must endure at all costs. (Bantick, cited in Nicoll 2001, 16)

The ANZAC character and all he has come to represent is only seen in triumphant terms, occluding the horror and grief and eliding the cultural specificity of a principally white and masculinist ideal of the Australian nation.

Militarism: a few bad apples?

The mythology of ANZAC is nested within a mythology of militarism – a mythology that only represents the military in positive terms. Australia's military, the Australian Defence Force (ADF), presents itself as an expression of the nation and its national character – it is everything Australian. Literally, the institution is 87 percent men, and most of them are of Anglo descent. Despite the culturally specific character of the institution and its cultural practices – authoritarian, hierarchical and regimented, the antithesis of liberal society – the ADF leadership and defence establishment presents itself in highly normalised fashion as a liberal democratic, culturally inclusive organisation.

However, over its history the institution has been marred by various scandals which have been governed through inquiries; all of which centred around the governing of masculinities – that is, the practices of men in fraternities. The series of scandals seem to be endless, yet they are also always forgotten – until the recent Skype affair at least.

Bastardisation, rituals of fraternity, racism and racist sects, alcohol and drug abuse in groups, and sex scandals against their female colleagues mark a history of military masculinities working for the purpose of self-identification and territorial identities. The orthodox representation of the military is an acultural institution, its role, function and place in Australia entirely taken-for-granted. This discussion looks at the forms of camouflage the institution adopts in order to maintain its highly naturalised state.

When the military 'messes up', that highly naturalised profile is decamouflaged. The most recent example of this is the 2011 Skype incident. In April 2011, the 'ADFA Skype Affair' generated widespread public concern. A male Australian Defence Force Academy (ADFA) army cadet broadcast himself having (consensual) sex with a female RAAF cadet to six of his peers in an adjacent room. Still shots were taken and distributed among other cadets. The female cadet became aware of the incident after the fact. The 'question of culture' once again was the focus of the public discourse, with commentators arguing over the structured or the aberrant character of such incidents. The question of culture refers to the question as to whether such incidents are an artefact of military culture or are aberrations by a few individuals.

Despite the implication of the institution in this act of sexual predation, the ADF command was horrified. However, it remained the act of a few young, misguided newly recruited cadets, as one former Chief of Army, General Peter Leahy, explained:

> Members of the press and other commentators should reconsider their unwarranted insinuation that this is 'defence culture'. The seven individuals involved have been at ADFA for barely two months.[1] You don't learn this sort of culture in that period of time. You bring it with you from your home, your school and the community. Australia as a whole is struggling with actions such as sexting, binge drinking and a general loss of the meaning of privacy, not just ADFA. (Leahy 2011)

For the ADF command, and the defence establishment more broadly, this was not an expression of military or organisational culture; indeed it was anathema to the core values of this proud national institution. In this rhetorical sweep, the predatory and criminal acts of these young men upon this unsuspecting woman were naturalised, blended into the fabric of broader society: camouflaged.

However, the act was an act of military performativity – an expression of the clumsy attempt to perform military fraternity. The act of becoming a soldier requires the violent demarcation from the previous life as a civilian. Moore explains the process of resocialisation:

> The objective is to purge the recruit's civil identity, including any preconceptions he may hold about his rights and personal freedoms, and supplant the civilian value system with that of the military. This is accomplished by various methods, including denigrating those outside the military system and at the same time stressing the virtues of military community; it is in effect a transformational approach where the recruit self-actualises the desire to become part of the military. (Moore 2009, 75)

The rebuilding occurs within a discourse of digger nationalism (Nicoll 2001), the embellished ANZAC mythology, a white, masculinist, aggressively heteronormative culture in

---

1 It was ten weeks in fact. This is two weeks shy of the 12-week recruit training at Kapooka. It is the time frame in which one is turned from a civilian to a soldier.

which men are the sole progenitors of national virility. Women, and others, are the intermediaries of their fratriarchal bonds.

The ADF, however, did not, and given its institutional identity, role, need and function could not, describe itself in such terms. To do so would be to decamouflage itself and render itself impotent. Military effectiveness would be named and to be named is to be exposed. The cultural reality of the institution must remain masked in order to retain its cultural puissance. The institutional accounts then become strategies of mimicry and camouflage.

Military media accounts of military misconduct have persistently argued that masculine predation is an aberration. If the organisation has a few 'bad apples', then it follows that the organisation is like any other: universities, football clubs or other similar collectivities. This is the technique of normalisation – a strategy of mimicry.

Homi Bhabha (1994) explains mimicry in terms of colonial–colonised relations. I argue that this can be used to explain civil–military relations, a set of relations where the state and military operate as distinct fraternities of men articulating the national interest using a feminised civil society as their intermediary. The military must mimic civil society – the community that it serves – in terms of values, norms and culture. Yet it is profoundly distinct – authoritarian, almost exclusively male, hegemonically masculine, white, nationalist and heteronormative. The military is a wolf in sheep's clothing, or a snake in the grass who speaks with 'a tongue that is forked', and produces a mimetic representation that 'emerges as one of the most elusive and effective strategies of [military] power and knowledge' (Bhabha 1994, 122).

This normalising discourse completely misses the highly gendered character of such institutions, as one example. Consequently, all organisations, not just the military are also marked by the poor conduct of selected individuals - this strategy of minimisation diffuses the culpability of the ADF. It follows then that the ADF is a predominantly honourable institution made up of hardworking, honourable individuals. This is the dazzle technique of glorification. And those that make wicked insinuations of a sick culture have an agenda, a grudge to bear or are generating a media moral panic. The critic is subsequently condemned and conceived as having an equally totalising notion of culture, but in this case a negative one. This is the technique of malignment or what Sykes and Matza (1957) describe as condemnation of the condemners: those that condemn the act or behaviours are condemned as hypocrites or holier than thou. The perpetrator may draw attention to the behaviour of the accusers and argue that their behaviour is similarly bad or worse; for example, all Australians are sexting, binging voyeurs (1957, 668).

These forms of camouflage are further elucidated in other forms of sociological theory, or the sociology of deviance. For example, Stanley Cohen (2001) describes three main ways in which organisations attempt to deny reality: outright denial (ADF members do not engage in misconduct); interpretive denial, in which raw facts are conceded but the meaning is disputed, often by renaming (a few bad apples); and justification: what has happened is necessary, justified by some higher purpose (soldiers are likely to be bad, or don't expect them to be 'goody two-shoes' – war is hell, or despite the WMD being a lie, it served the purpose of securing US interests).

These are strategies of camouflage, and they are evident in the ways in which war stories are represented. In a cultural sense, the discursive, identitary and truth regime implications of these governing elite and institutional accounts of cultural identity and cultural practice are informed by the study of the field of camouflage. They are also the practices of meconnaissance – a wilful or profoundly habituated disposition that refuses to acknowledge the source of its cultural dilemmas. The culture of the ADF is rendered invisible.

These techniques of neutralisation are an act of cultural prestidigitation. The sleight of logic results in the camouflage of the principal matter – the analysis of military culture. Our thoughts are led astray, our focus directed to broader society, to other institutions, to the aberrant individual, to places other than the military institution. As a result the broader public discourse falls for the illusion, trapped within the dialectic of all or nothing and its related oppositions, complacent in the mimicry that the military is just like broader society.

Conclusion

War and militarism are foundationally violent practices. War is organised violence, legitimised in relationship with the state and justified as protection of the people, or the nation. In the narratives and accounts that justify war, military action or the production and maintenance of a military, militarisation and the cultural specificity of the institution and its agents are naturalised. To render them in relief to their cultural circumstances would be to neutralise them, weaken their potency and undermine their authority.

The implications of war, militarism and state–military relations are authoritarianism and violence. The institutions, agencies, practices and cultural forms that sustain, and that are sustained by, militarism are culturally specific and exclusive, generating circumstances that maintain certain forms of racialised, gendered and sexualised subjects as dominant. Militarism and militarisation are instruments or forms of dominance and domination.

In order to maintain these positions, and relations of dominance, the institution and its actors must remain unquestioned and unquestionable – either because they are so heavily naturalised or they have the power or discursive or material force to resist questioning. Militaries and militarism are camouflaged, sustained through mythologies, of nation or protection of a way of life, or tropes of honour, duty, sacrifice and the national character. Moreover, the highly specific racial, gendered and sexualised expressions of those cultural forms must be invisible, naturalised so that they cannot be questioned as serving the interests of the few at the cost of the many.

Camouflage in this sense is a means of hiding but understanding it is a means of seeing. Eve Kosofsky Sedgwick (1985) explains that cultural critique, what we have expressed through the notion of cultural camouflage, diminishes cultural scotoma, and liberates cultural sight. It is:

> as in one of those trick rooms where water appears to run uphill and little children look taller than their parents, it is only when viewed from one vantage point in any society that sexuality, gender roles, and power domination can seem to line up in [a] perfect chain of echoic meaning. From an even slightly more eccentric or disempowered perspective, the displacements and discontinuities of the signifying chain come to seem increasingly definitive. (1985, 8)

Bringing the study of camouflage to cultural practice – at the site of discourse – contributes the suite of physical camouflage technologies to meaning making and representation.

Blending, dazzle or distortion are also adopted as technologies of representation working to shape cultural narratives through concealment, glorification or misrepresentation. Camouflage exposes the doubleness of cultural life where the impulse of domination is a rapacious singularity.

References

Adorno, T (1996). *Negative dialectics.* London: Routledge.
Barthes R (1972). *Mythologies.* New York: Hill and Wang.
Behrens R (2002). *False colors: art design and modern camouflage.* USA: Bobolink Books.
Bhabha H (1994). *The location of culture*, London: Routledge.
Bourdieu P (1977). *Outline of a theory of practice* (Vol. 16). Cambridge: Cambridge University Press.
Bourdieu P & Eagleton T (1994). Doxa and common life: an interview. In S Zizek (Ed). *Mapping ideology* (pp 265–277). London: Verso.
Cohen S (2001). *States of denial: knowing about atrocities and suffering.* Cambridge: Polity.
Cooke M (1996). *Women and the war story.* Berkeley: University of California Press.
Eisenstein Z (2006). Is 'W' for Women? In K Hunt & K Rygiel (Eds). *(En)gendering the war on terror: war stories and camouflaged politics* (pp 191–200). Aldershot: Ashgate.
Elias A (2012). *Camouflage Australia: art nature science and war.* Sydney: Sydney University Press.
Eng I (2000). Identity blues. In P. Gilroy, L. Grossberg & A. McRobbie (Eds). *Without guarantees: in honour of Stuart Hall* (pp 1–13). London: Verso.
Gare D & Ritter D (2008). *Making Australian history.* Melbourne: Thomson.
Harker R, Mahar C & Wilkes C (1990). *An introduction to the work of Pierre Bourdieu: the practice of theory.* London: Macmillan.
Hunt K & Rygiel K (2006). *(En)gendering the war on terror: war stories and camouflaged politics.* Ashgate: Aldershot.
Kosofsky Sedgwick E (1985). *Between men: English literature and male homosocial desire.* New York: Columbia University Press.
Leahy P (2011). *Get facts on scandal before firing begins.* https://au.news.yahoo.com/thewest/news/a/10805648/get-facts-on-scandal-before-firing-begins/. Accessed 21 May 2014.
Messerschmidt J (2010). *Hegemonic masculinities and camouflaged politics: unmasking the Bush dynasty and its war against Iraq.* Boulder: Paradigm.
Moore D (2009). *The soldier: history of courage, sacrifice and brotherhood.* NSW: Icon Books.
Nicoll F (2001). *From diggers to drag queens: configurations of Australian national identity.* Annandale: Pluto Press.
Razack SH (2004). *Dark threats and white knights: the Somalia affair, peacekeeping and the new imperialism.* London: University of Toronto Press.
Salusinszky I (2008). Keating rejects Gallipoli identity. *The Australian* October 31 [Online] Available: http://www.theaustralian.com.au/arts/books/keating-rejects-gallipoli-identity/story-e6frg8nf-1111117906152 [Accessed 21 May 2014].
Schippers M (2011). Review: Hegemonic masculinities and camouflaged politics by James Messerschmidt. *American Journal of Sociology,* 117(1): 342–344.
Sharma N (2006). White nationalism, illegality and imperialism: border controls as ideology. In K. Hunt & K Rygiel (Eds). *(En)gendering the war on terror: war stories and camouflaged politics* (pp 121–143) Aldershot: Aldgate.
Sykes GM & Matza D (1957). Techniques of neutralization: a theory of delinquency. *American Sociological Review,* 22(6): 664–70.
Wadham B (2013). Brotherhood: homosociality, totality and military subjectivity. *Australian Feminist Studies,* 28(76): 212–35.

Wadham B & Hamilton A (2009). Camouflage: how visual arts and sociology make sense of the military. *TASA Conference Proceedings,* Canberra: ANU.

13
Of mimicry and hipsters

Hsuan Hsu

'Of mimicry and man', Homi Bhabha's influential analysis of the contradictory role of mimicry in colonial discourse, established assimilative performance as a key strategic tool in the repertoire of subaltern cultural production. Along with theories of African American 'signifyin(g)', Asian American 'double agency', Native American trickster figures, gender performativity and queer 'disidentifications', mimicry promised to be an effective weapon of the weak – a surreptitious mode of satirising, critiquing, and reforming the discourses of power (Gates 1988, Chen 2005, Reesman 2001, Butler 1990, Muñoz 1999). While studies of colonial and ethnic mimicry have demonstrated the potential of camouflage as a vehicle for critiquing conventional racial and gender stereotypes, they've had less to say about the growing influence of liberal multiculturalism and 'post-racial' racism.[1] How has the social force of racial stereotypes shifted under contemporary conditions, when economic development consultants like Richard Florida tout multicultural diversity as a wellspring of creative capital and economic growth? The fact that much of the scholarship on mimicry was contemporaneous with discourses of liberal multiculturalism suggests that mimicry's subversive critique of biological and cultural racism may unwittingly serve to draw attention *away* from modes of racism grounded in structural violence rather than in the field of representation. Nevertheless, mimicry continues to play a key role in representing, appropriating and displacing persons and communities of colour as corporations and real estate developers capitalise on the surprising market appeal of qualities such as diversity, irony, and even depersonalisation.

According to Bhabha, the ambivalence at the heart of colonial mimicry is that, in demanding 'a subject of a difference that is almost the same, but not quite', colonial discourse 'must continually produce its slippage, its excess, its difference' (Bhabha 1994, 86). In a process of 'double articulation', mimicry simultaneously imposes cultural norms on colonial subjects and proliferates intentional and unintentional slippages that '[pose] an immanent threat to both "normalized" knowledges and disciplinary powers' (86). In the context of colonial discourse, mimicry is a tactical response to pressures of assimilation: mimics perform metropolitan conventions in partial, subversive ways. But what is the function of mimicry when the hegemonic discourse is not one of racial and civilisational

---

[1] On multiculturalism, see Melamed (2006), Fish (1997), and Lee (2004); on "post-race" racism, see Bonilla-Silva (2009) and Wise (2010).

hierarchy, but a liberal multiculturalism that values tolerance and turns diversity to profit? If, quoting Bhabha, 'the effect of mimicry on the authority of colonial discourse is profound and disturbing' (92), isn't the effect of mimicry on the authority of multicultural discourse profoundly affirming?

Addressing these questions requires a consideration of mimicry performed by the culturally privileged, rather than the culturally marginalised. There are countless examples of mimicry conducted from the centre, bristling with hypocrisy, exploitation, and hate: for example, 'playing Indian', blackface minstrelsy, CIA counterinsurgency practices, and camouflage marketing techniques like Starbucks Coffee's recent efforts to disguise new shops as local, independent cafes (Deloria 1999). Rather than catalogue such practices, however, this chapter will focus on one of the most widespread, contradictory and underexamined[2] instances of mimicry from above: *white mimics*. To understand white subjects who blend with relatively disempowered groups, we must shift our attention from spaces of colonial assimilation to the multiracial contexts of Western metropolitan centres, and from colonial subjects to hipsters. Drawing on the fields of race theory, cultural geography, and urban studies, I argue that hipsterism contributes to what Henri Lefebvre calls the 'production of space', as its emergent spatial practices (squat farming, biking, reinhabiting old warehouses) produce new perceptions of value in disinvested urban neighbourhoods.

White mimics

Rather than defining hipsters and mimics outright, I will consider a range of contexts and meanings for each term, stressing their points of intersection. Hipsterism, for example, has been described as a contact zone between white and black Americans, as a subculture whose members reject (or pretend to reject) mainstream fashions and media, and as an early wave of bohemian gentrifiers. Mimicry can be physical or psychological, tactical or sincere, subversive or appropriative. As Roy Behrens explains, camouflage can function through high similarity (imitating an object or background) or high contrast (using dazzle patterns to disrupt the visual field) – in hipster terms, we might consider a bar that occupies and resembles a warehouse to be an instance of similarity, and an outfit of clashing colours to be a case of contrast. Hipster practices of camouflage fall into three categories: young white people appropriating cultural objects frequently associated with people of colour; nostalgic appropriations of the signs of working class whiteness in post-industrial contexts; and a more abstract practice of self-deprecation associated with psychasthenia, environmental blending, and flat affect. The first part of this essay will consider how hipsterism functions as a practice of top-down assimilation or white mimicry, in which privileged, mobile whites appropriate a range of cultural signs from other groups in order to construct a sense of identity.

The earliest extensive analysis of white mimics who value and assimilate aspects of racial 'others' is Norman Mailer's controversial 1957 essay 'The white negro.' Mailer frames the hipster as an 'American existentialist' reacting to the awareness of mortality brought on by the atom bomb, concentration camps, and the 'slow death by conformity' he associates with post-World War II society (277). The hipster is the person who, under such

---

2 Bhabha's formulation – 'almost the same, but not white' – describes a context in which whiteness is always the target of mimicry, not its performer (86).

circumstances, chooses 'to live with death as immediate danger, to divorce [him]self from society, to exist without roots' (277). Mailer identifies African Americans as a central precursor and influence for hipsters choosing to live perilous, socially marginalised lives: 'the source of Hip is the Negro for he has been living on the margin between totalitarianism and democracy for two centuries' (278). Although Mailer's characterisation of 'the Negro' reductively equates blacks with danger, insecurity, physicality, jazz, lust, and the 'art of the primitive', Mailer deploys the term 'Negro' more as a projection of white anxieties than as a description of actual African Americans (279). He argues that blacks provided a cultural lexicon for whites who refused Cold War conformity: 'So there was a new breed of adventurers, urban adventurers who drifted out at night looking for action with a black man's code to fit their facts. The hipster had absorbed the existentialist synapses of the Negro, and for practical purposes could be considered a white Negro' (279).

In addition to describing hipsters as whites who mimic 'the Negro', Mailer describes the language and lived experience of the Hip as a continuous practice of blending in. Commenting on hipsters' affinity for 'words like go, and make it, and with it, and swing', Mailer describes Hip sociality as a form of intersubjective and environmental blending:

> to swing is to communicate, is to convey the rhythms of one's own being to a lover, a friend, or an audience, and – equally necessary – be able to feel the rhythms of their response. To swing with the rhythms of another is to enrich oneself – the conception of the learning process as dug by Hip is that one cannot really learn until one contains within oneself the implicit rhythm of the subject or the person. (286)

To illustrate this practice of black mimicry in action, Mailer introduces an anecdote about an overheard conversation between 'a Negro friend' and a young white woman:

> The Negro literally could not read or write, but he had an extraordinary ear and a fine sense of *mimicry*. So as the girl spoke, he would detect the particular formal uncertainties in her argument, and in a pleasant (if slightly Southern) English accent, he would respond to one or another facet of her doubts. When she would finish what she felt was a particularly well-articulated idea, he would smile privately and say, 'other-direction ... do you really believe in that?'
>
> 'Well ... No', the girl would stammer, 'now that you get down to it, there is something disgusting about it to me,' and she would be off again for five more minutes.
>
> Of course the Negro was not learning anything about the merits and demerits of the argument, but he was learning a great deal about a type of girl he had never met before, and that was what he wanted. (286–7)

Mailer's argument comes full circle here: what hipsters mimic about blacks is their capacity for mimicry – a capacity conditioned by centuries of social marginalisation and reduced access to literacy, education, and legal protections. While this passage reiterates stereotypes associating blacks with illiteracy, mimicry, and an inability to follow arguments, as a description of Hip philosophy it captures the importance of blending into the rhythms of a conversation, a social environment, and an interpersonal mood. This practice of 'swinging' helps explain why, in a society that overvalues individual achievement and holds individuals responsible for socially conditioned actions, hipsters are keenly aware of social context: 'Hip sees the context as generally dominating the man, dominating him because his character is less significant than the context in which he must function. [M]an is then not only his character but his context' (289). To the extent that hipsters view persons as products of their context, their understanding of character is profoundly attuned to the art of contextual blending and manipulation – that is, of mimicry.

Almost half a century after Mailer's essay, a new hipster subculture emerged in deindustrialised, lower-rent neighbourhoods in North American cities such as Brooklyn, Toronto, Seattle, Austin, Los Angeles, Oakland and Pittsburgh. In his contribution to the collection *What was the hipster? A sociological investigation* (2010b), Mark Greif traces this hipster efflorescence to 1999, and contextualises it amid hipster literature and film, the influences of punk and DIY culture, a sense of disillusionment with overt politics following the 1999 WTO protests, 'new zones of white recolonization of ethnic neighbourhoods', and new forms of online consumption. Whereas hipsters of the Beat Generation fetishised black culture, Greif argues that hipsters since 1999 fixate on:

> an only partly nostalgic suburban *whiteness*, the 1970s culture of white flight from the cities to the suburbs, of the so-called 'unmeltable ethnics', Irish, Italian, Polish, and so forth ... recolonizing urban neighborhoods with a new aesthetic. As the 'White Negro' had once fetishized blackness, the 'white hipster' fetishized the violence, instinctiveness, and rebelliousness of lower-middle-class suburban or country whites.' (Greif 2010b, 10)

Christian Lorentzen adds that 'hipsters, mostly white (the pastiest of whites), prided themselves on having ethnic friends, that they considered themselves "post-racial," and that when they told racist jokes they were being post-racist' (2010, 19). In the context of multiculturalism and 'post-racist' discourse, hipsters embrace whiteness as one ethnicity among others: to construct, perform, and consume working-class whiteness, hipsters sport 'trucker hats; the aesthetic of basement rec-room pornography, flash-lit Polaroids, fake wood panelling; Pabst Blue Ribbon; 'porno' or 'paedophile' moustaches; aviator glasses; Americana T-shirts for church socials, et cetera; tube socks; the late albums of Johnny Cash, produced by Rick Rubin; and tattoos' (Greif 2010b, 9). The *a priori* whiteness of 21st century hipsters is evident in the linguistically marked status of black hipsters (called 'blipsters'), the policing of hipster style enacted by the popular Tumblr 'Accidental Chinese Hipsters', and the convention of dissociation from racial 'others' in hipster narratives such as Miranda July's 'The boy from Lam Kien', Dave Eggers's *Heartbreaking work of staggering genius*, and Jonathan Lethem's *Fortress of solitude*. If this generation of hipsters does not define itself by appropriating black culture, it nevertheless mimics strategic non-white cultural nationalisms by constructing – through carefully curated clothing and accessories – an apparently working-class 'white' identity that is at once ironic and sentimentalised. 'By taking up the markers or feeling of a white ethnicity', writes Greif, 'they made it feel natural to engage in a subcultural separation, or de-integration, rather than bohemian integration, as they colonized neighbourhoods that were, in one way or another, really ethnic ' (Greif 2010a, 152). Hipsters – many of whom are employed in the service sector or 'creative' industries – thus camouflage their post-industrial existence in the trappings of industrial labour. Signs of working-class whiteness offer hipsters a form of class and ethnic camouflage that enables them to obscure – or at least disavow – their de-integrating colonisation of working-class and ethnic neighbourhoods. According to Neal Leach (2006), camouflage produces new social relations by operating 'as a mechanism for inscribing an individual within a cultural setting', as 'a medium through which to relate to the other', and 'as a form of connectivity'; these acts of inscription, relation, and connectivity also transform communities and places (240). But when mimicry makes connections across cultural and social inequalities, it risks making those inequalities invisible.

The lure of space

In addition to the assimilation of clothing, music, and other markers of ethnic and class identity, mimicry also involves a shift in spatial relations. Influential theorists of mimicry including Roger Caillois, Jacques Lacan, Homi Bhabha, Neal Leach and Hanna Rose Shell define the phenomenon as an identification with space or background. Noting instances of animal mimicry that serve no apparent evolutionary function, Caillois claims that 'the goal is indeed to *become assimilated into the environment*' (1936, 98). Succumbing to the '*lure of space*', the mimic undergoes 'a diminished sense of personality and vitality' as '*Life withdraws to a lesser state*.' As a form of environmental blending, mimicry illuminates not only cultural appropriations but also ways of inhabiting and reshaping one's surroundings.

Caillois' claim that mimicry involves a process of 'depersonalization through assimilation into space' resonates with common hipster practices. Hipsters blend in with existing spaces through practices of partial renovation that recall Bhabha's formula, 'almost the same, but not quite.' Thus, as they displaced ethnic stores selling discounted items in the Lower East Side, 'Hipster boutiques liked to keep the old, now ironic signage with Jewish names – as hipster restaurants kept signage from replaced Puerto Rican and Dominican restaurants in Spanish ' (Greif 2010a, 144). Hipsters also camouflaged the changes they introduced in urban space by 'develop[ing] a trend of not putting names on their restaurants or bars at all, giving everything an exclusive and unwelcoming aspect' (144). These acts of nostalgic appropriation transform spaces built or occupied by ethnic and working-class inhabitants into signs of authenticity and cultural capital.

An overview of hipster culture provides further examples of environmental blending. In an iconic shot from Zach Braff's *Garden state* (2004), the apathetic protagonist embodies the figure of the 'wallflower' by wearing a shirt that exactly matches the pattern of the wallpaper.[3] Practitioners of planking – the ironic riposte to the exhibitionist sport of parkour – perform flat affect (and also, perhaps, subtly critique the conventional practices of tourism and exercise) by awkwardly lying prone in public spaces. Blending into pre-existing spaces, hipsters appear to move into neighbourhoods quietly, passively, without transforming local culture or built space. Even the design of hipster establishments – bars, restaurants, cafes, boutiques – tends to take the form of open, flexible spaces. Communal tables, multiple seating areas, parklets, and pop-up shops provide indefinite, mutable spaces that can be used for multiple purposes. On the surface, hipster spaces appear to accommodate a diversity of bodies, interests and practices. Through the spatial camouflage of renovating and repurposing, hipsters and the businesses that cater to them insinuate themselves into neighbourhoods while minimising spectacular scenes of demolition and rebuilding. Consider, for example, the bicycle as a gentrification machine: though it appears to have no effect on urban space, it makes available to commuters residential neighbourhoods that are as yet underserved by public transit.

---

3   The image is reproduced in Joshua Tanzer, "Leaving Club Med," *Offoffoff.com* (Aug 1, 2004), http://www.offoffoff.com/film/2004/gardenstate.php.

This tendency to blend into urban environments takes on an affective register in hipster writing and films by Miranda July, Tao Lin, and so-called mumblecore directors such as Andrew Bujalski and Joe Swanberg. Hipster characters in these texts regularly engage in flat affect, self-deprecation, and the emotional register of mumbling. Caillois' oft-cited theorisation of mimicry as 'legendary psychaesthenia', or a psychic identification with one's surroundings, aptly describes the soft-spoken, anomic characters that populate hipster narratives. This flat affect and dissolution of will can be seen, for example, in a characteristic passage from Tao Lin's recent novel, *Taipei* (2003), describing a character reluctantly coming into consciousness one morning in Brooklyn:

He kept his eyes pressurelessly closed and didn't move, wanting to return – without yet knowing who or what he was – to sleep, where he could intensify and prolong and explore what he residually felt and was uncontrollably forgetting, but was already alert, in concrete reality, to a degree that his stillness, on his queen-size mattress, felt like a kind of hiding. He stared at the backs of his eyelids with motionless eyeballs, slightly feigning not knowing what he was looking at – which also felt like a kind of hiding – and gradually discerned that he was in Brooklyn … in the two-person apartment … (2013, 18–19)

The dissolution of individual identity that Caillois terms 'psychaesthenia' is evident here in both Lin's noncommittal, deadpan style and his protagonist's frequent wish to hide, disengage, or lie down. Lin explores such states of mind by conveying the mental processes of a protagonist who is alternately depressed, dissociative, semi-conscious, and under the influence of different drugs. Although both Lin and his protagonist are Asian American, his novel (and several of his other works) downplays race by focusing on hip urban locations (Think Coffee, Williamsburg, Washington Square, vegan restaurants, etc.) and his narrator's pathological self-detachment. If the novel invites a reading of Paul's experience as a diasporic New Yorker visiting his parents in Taiwan, it also foregrounds the anomie and flat affect that Paul shares with many of those closest to him. All his friends, he notes, share 'a self-consciously worried expression, seeming disoriented and shy in a distinct, uncommon manner indicating to Paul an underlying sensation of "totally yet failing" (as opposed to most people's "partial and successful") effort, in terms of the social interaction but, it would often affectingly seem, also generally, in terms of existing' (31). This blend of total sincerity, social detachment, and a tendency towards failure finds expression not only in Lin's writing style, but in his character's obsessions with death and disappearance: walking in the city street, for example, he 'imagined himself becoming physically faceted by rapidly facing different directions, in 15-degree movements, advancing blurrily ahead as a barely visible, wave-like curvature' (173). But if affective disengagement enhances his desire and capacity to hide, it also distances Paul from seriously considering political commitments or social problems. For example, when he contrasts Taiwan with New York, Paul quickly abandons a line of thinking that draws attention to racialised labour:

'I don't like places … where everybody working is a minority … because I feel like there's too many different … I don't know', said Paul with a feeling like he unequivocally did not want to be talking about what he was talking about, but had accidentally focused on it, like a telescope a child had turned, away from a constellation, toward a wall' (187).

In spite of his reluctance and the effects of MDMA, Paul still articulates a critique of the geographical conditions of race and labour in US cities: 'here [in Taipei], when you see someone, you don't know ... that ... they live like two hours away and are um ... poor, or whatever'(Lin 187). However, Paul's critique omits the role of relatively wealthy, educated urban youths – such as himself – in displacing 'minorities' and the 'poor' to affordable housing located 'two hours away' from neighbourhoods like Brooklyn and the Lower East Side.

The plague of artists

In a 2004 protest against the gentrification of Williamsburg, Brooklyn, Hasidic Jews handed out a flier calling on God to 'please remove from upon us the plague of the artists, so that we shall not drown in evil waters, and so that they shall not come to our residence to ruin it.' The tension between 'artists' and low-income housing fuels real-estate development in many US cities, where hipsters' practices of environmental blending often occur in neighbourhoods undergoing redevelopment. At the same time that hipsters appropriate and revise signs of white and non-white ethnic identity, they catalyse spatial transformations that displace lower-income inhabitants and reproduce racial hierarchies. Focusing on recent hipster memoirs and novels as well as the treatment of hipsters in ethnic fiction, this section will consider urban space and gentrification as important points of intersection between mimicry and hipster subculture.

In her bestselling memoir *Farm city: the education of an urban farmer* (2009), Novella Carpenter recounts her experiences as an urban squat-farmer after moving to a low-income Oakland neighbourhood known as Ghost Town: as the book's opening line puts it, 'I have a farm on a dead-end street in the ghetto.' Living near squatters, a black single mother, a Buddhist temple, a building 'filled with Vietnamese families', and a corner frequented by 'black kids', Carpenter reduces her dependence on industrially produced foods by farming and raising livestock on an empty lot. After several years, however, she learns that her squat farm will be evicted to make room for condos: as adventurous young people like herself move into what she calls the 'ghetto', investors begin to see the potential of real estate development in Ghost Town. Even as she enjoys getting to know her diverse, unruly neighbours, Carpenter unwittingly contributes to real estate dynamics that will eventually displace low-income residents from 'swing neighbourhoods' as urban homesteaders, hipsters, and condo residents move in. In fact, *Farm City* covers a period contemporaneous with the beginnings of Oakland's First Fridays – popular open-studio events which have attracted art collectors and real estate speculators to nearby areas like Temescal and the (newly named) Kono (Koreatown Northgate) and NOBE neighbourhoods. Ironically, Carpenter's description of squat farming perfectly describes the role of her activities (and other related DIY movements) in the real estate market: 'There was something captivating about making something useful again – resurrecting the abandoned' (26–7). Like squat farmers, hipsters produce new cultural capital and real estate values in urban areas abandoned by capital investment, simultaneously displacing prior inhabitants and appropriating their cultural diversity. Although it is apparently intended to announce that urban farming is hip, the urban homesteading tagline 'chickens are the new black' (see e.g., Casey 2009) also seems to acknowledge that such activities contribute to patterns of racialised displacement and rent increases in historically black and brown neighbourhoods. Ironically, gentrification also pushes Carpenter's own project out of the neighbourhood: 'And now I was just one of the many ghosts in Ghost Town. I sprang up here only because it was the perfect intersection of time and place ... I had arrived at a time when an abandoned lot could be taken over, a backyard turned into a place to keep animals, connections between humans made. This time had now passed' (267).

Jonathan Lethem's *Fortress of solitude* (2004) presents a darker account of the intersections between race, hipster subculture, and gentrification. The novel blends a *bildungsroman* about the interracial friendship of Dylan Ebdus and Mingus Rude with a chronicle of the gentrification of Brooklyn's Gowanus/Boerum Hill neighbourhood. As one of the only white children growing up in the neighbourhood, Dylan finds a friend and protector in Mingus. When he moves to New Jersey to attend 'the most expensive college in America' (272), Dylan adopts an 'urban' identity to impress his suburban schoolmates:

> nobody could question my street credibility here, where nobody had any street credibility whatsoever. I earned my stripe at Camden by playing a walking artifact of the ghetto ... Basically, I turned myself into a cartoon of Mingus. The schtick was a splendid container for my self-loathing, and for my hostility toward my classmates. And it made me popular (387)

Ironically, this appropriation of Mingus's blackness – which Dylan calls 'my minstrel show' (385) – occurs during the very years when Mingus is imprisoned for shooting his psychologically abusive grandfather and subsequently becomes addicted to crack.

Lethem's incorporation of magical plot elements highlights the theme of camouflage. A magic ring at first enables Mingus to fly and to fight petty crime disguised as Aeroman; when he moves to the Bay Area as a young adult, however, Dylan discovers that the ring's power has shifted from flight to invisibility: 'In truth, if it was still a flying ring I might never have tangled with Oakland. [But] Invisibility was sly and urban and might just do the trick' (410). Instead of offering flight's transcendence and the possibility of a momentary escape from geographical limits (things that a white man with means hardly needs), the ring endows Dylan with an invisibility that *entangles* him in the urban environment and enables him to access dangerous and predominantly black spaces. But if invisibility protects him from harm, it also allegorises Dylan's absence of identity apart from the appropriative minstrelsy of the 'white negro': 'Invisibility and Mingus's voice had flayed me bare. I had no secrets to conceal. I had no *mean face*, or any face at all .... . I wasn't thinking – my brain was invisible to itself' (490).

In the end, *Fortress of Solitude* critiques the political isolation of hipsters and bohemians as a nostalgic, utopian and self-consuming stance: an impossible attempt to inhabit the 'collapsing middle' (508): 'It was the same space the communists and gays and painters of celluloid imagined they'd found in Gowanus, only to be unwitting wedges for realtors, a racial wrecking ball. A gentrification was the scar left by a dream ' (508). But whose dream, and whose scars? Dylan's first-person narration expresses nostalgia for spectacles of racial and cultural difference:

> We all pined for those middle spaces, those summer hours when Josephine Baker lay waste to Paris, when 'Bothered Blue' peaked on the charts, when a teenaged Elvis, still dreaming of his own first session, sat in the Sun Studios watching the Prisonaires, when a top-to-bottom burner blazed through a subway station, renovating the world for an in-

stant, when schoolyard turntables were powered by a cord run from a streetlamp, when juice just *flowed*. (508)

Invoking the appropriation of public electricity so central to Ralph Ellison's *Invisible Man*, Lethem's nostalgic litany of 'middle spaces' is aligned with a white 'we' – with those who (not unlike Novella Carpenter's squat farm) benefit from 'renovating the world.' Although Dylan opposes the 'social mimicry' of white gentrifiers like his friend Arthur Lomb (429) – who adapted to living among black neighbours in order to later profit from their displacement – he nevertheless appropriates Brooklyn's pre-gentrified past as a source for his own sense of authenticity. As Matt Godbey writes, Dylan's conflicted identification with Gowanus' black community 'is an act of appropriation that begins to suggest how individual pursuits of identity and authenticity are reshaping inner-city neighbourhoods by eschewing concerns for social welfare in favor of a self-directed focus on the stylization of life.'

Whereas texts like *Farm city* and *Fortress of solitude* focus on white gentrifiers, several recent anti-gentrification texts foreground the stories of Chicano/a, African American, and other minority residents who are either physically or culturally displaced by urban redevelopment. For example, Dinaw Mengestu's *The beautiful things that Heaven bears* (2007), Nathan McCall's *Them* (2007), and Brando Skyhorse's *The Madonnas of Echo Park* (2011) dramatise tensions between ethnic communities and new white residents in Washington, D.C., Atlanta, and Los Angeles; Linda Goode Bryant and Laura Poitras' documentary film *Flag wars* (2003) chronicles the conflict between African American communities and gay white homebuyers in Columbus's Olde Towne East neighbourhood; Barry Jenkins's *Medicine for melancholy* (2008) appropriates the understated style of 'mumblecore' film (a style often associated with hipsters) to explore how two young black San Francisco residents position themselves in relation to capitalism, gentrification, race, and the historic displacement of the city's black communities; and the music video for George Watsky and Chinaka Hodge's *Kill a hipster* (2013) depicts gentrification as a violent zombie invasion spreading through black and Chicano neighbourhoods in Brooklyn, Oakland and Los Angeles.[4]

The Madonnas of Echo Park offers a nuanced, deeply historicised, and formally sophisticated topography of the gradual influx of hipsters into the L.A. neighbourhood of Echo Park. In one climactic scene, Skyhorse presents a stark barroom encounter between Freddy (a Chicano hustler returning to the gentrifying neighbourhood of Echo Park after a long prison term) and two white hipsters:

> I order the cheapest beer they have, a PBR, and search for my mark. Over by the pool table with a young white girl who'd be gorgeous if not for her tattoos and shaved head is a white guy in his thirties with thick Buddy Holly-style glasses, a short-sleeve shirt that changes color depending on what angle I look at it from, baggy black pants with a chain dangling from his right pocket, and spotless black 'work' shoes. (120)

Skyhorse satirises hipsters' class camouflage by contrasting Freddy's purchase of PBR ('the cheapest beer') with the white man's spotless 'work' shoes. The white man's chameleonic shirt, which 'changes color depending on what angle I look at it from', also hints at his po-

---

[4] George Watsky with Chinaka Hodge, *Kill a hipster* (2013), music video directed by Jackson Adams http://www.youtube.com/watch?v=6LTLuzkqpZc&feature=kp&noredirect=1

tential for camouflage. By the end of this scene, Freddy's attempt at subversive hustling backfires: when Freddy demands the five hundred dollars he has won, the man in the Buddy Holly glasses brutally beats him and takes his wallet. The ex-convict's attempt at deception is trumped by the hipster's own array of chameleonic signs – signs that extend beyond this individual case to the entire neighbourhood that is being transformed by the influx of queer and liberal white residents, English-language graffiti, and hip cafes.

More broadly, *The Madonnas of Echo Park* explores the theme of mimicry by repeatedly featuring Madonna's music video for 'Borderline', in which the artist masquerades as a young Chicana on a street corner in Echo Park surrounded by 'Mexican break-dancers, Latin boyfriend, Madonna's girlfriends dressed in retro *chola* girl outfits.'(Skyhorse, xviii) In Skyhorse's novel, seeing this video regularly on MTV inspires Chicana girls in Echo Park to dress up in 'Madonna-style outfits' and dance on the street corner where Madonna's music video was shot. To some extent, *Madonnas* explores the appeal of hybridity for young Chicanas moving back to Echo Park: several central characters imitate and identify with popular singers like Madonna, Gwen Stefani and Morrissey. When the book's central character, Aurora, returns to the neighbourhood after spending a few years away, she is at first disoriented by the '*gringo* hipster stores' and the related real estate boom: 'It is as if an antimatter explosion had detonated high above Echo Park, reconstructing decay into a glittering faux affluence, a Willy Wonka neutron bomb coating the landscape in radioactive smiley face yellows and Wellbutrin blues' (189). By the end of the book, however, she has resolved to move back to the neighbourhood. Aurora envisions urban redevelopment not only as displacement, but as an opportunity for Chicano/a resettlement and renewal, describing Echo Park as 'an amaranthine valley of orange groves that bloom from here to the ocean, a land rich with roots that grow, thrive, burn, are razed, heal, then grow again, deeper and stronger than before.'

But while many of Skyhorse's characters experiment with hybridity, the book as a whole historicises the real estate boom by connecting it with the Battle of Chavez Ravine (1951–61)[5], in which the predominantly Mexican American residents of Chavez Ravine were displaced to make room for L.A.'s Dodger Stadium. The character Aurora is named after her grandmother, Aurora Salazar (based on Aurora Vargas), who was forcibly removed from her home in a widely publicised eviction in 1959. If Aurora views her decision to move back to Echo Park as an opportunity to restore lost roots, Skyhorse's narrative also foregrounds the devastation of family and collective memory suffered by her family and neighbours. The book's distinct chapters – each featuring a different first-person narrator – chronicle the experiences of characters who are frequently unaware of the complex ways in which they're interrelated: in the last chapter, for example, Aurora walks right past her estranged father, her half-sister, her mother, her grand-uncle and her estranged grandmother without recognising or being recognised by any of them. Only the reader knows that her biological father is being deported at the very moment that Aurora thinks, 'This is the land we dream of, the land that belongs to us again' (199). Another key scene – in which the young Aurora and other girls dress up like Madonna and dance outside one of the locations featured in Madonna's music video – ends up highlighting the racially divergent outcomes of mimicry: whereas Madonna accumulates cultural capital by masquerading as a Chicana, one of the girls dancing on the street is accidentally killed in a drive-by shooting. By contrasting the material conditions of Echo Park's residents with numerous

---

5 On the Battle of Chavez Ravine, see Avila (2004), 145-84.

instances of hybridity and interracial intimacy, *Madonnas* critiques attempts to redress the injuries of mass displacement through cultural hybridity.

Geographically located at the fleeting urban borderlands between white and non-white communities, hipsters engage in mimicry at the levels of both cultural identity and spatial blending. The cultural representations of hipsters I've examined here demonstrate that mimicry, far from being an essentially subversive defence mechanism or weapon of the weak, has become an important tool for aggressive acts of cultural appropriation and urban renewal. The adaptive display of cultural and ethnic signs camouflages the economic and geographical truth of hipsters: that they convert underemployment, disaffection, and cultural marginality into cultural capital and real estate value. This dynamic raises broad questions about the spatial effects of mimicry: mimicry transforms environments by blending with them. Particularly now, when camouflage has become highly visible as both fashion statement and marketing strategy, cultural mimicry attracts aesthetic appreciation and capital investment to areas associated with cultural 'authenticity.' In the process, both low-income residents and, eventually, many hipsters themselves are displaced from the places to which their spatial practices have added value. After performing and aestheticising their disappearance *into* space, hipsters too eventually disappear *from* these places, pushed by elevated real estate prices to the next frontier of urban redevelopment.

This analysis of hipsters' various forms of cultural and spatial assimilation indicates the importance of contextualising the aesthetics of camouflage. If camouflage aestheticises points of contact between self and other and between bodies and space, it does so under particular economic and political conditions and in the service of particular interests. Given the extent to which power functions through the production and reproduction of particular kinds of spaces (Lefebvre), the spatial arts of camouflage may play an increasingly important role in resolving spatial tensions and transforming existing spaces. As a technique for resolving spatial contradictions, camouflage frequently has geographically conservative effects. Although it may be mobilised in the service of subversion, parody, or individual liberation, camouflage hides spatial tensions and conceals – and at times privatises – political struggle.

However, it is important to note that these social and economic effects of hipster subculture are generally unintended, and the question remains whether hipster practices can also support generative forms of identity and space. Can what Lethem lyrically describes as the 'middle space' that precedes gentrification lead to something other than capitalist co-optation and real estate development? In the fleeting middle space, contacts are made across the lines of race, class, and sexuality; organisations such as the 826 tutoring centres initiated by Dave Eggers provide education to underprivileged children in and around gentrifying neighbourhoods; new coalitions such as the Occupy movement emerge and struggle to keep urban space in the hands of the 99 percent; and writers and artists produce critical works engaging with the dynamics of gentrification. These writers, artists, and organisations have no illusions about passively blending into space, moving into different neighbourhoods without friction or incident. Instead, they politicise the very process of environmental blending by acknowledging that their presence has a transformative effect on urban space, and by struggling to shape the course of urban transformation. They acknowledge the new proximities and contacts that emerge in the middle space, and attempt to build coalitions that might provide alternatives to the conventional paths of gentrification and displacement.

References

Avila E (2004). *Popular culture in the age of white flight: fear and fantasy in suburban Los Angeles*. Berkeley: University of California Press.

Behrens R (2002). *False colors: art, design, and modern camouflage*. Dysart, IA: Bobolink Books.

Bhabha H (1994). Of mimicry and man: the ambivalence of colonial. In H Bhabha. *The location of culture* (pp.85–92). London: Routledge.

Bonilla-Silva E (2009). *Racism without racists: color-blind racism and the persistence of racial inequality in America*. Lanham, MD: Rowman & Littlefield.

Butler J (1990). *Gender trouble: feminism and the subversion of identity*. New York: Routledge.

Caillois, R (1936 [2003]). Mimicry and legendary psychasthenia. In C Frank (Ed), *The edge of surrealism: a Roger Caillois reader* (pp.89–103). Translated by C Frank and C Naish. Durham: Duke University Press, 2003.

Carpenter N (2010). *Farm city: the education of an urban farmer*. New York: Penguin.

Casey L (2009). Clucking about backyard chickens. Insidebayarea.com (June 19, 2009). http://www.insidebayarea.com/homeandgarden/ci_12611151. [Accessed 21 May 2014]

Chen T (2005). *Double agency: acts of impersonation in Asian American literature and culture*. Palo Alto: Stanford University Press.

Deloria P (1999). *Playing Indian*. New Haven: Yale University Press.

Fish, S (1997). Boutique multiculturalism, or why liberals are incapable of thinking about hate speech. *Critical Inquiry* 23:2 (Winter 1997) 378–95.

Gates HL (1988). *The signifying monkey: a theory of African-American literary criticism*. New York: Oxford University Press.

Greif M (2010a). Epitaph for the white hipster. In M Greif, K Ross & D Tortorici (Eds). *What was the hipster? A sociological investigation* (pp.136–67). New York: n+1.

Greif M (2010b). Positions. In M Greif, K Ross & D Tortorici (Eds). *What was the hipster? A sociological investigation* (pp.4–13). New York: n+1.

Leach N (2006). *Camouflage*. Boston: MIT Press.

Lee J (2004). *Urban triage: race and the fictions of multiculturalism*. Minneapolis: University of Minnesota Press.

Lethem J (2004). *The fortress of solitude*. New York: Vintage.

Lin T (2013). *Taipei*. New York: Vintage.

Lorentzen C (2010). I Was Wrong. In M Greif, K Ross & D Tortorici (Eds). *What was the hipster? A sociological investigation* (pp.14–23). New York: n+1.

Madonna (1984). Borderline (1984), music video directed by Mary Lambert. http://youtu.be/rSaC-YbS-Dpo

Mailer N (1957). The White Negro: superficial reflections on the hipster. *Dissent* 4(3): 276–93 (Summer 1957).

Melamed J (2006). The spirit of neoliberalism: from racial liberalism to liberal multiculturalism. *Social Text*, 24(89): 1–24.

Muñoz J (1999). *Disidentifications: queers of color and the performance of politics*. Minneapolis: University of Minnesota Press.

Reesman J (Ed) (2001). *Trickster lives: culture and myth in American fiction*. Athens: University of Georgia Press.

Skyhorse B (2011). *The Madonnas of echo park*. New York: Free Press.

Tanzer, J (2004). Leaving Club Med. *Offoffoff.com*. http://www.offoffoff.com/film/2004/gardenstate.php

Watsky G & Hodge C (2013). *Kill a hipster*. Music video directed by Jackson Adams. http://www.youtube.com/watch?v=6LTLuzkqpZc&feature=kp&noredirect=1

Wise T (2010). *Color-blind: the rise of post-racial politics and the retreat from racial equity*. San Francisco: City Lights Books.

14
Camouflage/fashion/performance: a case study of Leigh Bowery

Jacqueline Millner

According to architect and theorist Neil Leach writing in his 2006 book *Camouflage*:

> Camouflage does not entail the cloaking of the self so much as the relating of the self to the world through the medium of representation … The role of camouflage is not to disguise, but to offer a medium through which to relate to the other. (2006, 240)

In part, Leach bases his argument on French surrealist Roger Caillois' observation that creatures at different times wish either to stand out or blend in with their environment, and their identity is dependent on this process (Caillois 1935). Using these ideas as a point of departure, I will consider the intersection between camouflage, fashion and performance through a case study of the pioneering genre-bending Australian artist Leigh Bowery. Bowery's conflation of self and image, and his delight in 'becoming invisible' during off-show appearances, raise interesting questions about the negotiation of the process of conformity versus standing out that is at the heart of camouflage.

Camouflage as a motif can give us insight into the power and singularity of Bowery's oeuvre, and perhaps help explain its enduring fascination. It allows us to pinpoint the apparent paradox at the core of his work: on one hand, the urge for total abandon and permissiveness, to dissolve the self, rip it apart or cause inside and outside to leak in the ultimate blending; and on the other, the urge to ascesis and negation, to discipline and structure the self to the point of violence in costumes that transformed Bowery's body into impenetrable sculptures. These paradoxical urges are related to the oscillation between vulnerability and defence inherent in camouflage. Bowery laid bare his lacerations of the outsider, the pain of not belonging for all to see, but also perfected the intimidating carapace of the late 20th century dandy, safe in his 'look', his armour of disdain and cultural superiority. And yet, ironically, towards the end of his short life – he was diagnosed HIV positive in 1988 and died in 1994 aged 33 – Bowery apparently considered his favourite 'look' to be his naked self as portrayed by British painter Lucien Freud (Als 1998, 25).

A life

Leigh Bowery may have died almost 20 years ago, but his work still bristles with currency. His legacy has been increasingly acknowledged, including in a major retrospective in 2012 entitled 'Xtravanganza: staging Leigh Bowery' at the Kunsthalle Vienna.[1] Nonetheless, it is true that perhaps on account of the genre-defying and restless nature of his practice, Bowery's place in the canon of contemporary art is yet to be definitively secured. His immediate influence went well beyond the art world, to fashion, design, club culture, and dance. Certainly his collaborators in the 1980s and 1990s – such as choreographer Michael Clark and pop musician Boy George – all attest to his ground-breaking ideas and sensibilities that fuelled the innovation in those creative fields during that period in London, while others note that Bowery anticipated many of Alexander McQueen's signature designs by several years.[2] But arguably his influence on art practice has been a slow burn that has only more recently garnered closer attention. Some convincingly claim that Bowery's playfulness and experimentation with a variety of media, without concern for disciplinary boundaries, influenced the strategies taken up by the yet to be anointed Young British Artists, such as Damien Hirst and Sarah Lucas (Carsley 2003, 17) as well as others like Yinka Shonibare and Gillian Wearing (Als 1998, 22). The recent turn to performance in contemporary art has also reignited interest in the form's varied historical forebears. While Bowery remains decidedly one-off, it is evident that his witty but physically intense and confronting approach paved the way for many contemporary strategies.

Leigh Bowery was born in 1961 in the singularly nondescript outer western Melbourne suburb of Sunshine. Given the desire to outrage at the heart of his work as a fashion designer and performer, biographers have made much of this, although once he left for London at age 19 he made little mention of his Australian origins (Als 1998, 14). Nonetheless, the lower-middle-class primness and hypocrisy that mark Bowery's formative years are important in the role that camouflage played in his art: Bowery decidedly did not blend with his social surroundings, and was acutely aware of this from an early age. The photograph of Bowery and his parents, Evelyn and Tom Bowery, on their first visit to his council flat in London in 1984 is telling. His mother, a portly middle-aged marm with a permanent wave and checked blouse, and his father, greying at the temples, sporting a short sleeved white shirt, tie and pen in his breast pocket, stand smiling at the camera on either side of their son. Their drab 'normality' is all the more apparent in contrast to the radical otherness of Bowery's attire: his face is flattened to a mask by kabuki-like make-up, his bald head dribbled in black glue, his jacket all beads and lamé, yet his smile the well-rehearsed gesture of the dutiful son in family happy snap. He has staged his own camouflage – belonging and non-belonging – to negotiate his identity. His oscillations between blending in and standing out are literally played out in the décor of this same council flat: the photographs that record Bowery posing against the Star Trek wallpaper that covered his walls, his face and outfit uniformly 'disguised' in large spots that both carry into and disrupt the broader pattern, are a study in camouflage. Robyn Healy notes that Bowery's obsession

---

1 Xtravaganza: staging Leigh Bowery, curated by Angela Stief, Kunsthalle, Vienna, October 19, 2012 – February 3, 2013. This is the first major exhibition dedicated to Bowery since the 1994 show at the Museum of Contemporary Art, Sydney, in 2003–04, Take a Bowery: the Art and (larger than) life of Leigh Bowery, curated by Gary Carsley.
2 Hilton Als claims, for example, that Bowery did 'bumsters' eight years before McQueen (Als 1998, 22).

with spots began as 'a device to highlight rather than disguise his pimples' and developed into a signature style in its evocation of disease and pestilence on one hand, and clean and jolly modernist design on the other (Healy 2003, 80).

Several interviews reveal Bowery's early sensitivity to the aesthetics of his everyday reality and his innovative efforts to play around with them. Bowery recalled rearranging his childhood domestic environment, including uprooting and replanting the garden, so that his parents needed 'a road map' when they came home from work (Als 1998, 12). He attempted to re-make the environment to better reflect his own reality, but also to disorient the reality of those who posed a threat. As a teenager, Bowery began to partake of ever more conspicuous displays of difference, from the gaudy outfits he made while a fashion undergraduate at the Royal Melbourne Institute of Technology which he wore amid the crowds of the busy city centre, to his rejection of mass produced fashion, to his open engagement with Melbourne's cruising scene (Als 1998, 13).

Those overt gestures of not belonging led soon enough to his complete rejection of the Australian suburban context by emigrating to England in 1980. Within a year or so of landing in London – after a stint at Burger King from which he was fired for pilfering from the till – Bowery had discovered the milieu in which he did fit in: the nightclubs and fashion circles of New Romantic London. He picked up a Cockney accent (although he changed it again to 'upper class posh' when posing for Lucien Freud), and never mentioned his Australian origins. Despite his rejection of the term 'designer', it was as a designer that he first made his mark, from Kensington markets to a major show, insisting on making every item himself so that he was unable to ever meet orders from retailers (Als 1998, 15).

Before long, Bowery was collaborating with and providing the inspiration for the likes of choreographer Michael Clark, designers Vivienne Westwood and John Galliano, and pop icon Boy George. He became a regular cabaret performer and host at the new club Taboo; this was a mode of performing in which he was able to continually innovate and do outrageous things in a bid, as he explained, to make the crowd less inhibited themselves (Als 1998, 17).

Bowery observed that in his life and his work he was driven to seek out shame and embarrassment because he found these more memorable and intense than pleasurable things. (Bowery 1998a, 198) He considered shame the least explored of the human emotions, and confessed that the urge to experience and cause shame in others was compulsive (Als 1998, 18). In one excruciating letter to a friend, written in a hotel room in Melbourne during his first trip back to Australia with the highly acclaimed Michael Clark dance company, he can hear his mother crying in the next room: it is the aftermath of his performance at the Melbourne Town Hall, which his proud mum had attended with several of her Salvation Army friends and relatives, only to be confronted with Clark being fellated while sporting a giant dildo and her son's 'as camp as Christmas' romping about naked on stage. Bowery writes, 'What was planned by my mother to be the *piece de resistance* of a triumphant homecoming turned out to be the most mortifying experience of her life' (Bowery 1998b, 59).

Shame

According to Silvan Tomkins – the psychologist who pioneered affect theory in search of an overarching framework of human emotion – shame, of all the affects, positive and negative, is the most deeply felt:

> If distress is the affect of suffering, shame is the affect of indignity, of defeat, of transgression, and of alienation. Though terror speaks to life and death and distress makes the world a vale of tears, yet shame strikes deepest into the heart of man. While terror and distress hurt, they are wounds inflicted from outside which penetrate the smooth surface of the ego; but shame is felt as inner torment, a sickness of the soul. It does not matter whether the humiliated one has been shamed by derisive laughter or whether he mocks himself. In either event he feels himself naked, defeated, alienated, lacking in dignity and worth. (Tomkins in Sedgwick et al. 1995, 133)

Shame is a negative affect that, according to affect theory, makes us feel bad when something or someone we are interested in or enjoying is withheld from us:

> Shame is an innate auxiliary affect and a specific inhibitor of continuing interest and enjoyment. Like disgust, it operates ordinarily only after interest or enjoyment has been activated, and inhibits one or the other or both. The innate activator of shame is the incomplete reduction of interest or joy. Hence any barrier to further exploration which partially reduced interest or the smile of enjoyment will activate the lowering of the head and eyes in shame and reduce further exploration or self-exposure powered by excitement or joy. (Tomkins in Sedgwick et al.. 1995, 134–5)

Tomkins linked shame to disappointment and humiliation, and theorised that this innate affect evolved in order to trigger action to overcome obstacles to interest and enjoyment. Since human behaviour generally aims to maximise positive affect and minimise negative affect, shame usually provokes the desire to escape from the gaze of others. As Tomkins puts it, 'the shame response is an act which reduces facial communication … The individual calls a halt to looking at another person, particularly the other's face, and to the other person's looking at him, particularly at his face'. (134)

But Bowery did the opposite. As he explained:

> I try to make myself embarrassed all the time and to put myself in embarrassing situations. I think for me it was a good thing to be shy because it meant that I was embarrassed all the time, so it meant that I would go through all the things that I found difficult and then try to make myself even more embarrassed and even more nervous and it would give the ideas a kick start. (Bowery 1998a, 198)

For Bowery, it appears, shame was a creative stimulus. He would contrive situations and relationships where he could encounter shame, both his own and that of others, in a manner that is counter-intuitive to the care of self. Such situations harnessed not only the critical gaze of others but also that of the performer himself, that is, they brought on, or perhaps staged, intense self-consciousness. To use Tomkins' words, Bowery deliberately left himself 'naked, defeated, alienated, lacking in dignity and worth', like a creature in a hostile environment without the cover of camouflage.

According to filmmaker Baillie Walsh, it was Bowery's background as a 'well brought up boy someone else raised him to be' that fuelled the desire to make a spectacle of himself: 'He was really horrified by what he was … [so] he wanted to tell the joke, he didn't want to be the joke'. (Walsh cited in Als 1998, 14) This is a fairly standard reading of the desire to outrage and self-deprecate as a form of pre-emptive strike. I would argue, however, that

Bowery's strategy was far more complex, and that using camouflage as a motif and shame as a motivator allows us to explore it.

Bowery's manoeuvres can be read less as 'making a spectacle of his *self*' than as different forms of *obliterating* his self, in effect, making the self 'disappear'. Whether by those actions and performances that seek effectively to dissolve the self by breaching its boundaries, or by his transformation into 'The Look', Bowery's desire to differentiate who he was even from his very self is at the core of his work, suggesting that realising the self means destroying the existing subject. As gender studies scholar Alison Bancroft has argued, we could see Bowery's work as marking 'the obsolescence of a particular understanding of masculine subjectivity or selfhood'. Bancroft cites Leo Bersani's argument:

> that 'male homosexuality advertises the risk of the sexual itself as the risk of self-dismissal, of losing sight of the self, and in doing so it proposes and dangerously represents jouissance as a mode of ascesis'. [This] can be seen to be following the point made by Lacan … regarding the proximity of the death drive and the obliteration of the subject to that subject's self-realisation … The negation of the self that Bersani identifies suggests an instance of the jouissance of transgression. This negation of the self that is central to queer jouissance, or even the suggestion of such negation, is profoundly transgressive because it ecstatically breaches the boundaries of the self, at the same time as it destroys the very limits of sociality. (Bancroft 2012, 68–9)

Remembering that 'camouflage conceals by the obliteration of visual signs' (Martha Banta cited in Behrens 2009, 80), let us now consider Bowery's strategies in turn: the purported obliteration of the self through, first, the construction of the impermeable carapace of his 'look', and second, the breaching of the body's boundaries and effacement of the traditional social markers of identity, in particular the face and gender-specificity.

The carapace

According to critic Hilton Als, Bowery 'was a complete reinvention of that much beloved and often reviled figure: the English dandy'. (Als 1998, 12) The French dandy is steeped in melancholy and the abrogation of passion, dresses in black and invisibly blends in all spheres of modern life as Baudelaire described him:

> … to see the world, to be at the centre of the world, and yet to remain hidden from the world … The spectator is a prince who everywhere rejoices in his incognito. (Baudelaire in Mayne 1995, 9)

By contrast, the English dandy is driven by his inability to abide Englishness and its distrust of self-expression. The English dandy, writes author Martin Green, 'dances between serious moral principles and defiant amoralism', an amoralism 'marked by cruelty, violence, sexual experiment, and an assertive ugliness of sprit'.[3] Bowery's 'looks' – literally and metaphorically – fused dress and wearer, so that the surface became the essence of who

---

3   Martin Green, *Children of the sun: a narrative of decadence in England after 1918*, cited in Als 1998, 15.

he was: he did not wear gloves, but dipped his hand in glue and glitter instead; he did not wear masks so much as used his face as another sculptural surface. This recalls the way the original English dandy, Beau Brummell, is described by fashion scholar Elizabeth Wilson:

> The originality of Brummell [was that] he fused the wearer and the dress. The dandy was not just a style of dressing, nor was it just a certain kind of person; it was the combination of the two, united in a stance of combined disdain, provocation, and indifference towards the world. (Wilson 2007, 98)

Through this combination, the dandy 'creates a seamless perfection, as impenetrable as the carapace of a beetle. It is not surprising that this mode of being led to the idea that dandies were androgynous, asexual, and even if deviant, deviant in an opaque and hidden way'. (Wilson 2007, 98) Bowery, writes Wilson, went even further in his fusion of self and surface: he 'defied nature and biology to create a wholly artificial self, going far beyond gender, let alone mere drag, to transform his being into a parody of glamour that astonished with its effrontery'. (Wilson 2007, 103) This is echoed in curator William Lieberman's remark when Bowery attended the opening of Freud's exhibition of his nudes at the Metropolitan Museum of Art in New York dressed in a floral camouflage ball gown and Kaiser helmet: 'The extraordinary thing was that it was never drag. He wasn't trying to imitate or personify anyone else. He was simply creating a new being' (Als 1998, 25).

Bowery's hyperbolic flamboyance operates as both a means of concealing and revealing. It sharpens our focus on social hypocrisy, including problematising the socially acceptable form of the homosexual body, what Als describes as 'the velvet and lilies of Oscar Wilde': 'Bowery was the dandy who soiled Wilde's velvets with vomit', Als writes. (Als 1998, 16–18) Boy George observes, 'The rest of us used drag and make up to disguise our blemishes and physical defects. Leigh made them the focal point of his art' (George 1998, 236). Anthony d'Offay, who invited Bowery to do an extended performance in his gallery, thought that Bowery was like a mirror in which others saw their conscious and unconscious thoughts, the carapace so polished as to become a hyperbole of the self. In this 1998 performance, Bowery spent from six till eight every evening for five days in the gallery playing out a succession of his looks in a room divided by a two-way mirror. Where the artist lay on a chaise longue was brightly illuminated, while the audience sat in semi-darkness: the crowd could see him, but Bowery could see only himself.

Bowery's dandy may have revealed much about the artificiality and hypocrisy of social conventions and roles, but he also diverts our attention from the vulnerabilities of the naked subject. That notion of the dandy's body and persona as an impermeable carapace that repudiates the gaze by attracting it is particularly relevant to the development of Bowery's sculptural look as the eighties passed into the nineties. Already in 1983, on his return to London from New York, Bowery 'radicalised his look to make it total' through his creation of what he called 'the Paki from outer Space'. Bowery went beyond make-up and *accoutrements* to completely inhabit the character, which entailed:

> then out-of-date platform shoes painted silver, brightly coloured striped stockings, oversized striped tunics, hexagonal hats with a switch of fake hair, a face painted blue with Hindi inscriptions across the forehead, and a nose ring with chain from nose to ear. (Als 1998, 15)

By the late eighties, Bowery's 'total look' had become increasingly sculptural and extreme. As Gary Carsley describes it:

> Bowery's re-inscription of his body included flaring one leg with a monstrous club foot, filling out parts of his buttocks with foam, hauling his stomach up into a pair of tits gaffer-taped in place, and changing the silhouette of his waist and neck with a series of corsets and extravagant padding. (Carsley 2003, 18)

That re-inscription was in essence a form of camouflage: Dutch critic Anna Tilroe suggests that Bowery's images 'show flesh that is not flesh, a head that is not a head, genitals that are not genitals'. (Tilroe 2003, 125)

Perhaps the total look's most innovative aspect was the use of the face as simply another surface. Bowery denied, however, that he was *hiding* his face; he asserted rather that, 'I think about the body as just supporting different shapes and so I'm not making any special concession for the head'. (Bowery 1998a, 207) According to Als, Bowery's 'vacillations between masking and unmasking became ever more extreme ... thick facial make up gave way to hoods and neck corsets that covered the head entirely ... his costumes became increasingly sculptural, with spherical arms, misshapen legs and built in breasts'. (Als 1998, 23) It is fascinating how like the paint-splattered hooded cloaks or *cagoules,* developed by the first French camoufleurs during the First World War, are some of Bowery's face sculptures. As historian Elizabeth Kahn described them, 'Hidden beneath camouflaged cagoules ... was a ghoulish image of the modern soldier ... [whose] amorphous costume of drab greens and browns ... turned the individual into a frightening form'.[4] Bowery's full-face looks were similarly ghoulish at times.

An interesting effect of this full head coverage was that it severely impaired his vision: as his widow Nicola noted in an interview, 'Leigh would be visually handicapped at the same time as he was the most extraordinary thing to look at'. (Bowery 1998, 151) She goes on to say that as his performances evolved, 'Leigh liked to be more and more obscure, more untouchable'. This squares also with Wilson's analysis of glamour which she says is 'tragic', 'achieved through suffering', the result of artfully concealed effort, and dependent on what is withheld, on what is hidden. (Wilson 2007, x)

In Bowery's hyper-sculptural costumes, the body of the performer its perception impaired, its bulges and creases manipulated like brute matter – becomes more and more thing-like, more and more inanimate. It is as if the costume-cum-body has structured and disciplined the subject to the point of obliteration.

Underlining this notion of the obliteration of self through the construction of the look – what we could call the endgame of Bowery's camouflage strategies – is the fact that there was eventually no escaping the look even in the off times. When not on stage or at the club, Bowery apparently 'just tried to look like people', to blend in according to the way he did with his chameleon-like habit of speaking like people he spent a lot of time with. (Ozbek 1998, 125) His inherently articulate and polite ways often surprised those who had only seen him 'in persona'. Yet even in his daywear, Bowery managed to hold off the gaze. With his shop dummy wig and child molester clothes – what Boy George described as his Benny Hill day look (George 1998, 236) – Bowery evinced a persona that oozed such potential for

---

4   Elizabeth Kahn, 1984, cited in Behrens 2009, 79.

emotional violence that even construction workers would cross the road to avoid him. As Als notes:

> The dichotomy between being seen and not seen, ashamed and brazen, also played itself out in his day look which was in a sense more threatening than anything Bowery invented for night, since it was meant to approximate his feelings of his own normality in relation to the everyday and its citizens. (Als 1998, 19)

Dissolution

Another way that we might think of Bowery as obliterating the self as a way of self-realisation is through his performances and costumes that breach the boundaries of the self, and obscure key markers of identity, in particular his gender and his face. We've already considered how Bowery obscured the principal sign by which the social world usually recognises people as both human and as sexed: the face. Gender-specific physical characteristics such as breasts and genitals are probably the next most immediate sign of identity and difference: these Bowery artificially created through deception and concealment, taping his chest to create breasts, or slinging his penis between his buttocks and wearing a merkin to give the impression of female genitalia.

As already suggested, what Bowery did was beyond drag: he never aimed for the usual idiom of a man in women's clothing. Indeed, as Bancroft argues, he deliberately failed to manifest either masculine or feminine bodily traits to any degree of satisfaction: 'His body, despite its distortions, remained resolutely male, but it was a male body that had breasts and lacked a penis'. (Bancroft 2012, 72) And in one notorious performance, it was a male body that could also give birth.

Apparently inspired by the birth scene in bad-taste epic *Female trouble* starring Divine (dir. John Waters 1974), Bowery's birth performance (1993–94) was a collaboration with his wife Nicola and the band Minty. Nicola was curled foetus-like, upside-down and naked, strapped onto Bowery's body and concealed beneath his costume. Bowery walked onstage, music blaring, and began moaning and panting in simulated labour before laying down on a table, legs akimbo, and 'giving birth' to Nicola who emerged from between his legs through a gradually enlarged hole in Bowery's stockings. At this, the audience cheered: 'Behold the man! A body that splits in two and creates new life!'(Tilroe 2003, 124).

As Bancroft argues, Bowery's 'distortion of his own body confounds any suggestion of corporeal integrity'. (Bancroft 2012, 71) The many and varied manipulations seriously challenge the idea of the body having any boundary at all. This is literally enacted in Bowery's endurance performances such as *The enema performance* (The Fridge 1990), where the artist, unable to control his bowels after an enema, sprayed the audience with faeces, and *The laugh of no. 12* (1994). In this performance, Bowery recreated the Tarot card of The Hanged Man. Suspended upside down, trussed and hooded, his penis a 'coxcomb' of clothes pegs, Bowery sang and Richard Torry played guitar before pulling and releasing a rope that sent Bowery to 'meet the world head-on' by crashing through a glass pane. (Tilroe 2003, 120–4) Bleeding from several wounds, Bowery laughed off his injuries, calling out at the performance's climax, 'No embarrassment at all! Oh, my God, this fantastic feeling!' (Tilroe 2003, 120) To cite Bancroft, 'If Bowery constituted his subjectivity as performance art, which, uniquely, he did, this means that Bowery was enacting in his own life/art the very dissolution of the subject'. (Bancroft 2012, 73) The ultimate camouflage …

Conclusion

'To be natural is such a very difficult pose to keep up', to quote one of Bowery's inspirations (Wilde 1895). I'd like to conclude with the look that Bowery's widow says became his favourite: his naked self as painted by Lucien Freud.

At one level, we might think that this operates as complete exposure that eventually enables Bowery to come to terms with his self: 'My physical features which so worried me in the beginning? They are now in paintings which are housed in the great collections and museums in the world!' (Bowery 1998, 25). Yet on another level, we might read this as yet another carapace that camouflages the vulnerable self, cloaking it in the language of high art. Bowery clearly revered Freud, paying him the highest compliment by imitating the way he spoke and even the way he ate. He relished the mantle of cultural respectability, and the potential longevity, that this association brought him. But he also played up: he allegedly stole from Freud – not only money but two unfinished paintings that were only returned after Bowery's death – and ridiculed him in public. Even in these nude portraits, which supposedly lay the artist bare, Bowery exceeds and eludes his own representation in a fascinating evocation of camouflage.

References

Als H (1998). The cruel story of youth. In R Violette (Ed). *Leigh Bowery*. London: Violette Editions.
Bancroft A (2012). Leigh Bowery: queer in fashion, queer in art. *Sexualities*, 15(1): 68–79.
Behrens RR. (2009). *Camoupedia: a compendium of research on art, architecture and camouflage*, Dysart, Iowa: Bobolink Books.
Bowery L (1998a). What about your sex life: Interview with Richard Torry. In R Violette (Ed). *Leigh Bowery*. London: Violette Editions.
Bowery L (1998b). Letter to Sue Tilley. Reprinted in R Violette (Ed). *Leigh Bowery*, London: Violette Editions.
Bowery N (1998). Interview with Cerith Wyn Evans. In R Violette (Ed). *Leigh Bowery*, London: Violette Editions.
Caillois, R. (1935). Mimicry and legendary psychasthenia. Reproduced in Claudine Frank (Ed). *The Edge of Surrealism: A Roger Caillois Reader*, Durham and London: Duke University Press, 2003.
Carsley G (2003). All his own make up. In G Carsley (Ed). *Take a Bowery: the art and (larger than) life of Leigh Bowery*. Sydney: Museum of Contemporary Art.
George B (1998). Afterword. In R Violette (Ed). *Leigh Bowery*, London: Violette Editions.
Healy R (2003). Where the sun shines: Leigh Bowery, fashion heavyweight. In G Carsley (Ed). *Take a Bowery: The Art and (larger than) life of Leigh Bowery*, Sydney: Museum of Contemporary Art.
Leach N (2006). *Camouflage*, Cambridge, MA: MIT Press.
Mayne J (Ed) (1995). *The painter of modern life and other essays by Charles Baudelaire*. London: Phaidon Press.
Ozbek R (1998). Leigh Bowery. In R Violette (Ed). *Leigh Bowery*, (p 125). London: Violette Editions.
Kosofsky Sedgwick E, Frank A & Alexander IE (Eds) (1995). *Shame and her sisters: a Silvan Tomkins reader*, Durham and London: Duke University Press.

Tilroe A (2003). The laugh of No. 13. In G Carsley (Ed). *Take a Bowery: the art and (larger than) life of Leigh Bowery*. Sydney: Museum of Contemporary Art.

Wilde O (1895/1990). *The importance of being earnest*, London: Dover Publications.

Wilson E (2007). A note on glamour. *Fashion Theory*, 11(1): 95–108.

15
Hiding in the cosmos

Nikos Papastergiadis

The most obvious place to hide is in the front. Hiding in front of one of the key concepts that is framing contemporary discussions on art and culture is the word cosmos. Cosmopolitanism is an idea of our place in the world and an ideal of how to belong with other people. At its most utopian level cosmopolitanism proclaims a form of belonging that is free of boundaries and is open to the sensory awareness of the universe. It proposes the widest possible sphere of belonging and freedom. In this chapter I seek to explore the extent to which the world-making activity of contemporary art is expressive of an immersive form of the cosmopolitan imaginary. I will focus on the idea that a certain view of the cosmos has been hidden for over two millennia, even though it is manifest in the texture and form of all art practice. Art is a world-making activity and the cosmos is revealed in every instance even if our focus is on everything else. Art can camouflage an emergent world, or the coming world, as it reconfigures the elements in the existing world. The dynamics between visibility and invisibility, the process of concealing in the midst of revealing, is at its most exquisite when it is articulated through an immersive environment. When the message is everywhere it can be nowhere. The cosmos is such a ambient environment. I will therefore address the process of camouflage by bringing into play the term cosmos in cosmopolitanism:

1. cosmos – as aesthetic: an assemblage that pleases, an order that is attractive and hospitable to others
2. cosmos – as cosmology: a place that is larger than the earth but only one of the parts of the boundless universe
3. cosmos – as political philosophy: all humanity to which we all belong, and hence the phrase citizen of the world, cosmopolitan.

Exploring the cosmos of art is not the same as the now common surveys of the global art world. The ambitious surveys of artistic developments across the world, whether they are conducted by teams that are distributed across different regions (Belting & Buddensieg 2009), or directed by a solitary figure who has sought to integrate emergent trajectories and classify diverse practices into a new hierarchy (Smith 2011), have stumbled before a fundamental problem (Papastergiadis 2012). To have a total worldview of contemporary art is now impossible. It is produced at such a rate and in so many different places that no one can ever see the whole. The events and horizons of contemporary art have become resistant to any totalising schema. However, by bringing into closer focus the elemental terms of globe and cosmos, we can begin an alternative exercise in imagining the forms of connection and being in the world. A simple distinction may help. In the most banal uses of globalisation there is very little significance given to the key term globe. The world is treated as a flat square surface upon which everything is brought closer together and governed by a common set of rules. Globalisation has an integrative dynamic, but a globe without a complex 'ecology of practices' (Stengers 2011) would not have a world. A world is more than a surface upon which human action occurs. Therefore the process of globalisation is not simply the 'closing in' of distant forces and 'coordination between' disparate elements that are dispersed across the territory of the world.

As early as the 1950s Kostas Axelos made a distinction between 'mondialisation' and globalisation. He defined mondialisation as an open process of thought through which one becomes worldly (Elden 2006). He thereby distinguished between the empirical or material ways in which the world is integrated by technology from the conceptual and subjective process of understanding that is inextricably connected to the formation of a worldview. This tension highlights the camouflaging of the cosmos. The etymology of cosmos also implies a world-making activity. In Homer the term cosmos is used to refer to an aesthetic act of creating order, as well as referring to the generative sphere of creation that exists between the earth and the boundless universe.

Cosmopolitanism is now commonly understood as an idea and an ideal for embracing the whole of the human community (Delanty 2009, 20). Everyone who is committed to it recalls the phrase first used by Socrates and then adopted as a motif by the Stoics: 'I am a citizen of the world.' Indeed the etymology of the word – as it derived from cosmos and polites – is expressive of the tension between the part and the whole, aesthetics and politics. In both the Pre-Socratic and the Hellenistic schools of philosophy, this tension was related to cosmological explanations of the origin and structure of the universe. In these early creation stories the individual comes from the abyss of the void, looks up into the infinite cosmos and seeks to give form to their place in the world. It is also, in more prosaic terms, a concept for expressing the desire to be able to live with all the other people in this world. However, the idea has always remained as an ideal, because there is no unified state of the cosmos that can distribute citizenship to all. Nevertheless for many the ideal does not diminish just because such a cosmos has never materialised as a political institution. They still insist on the necessity and validity of the idea. We claim that artistic expression is in part a symbolic gesture of belonging to the world. Art is poised somewhere between the ancient cosmological ideas and the modern normative cosmopolitan ideals.

For the Stoic philosophers in the Hellenistic era, the concept of cosmopolitanism was expressed in an inter-related manner – there was spiritual sense of belonging, and aesthetic affection for all things, as well as political rumination on the possibility of political equality and moral responsibility. Since the Stoics the spiritual and aesthetic dimensions of cosmopolitanism have been slowly disregarded. By the time Kant adopted cosmopolitanism as a key concept for thinking about global peace, the focus was almost entirely on de-provincialising the political imaginary and extolling the moral benefits of extending a notion of equal worth to all human beings. Since Kant the debates on cosmopolitanism have been even more tightly bound to the twin notions of moral obligations and the virtue of an open interest in others.

Cosmos, in my mind, refers to the realm of imaginary possibilities and the systems by which we make sense of our place in the world. What sorts of worlds are made in the artistic imaginary? The classical pronouncement of cosmopolitanism, 'I am a citizen of the world', is from our perspective not just a statement of belonging to the whole of the world, and an expression of solidarity with all in this world, but also an aesthetic process for the expression of both the artist's vision of the world, and the worlds made through art. This wider conception and affirmative embrace of the cosmos is nowhere to be found in modern and contemporary discourses on cosmopolitanism. Cosmology has long since been banished from the realm of philosophy, but it seems to have survived in the sensibilities of art. Deep in the sensibility of art there is hidden a secret vision of the world. This 'coming' world is camouflaged in the existent world of things. Consider this quotation from the Russian avant garde artist Malevich in which he elevates the function of machines to the role of being a *new* context that would crack open an *ancient* secret that had perdured in art but almost vanished from popular consciousness. Malevich says:

> The new life of iron and the machine, the roar of automobiles, the glitter of electric lights, the whirring of propellers, have awoken the *soul*, which was stifling in the catacombs of ancient reason and has emerged on the roads woven between *sky and earth*. If all artists could see the crossroads of these *celestial* paths; if they could comprehend these monstrous runways and the weavings of our bodies with the clouds in the sky, then they would not paint chrysanthemums. [emphasis in the original] (2003, 177)

The widening of perspective

Camouflage is a matter of perspective. Setting art in a broader frame is in part a response to the innovations in pictorial perspective. There have been a number of ways in which artists have adopted an imaginary vantage point for viewing the world, or experimented with the use of new media to enhance or multiply the experience of perspective. In this brief section I will outline four fundamental innovations in the ways of seeing. These are instances that have necessitated a shift in worldview. I will categorise these shifts in perspective – and the complex interplay between hide and seek, visibility and invisibility that are central to the concept of camouflage under four key terms: aerial, archaeological, ambient and activist.

One of the great innovations that has come from contemporary Aboriginal painting in Australia is the aerial perspective of the land. Most contemporary Aboriginal paintings are produced with the large canvas flat on the ground. The artist, or a collective, move around it and the image usually follows from the humming of a song cycle that evokes the interconnectedness of a place, an ancestor figure and a journey. In the case of Doreen Reid Nakamarra we are invited to look down on the paintings that have been carefully installed on the floor. We see the intricate patterning and colouring of the canvas surface from an angle that is partly to the side and telescopically reduced.

This intimation of a wider viewpoint can be compared to the vertical axes proposed in a work by the American First Nations collective Postcommodity. In their installation *Do you remember when* (2012) the four person collective cut a four-foot hole to expose the land of the Gadigal people that lay below the polished floors of the Art Gallery of New South Wales. The hole in the floor of an institution that hosted the 2012 Sydney Biennale thus also served as an archaeological frame for the absent history of the local indigenous people.

The gaze that contemplates a painting still operates as if it is looking through a window. Aboriginal painting alters this viewpoint. New media installations now have the capacity to create an ambient perspective where the virtual window cascades into a near infinity of viewpoints. Unlike the gaze that operates through a fixed window that is always defined in relation to the spectator's grounded placement before the window, the virtual window does not presuppose that the spectator's gaze is bound to any fixed position, but it is implicated within the 'infinite infinity' of virtual horizons. In *T_Visionarium II* (2006)[1] produced by the iCinema group of artists (Centre for Interactive Cinema Research at the University of New South Wales, College of Fine Arts), the spectator is enclosed in a 360-degree cylindrical screen that is composed of 300 'windows' that hover against a black screen. Each window is a screen. The resulting panorama is not one that is evocative of an encounter with the awesome sublime but rather a field of focused activity. The spectator enters the realm with a remote control device and can select a screen to 'drill' deeper into the archive that is contained in each window. The characteristic feature of a contemporary work of ambient art is that an emergent image never appears in the same work twice. The exact view or point of revelation cannot be found twice, therefore it can never be verified. It is always a relational view. It is shaped by its own iterative dynamics of self-formation, and the feedback from the specific points of entry and modes of participation of the viewer. No viewer ever completes this kind of work, but no two viewers have exactly the same experience. In general, the ambient perspective appears more in the form of assemblage where the viewpoint is as much formed by the complex cluttering together of bits as it is by the spaces left between these bits and pieces.

Finally we have the example of artists that are either part of collectives or align their practice with specific groups in order to deepen and widen their engagement with social and political practices in everyday life. In Documenta XIII there were a number of examples such as Maria Theresa Alves and Mark Dion whose installations were the consequence of a particular project concerning the threats to planetary ecology. In their art practice there is an acknowledgement that such issues are of a scale that they exceed the capacity of any individual or even a collective, therefore what they provide is the traceline of an invariably incomplete but much bigger picture. The activist perspective is not developed in opposition, but as an extension of what art is and what sort of worldview it constructs. Numerous examples can be drawn from collectives such No-one is Illegal. In the 2008 Taipei Biennale there was a strong representation of such activist perspectives, most notably in the work by The International Errorists and the subsection curated by Oliver Ressler.

The cosmos of art is as diverse as the media and social practices through which art is expressed. This relationship between the media and the world is at the crux of what is possible. Our insight into the world-making activity of art is dependent on our capacity to train the imagination to find its place in the cosmos. It is from this perspective that it is useful to zoom in on the aesthetic dimensions of cosmopolitanism. In fact, I will claim that the dominant emphasis on the moral framework and the disregard for the aesthetic process has constrained the scope of being cosmopolitan. The expression of interest in oth-

---

1   iCinema: *T_Visionarium II*, 'Scientia': University of New South Wales, Sydney, 2006.: Project directors: Neil Brown, Dennis Del Favero, Matthew McGinity, Jeffrey Shaw and Peter Weibel. Produced by iCinema Centre and co-produced by ZKM, Karlsruhe.

ers, or the willingness to recognise the worth of other cultures, is no doubt a worthy moral stance, and a necessary stance if we are to engage in any dialogue about what is possible in a world in which rival viewpoints jostle for space. However, if this approach is defined exclusively in a moral framework, it also performs another level of camouflage: it constrains the very visibility of the aesthetic interest in others. In short, if interest in others is subsumed under the moral imperative of feeling obliged to respect others, then the possibility of an aesthetic engagement is subordinate to a normative order.

But from where does the impulse of conviviality come? Let us take a few steps back to the idea that cosmos is an order-making activity. Cosmos is not just a counter to the condition of chaos, and an intermediary zone between the material earth and the boundless space of the universe, but is also the fundamental activity of making a space attractive for others. I suggest that it starts in the primal desire to make a world out of the torsion that comes from facing both the abyss of the void and the eternity of the cosmos. This act of facing is a big bang aesthetic moment, filled with the horror and delight. Our aesthetic interest in the cosmos is therefore inter-linked to the social need for conviviality. The everyday acts of curiosity, attraction and play with others does not always come from a moral imperative, but also from aesthetic interest. Do we possess a language that can speak towards the mystery of this interest? Art history, and the humanities in general, have struggled to develop a language that is suitable for representing the mercurial energy of aesthetic creation. The pitfalls of the two extremes – narcissistic mystical illusionism and empirical instrumentalism – are most evident in the contrast between Romanticism and Marxism.

In conclusion I would now seek to turn to the questions: 'How do we give voice to the experience of awe and wonder when we encounter creation?', and, 'Why do we jump for hyperbole and mysticism when we confront the abyss of death'? In an essay that has nothing to do with cosmopolitanism, but examines the reaction to the experience of witnessing childbirth, Jacques Derrida states that this moment of creation is a kind of world shaking and cosmic re-making event.

> Families prepare for a birth; it is scheduled, forenamed, caught up in a symbolic space that dulls the arrivance. Nevertheless, in spite of these anticipations and prenominations, the uncertainty will not let itself be reduced: the child that arrives remains unpredictable; it speaks of itself as from the origin of another world, or from an-other origin of this world. (2002, 95)

Is this what happens when art imposes itself as another world? Does art refuse to be 'caught up in a symbolic space' and manage to leap out of a void and hit us in a flash? Can a voice also convey a cosmos? How does the rhythm of human breath and the element of wind, the authority of speech and allure of music, all come together into some kind of material presence? If the 'arrivance' of birth can shatter the symbolic, so can death. What is on the other side of death will never be visible in this world. But can we retrieve that last image before the threshold has been crossed? The mystery of this moment in time has haunted photography. Think of the fascination with the revelation of spirits in the early history of photography, or the obsession with the killer that is camouflaged in the bushes in Michelangelo Antonioni's *Blow up* (1966). These issues resurfaced in Rabih Mroué's installation at Documenta XIII. It is a piece that situates the archival nexus of documentation alongside the experience of complicity and mystery. This work is situated in two rooms. Upon entering the first room there is a set of flicker books and headphones. The audio comprises of recordings of riotous street scuffles and the sound of gunfire. You are given the task of trying to match sound and image. It is a mesmerising but ultimately futile act. The books sit inside blue inkpads, and as you handle them your thumbs and fingers become stained. In the other half of this room there are four large photographic prints of ambiguous silhouettes that slightly sway away from the wall and cast a strange flowing reflection at your feet. Opposite is an abstracted video revealing images of a man who keeps falling. The closer you look the more you realise that there is always a subtle change in the details – a different personal item also falls as he falls – cigarettes, phone, lighter. Could it be different people in these images?

In the second room there is a video recording of a lecture by the artist entitled *The pixelated revolution*. It commences with the comment that inspired the project: 'The Syrians are recording their own death.' Mroué explains his investigation into the phenomenon of people recording the violence of the civil war on their mobile phones, and his fascination with the perplexing instances where the witness with the camera comes into eye contact with a person whose rifle is pointing straight at his body. The viewfinder of the gun and the lens of the camera are aligned in a deadly symmetry. Remarkably, the unarmed civilian continues recording, remains stationary, and is shot dead.

This dreadful event provokes many questions. Was it a futile act of sacrifice? Is this evidence of an expression of immunity of the virtual from the real? Can we now resurrect the discredited science of optography to reveal the truth of the final image that occurs at the moment of death? In other words, does the image of the assassin appear in the final frame of the camera? Is this image the same as the final image that would be experienced in the retina of the eye? Mroué becomes obsessed with these questions. He replays the scenes countless times. He isolates the frames and analyses each detail like a scientist. He speculates on why the cameraman continues to film at this point of such palpable risk. He wonders whether the eye that is behind the camera experiences itself as being immune from the battle scene, as if the camera could serve as the 'prosthesis between life and death'. He suspects that the eye of the cameraman operates as if it is in a virtual world. He then comes to the conclusion that the exact, or what he calls the 'vital', moment of the occurrence of death is not visible to the naked eye. It can only be seen as a blank: a void. This seems like a reasonable conclusion, but then he makes a truly astonishing aesthetic proposition on the invisibility of the vital scene: 'The vital moment is stretched in two dimensions simultaneously, towards life and death.'

Such a statement can never be verified. It does not conform to the normal rules of truth claims. What is Mroué offering by ending with this vast declaration? At one level he articulates a profound empathy and solidarity with the dead. The questions that motivate the artist and the final declaration are expressions of support towards the one who kept staring at the violence when the logic to flee should have overcome their sense of curiosity and outrage. Hence the solidarity is not just for the suffering but for the commitment to defy the executioner. From where does this crazy commitment come? Is this also, as Derrida speculated, the 'origin of another world, or from an-other origin of this world'.

It should be noted that the wild leap constituted by this final artistic statement is in stark contrast to the whole tone and structure of the lecture. The lecture was expressed with exemplary calm reasoning. No lawyer could fault his logic, just as many scientists would appreciate the precision of his observations. The declaration that 'the vital moment is stretched in two directions simultaneously towards life and death' creates a complete break. It is not part of any process of deduction. It is just an assertion. Yet it has the truth claim of artist fire. To describe the timing of the moment with the term 'vital' introduces elemental forces that are again distinct to the tradition of thought that pinned the responsibility of the cameraman to a mast that compels him to photograph everything, even if it makes him feel like an accomplice in the scene of violence. The 'decisive moment' in which the whole scene captured in an instant is not just the opportunity to punctuate time but also a declaration of the photographer's duty. The photographer was there to document the event. The decisive moment was also meant to display the most exquisite form of judgment – brutal and elegant in its precision. However, the war photographer's dilemmas have suddenly vanished. They are no longer faced with the solitary burden of representing the horror. The soldiers go to battle with cameras on their weapons just as other participants and civilians caught in the cross-fire all have mobile phones in their pockets. Moral outrage and complicity have been 'stretched' by the blurring of the distinction between actors and witnesses. By focusing on the recordings made on mobile phones Mroué is also considering how the body of participants in this war have also changed. The mobile phone is described as a prosthetic. It is not there to replace a missing limb but to capture the last moment in a life that will disappear. The twitching union of mind and eye is now transfigured into a vital force that stretches time along the spectrum of opposing drives for life and death.

Mroué concludes his lecture with a reflection on the presumption of immortality. Why does the person who is capturing the image of the battle in Syria not drop his camera and run when the sniper points his gun to him? Why does he think that the catastrophe that is happening before his feet will not rise up and engulf him? This example is clearly a limit case when we consider the hide-and-seek connection between sensory awareness and art as a world-making activity. The illusion of camouflage is both exposed and sustained. The holder of the camera continues with the presumption of invisibility even as he captures the image of himself in the sightline of the shooter.

References

Belting H & Buddensieg A (Eds) 2009. *The global art world: audiences, markets and museums*. Ostfildern: Hatje Cantz.
Delanty G (2009). *The cosmopolitan imagination*. Cambridge: Cambridge University Press.
Derrida J (2002). The deconstruction of actuality. In E. Raffenberg (ed. & transl). *Negotiations: interventions and interviews, 1971–2001*. Palo Alto: Stanford University Press.
Elden S (2006). Introducing Kostas Axelos and the 'world'. *Environment and planning D: society and space*, 24(1): 639–42.
Malevich K (2003). From cubism and futurism to suprematism: the new realism in painting [1913]. In C Harrison & PJ Wood (Eds). *Art in Theory 1900–2000*. Oxford: Blackwell Publishing.
Papastergiadis N (2012). *Cosmopolitanism and culture*. Cambridge: Polity Press.
Smith T (2011). *Contemporary arts: world currents*. London: Laurence King Publishing.
Stengers I (2011). *Cosmopolitics II*, transl. R. Bononno. Minneapolis: Minnesota University Press.

Afterword
Shifting ground

Ross Gibson

Over the past 20 years, many scholars from the various disciplines that comprise complexity science have provided insights into the emergent, almost chaotic qualities that seem to define large portions of everyday experience, be that experience physical, psychic or sociological. Sometimes the dynamic behaviour that such studies monitor is not immediately visible, for the changefulness that animates complex circumstances often occurs behind observable surfaces, in qualities of reality that are not optically explicit or instantaneously discernible. Instead the defining impulses might be found seeping in chemical, audible, haptic, morphological or olfactory dynamics. For the world presents and conceals itself via many facets and levels.

To the extent that changefulness characterises the world, therefore, and given that camouflage is an art for masking some patent characteristics of the world, this chapter asks how might an interrogation of the assumptions behind old and new camouflage practices challenge us into thinking in fresh ways about the complex systems and 'changescapes'[1] that host most contemporary occurrences?

It is generally agreed that because complex-dynamic systems are active and ever-altering, they cannot be 'frozen' by analysts using prescriptive models, nor can they be conclusively understood.[2] Complexity must be grasped contingently, impressionistically. Investigating complexity, one can best hope to get a feeling for what is going on, using continuous narrative accounts, speculative animations and open-ended 'possibility charts'. To still these kinds of systems renders them no longer complex or dynamic. For as William Wordsworth observed centuries ago, 'we murder to dissect'.[3] And as Joseph Margolis has reminded us more recently, invariant objects are not necessarily the basis of reality, even though the post-Socratic Classical tradition (represented by Plato and Aristotle particularly) has long distracted us from the crucial pre-Socratic assertions (espoused by Thales and Heraclitus most notably) that everything stems from water and no assayer can enter the same river twice.[4]

---

1 For an account of this notion, see my chapter entitled "Changescapes" in Rutherford and Holloway (Eds) (2010).
2 For an excellent introduction to these themes, see Cilliers (1998).
3 Wordsworth (1936), 377.
4 See Margolis (1993).

Afterword

Trying to keep faith with the live-ness of the world, therefore, this chapter seeks some fresh insights from the ways various processes of camouflage need to warp when they align to the changeful systems of present-day experience. This is mainly an investigation of the given world, therefore. I have nothing much to say about camouflage; but I might be able to offer something *through* it, to say something about the phenomenal and unstable domains that camouflage tries to mask.

Definitions

Camouflage is used for concealing. This is obvious. But can it be used also for revealing? Given that camouflage plays the apparent against the existent, we have a chance here to examine some basic precepts of sense-making. Rather than investigating what camouflage *is*, therefore, let's ask: what can be thought with it and through it? We can use it to ponder what can be thought about the status of individual things, to what extent can such things also be understood as events when examined over time, and specifically how does an assemblage of event-things tend to engender communities, with all their structured but unruly characteristics? In other words let's ask what fresh insights we might generate, via camouflage, into individual sovereignty and psychology as well as into the communal systematics of politics.

To get started, we need to share definitions. First, what is camouflage? It is a process that encourages the misapprehension of something perceptible. By studying how this misapprehension proceeds, we stand a chance of grasping better how its opposite – apprehension – occurs. So camouflage is a prompt for re-thinking ontology and hermeneutics.

As Roy Behrens has observed, with camouflage most things tend 'to become less thing-like'.[5] The thing being camouflaged might be a haze of pulsing colour viewed as a shadow; it might be a loss of temperature; or some aromatic intensification. More than just a trick to the eye, most camouflage operates as an event, as a series of actions applied to objects and intensities occurring in space and time. With their inherent changefulness, events tend to bring motion. And to quote Behrens again, thinking principally of optical duping, motion has always been 'the great spoiler of camouflage'.[6] Or to say this in other words, applying a contemporary focus: camouflage itself is changing nowadays, what with the preponderance of algorithmic tracking and emergence systems now making environments that are supported and activated by ubiquitous computing.

Therefore motion and changefulness must be a major preoccupation for avant-garde camouflagists as they try to produce an ever-altering match for the 'shiftiness' that defines so much contemporary experience. Magicians, capitalists and camouflagists, it seems, all want to finesse similar kinds of transactional powers as they seek to extract advantage while matter and moments go morphing from instant to instant. To mask things as they evolve and devolve, as they emerge and submerge in patterns over time: this is the great quest of contemporary camouflage. The task is to track and trick conglomerations of things behaving together as unpredictable events.

---

5 Roy Behrens, Public keynote lecture, 'Camouflage Cultures: surveillance, communities, aesthetics, animals', an international conference and exhibition co-convened an co-curated by Ann Elias and Nicholas Tsoutas, Sydney College of the Arts at The University of Sydney, 8 August 2013.
6 Behrens, Keynote, 'Camouflage Cultures'.

As noted already, senses other than vision can be cajoled into misapprehension. Optical camouflage is just a sub-set of a larger venture. Indeed, as several delegates observed during the *Camouflage Cultures* conference at The University of Sydney in 2013, even language can be understood as a camouflage ground. Irony, for example, is really a verbal and performative mode of camouflage. Many senses and many modes of sense-making – from the personal to the political, from the visual and kinetic to the linguistic and intuitive – can therefore get beguiled through camouflage. And by examining these multi-modal duping practices we might know our sensibilities and consensualities in new ways.

Relations

It's a commonplace to say that camouflage operates in the shimmer between figure and ground, between sense and non-sense, signal and noise, self and other. Moreover, by focusing attention on the significance of *events*, we begin to understand how camouflage might also operate in the stutter between stasis and dynamics. Camouflage used to be principally a graphic and static form – patterns painted on boats, netting and screens that blur contours, and so on; but now it needs dynamics, it needs to be multi-modal, cinematic and also interactive, reflexive and emergent. This is because every present moment is always cohering while it's disappearing in front of, around and within people who deploy the panoply of their senses for perceiving the nuances of experience. And these perceivers cohere and disappear somewhat too, as they attempt to sense the full store of relations that are possible between themselves (understood to be independent but also interdependent figures) and their shared environment (perceived and interpreted as shifting ground) all contending in space and time. Freedom flexes with connectedness, singularity vies with communality to make the structured but loose dramas that comprise sociability and politics, with the result being that experience arises in the simultaneously physical, psychic and social realm that we all inhabit, that we all try to influence even as it shapes us too.

Speculating about what contemporary camouflage needs to be, we end up prying into politics therefore; into the commonsense understanding of integrated, communal experiences in a world full of motion. Speculating about the challenges for contemporary camouflage leads us to think anew about how the perception of things occurs through time, how this perception is necessarily changeful, ever-emergent and eventful, and how each perceiving individual has to be understood as a component or 'community member' within the larger and shifting system that comprises experience in the phenomenal world. What's more, there are machines now performing so much surveillance for us and these machines, of course, can be duped even as they work to give the impression that we are well-served with vigilance. In such a context – human and machinic – community can be defined as a volatile system of entities, a system that is not so much an object as an event insofar as society is an interconnected and contentious assemblage of interactors combining, recoiling, altering and unfolding as a perceptible phenomenon in time. And given that camouflage manipulates apprehension, we find ourselves asking: what must it track when its quarry is on the move and not entirely 'natural', when it is applied to systems – not only organic but also mechanical and computational – that are *complex and dynamic*? Answer: the camouflagist has to mask the apprehension of intricate and contingent *relationships* rather than (or in addition to) the apprehension of discrete and stabilised *objects*.

Poets have long understood experience thus. For example, the modern Japanese haiku master Seishi Yamaguchi had this expansive view: 'because objects are already in existence, it is not necessary to create them ... all we have to do is grasp the relationships among them.'[7] And Henry James, ruminating on the magic tricks required of a novelist, was similarly outreaching: 'Really, universally, relations stop nowhere, and the exquisite problem of the artist is eternally but to draw, by a geometry of his own, a circle within which they shall happily *appear* to do so.'[8]

Fields and lines, grounds and figures

So by speculating about the challenges facing 'eventful' or 'changeful' camouflage practices nowadays (recalling that camouflage has conventionally been 'spoiled by motion') we have to think in fresh ways about what an individual actually experiences within complexity. The old camouflage theme of the figure–ground relationship is pertinent here, with the added intrigue that we come back to this dyad now knowing that the ground is rarely solid and the figure is almost never static or in focus or necessarily natural.

Recent studies in neurology are useful in this regard. For example, Benjamin Libet's *Mind Time* proposes that consciousness is formed in a constantly arising-and-altering moment that is generated within each individual psyche as it negotiates the risky edge between itself and the larger world (which larger world includes, of course, oneself and other selves also).[9] This is another version of the figure–ground drama. For Libet, consciousness is comprised of a stream of present instants that coruscate in 'mind time', in an urgent, ever-progressing 0.3-second interval of lived experience between when stimuli are first registered in one's broad-but-almost-formless awareness and then interpreted within the structured flow of inchoate personality. As these 'pre-conscious' stimuli are constantly processed within the 0.3-second intermission of burgeoning awareness, the present arises for each individual within the fleeting-unfurling 0.3-second interval; and socially the several individuals who comprise a community at any given moment more or less agree that experience is unfolding in sync for them all. This is how long the present lasts: 0–0.3 seconds.

At a social level, the present moment is a kind of structuring fiction that normally allows us to get on with things while each person's emerging consciousness gets extracted, instant by instant, as a line drawn out of time from the deep, volumetric flux of threats and opportunities that constitute existence in a vast world of phenomena and stimuli. Libet's experiments show that for every human being attempting to make his or her particular way through the engulfing world of threats and opportunities, the brief 'moment' of less than half a second lets the individual scan for information before beginning consciously to interpret the raw stimuli; in other words, the individual scans for threats and options before asserting the figure of itself against the ground of the shifting stimuli.

This scanning-process is a rapid-fire, continuous 'snapshotting' of everything perceptible. It is a survey of the 'ground' from which the figure of one's consciousness must step

---

7   See Yamaguchi, 'Preface' (1993), xix.
8   Henry James, 'Preface' to his *Roderick Hudson*. (The novel was first published by James in serial form in the *Atlantic Monthly* in 1875. The 'Preface' was first published by James in 1907). See the online creative commons version: http://www.henryjames.org.uk/prefaces/text01.htm.
9   Libet (2004).

and step again and again. The snapshotting is wide-angle and non-hierarchical, because all threats and opportunities must be treated as equal until interpretation offers shape to the data and gives sequential actions a real urgency in a kind of survivalist 'workflow' or storyline. Interpretation is thus 'figural' because interpretation is the application of structure on the basis of your memory prompted by your extant personality while you monitor the profuse array of possibilities or prospects that will emerge from the ground where you have retrospectively stored your past experiences. Memory, desire and imagination jostle to make a contest with fate, all of which produce perceptible experience. Thus consciousness arises even as it stumbles. The self lives in a kind of shimmer where a somewhat-formed figure jigs in the ground of the messy world. Another way to understand this drama of consciousness, therefore, is to construe *a field* of received experience out of which *a line* of enacted sovereignty is drawn by each conscious subject. The line is drawn by the conscious figure; the field is delimited in the larger ground of worldly experience and memory.

Iain McGilchrist's *The Master and his Emissary* presents a comparable worldview.[10] McGilchrist explains how the 'bi-cameral' brain, with its symmetrical but differently operational halves, offers the chance for each conscious mind to be formed in a dynamic oscillation between right-brain and left-brain predispositions, between hyper-observant contingency-scanning and super-efficient prescriptive processing. Pattern-apperception combines with narrative-imposition. Although most people and cultures tend to be dominated by one or the other of these two dispositions, McGilchrist contends that the most vibrant and capable consciousness maintains its best stability almost gyroscopically, by actively spinning or oscillating the two modes, each around and through the other, so that the world is perceived and interpreted both extensively (as an open field of contingencies) and intensively (as an assured line of prescribed reasoning). Figure, ground, focus, breadth, change, adaptation, action, alteration, emergence: consciousness and the vast, immanent world chase each other through these turnpikes.

Connectedness and a conclusion

With astonishing prescience, Ralph Waldo Emerson saw it and said it vividly in the 1840s:

> Really, all things and persons are related to us, but according to our nature they act on us not at once but in succession, and we are made aware of their presence one at a time. All persons, all things which we have known, are here present, and many more than we see; the world is full … No sentence will hold the whole truth, and the only way in which we can be just, is by giving ourselves the lie; Speech is better than silence; silence is better than speech; – All things are in contact; every atom has a sphere of repulsion; – Things are, and are not, at the same time.[11]

This is how we can be goaded into re-thinking and stretching our solid-state models of the world: by considering what camouflage really needs to be. Sensing the limits of good

---

10   See McGilchrist (2009).
11   Ralph Waldo Emerson, 'Nominalist and realist', in *The complete prose works*, London: Ward, Lock and Co, 1891, 150. (First published in 1844.)

duping, we too can sense the duplicity of the solid old world. Which is where the examination of camouflage can lead us, into fresh considerations of phenomenology. It can help us apprehend afresh how every figure really does seem to stem from water even while it yearns to be on solid ground. Everything that seems solid wants to absorb each of its others. The figure and the ground give rise to each other.

References

Behrens R (2013). Public keynote lecture, Camouflage Cultures: surveillance, communities, aesthetics, animals, an international conference and exhibition co-convened an co-curated by Ann Elias and Nicholas Tsoutas, Sydney College of the Arts at The University of Sydney, 8 August 2013.

Emerson RW (1891). *The complete prose works*. London: Ward, Lock and Co.

Gibson R (2010). 'Changescapes'. In J Rutherford & B Holloway (Eds). *Halfway house : the poetics of Australian spaces*. Crawley, WA: UWA Publishing.

Henry J. 'Preface' Roderick Hudson. http://www.henryjames.org.uk/prefaces/text01.htm.

Libet B (2004). *Mind time: the temporal factor in consciousness*. Cambridge MA: Harvard University Press.

Margolis J (1993). *The flux of history and the flux of science*. Berkeley: University of California Press.

McGilchrist I (2009). *The master and his emissary*. New Haven: Yale University Press.

Wordsworth W (1798). The tables turned. In T. Hutchinson & E. de Selincourt (Eds) (1936). *Wordsworth: poetical works* (p 377), London: Oxford University Press.

Yamaguchi S (1993). *The essence of modern haiku*. Atlanta: Mangajin.

About the contributors

Roy R Behrens is a writer and designer who has taught graphic design and design history for nearly 40 years, at the University of Wisconsin-Milwaukee, Art Academy of Cincinnati and other schools. Since 1990, he has taught at the University of Northern Iowa, where he is a professor of art and distinguished scholar. He has published hundreds of essays and articles on art- and design-related subjects. He is the author of *Art and camouflage: concealment and deception in art, nature and war* (1981), regarded as one of the earliest books about the role of artists in the development of modern camouflage. His most recent books include *False colors: art, design and modern camouflage* (2002); *Cook book: Gertrude Stein, William Cook, and Le Corbusier* (2005); *Camoupedia: A compendium of research on art, architecture and camouflage* (2009); and *Ship shape: a dazzle camouflage sourcebook* (2012). Described by *Communication Arts* magazine as 'one of the most original thinkers in design', he was a nominee for the Smithsonian Institution's National Design Awards in 2003.

Donna West Brett is lecturer, modern art at the University of Sydney, an independent curator and museum professional. Her current research interest focuses on modernist and Cold War photography and the state of exile. Exhibitions include 'Joseph Beuys and the "Energy Plan"' (2012) and 'The stranger's eye' (2010). She has published in *Memory Connection*, *Photographies* and Art Gallery of NSW collection publications. Her forthcoming book *Photography and place: seeing and not seeing Germany after 1945* (2015) presents a theoretical and historical analysis of German photography and place. She is also a member of the editorial committee and reviews editor for the *Australian and New Zealand Journal of Art*.

Paul Brock is a world authority on Phasmida (stick and leaf insects), author of several popular books covering taxonomy, rearing, catalogues, and the continually updated Phasmida Species File http://phasmida.speciesfile.org as well as *Insects of the New Forest* (2011) a major reference source for photographers and conservationists. He has published over 200 scientific papers in many different journals. Latest books are *A photographic guide to insects of the New Forest and surrounding area* (2011) and *The complete field guide to stick and leaf insects of Australia* (2009).

About the contributors

Ann Elias is Associate Professor in Critical Studies at Sydney College of the Arts, the University of Sydney. Current research activity concentrates on camouflage, representations of flowers, and imagery of the Great Barrier Reef. Publications include *Camouflage Australia: art, nature, science and war* (2011) and *Useless Beauty: flowers and Australian art* (2015). Journal articles on camouflage, flowers, the Barrier Reef, and underwater space are found in *Papers of Surrealism, Leonardo, 19th Century Art Worldwide,* and *Antennae*.

Ross Gibson is Centenary Professor in Creative & Culture Research at the University of Canberra. As part of his research he makes books, films and art installations and he encourages postgraduate students in similar pursuits. His main interests are environmental consciousness and cross-cultural negotiations throughout colonial history, particularly in Australia and the Pacific. His work spans several media and disciplines. Recent projects include the books *26 views of the starburst world* (2012) and *The summer exercises* (2009), the video installation *Street x-rays* (2005), and the minimalist, photographic poem: 'Accident music' which appears weekly in the form of a blog that is published by the Justice & Police Museum in Sydney (since 2010).

Amy Hamilton is a visual artist and an arts educator. Her principally figurative work is in acrylic or oil on canvas as well as linocut and silk screen prints. Amy's recent art work is influenced by the relationship between visual camouflage and discursive representation technologies. She has been involved in art-education projects that involved contributing to the national arts curriculum, and integrating arts-based pedagogies across different curriculum areas.

Pamela Hansford has previously taught in Art Theory programs at the University of Sydney and University of New South Wales and she works as a freelance writer who publishes on contemporary art and culture. Her books include *Wits End: Black Humour in Contemporary Art* (with Kay Campbell,1992), and *Dagger Definitions* (1987). Her current research interests are focused on adaptive bodily and cultural configurations that emerge in response to rapid change. She is the recipient of several awards including a NSW Premiers Award (in conjunction with Sydney University), an Australian Writers & Designers Guild Book of the Year award for *Wits End*, and a Pascal Prize for Art Criticism (highly commended).

Ross Harley is an award-winning artist, writer and educator whose career crosses the bounds of traditional and creative arts research. He is a professor and dean of the Faculty of Art & Design at the University of NSW.

Jack Hasenpusch is a specialist of Australian Phasmida (stick and leaf insects). He specialises in breeding and studying life histories of Phasmids and Coleoptera, and has authored and co-authored numerous papers. He is director of the Australian Insect Farm which was initially established to supply insect specimens and breeding/life cycle insect kits. He is co-author of *The complete field guide to stick and leaf insects of Australia* (2009).

Ian Howard is an artist and professor at UNSW Faculty of Art & Design, Sydney. He was Dean of the College of Fine Arts from 1998 to 2013 and prior to that was Provost and Director of the Queensland College of Art, Griffith University. He trained in Sydney

(Diploma of Art Education), London (Graduate Diploma of Advanced Studies, Film and Television) and Montreal (Master of Fine Arts). His artwork progresses a cultural relationship between civilian and military institutions concentrating on borders and their enforcement mechanisms and vehicles. He works and exhibits internationally and is represented by Watters Gallery, Sydney. He has been the chairperson of the National Association for the Visual Arts, a member of the Visual Arts Board of the Australia Council; a board member of the Australian Centre for Photography and chairperson of the Visual Arts Committee, Arts Queensland.

Hsuan L. Hsu is an associate professor of English at the University of California, Davis. His interests include 19th- and 20th-century US literature, Asian-American literature, visual culture, cultural geography, comparative racialisation, and environmental justice literature. He is the author of *Geography and the production of space in nineteenth-century American literature* (2010) and *Sitting in darkness: Mark Twain, Asia, and comparative racialization* (2015). He serves on the editorial board of *Literary Geographies*, the advisory board of the *Journal of Transnational American Studies*, and the Executive Council of the MLA's American Literature Section.

Bernd Hüppauf is professor emeritus of New York University. He taught modern literature, theory of culture, and comparative literature at the universities of Tübingen, Regensburg, at University of New South Wales, and from 1993 at New York University. He was director of Deutsches Haus at NYU until 2003. Bernd's research areas include word and image, representations of war in literature and photography, literature and philosophical anthropology, and aesthetics of scepticism. His books in English include *War, violence and the modern condition* (1997), *Globalization and the future of German* (2004), *Vernacular modernism*: Heimat, *globalization, and the built environment* (ed. with Maiken Umbach) (2005), *Science images and popular images of the sciences* (ed. with Peter Weingart) (2008), *Dynamics and performativity of imagination* (ed. with Christoph Wulf) (2009).

Ian McLean is research professor of contemporary art at the University of Wollongong, and a well-known commentator on Australian art. His books include *Art of Gordon Bennett* (with a chapter by Gordon Bennett) (1996), *White Aborigines: identity politics in Australian art* (1998), *How Aborigines invented the idea of contemporary art* (2011) and *Double Desire: Transculturation and Indigenous Contemporary Art* (2014).

Dr Jacqueline Millner is Associate Dean Research at Sydney College of the Arts, University of Sydney, where she also lectures on contemporary art theory and history. She has published widely on contemporary Australian and international art in key anthologies, journals and catalogues of national and international institutions. Her books include *Conceptual Beauty: Perspectives on Australian Contemporary Art* (2010), *Australian Artists in the Contemporary Museum* (with Jennifer Barrett, 2014) and *Fashionable Art* (with Adam Geczy, 2015). She co-convenes the research group Contemporary Art and Feminism at the University of Sydney.

Jonnie Morris is a writer, director, and editor with a passion for filmmaking and biology. She has a diverse background ranging from high end advertising campaigns to multimedia and broadcast documentary projects. Since 2008 Jonnie has freelanced for international broadcasters such as Al Jazeera, VICE media, and BBC. She has also worked on extensive cross-platform documentaries including Alexandra Cousteau's Expedition Blue Planet North America (2010) and SXSW finalist Ringbalin Riverstories (2013).

In 2011 she began researching an original documentary on the evolution of camouflage design - 'Dazzle: The Hidden Story of Camouflage' is a 56min film produced by Jonnie & Kate Films for ABC TV. It will air in Australia and internationally in 2015.

Brigitta Olubas is associate professor of English in the School of the Arts and Media at the University of New South Wales, Sydney. She is the 2013–15 president of ASAL (the Association for the Study of Australian Literature), editor of ASAL's scholarly journal *JASAL*, and a founding executive member of the new peak English body AUHE (Australian Universities Heads of English). She has published widely on Australian literary and visual culture studies, including essays on the writing of Nam Le, Patrick White, Raimond Gaita and Antigone Kefala and the artwork of Tracey Moffatt, Marian Drew, Donna Marcus, Sebastian di Mauro and Bruce Reynolds. Recent book publications include a scholarly monograph and an edited collection of critical essays on author Shirley Hazzard (Cambria Press and Sydney University Press). In 2016 her edited collection of the nonfiction writings of Shirley Hazzard will be published by Columbia University Press.

Nikos Papastergiadis is professor at the School of Culture and Communication at the University of Melbourne. Throughout his career, Nikos has provided strategic consultancies for government agencies on issues relating to cultural identity and worked on collaborative projects with artists and theorists of international repute, such as John Berger, Jimmie Durham and Sonya Boyce. His current research focuses on the investigation of the historical transformation of contemporary art and cultural institutions by digital technology. His publications include *Modernity as exile* (1993), *Dialogues in the diaspora* (1998), *The turbulence of migration* (2000), *Metaphor and tension* (2004) *Spatial aesthetics: art place and the everyday* (2006), *Cosmopolitanism and culture* (2012). He also authored numerous essays which have appeared in major catalogues such as the Sydney, Liverpool, Istanbul, Gwanju, Taipei, Lyon and Thessaloniki Biennales.

Tanya Peterson's practice encompasses writing, art making and criticism. Her exhibition profile spans over a decade and she publishes widely on contemporary art. She currently lectures at UNSW Art & Design and the National Art School, Sydney.

Nicholas Tsoutas is is Zelda Stedman Lecturer in Visual Arts at Sydney College of the Arts. He was a director of four major art centres in Australia – Artspace, The Institute of Modern Art, The Performance Space and The Casula Powerhouse, as well as an independent curator and writer. His main areas of interest are in the areas of conceptual and installation art, performance art, contemporary postmodern theory and criticism, with a particular emphasis on postcolonial critique in relation to globalisation, mobility, cultural exchange, hybridity and cultural diversity. His practice has been informed through the intertextual processes of interdisciplinary border crossing and intervention. His professional commitments have been defined through his privileging of and emphasis on the creative capacities of artists and an innovative approach to shaping the critical transaction of their ideas.

About the contributors

Linda Tyler is associate professor and director of Gus Fisher Gallery at the Centre for Art Research in the National Institute of Creative Arts and Industries at the University of Auckland. In 2011 she won the Robert Lord Writers' Fellowship, Dunedin. She is currently associate investigator on a Marsden Fund Research Project 'Pornography perturbed'.

Ben Wadham is a sociologist interested in civil–military relations and critical military studies. He has researched the way in which the camouflage movement of the 20th century is an expression of civilian and military relations, in terms of the militarisation of democratic life and the civilianisation of the military. He is also interested in the ways that techniques of visual camouflage can be applied to discourse, hegemony and naturalisation. Ben has worked with the visual artist Amy Hamilton to exhibit on the theme of camouflage and the hegemony of militarism.

Index

active escape 50
accidental perspective *see* Ames II, Adelbert: accidental perspective
adaptation 20, 21, 25, 29, 48, 56, 57, 63, 65, 88, 92
ADAPTIV technology 68
Adorno, Theodor 162
Ames II, Adelbert 4–7
  accidental perspective 6
  Ames room 4, 12
  architect's room 4
  forced perspective 6
Andre, Carl 80, 84
animals ix, 4, 18, 21, 24, 28, 33–44, 66, 88, 98
  animal camouflage 7, 11, 22
  animal colouration 25
  wild animals 33, 52, 63
  zoo animals 33
anti-camouflage 78, 84
ANZAC mythology 163–167
Arnheim, Rudolf 13
assimilation 90, 171, 172, 175
  spatial assimilation 181
  assimilative performance 171
authorised concealment 136

BAE systems 68, 68
Barthes, Roland 17, 79, 102, 163
beauty 28
Behrens, Roy 19, 35, 135, 172
Berger, John 33, 42
Berlin Wall 148
Bhabha, Homi 166, 171, 175
blending camouflage 1, 22, 162, 181
  environmental blending 172, 175
Bowery, Leigh 183–191

Bucklow, Christopher 102
butterflies *see* Lepidoptera

Caillois, Roger 42, 91, 97, 175, 183
calculated deception 18
camouflage
  and religion 22
  as a motif 129, 183, 187
  as adaptation 20; *see also* adaptation
  installations 40, 116
  magical concept of 20, 23, 35
  man-made 19
  patterning 36, 96, 111, 117, 129, 130, 195
camoufleurs 2, 6, 9, 66, 127, 189
cephalopods 65–71
chromatophores 68
  artificial chromatophore 70
concealment 11, 25, 88, 91, 94, 118, 156; *see also* authorised concealment
conditional effects 92
conformity 172, 183
cosmopolitanism 193
costume 11, 95, 135, 183, 189
Crimp, Douglas 77
crypsis 26, 42
cubism 21
cultural evolution 21
cuttlefish *see* cephalopods

Dakin, William 2, 35, 36–39
Darwin, Charles 25
  theory of biological evolution 18–19, 24, 25, 30, 35
Dawkins, Richard 21, 77, 79
dazzle camouflage 7, 8, 65, 116, 128, 161, 164

Index

de-camouflaging 23, 77, 162
deception 17–18, 26, 27, 91, 92, 163, 190
　visual deception 72
defensive strategies 47, 52, 53
　defensive secretion 50
deflection 18
Demand, Thomas 107–112
detection 22
disruptive patterns 2, 36, 42, 70, 74, 121; *see also* dazzle camouflage
Dupain, Max 35, 40
Dwyer, Mikala 94

ecology vii, 33, 52
Elias, Ann 2, 91, 128
e-paper technology 71
evolution vii, 18, 22, 26, 27, 29, 80, 90; *see also* Darwin, Charles: theory of biological evolution
　evolutionary anthropology 24
　evolutionary ethics 24

Freud, Lucien 183, 185, 188, 191
Freud, Sigmund 25, 91, 94
Fried, Michael 107
femininity 118, 122, 190

Gargantuan Stick-insect 48, 49
gendered identity 118, 160, 171, 187, 190
genetic engineering 88
gentrification 172, 175, 177–179, 181
Gröschner, Annett 148

Hanlon, Roger 66, 69
Heidegger, Martin 81, 84, 128
Hinder, Frank 35, 40
Hochberg, Julian 10
Howard, Ian 127–144
hybridity 121, 180
　cultural hybridity 181

immune system processes 87–90
insects 47–63, 90
invisibility cloaks 70

jungle warfare 36
Junqin, Colonel Xing 127–144

Key, Kenneth 51
Koestler, Arthur 9
kowhaiwhai 115, 118, 122, 124
Krauss, Rosalind 77, 83, 102

Leach, Neil 9, 91, 104, 148, 153, 174
Lepidoptera 72
Levine, Sherrie 78
light
　interplay of light 102
　superadded light 104
　residual sensitivity 104
　indexing of light 101–104
Lévy-Bruhl, Lucien 24

Macleay's Spectre 52
Mailer, Norman 172
masculinity 37, 160, 164, 187, 190
masks and masking 20, 26, 95, 161, 164, 184, 188
Massumi, Brian 111
meme 79
　variant memes 80
Messerschmidt, James 160
Messmer, Arwed 147, 148
metamorphosis 20, 23, 50
Michals, Duane 101
military camouflage 27, 35, 40, 71, 87, 115, 128, 133, 160, 165
mimesis 17–19, 26, 77, 79, 88
　mimetic realism 17
　mimetic imitation 17
mimicry vii, 19, 25, 42, 50, 57, 66, 79, 88, 91, 127, 162, 166
　biomimicry 66, 70, 72
　black mimicry 173
　colonial mimicry 171
　ethnic mimicry 171
　hipster mimicry ix, 172
misrepresentation 28, 142, 164
mondialisation 194
Monteith's Leaf-insect 47, 58
moths *see* Lepidoptera

Nagel, Thomas 28
natural selection 19, 22, 25, 29, 77, 90; *see also* Darwin, Charles: theory of biological evolution
naturalisation 160, 164
naturalistic animal enclosures 38, 43
New Zealand 115, 118
Nietzsche, Friedrich 25, 27

overt camouflage 142
octopus *see* cephalopods
owls *see* strigiformes

Penrose, Roland 128
perception viii, 4, 18, 22, 110, 121, 147, 161, 195

Index

phasmids 47
Portmann, Adolf 1, 13
procrypsis 50
psychological camouflage 156, 172

retro-reflective technology 70
Reynolds, John 115, 117
rubbings 130, 135, 136, 140
Rudd, Kevin 143
Ruff, Thomas 105

seeing eye 2, 6
self-deception 24, 28, 41; *see also* deception
sexual selection 30, 43, 83
shading 3, 13
  countershading 13, 25, 162
shinkansen bullet train 73
sound 26, 29, 50, 53, 72, 116
  sound suppression 73
squid *see* cephalopods
Stein, Gertrude 137
Steiner, George 19
Steyerl, Hito 109–112
strigiformes 72–73
structural colouration 71

surveillance viii, 1, 2, 38, 40, 95, 152
  surveillance photography 147, 154

Taronga Zoo 34, 35–43
Taussig, Michael 128
Thayer, Abbott 2, 7, 11, 21, 25
Thayer, Gerald 11, 12
Tillers, Imants 79–85
transformation 18, 24, 92, 105, 124, 128, 177, 187
Trivers, Robert 27
Tessellated Stick-insect 51

u-boat 6
unseeing 147

visual disorientation strategies 118

Warner, Everett Longley 7
Weiss, Paul 8
World War I 6, 11, 19, 25, 65, 127, 189
World War II 2, 11, 36, 65, 127
Wright, Frank Lloyd 10

xenotransplantation 89